WOODCRAFT magazine

TIPS & TRICKS
FOR WOODWORKING

TECHNIQUES / **TOOLS** / **WORKSHOP**

FROM THE EDITORS, CONTRIBUTORS,
AND READERS OF *WOODCRAFT MAGAZINE*

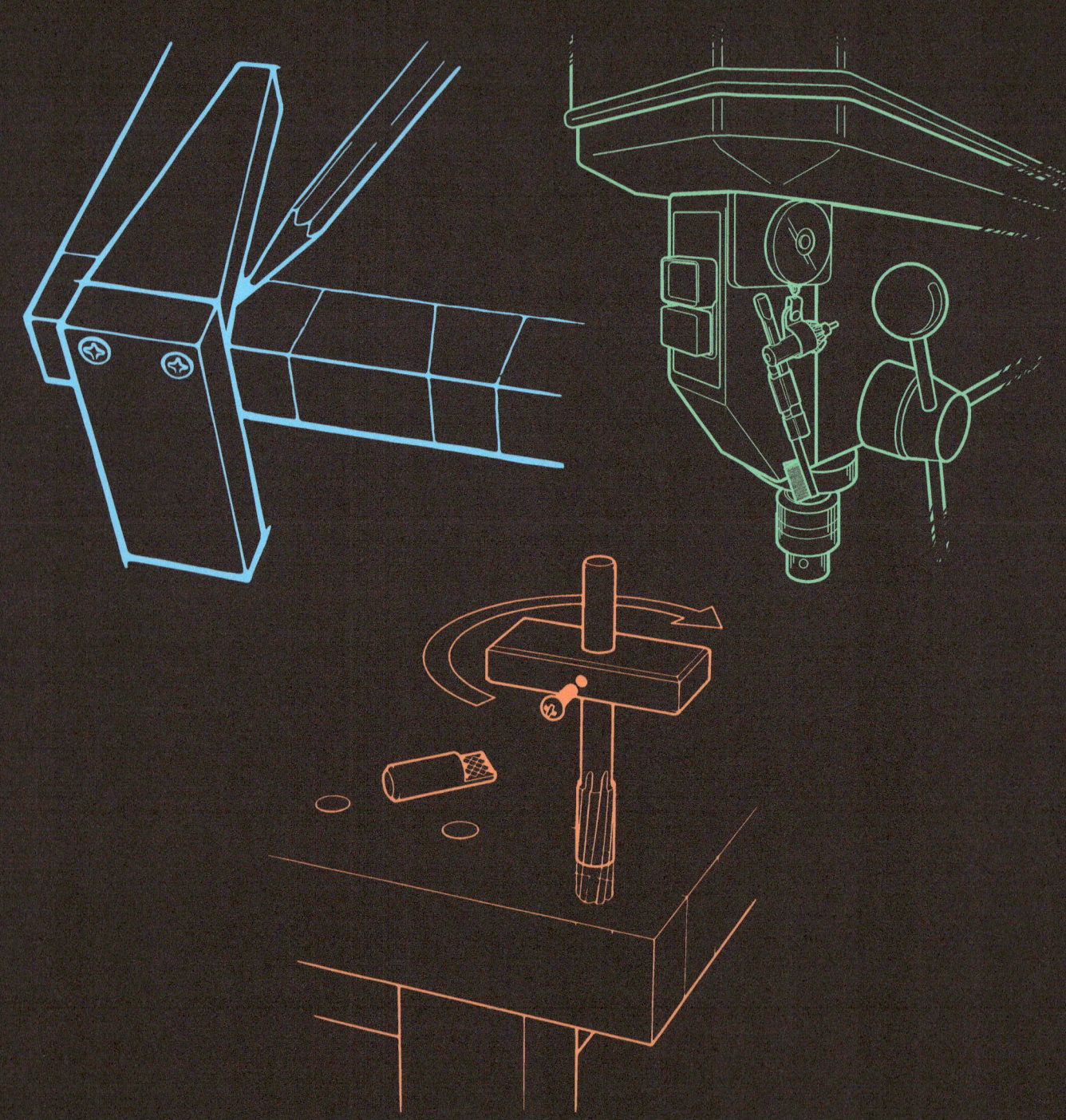

CONTENTS

TECHNIQUES

ASSEMBLY	6
FINISHING	14
FURNITURE CONSTRUCTION	25
GLUING	29
JOINERY	37
MEASURING & MARKING	47
SANDING & SHAPING	61
SHARPENING	72

TOOLS

BANDSAW	82
DRILL & DRILL PRESS	90
JOINTER	113
LATHE	116
MITERSAW	125
OTHER POWER TOOLS	129
PLANER	135
ROUTER	138
TABLE SAW	151

WORKSHOP

CLAMPING & WORK-HOLDING	182
CLEANUP	206
DUST COLLECTION	210
ORGANIZATION & STORAGE	214
SHOP	228

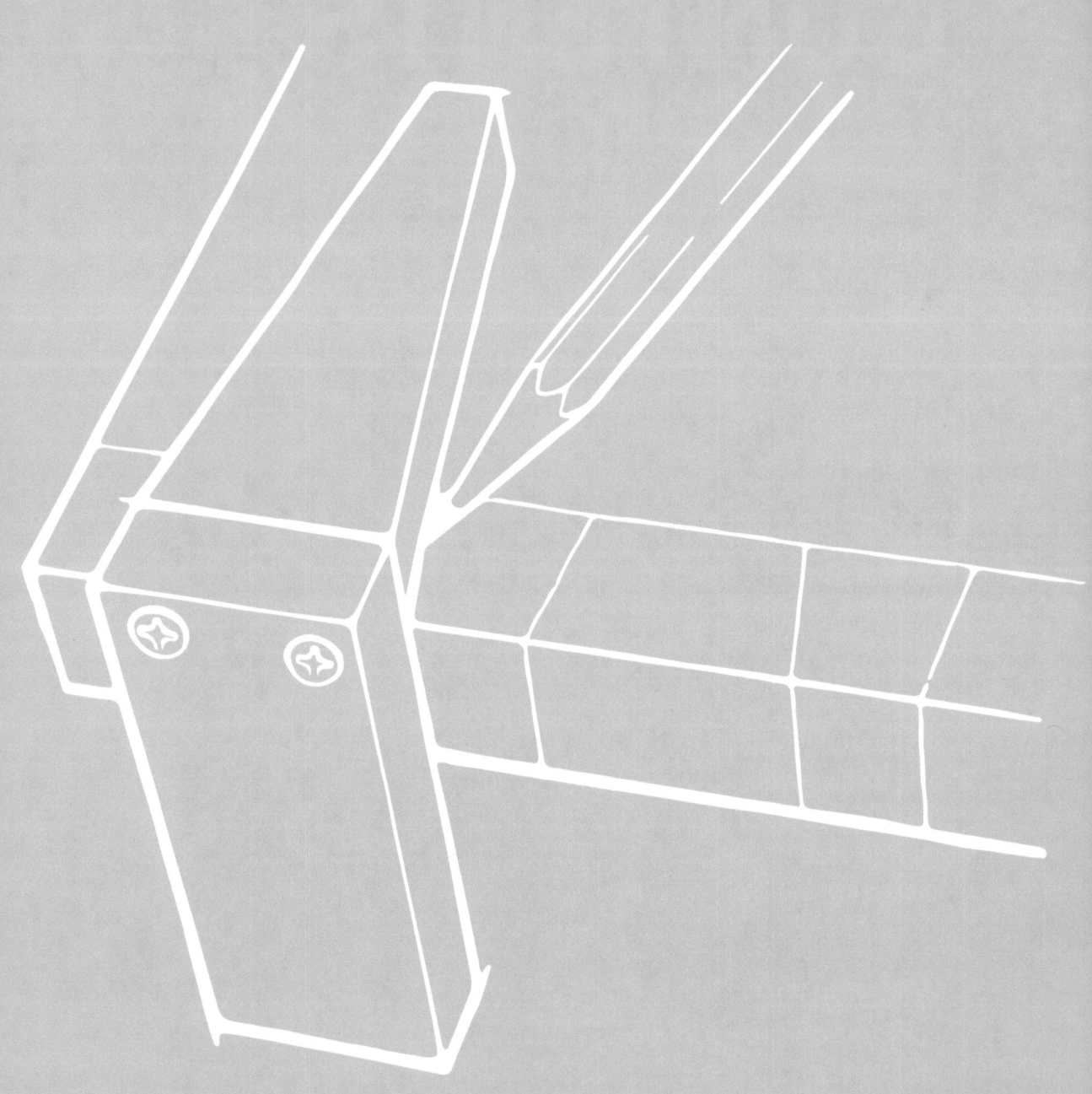

TECHNIQUES

ASSEMBLY **6**

FINISHING **14**

FURNITURE CONSTRUCTION **25**

GLUING **29**

JOINERY **37**

MEASURING & MARKING **47**

SANDING & SHAPING **61**

SHARPENING **72**

ASSEMBLY

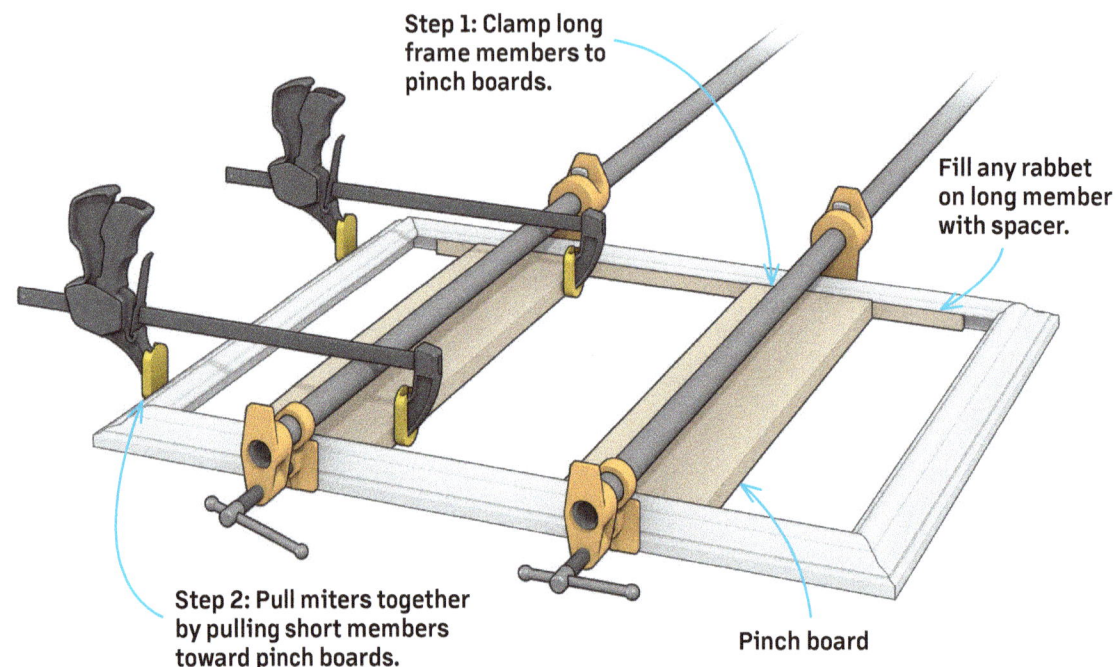

Clamping mitered frames in a pinch

If you don't have commercial miter clamps, here's an effective way to glue up a mitered frame without them. First, dry fit the pieces to ensure that the frame is square and the miters are tight. Make two square-crosscut boards a few inches wide, and as long as the shortest inside dimension of the frame. Tightly clamp these "pinch boards" between the long frame members, offsetting them from the ends to allow for glue squeeze-out. Double-check the joint fit, making adjustments if necessary, then apply glue to the joints, and clamp the miters together as shown. Note that for frames with an inside rabbet, you'll need to temporarily fill in the rabbets on the long members to prevent the pieces from cocking under clamp pressure.

—*Rick Melpignano, Enfield, CT*

How to grain-wrap a box

A mitered box looks best when the grain runs uninterrupted around the corners. To perform this trick, begin with stock that's twice the desired thickness of your finished wall, plus 1/4" or so for milling. Rip it to finished width, and about 1/4" longer than the combined length of 2 contiguous walls. Lay the walls out to length in the order shown in the top drawing, lettering the individual parts for reorientation later. After resawing the stock, plane it to final thickness, and then cut the pieces to length. To lay out the miters, first swap the pieces as shown in the top two drawings, which effectively turns the blank inside-out. After cutting the miters and joining the letter-matched ends, one pair of diagonally opposed box corners will exhibit continuous grain, and the opposite corners will be book-matched. Nice!

—Geoffrey Noden, Trenton, NJ

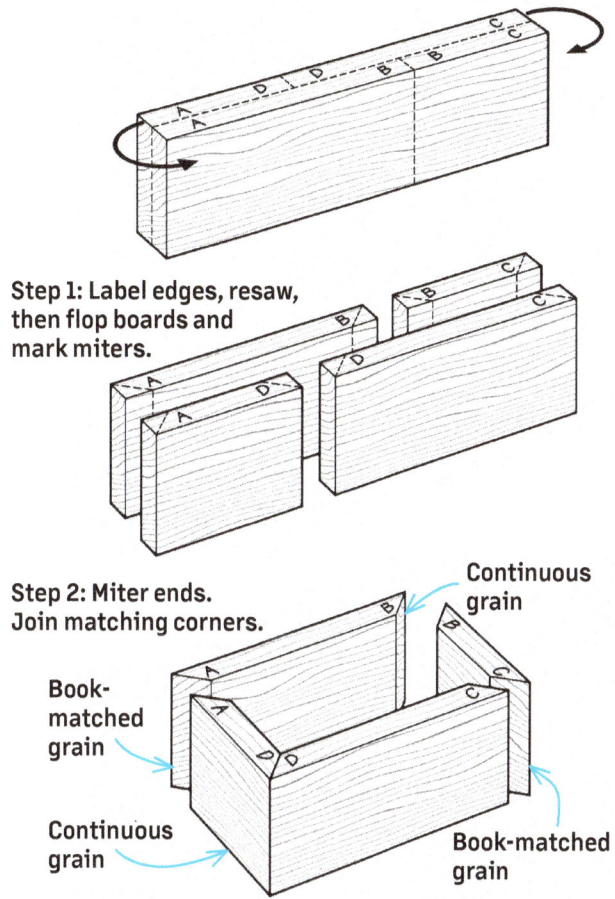

Step 1: Label edges, resaw, then flop boards and mark miters.

Step 2: Miter ends. Join matching corners.

Continuous grain

Book-matched grain

Continuous grain

Book-matched grain

Hammerless nailing

It probably won't happen often, but there may come a time when you need to drive a small nail and absolutely can't find the room to swing a hammer. Try using a C-clamp instead. Position the nail so that the fixed pad of the C-clamp is fitted on the nailhead, and the clamp is tightened to force the nail into the piece of wood. Use nails of a length that will not go into the second piece of wood and end up against the movable pad of the clamp. If the blocks of wood being nailed are also glued, the clamps can be left in place until the glue has set.

—Alan B. James, Phoenix, AZ

Lipstick for locks

Over the years, I've swiped a few items from my wife's makeup kit in the service of my craft. I'm particularly fond of lipstick, which I keep in my toolbox for marking lock mortise locations in door jambs. For example, after installing a deadbolt in a door and attaching the door stop, I wipe the lipstick across the end of the bolt. I retract it, close the door, and then throw the bolt, letting it kiss the door jamb to indicate the best placement for the bolt mortise and striker plate.

—Paul Anthony, Riegelsville, PA

TECHNIQUES > ASSEMBLY

Corral fasteners in a magnetic bowl

A magnetic mechanic's bowl—available at any auto-parts store—is a woodworker's spill-proof solution for screws, nails, or other ferrous hardware items. Even sideways or upside-down, the fasteners stay put until you need one. While the bowl's strong grip solves one problem, it can create another, making it difficult to remove the leftover fasteners to return them to storage. But you can sidestep this inconvenience with a plastic container such as a baby food dish with a clear snap-on lid. Even with this insert, the magnetic attraction is still strong enough to prevent most spills.

—Anna Martin, St. Louis, MO

Small brad holder

We've all seen tips for holding brads and small nails to avoid whacking your fingers—including using a slotted piece of cardboard, a comb, etc.—but here's a better approach. It's a holder that's very quick to use, and one that easily positions the brad in a vertical position for accurate starting taps. All you need is a tongue depressor or popsicle stick and two 1/4"-diameter rare-earth magnets. Simply cut a small V-shaped notch in one end of the stick, and then epoxy a magnet in place so that its edge is tangent to the bottom of the notch. To use the tool, position the brad against two stacked magnets, as shown, to hold it in place as you give it a starting tap or two.

—John Cusimano, Lansdale, PA

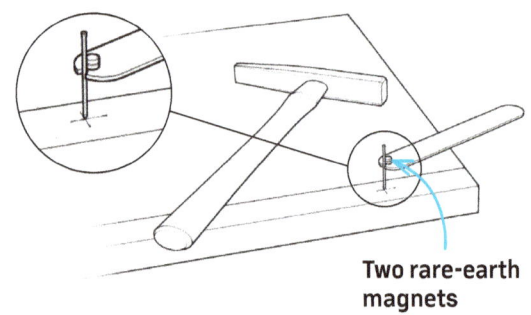

Two rare-earth magnets

Honing hardware to fit

Stamped hinges are often bowed across the face or distorted around the screw holes. This can complicate mortise layouts and can even interfere with precise installation. To correct problems before they occur, I hone my hardware before layout. Running the bottom face over a sharpening stone or mill file quickly identifies and then flattens minor bows or bumps.

—Tommy MacDonald, Boston, MA

Frame assembly jig

When nailing or screwing together the corners of picture frames or even small boxes, you need a way to hold the parts together for fastening. This simple assembly jig does the trick nicely. It's nothing more than an MDF panel with two rails attached at precisely 90º to each other. The ends of the rails are set back from the business corner of the panel to allow tool access when the frame pieces are positioned and clamped in place for fastening. The part dimensions are not critical, but I find that the sizes shown work well in most cases. What is important is that the panel is dead flat and that the rails sit square to it. I attached a clamping cleat to the underside to secure the jig to a bench vise when in use.

—Tom Washington, Billings, MT

Turn of the screw

Although they're extremely attractive in a variety of projects, brass screws are notoriously soft and easy to break if not installed carefully. Taking three easy preparatory steps before attempting to drive a brass screw into wood can help.

First, drill a pilot hole of the correct size. Then drive and remove a steel screw of the same size into the hole to create threads.

Finally, wax the brass screw with beeswax and drive it home.

—Don Guillard, Parkersburg, WV

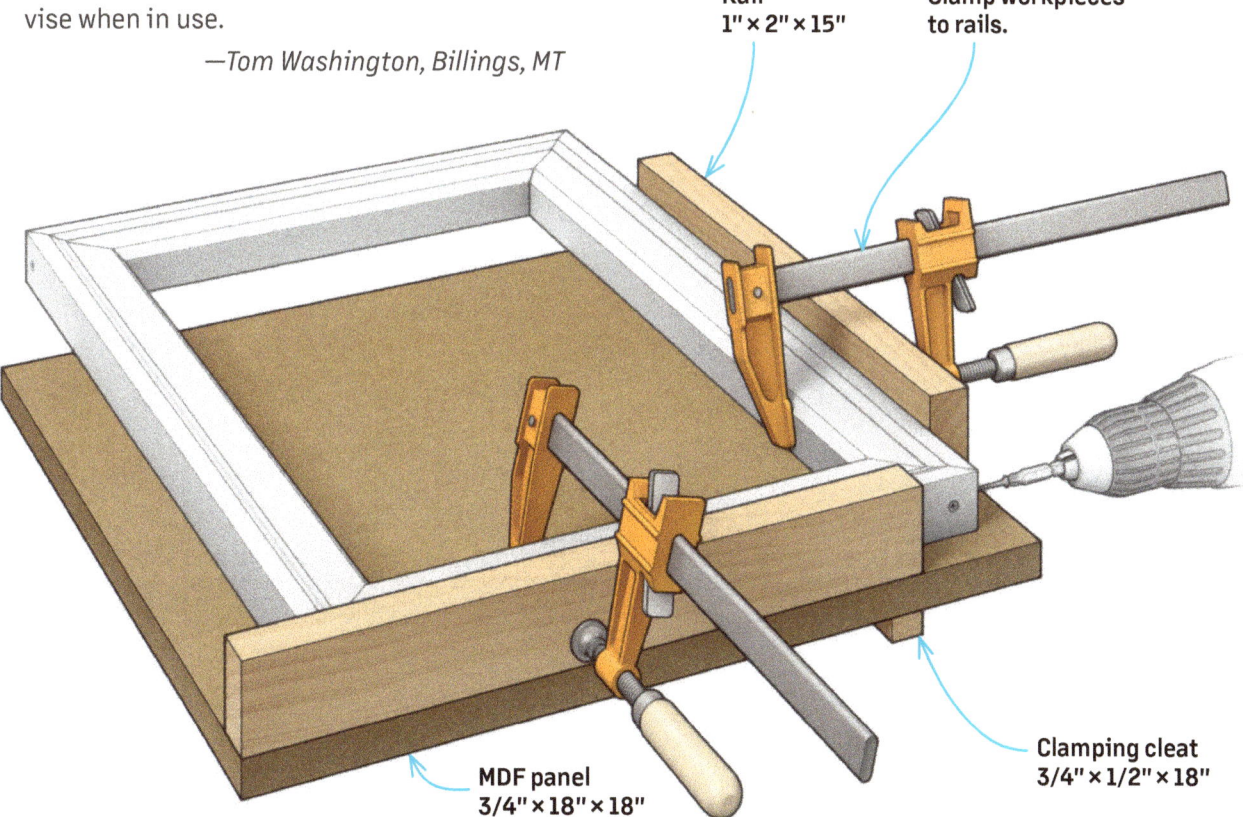

Rail
1" × 2" × 15"

Clamp workpieces to rails.

MDF panel
3/4" × 18" × 18"

Clamping cleat
3/4" × 1/2" × 18"

TECHNIQUES > ASSEMBLY

Door-hanging supports

When hanging cabinet doors with European hinges, I first screw the cup halves to the door and then attach the mounting plates to the hinge arms. Next, I hold the door in open position against the cabinet box in order to mark the locations of the mounting plates on the cabinet side. However, it can be a little tricky to hold the door while doing this. To make the job a lot easier, I cobbled up these door supports—one for a right-hand door, and one for a left-hand door. To use one, clamp it to the cabinet bottom as shown, positioning the shoulder to hold the door laterally about where you want it. This allows you to easily mark the hinge plate locations.

—Dan Martin, Galena, OH

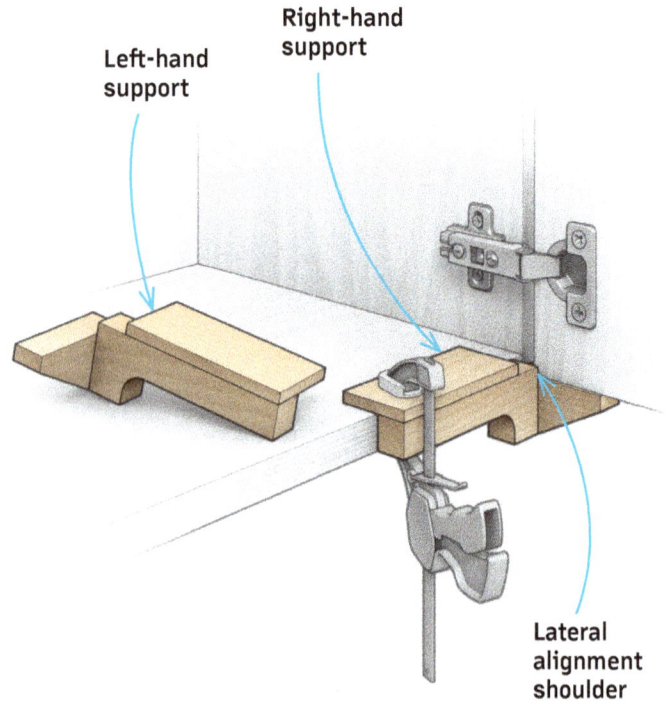

Left-hand support
Right-hand support
Lateral alignment shoulder

Brass ball catch upgrade

I like to use brass ball catches for fine furniture because they're classy looking, secure, and they can be mounted in a variety of orientations. However, I've experienced two problems with them. The first is that their springs are so stout that you really have to tug on the door to open it. (Even adjusting the spring caps outward doesn't help.) To fix the problem, I replace the stock springs with ballpoint pen springs cut to about the same length. The second issue with these catches is that, when mounted vertically, the bottom spring cap can back itself out from repeated use, ejecting the spring and ball. The solution? Unscrew the cap, apply a dab of fingernail polish to the threads, and reinsert while wet.

—Paul Anthony, Riegelsville, PA

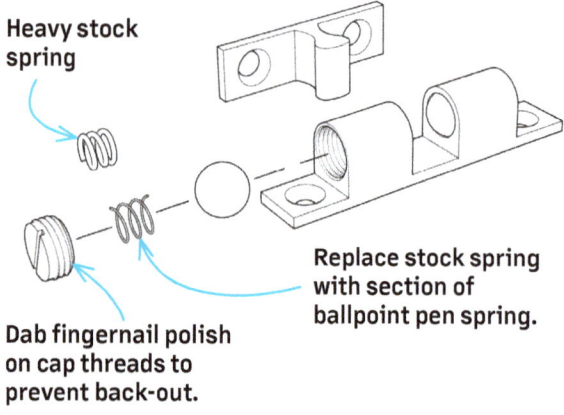

Heavy stock spring
Replace stock spring with section of ballpoint pen spring.
Dab fingernail polish on cap threads to prevent back-out.

Hands-free nailing

When using small nails, brads, tacks, etc., and it's hard to hold them with fingers while driving, put the nail in the open end of a bobby pin. Put the head down close to the pin to make it easier to hold.

—Jeremy Weston, Chicago, IL

ASSEMBLY < TECHNIQUES

Magnetic brad support

Holding small brads for hand-nailing can be a bruising experience. In an effort to find something to keep my fingers out of harm's way, I started digging through my miscellaneous hardware. When I came across an old magnetic catch that had fallen apart, I knew I had found the answer. In this type of common catch, the rectangular magnet has notched corners, into which a brad can nestle standing up. Holding the magnet instead of the brad keeps your fingers safe during those first few hammer taps. If you don't have this type of catch on hand, you can use any relatively thick magnet by filing a notch into it.

—Barry Goldwin, Springfield, MA

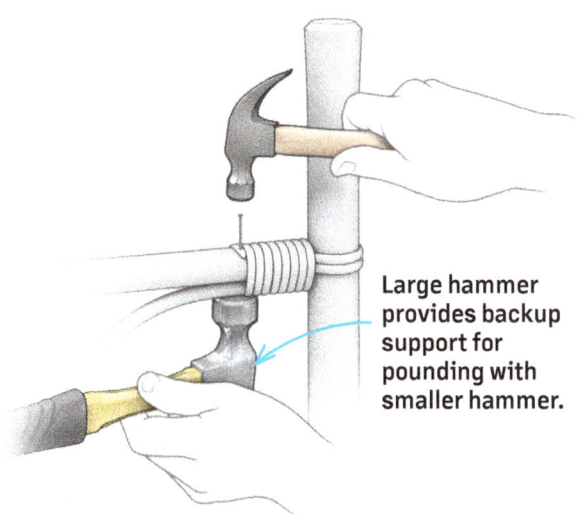

Large hammer provides backup support for pounding with smaller hammer.

Nailing backup

This tip came to mind the other day when I was tacking a strip of loose rattan back onto its table leg. There are times when you need to hammer against something like an upended table leg or a cantilevered chair arm that can't be laid on the bench for solid support. In those cases, you can bring backup to the piece in the form of another (preferably larger) hammer, small anvil, or any other chunk of heavy metal. It makes a world of difference, and often is the only way to smack the piece sufficiently without breaking it.

—Charles Fitzenberger, Mobile, AL

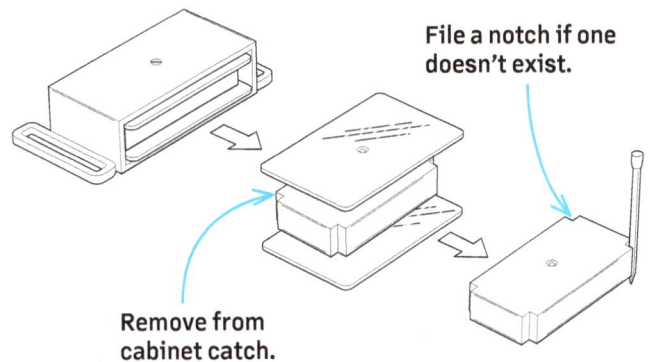

File a notch if one doesn't exist.

Remove from cabinet catch.

Instant soft-faced mallet

Need to knock something apart or tap something together and don't have a soft-faced hammer or mallet? Outfit the head of your hammer with an inexpensive rubber tip made for chair legs.

—Craig W. Bentzley, Chalfont, PA

TECHNIQUES > ASSEMBLY

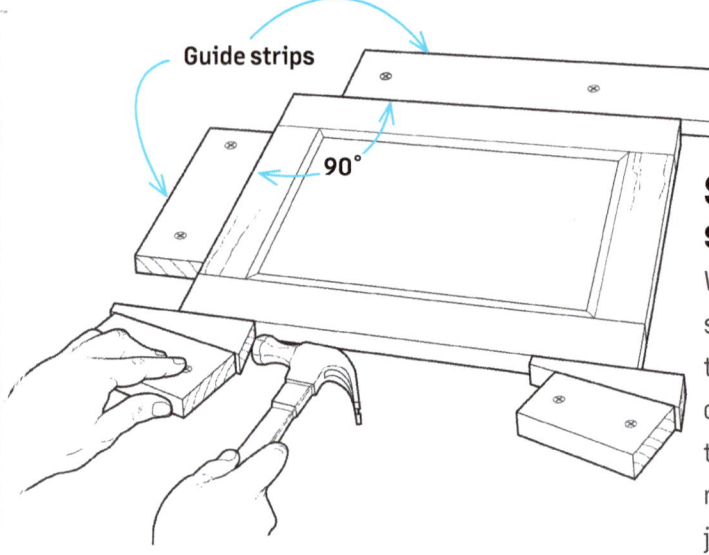

Guide strips
90°

Self-squaring, clamp-saving door assembler

While assembling some doors for my new shop cabinets, I found myself working faster than the slow-setting glue and my humble collection of clamps would allow. Not ready to call it quits for the day, I came up with this no-clamp setup that enabled me to finish the job in less time, and for less money, than it would have taken to buy more clamps. This tip can be applied to any 3/4"-thick piece of scrap plywood, hardwood, or melamine, but I liked it so much that I outfitted my assembly table with a similar set of clamping guides.

Starting with a panel surface several inches larger than the door, use a framing square to position two perpendicular guide strips. Next, cut a pair of 15° wedges (the actual angle isn't terribly critical). Place a door into the assembly corner and position the wedges along the door's outside corners. Screw two blocks near the corners of the door so that when the wedges are tapped, the pressure is directed against the joint.

As an extra benefit, the table keeps the doors square and flat, and the wedge clamps are less likely to dent the wood. Just make sure to wax the table and the guides to prevent the assembly from sticking to your clamping table.

Spray adhesive helping hand

My partner, a 60-year-old, and I do a lot of wood finishing in houses such as installing vanities. As he is older, he gets frustrated putting in corner brackets underneath the vanity; the brackets keep falling out of his hands due to the awkward position required. This also happens when he is trying to straighten and screw a hook on the wall or attach a hinge to a door and so on.

We solved the problem by putting a small amount of high-strength spray adhesive contact glue on the bracket, putting it in place, and then screwing it on with the use of one hand. No more having things fall. We carry a can of the glue with our tools. This idea makes work twice as easy.

—Fred Mandel, Dinsmore, Saskatchewan

—David Miller, Clemmons, NC

ASSEMBLY < TECHNIQUES

Help with keyhole hanging

Keyhole slots provide a great way to hang small cabinets and other projects. A pair of keyhole slots are also often integrated into commercial power strips and other accessories for mounting purposes. The problem with paired slots is that the screws must be laid out precisely on center to work, and misalignment can be hard to correct. I've found that commercially available dowel centers do the trick nicely. Just insert the appropriately sized dowel center into each keyhole slot, and then press the item to be mounted in place. Voila! You now have perfectly located centerpoints for your mounting screws.

—John Crouse, Wolcott, NY

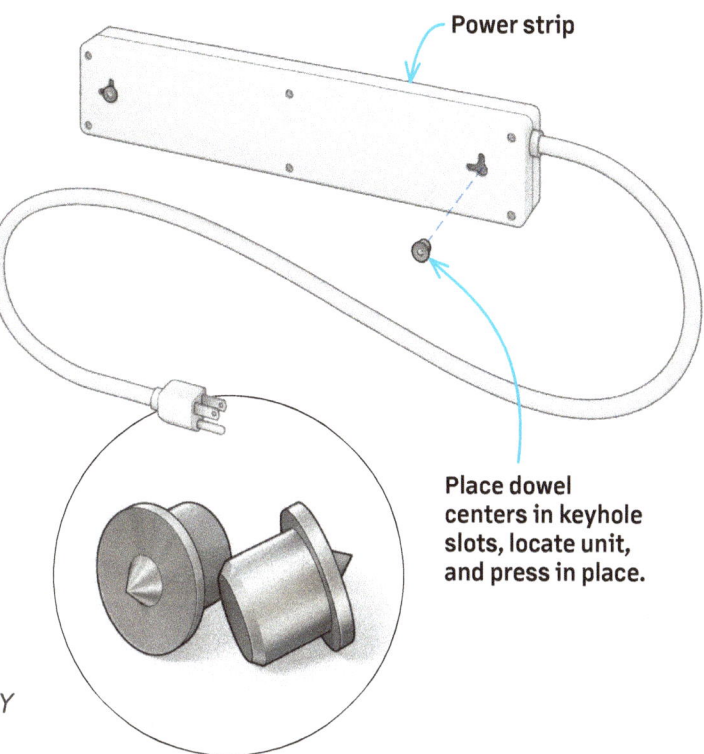

Place dowel centers in keyhole slots, locate unit, and press in place.

Easy ball catch location

I like using brass double-ball catches. The only problem is that they can be tricky to install, as there's virtually no allowance for misalignment. Here's an approach that I've found works well. First, screw the catch receiver to the cabinet. Then make a spacer that's at least as long and wide as the prong plate and a bit thinner than the length of the prong screw. After drilling pilot holes, screw the prong plate to the spacer, allowing the screw tips to project from the rear. Press the prong into the receiver and close the door. A few smart raps against the door will create divots that precisely locate the prong screws in the door's back side.

—Robert Wapp, Viroqua, WI

Step 1: Screw receiver to cabinet side.
Step 2: Screw prong plate to spacer with screw tip projecting.
Spacer
Step 3: Insert prong in receiver.
Step 4: Close door and tap on it to locate prong plate screws.
Receiver
Prong plate

WOODCRAFT MAGAZINE TIPS & TRICKS FOR WOODWORKING 13

FINISHING

A smarter way to spray small

I've always loved using my HVLP sprayer, except when finishing small projects. That's because it's inconvenient and wasteful to mix up small amounts of finish for the large can, which also doesn't work as well when it's mostly empty. I was agonizing over this when my 6-year-old granddaughter wandered into my shop sipping from a small 8-oz. water bottle, and I realized the answer was right in front of me.

I dried out the bottle and drilled a hole in the cap that would create a tight fit for my gun's siphon tube. Drilling part way through from each side with a brad-point bit created a very neat hole. I filled the bottle with finish, screwed on the top, and inserted the siphon tube. After slipping the bottle into the can and dogging down the lid, I found that the gun worked very well. Even when I tilted it sideways, the finish did not leak out. When done, I simply removed the bottle, sealed it with another cap, and set it aside to wait for the next coat. I didn't even have to clean out the can. No muss, no fuss.

—Thomas Moss, Bradenton, FL

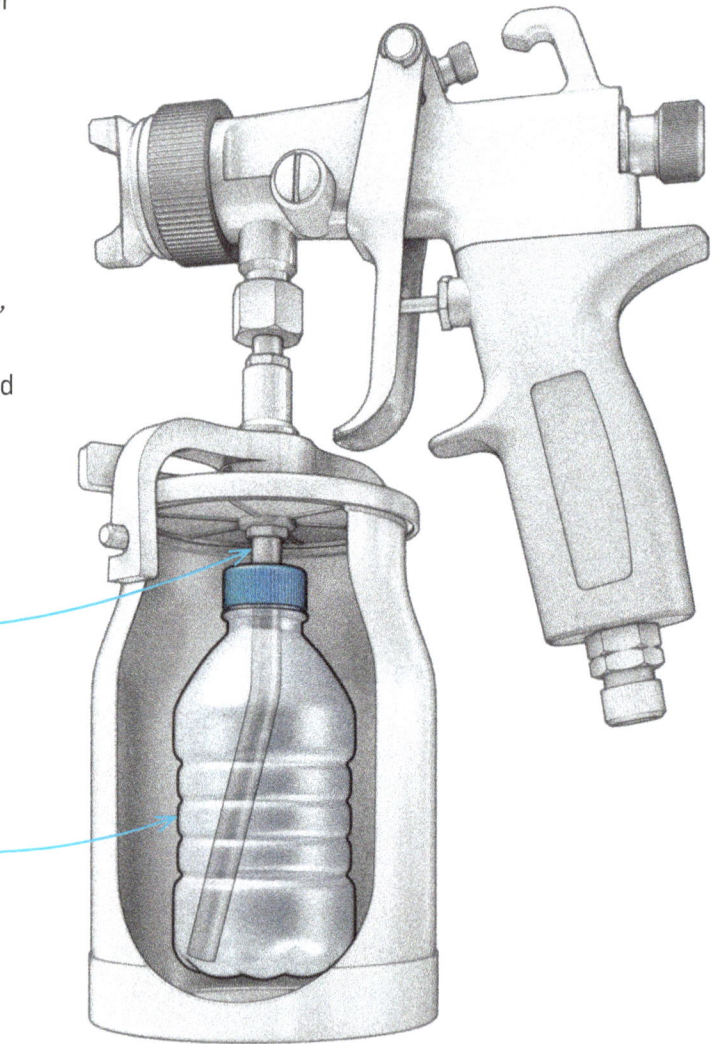

Slip siphon tube into hole in cap.

8-oz. water bottle

FINISHING < TECHNIQUES

Quick two-faced finishing

Solid-wood door panels should be finished before installing them in their grooves during frame assembly. The fact that the panel edges will be hidden in the assembled door means that you can avail yourself of a neat trick for efficient finishing. Set up for the job by pressing two widely spaced push pins into one end of your panel, and one in the center of the opposite end. Rest the pinned panel on a pair of 2×4s as shown, and apply finish to one panel face. Then grab the pair of pins on one end, and flip the panel over, rotating it on the single pin at the opposite end. You can now finish the second side without having to wait for the first to dry. The same basic approach can be used for any tall door whose top and bottom won't show in use. But instead of push pins, use nails or screws.

—Tim Markinson, Tulsa, OK

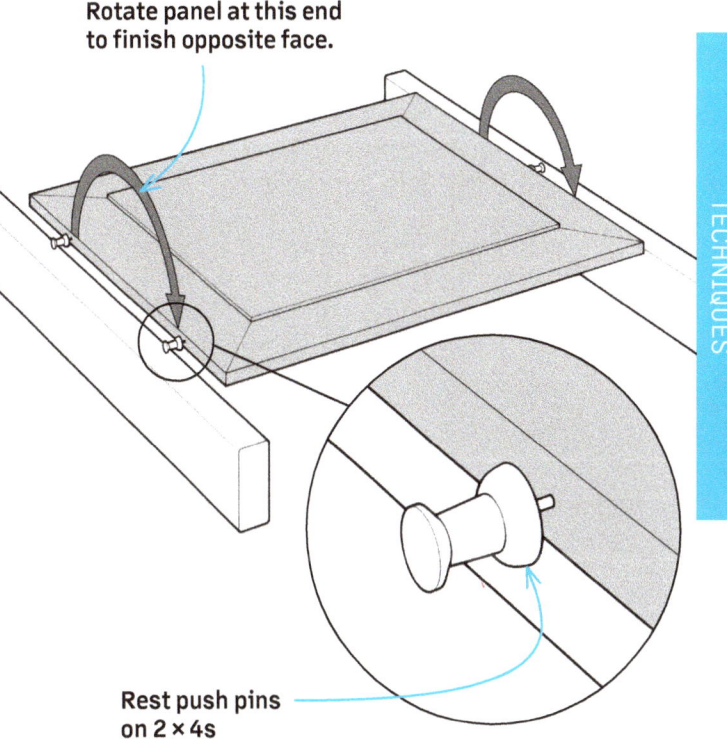

Rotate panel at this end to finish opposite face.

Rest push pins on 2 × 4s

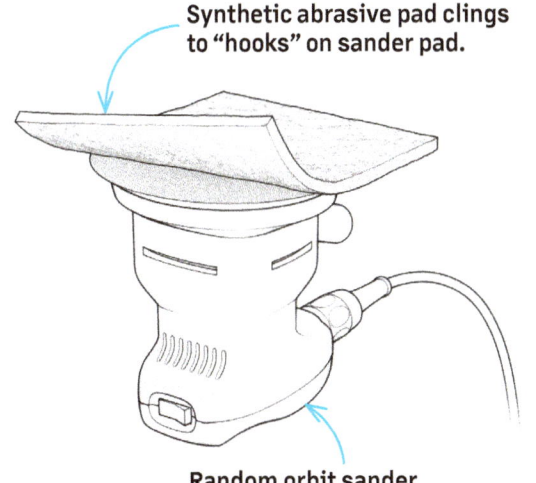

Synthetic abrasive pad clings to "hooks" on sander pad.

Random orbit sander

Random orbit rubout

Sometimes I like to use synthetic abrasive pads to rub out finishes. When working large panels, which can demand a lot of time and elbow grease, I pull my random orbit sander into service. Its hook-and-loop-faced disc grabs a synthetic pad firmly without slippage as long as the weight of the sander is on the pad. It sure makes easy work of an otherwise tedious chore.

—James Capstick, St. Louis, MO

WOODCRAFT MAGAZINE TIPS & TRICKS FOR WOODWORKING   15

TECHNIQUES > FINISHING

All-purpose alcohol swabs

Single-use alcohol swabs are good for more than just cleaning minor cuts. In the shop, these inexpensive spill-proof pads are useful for erasing smudges and pencil marks, stripping the adhesive off sanding plates, and removing pitch from tools (especially thickness-planer feed rollers). Denatured alcohol won't stain or raise wood grain and, compared to most other solvents, is safe to handle, as long as you follow the manufacturer's safety precautions.

—*Kevin Strider, Sparta, NC*

Wipe-on shop-safe rust blocker

A thin coat of shellac is an easy (and easily reversible) way to keep rust from getting a toehold on metal hand tools such as planes, rules, and chisels. Simply mix up a fresh 2-lb. cut, wipe on with a rag, let it dry, and you're done.

The thin film will eventually rub off surfaces that receive regular wear, but for spots that don't see metal-to-metal or metal-to-wood contact, or tools that spend most of their time sitting on a shelf, the hard film finish provides long lasting protection. Unlike some oils or heavy film protectants, shellacked tools don't require any special cleanup when you want to put them to use. To dissolve and completely strip off any shellac residue, use denatured alcohol and a clean rag.

—*Peter Tomlinson, Cullman, AL*

A lattice drying rack

I was wondering what to do with a couple of PVC lattice panel scraps left over from a deck project, when I realized they would make great drying racks. I hung them from screws on ceiling joists (they could be screwed to wall studs instead), and slipped square sticks into their openings to serve as supports for work being finished. The sticks, which can be arranged in any configuration, rest diagonally so there's minimal contact with the finished underside of a workpiece. If necessary to keep the lattice panels from flopping, you can attach a spring clamp at each end of at least one stick.

—*Serge Duclos, Delson, Québec*

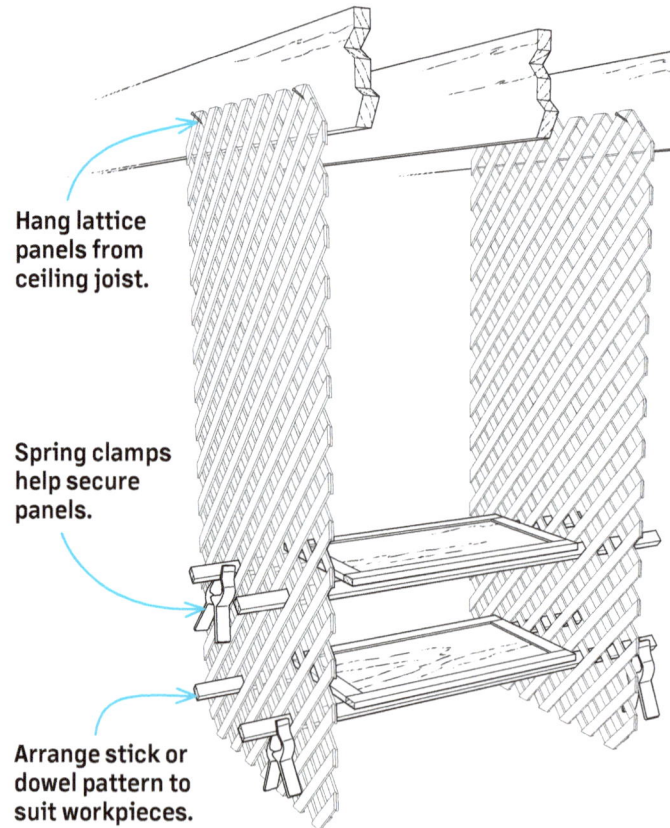

Hang lattice panels from ceiling joist.

Spring clamps help secure panels.

Arrange stick or dowel pattern to suit workpieces.

Disposable mixing cup

Good kitchen measuring cups don't belong in the shop, or any place where you might feel tempted to use them for mixing epoxy, two-part finishes, or other nasty chemicals. If you can convince the cook of the house to let you borrow the good measurer just once, you can make a decent shop-grade substitute from a plastic cup.

Using water, carefully pour set amounts, then mark the side of the cup with a permanent pen. Instead of repeating that measuring and marking process with each mix, simply slide a second cup inside the first. If you can keep the master cup clean, you can mix a boat's worth of epoxy without needing to redo your measurements.

In addition to preserving domestic harmony, my disposable measuring cup prevents the accidental contamination that can occur when mixing chemically reactive ingredients in the same container.

—Joe Roscoe, Rochester, NY

Dying in small measures

When making custom dyes from powders or liquids, I blend together primary and secondary colors that I've mixed up in 8-oz. containers. When trying to hit a color target, I combine very small amounts to test on my project wood. For best results, I use a cough syrup cup as a measure because it includes increment markings on the side, allowing me to keep accurate records of mix ratios that I can record in a notebook or on my stain samples.

—Jeff Peters, Redgranite, WI

Sawdust filler tips

To fill in gaps, I have often mixed up my own filler from glue and sawdust. I was never quite satisfied with the result, because the glue residue affected the finish. Now I use stainable glues mixed with sawdust. The fine sawdust from my palm sander's dust collection bag is excellent for mixing.

I also found that rubbing the joint with sawdust gives a slightly rounded and smooth edge that stains well. I store the sawdust in containers labeled by type of wood.

—Jay Williams, Shirleysburg, PA

TECHNIQUES > FINISHING

Make dust for filler

Here's a method for getting a great color match to make wood filler with sawdust for small parts. Cut a small block from scrap that matches the wood where the defect is. On the table saw, make a series of parallel cuts about 1/4" apart and at least 1/2" deep. Use masking tape to cover where those cuts exit the block and find the finest, most worn-out belt you have for your belt sander. Hold the block against the belt for a few seconds and turn the sander off with it still held in place. Lift the block off gently; static electricity will have held a nice amount of dust in the saw cuts. I label and save the blocks so I always have a source for fresh dust of the woods I use most often. The small amount of tape in the mix won't affect your color match at all.

—William McDowell, Syracuse, NY

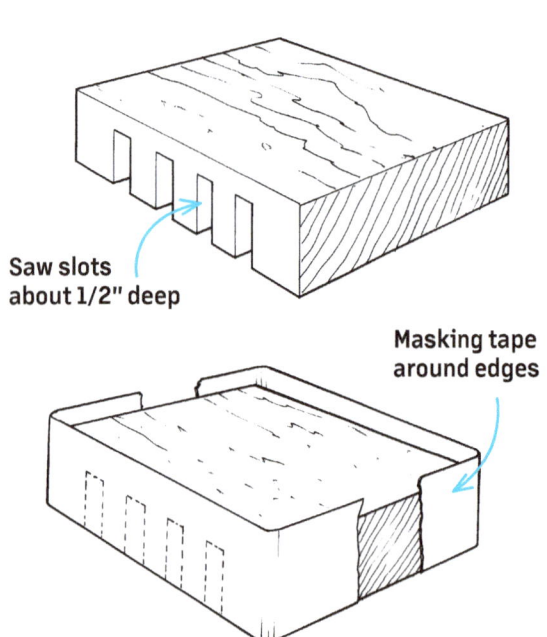

Saw slots about 1/2" deep

Masking tape around edges

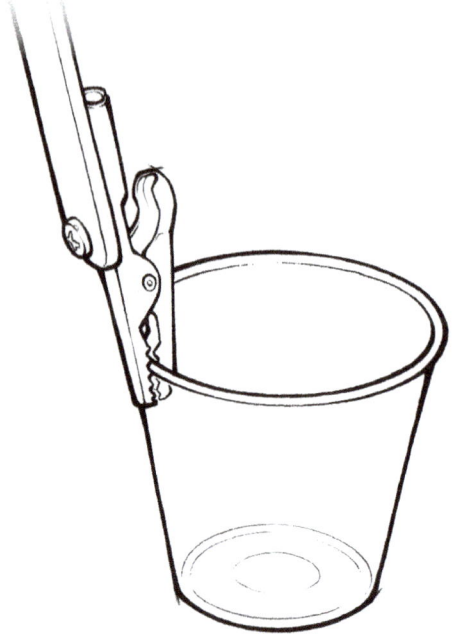

Lil' dipper for finishes

I use expensive varnish on the natural-edge tables I make. I have found that dipping finish from the container is easier and less messy than trying to pour small amounts into another container. You also eliminate getting finish in the rim of the can, which we all know makes it impossible to remove, and eventually finds its way into the finish.

To make the job easier, I use little plastic shot glasses. They are available at party stores and drug stores. To hold the cups for dipping, I made a little jig using a small piece of wood and an electrical alligator clip. The cups are inexpensive and disposable, and they eliminate another possible opportunity for contamination. They are also handy for mixing small quantities of epoxy, paints, and stains—just be careful that the solvent from whatever material you are using doesn't dissolve the cup. Liquid levels easily show through the clear sides, so keep a permanent marker handy.

—John Esposito, Foster, RI

Finishing turntable

When faced with spray-finishing a half-dozen Windsor chairs, I realized that I needed a rotating platform. When I remembered seeing a design for a turntable built around the concept of one pipe slipped inside another, I headed to the hardware store to buy the parts, and found that 3/4" ID galvanized pipe can nestle nicely inside 1" ID galvanized pipe. (But double-check, because some pipe diameters vary.) I had one end of each pipe threaded, and bought the appropriate pipe flanges and mounting screws, along with a 3/16" × 2" bolt.

Back at the shop, using a scrapwood V-cradle at the drill press, I drilled a row of 7/32"-diameter holes through the larger pipe, screwed each pipe flange to a piece of 3/4" plywood, and slid the pipes together. Voila! A turntable! To adjust the height for comfortable spraying of smaller pieces, I simply slip the 3/16" bolt into the chosen pipe hole, where it serves as a rest for the bottom of the 3/4" ID pipe.

—Marlon Rappaport, Newport, RI

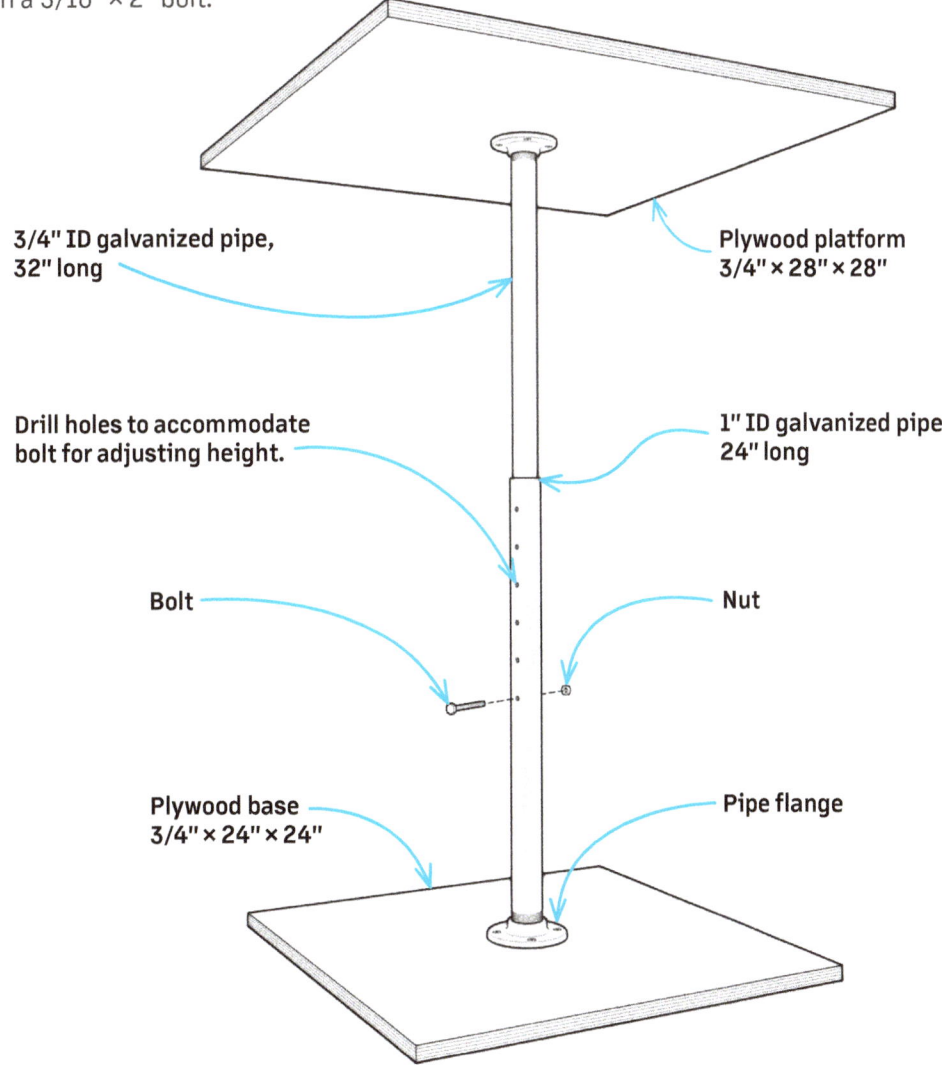

TECHNIQUES > FINISHING

Parallelogram screw strips

Like many woodworkers, I often use "screw strips" to support panels and other project parts when finishing them. With flat-head screws driven through them, these screw strips essentially hold the inverted screws upright so "wet" work can rest on the tips without damage, allowing you to finish to both faces of a piece in immediate succession.

The problem I've found with most screw strips is that they're prone to tipping. To solve the problem, I took inspiration from the concept of parallel rulers. I simply connected a pair of screw strips using two 1/4"-thick strips of hardboard and a couple 3/4" pan-head screws with washers, as shown. When spread apart, the parallelogram unit has firm footing for supporting workpieces. When not in use, a unit can be folded shut and safely stacked together against another unit with the screws facing inward toward each other.

—*Mark Dean, Dade City, FL*

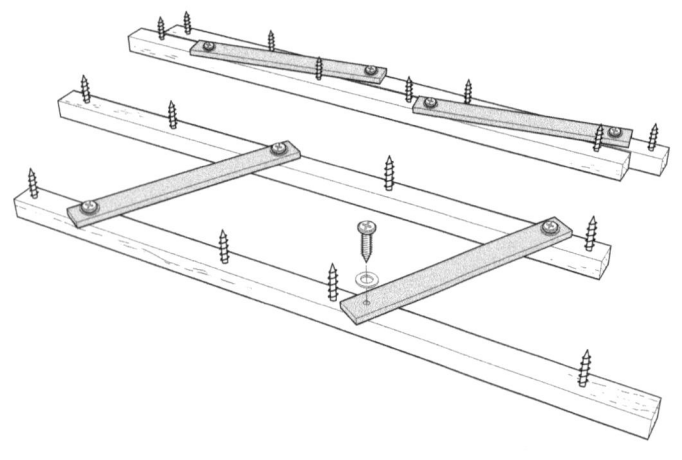

Transform blind slats into finishing standoffs

The quest for the perfect standoff for raising freshly finished projects off a dust-ridden shop surface never ends. I stumbled across this cost-free solution. I took old plastic venetian blind slats, shaped a section into a rough circle shape, and pinned the ends together with a single staple (the slats tend to take their own shape.) The stapled slats provide all the compressive strength you need to hold most any reasonable size workpiece during the curing process. After use, I hook the standoffs on a long hook or nail or discard used-up ones.

—*Bob Klelland, St. John's, Newfoundland*

Scaling down "pound cuts"

When giving instructions on mixing your own shellac from flakes, many woodworking articles refer to "pound-cut," which indicates how many pounds of flakes are mixed into one gallon of denatured alcohol. Unfortunately, the math for scaling down the dry- and fluid-ounce measurements when mixing smaller amounts can be confusing. To simplify matters, remember that a "pound cut" ratio is the same as an "ounce/cup" ratio. (One ounce of flakes to one cup of alcohol yields a 1-lb. cut; two ounces of flakes to one cup of alcohol for a 2-lb. cut, etc). I find that a cup or two is enough for mid-sized projects. If not, it's easy to mix up more at the same cut.

—*Mike Buchanan, Franklin Lakes, NJ*

FINISHING < TECHNIQUES

A tacky uplift

Nail dome-headed upholstery tacks into a board to create a stand-off platform for finishing. The tack heads minimize contact with the surface without scarring and allow airflow under the workpiece.

—Rob Spiece, Berea, KY

Simple spindle spraying

When faced with spray-finishing a bunch of spindles, I find that it's well worth the time to set up a simple rack for hanging the parts. It's nothing more than a suspended 2 × 4 outfitted with cup hooks. I then install a screw eye into the end of each spindle to hang it from a cup hook. (No harm done since spindle ends are seldom exposed in a finished piece.) The setup allows me complete spraying access, and eliminates handling the pieces during the process.

—Joe Hurst-Wajszczuk, Birmingham, AL

Cup hook in 2 × 4 accommodates screw eye in end of spindle.

Ladders provide convenient support.

WOODCRAFT MAGAZINE TIPS & TRICKS FOR WOODWORKING   21

TECHNIQUES > FINISHING

An adjustable brush

When a finishing brush started falling apart, I decided to hold it together with a rubber band, which worked pretty well. In the process, I realized that I was converting my floppy-bristled brush into a firm-bristled brush, which I find works better when applying thicker finishes. Now I don't have to buy such a wide variety of brushes. I simply "adjust" the bristle stiffness with a thin rubber band, placing it closer to the ferrule for best flexibility, and closer to the far end for more stiffness.

—Ethan Talbert, St. Augustine, FL

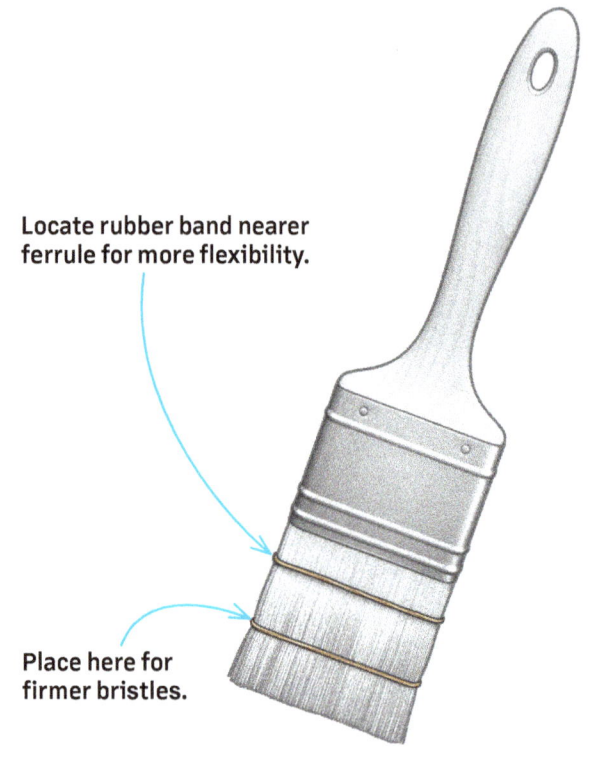

Locate rubber band nearer ferrule for more flexibility.

Place here for firmer bristles.

Paper bag trick

The problem with slow-drying finishes, such as oil-based polyurethane, is that no matter how carefully you clean your shop, a few dust specs are bound to land onto the surface before the finish has completely dried.

Before you resort to sanding out the finish and applying another topcoat, try rubbing the last coat with a piece of brown paper shopping bag. As an abrasive, brown paper is finer than even #0000 steel wool. As long as the finish is thoroughly dry, the paper will level dust nibs without scratching the surface. Once the finish feels satisfactorily smooth, top it off with a coat of wax to give it extra sheen.

—Tommy MacDonald, Boston, MA

FINISHING < TECHNIQUES

Sanding against the grain for a smoother finish

Pre-raising the grain before applying a water-based dye or topcoat is a good way to deal with the fibers that pop up when you add water, but if you're not careful, you could only press down the fibers you want to remove. My approach may sound unconventional, but it works.

After finish-sanding and wiping the surface with a wet sponge, wait until the surface dries. Now using your final grit, very lightly sand across the grain. Next, sand diagonally across the grain in one direction, and then in the other. This cross-grained sanding breaks away the fibers cleanly. Finish up by sanding parallel to the grain, using similar pressure to erase any cross-grained scratches.

—Peter Christian, Little Rock, AR

Practice new methods

When you're trying some new technique or finish on a project, start off in a discreet area like the back, an underside, or low at the rear of the piece to let you get the feel of it. That way, if you happen to screw up, you won't be loudly announcing the flaw. And when you do make a mistake on a piece, for gosh sake, don't ruin someone's compliment of your work by immediately pointing out and apologizing for the goof. Well, try not to, anyway.

—Uncle Remus, Truth or Consequences, NM

Combustion prevention

Drape flattened solvent-finish rags over ladder steps to allow air circulation as they dry. If left crumpled up, heat-releasing drying agents trapped in air pockets can lead to spontaneous combustion. Those warning labels are no joke.

—Larissa Huff, Schwenksville, PA

Final polish

Tinted wax-type shoe polish can be used for final polishing and as color-matching filler for fixing finish nail holes. Unlike lighter wax, leftover residue won't leave a white haze.

—Tristan Juday, Portsmouth, ME

TECHNIQUES > FINISHING

Tabletop spray booth

The availability of water-based finishes and affordable small-scale spray units these days makes finishing moderately sized projects easier than ever. If you're spraying in your shop, however, you do need a spray booth of some sort to manage the overspray. I have a simple, inexpensive setup that does the job nicely. I created a booth by slicing and taping together pieces of inexpensive 1/2"-thick rigid foam insulation, available at home centers. I cut out a ventilation window in the rear panel, to which I taped a small furnace filter. Placed on a table near an open window with a small box fan in between, the setup safely corrals and evacuates water-based overspray. (I don't recommend spraying solvent-based finishes through an electric fan.) When I'm done finishing, the booth is quickly disassembled for compact storage.

—Sarah Frank, Lake Charles, LA

Tape together rigid insulation panels to create a box.

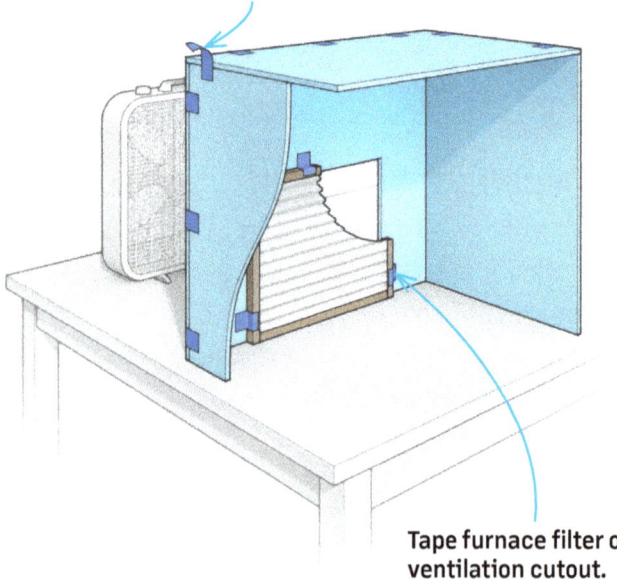

Tape furnace filter over ventilation cutout.

Finish flip seal

Partially used cans of finish can be hard to seal properly, causing the finish to go bad. A good way to prevent this is to wipe the lid contact areas clean, tap the lid down well, and then flip the can upside down for storage. This way, the finish itself will form an airtight seal around the rim.

—Jonah Talbert, St. Augustine, FL

Shellac and linseed combo for turners

To achieve an instant finish on your woodturnings that is hard, smooth, and beautiful, mix a solution of 50% shellac and 50% linseed oil. Soak the end of a cloth, turn on your lathe, and while the piece is turning, "burn it in." As the finish heats up, it will harden and dry for an instant and awesome finish!

—James J. Olszewski, Tigard, OR

Free distilled water

Because it's free of chemicals, distilled water is often recommended for mixing dyes and for raising grain prior to one final finish-sanding before applying a water-based finish. If you own a dehumidifier, you have a free source of this water. Just note that it's not safely drinkable.

—Perry Walker, Salem, MA

FURNITURE CONSTRUCTION

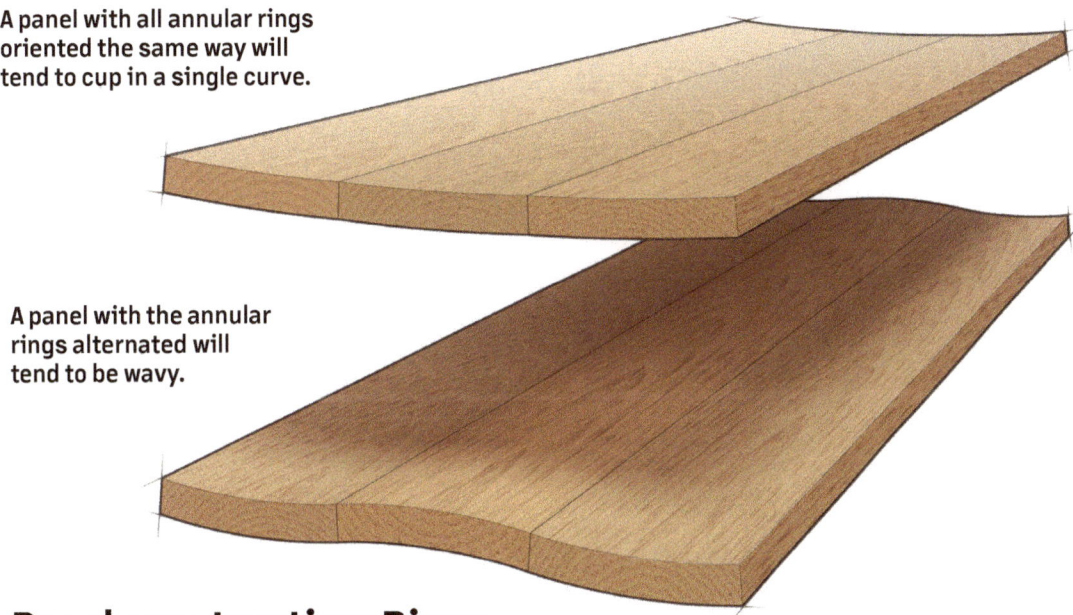

A panel with all annular rings oriented the same way will tend to cup in a single curve.

A panel with the annular rings alternated will tend to be wavy.

Panel construction: Rings up or rings down?

There is conflicting advice regarding how to orient the annular rings on boards when edge-gluing them to make up wide panels. Some say to alternate the direction of the rings; others say to keep them all oriented the same way.

The debate goes back to the days when woodworkers had wider, but inconsistently dried stock to work with. Flat-sawn boards tend to cup opposite the orientation of their annular growth rings, so if all the rings of the boards that make up a panel are oriented in the same direction, the panel will tend to curl like a potato chip as it adjusts to its environment. This tendency can be overcome by fastening the panel to an apron, adding breadboard ends, or trapping it within a frame.

If the rings in the boards are alternated, the panel will tend to develop waves, or ripples across its surface. But overall, the panel will remain flatter. I take this approach when making unsupported panels such as table leaves, using riftsawn or quartersawn stock if possible for best stability.

For panels that will be supported in some manner, I simply arrange the boards for the best face grain match, and ignore the annular ring orientation.

—*Kirby Hastings, Kansas City, MO*

TECHNIQUES > FURNITURE CONSTRUCTION

Hinge as a drawer stop

When I make a project with simple wooden drawer guides, I like to add an outward stop to prevent the drawer from accidentally being pulled all the way out and spilling its contents on the floor. Of all the techniques I've tried, one of the simplest and most effective is to screw a hinge to the rear edge of the top rail. Locating the hinge so that only part of the lower leaf extends below the rail creates an effective stop that can easily be lifted up out of the way when you want to remove the drawer.

—James Hoyt, Lexington, NE

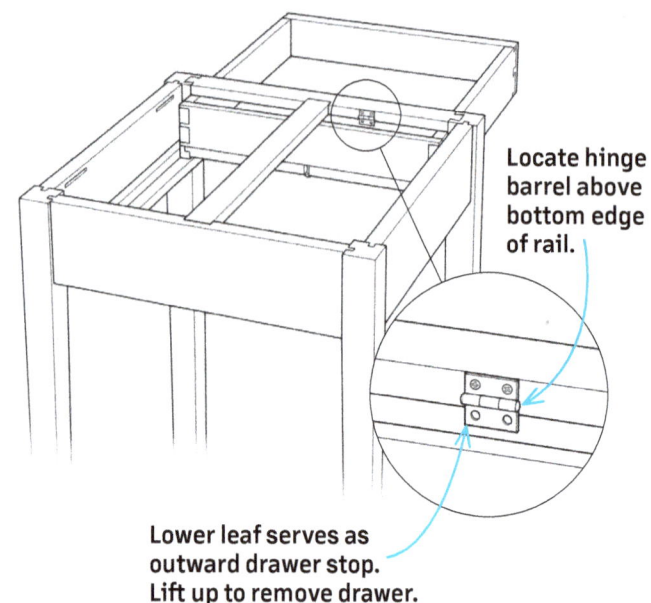

Locate hinge barrel above bottom edge of rail.

Lower leaf serves as outward drawer stop. Lift up to remove drawer.

Book-matching legs

When making a project with four square legs, a nice visual touch is to configure the legs to display book-matched grain when viewed from any side of the piece. Here's how to do it: Begin with a square piece of riftsawn stock the length of the legs. It should be twice the thickness of a finished leg, plus about 1/4". Draw a triangle on one end, and then rip the piece into quarters to make four individual leg blanks. Using the triangle as a reference, reconstitute the pieces back into their original order, and number the ends as shown. Then switch the position of two diagonally placed legs, and rotate the remaining two legs 180°. Maintaining this relationship of the legs on the project will create book-matched leg grain on each face of the piece.

—Geoffrey Noden, Trenton, NJ

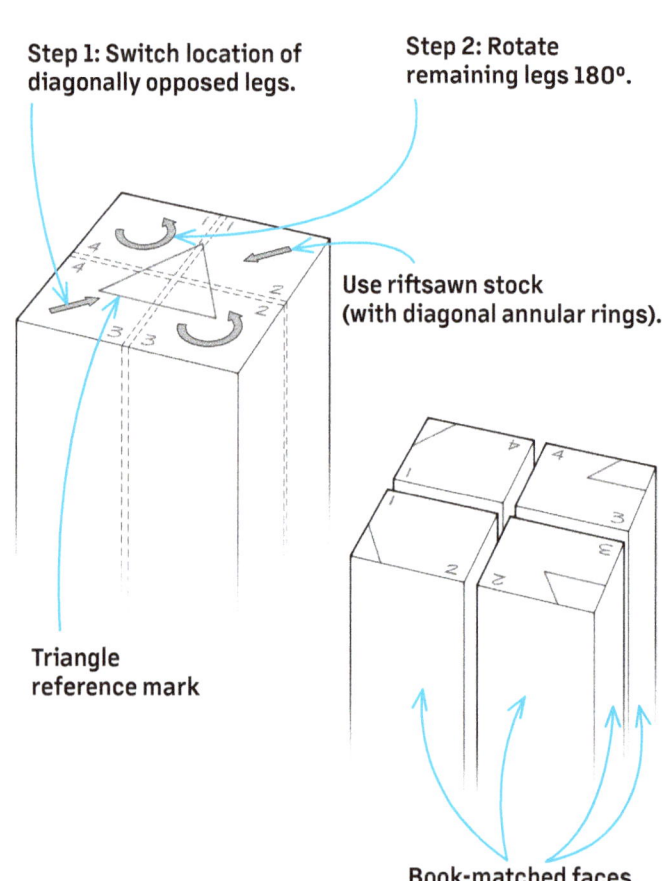

Step 1: Switch location of diagonally opposed legs.

Step 2: Rotate remaining legs 180°.

Use riftsawn stock (with diagonal annular rings).

Triangle reference mark

Book-matched faces

Adjustable drawer stop

A traditional method for creating drawer stops for inset drawers is to glue two small blocks of wood—one on each side—to the front rail of the drawer's supporting web frame. The tricky part is aligning the stops perfectly so that the drawer front face sits precisely flush with the cabinet face. A typical approach is to first measure back from the front edge of the rail on the web frame, then scribe a line at the location of the rear face of the drawer front. Wipe glue on the stops, set them a bit forward of your line, and then carefully install the drawer, aligning it perfectly with the case front. Make sure to remove the drawer before the glue sets to prevent any squeeze-out from locking it in place.

Unfortunately, the blocks can slip out of alignment during installation. My fail-safe trick? I cut a small rabbet in my stop material, and install each stopblock with the rabbeted face forward, as shown. Then, if the drawer front sits a bit proud of the case after the glue sets, a swipe or two with a shoulder plane across the stop is all it takes to cleanly line things up. Alternatively, I can glue on a sliver of veneer to pack out a recessed stop, planing it perfect afterward if necessary.

—Mario Rodriguez, Philadelphia, PA

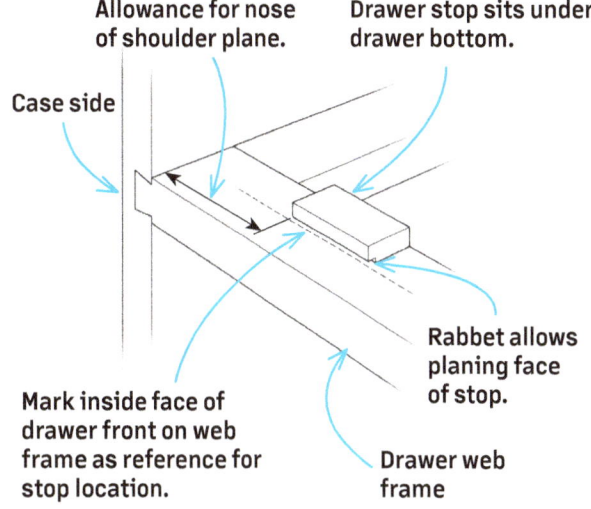

Simple drawer stops

A while ago, I made some utility drawer cabinets for my shop, using face frame construction and wooden drawer slides. Unfortunately, I sometimes found myself pulling the drawers out too far and spilling their contents on the floor. To prevent that nonsense, I drove a screw into the upper rear corner of each drawer side so that it would catch against the rear of the face frame to serve as a stop that can easily be removed when necessary. Not pretty, but effective. For nice furniture of similar construction, you could take a classier approach and use snug

—Bill Wells, Olympia, WA

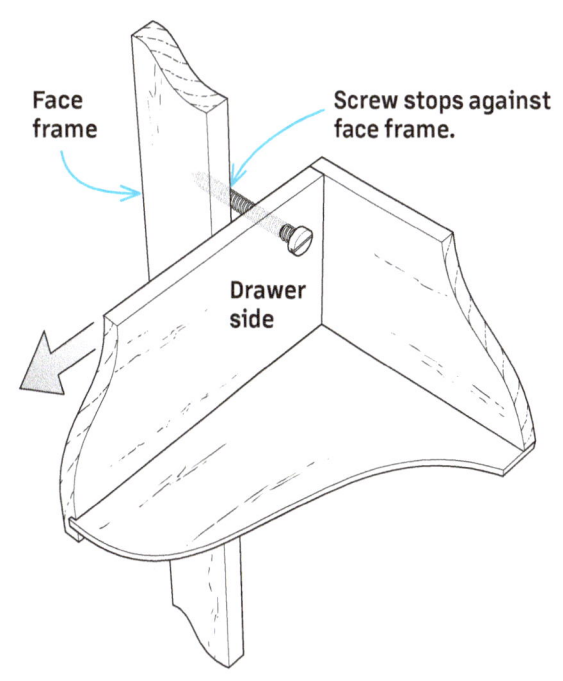

TECHNIQUES > FURNITURE CONSTRUCTION

Leather-faced outward drawer stop

An outward drawer stop prevents content spills while still allowing intentional drawer removal. Here's a clever version of an outward stop that's unobtrusive and simple to make. It consists of two blocks of wood, each mitered to 20° at one end and glued to a scrap of leather that serves as a hinge of sorts. One block is screwed to the case partition above the drawer, while its partner is free to drop down and butt against the inside face of a withdrawn drawer back. When installing a stop, center it across the width of the opening, and make sure to locate it far enough back to clear the drawer front. Alternatively, for a frameless opening with no space above the drawer, notch the drawer back to clear the stop. To remove the drawer, simply reach inside and lift the pivoting block out of the way of the drawer back.

—Andy Rae, Asheville, NC

Glue leather to both blocks.

Pivoting block 1/4" × 1" × 1-1/2"

Fixed block 1/4" × 1" × 1-1/2"

20°

Screw stop to partition above drawer, with miters to rear.

Adjustable drawer-planing perch

To plane a drawer side, you typically need to hang it on a support board that's cantilevered off the edge of your bench. The problem is that the work can shift around on a board whose width doesn't exactly match the inside dimension of the drawer box, and clamps can get in the way of planing.

Instead of a single board, I use sticks because they can be wedged to apply pressure against the sides of any sized drawer to secure it without clamps. To create the setup, extend three stout sticks across your bench as shown, with one of them resting against a projecting bench dog. With the drawer hanging on the cantilevered ends of the sticks, clamp their opposite ends to the bench, and then wedge a couple of cross sticks between them to create pressure against the sides of the box. (Note that the center cantilevered stick supplies support for full-length planing of the drawer side. If you're just cleaning up the joints at the corners, you can omit it.) When planing, work in the direction of the bench dog.

—Philip Houck, Boston, MA

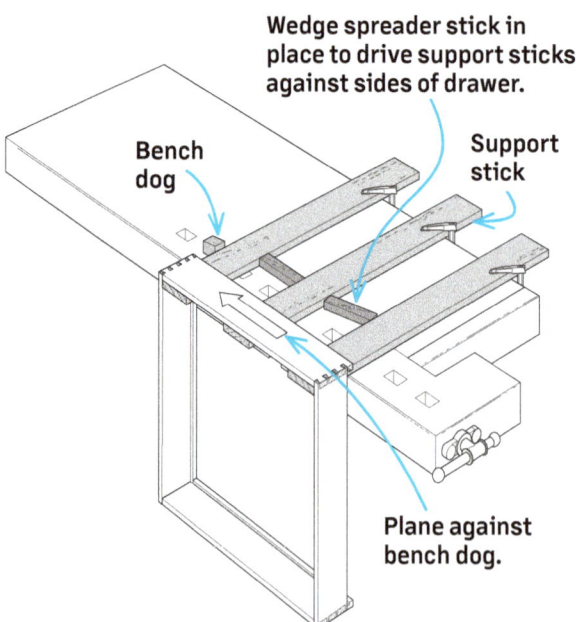

Wedge spreader stick in place to drive support sticks against sides of drawer.

Bench dog

Support stick

Plane against bench dog.

GLUING

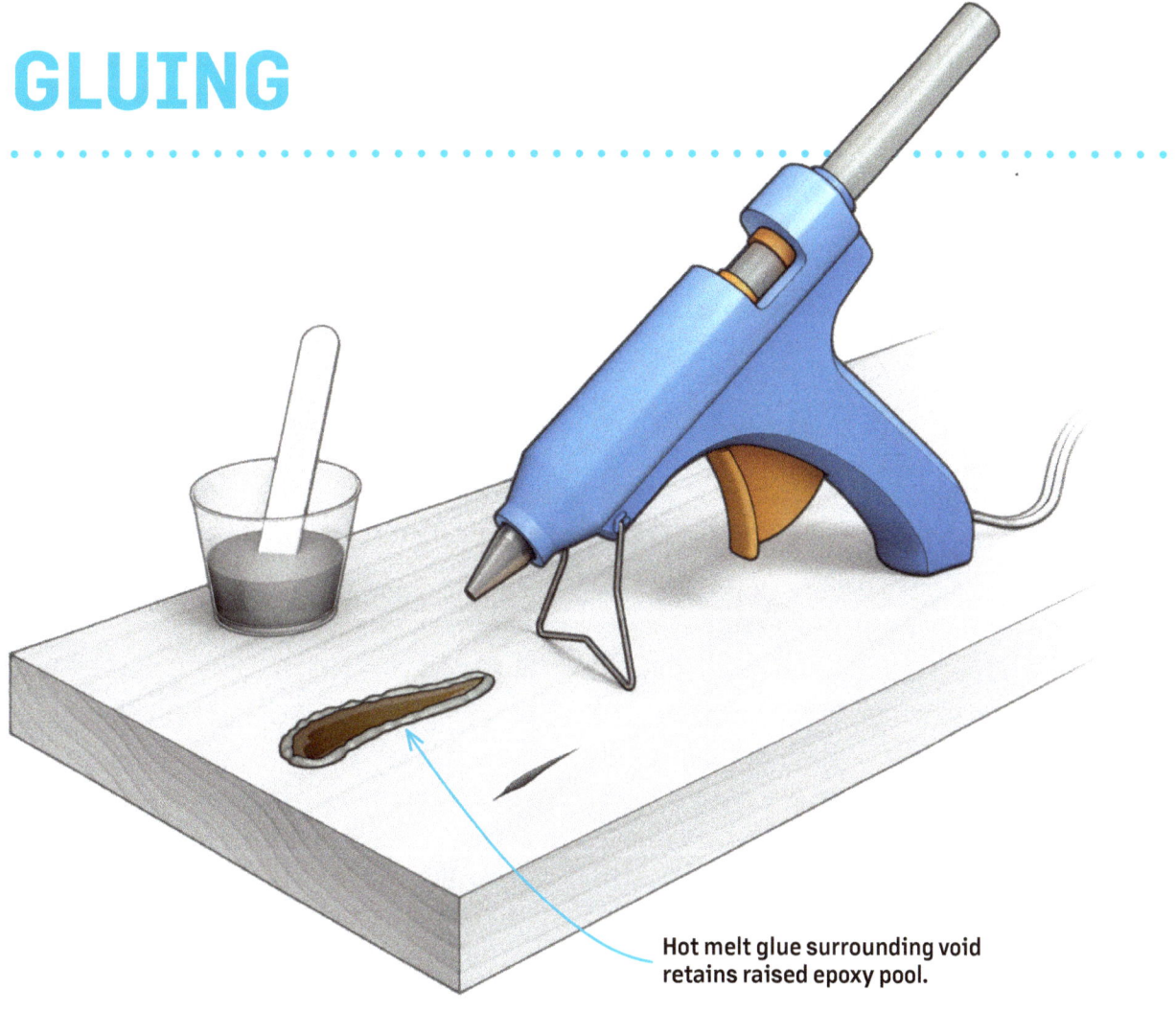

Hot melt glue surrounding void retains raised epoxy pool.

Hot-melt epoxy shortcut

Like many woodworkers, I use slow-curing epoxy to fill cracks and voids in slabs and other boards. The problem is that you have to babysit the application, often refilling it multiple times as it settles and seeps into the void, which is time consuming. I've discovered that you can use hot-melt glue to create a "dam" around the recess that creates a reserve to replace seepage. It also keeps the epoxy from oozing across the surface where it's not needed. After the epoxy cures, just use a card scraper to remove the hot melt glue and epoxy overfill for a flat, smooth, void-free surface.

—Brett Whited, Washington, WV

TECHNIQUES > GLUING

No-tip cup holder

I use disposable paper cups to hold glue, filler, and finishes. They're inexpensive, readily available, and easy to dispose of. Their only drawback is that they are very lightweight and prone to tipping, especially when drawing a brush over the rim of the cup to remove excess material. I've made several no-tip cup holders that work well in my shop.

Start with a 1-1/2" × 4" × 4" wood block—a scrap of 2×4 will also work fine—and cut a hole in the center sized to accommodate the cup of your choice. You can cut the hole with a hole saw, Forstner bit or scroll saw, or just cut it out on the bandsaw. (If you use the bandsaw or scroll saw, you can adjust the saw table to angle the sides of the hole to match the shape of the cup.) Then hold the block upright and cut out a V-shaped groove along one edge of the top to use as a brush holder.

—Frank LaRoque, The Dalles, OR

Glue-sizing end grain

When gluing miter or butt joints, the end grain can quickly absorb the glue, causing a starved joint after assembly. The solution is to spread a thin "size coat" of glue first, let it soak in, then apply more before clamping up the joint. This trick even works for joints with both end-grain and face-grain surfaces. For example, when gluing a tenon, size the shoulders, wait a minute or so, then apply glue to the cheeks and a bit more to the shoulders before assembling the joint.

—Ross Gruber, Oklahoma City, OK

A positive note

For years, whenever I needed to mix up a small amount of epoxy, I'd use a piece of scrap wood or cardboard as a mixing surface. Afterward, I'd decide if I could reuse the wood/cardboard or throw it away. I recently found that all I have to do is mix it on the top sheet of one of those little sticky notepads, and then tear it off and trash it when done. It works great and saves both time and cleaning up a small mess. I wish I had thought of this years ago.

—Jack C. Clark, Tucson, AZ

Avoid glue line depressions

After edge-gluing panels, give them at least a day or two to dry thoroughly before flattening them. Otherwise, any areas slightly swollen with moisture may shrink as they finish drying, creating glue-line depressions.

—Paul Anthony, Riegelsville, PA

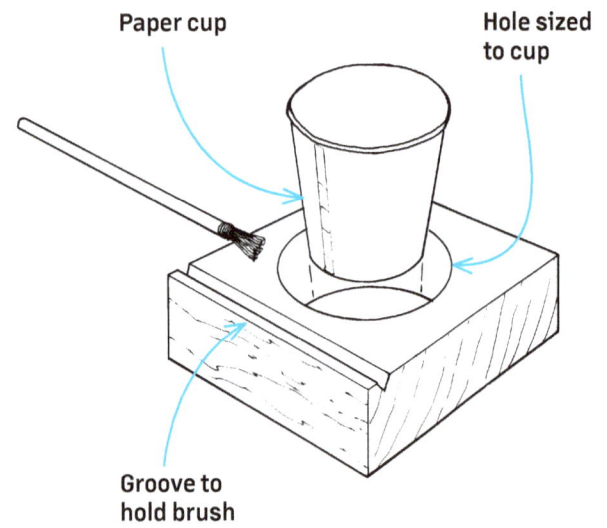

Paper cup
Hole sized to cup
Groove to hold brush

WOODCRAFT MAGAZINE TIPS & TRICKS FOR WOODWORKING

Corral that bottle cap

Do you spend a lot of time searching for the top to your glue bottle? Here's my answer to this pesky problem.

Cut a piece of dental floss 6" long. Take the cap off the glue bottle and pierce a small hole in the top of the cap. Push the dental floss through from the top. Tie a bulky knot in one end, and pull it up into the cap to make sure the knot is big enough. Tie a noose in the other end and place it around the top portion of the glue bottle. Now you can rest assured you will always be able to find the cap after you use your glue.

I tried other materials such as fishing line, but I found dental floss worked better because of its strength and flexibility for tying.

—Frank LaRoque, The Dalles, OR

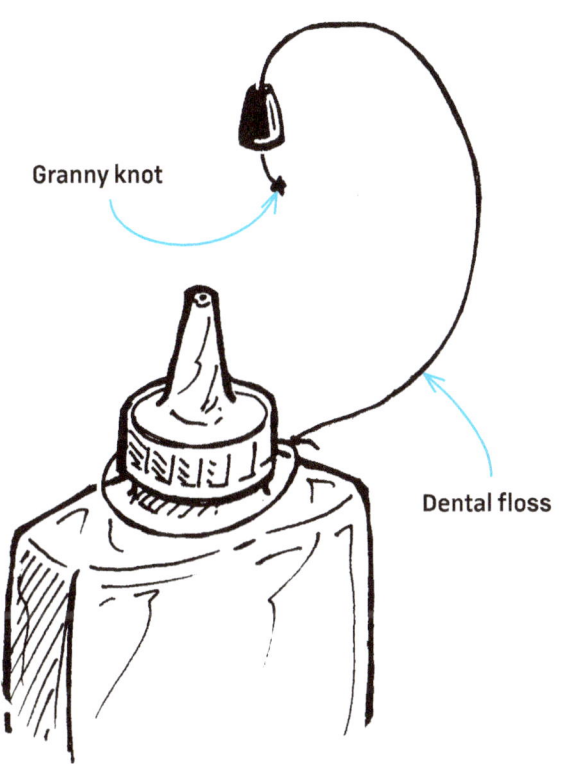

Granny knot

Dental floss

Jelly jar glue pot

Too often, glue bottles become clogged and/or glue brushes roll off the bench and get caked in sawdust. Inserting a brush through the lid of a small jar solves both problems quite neatly. Apply a bead of hot-melt glue on both sides of the lid to lock the brush in place and create an airtight fit.

—John Caccia, Platteville, WI

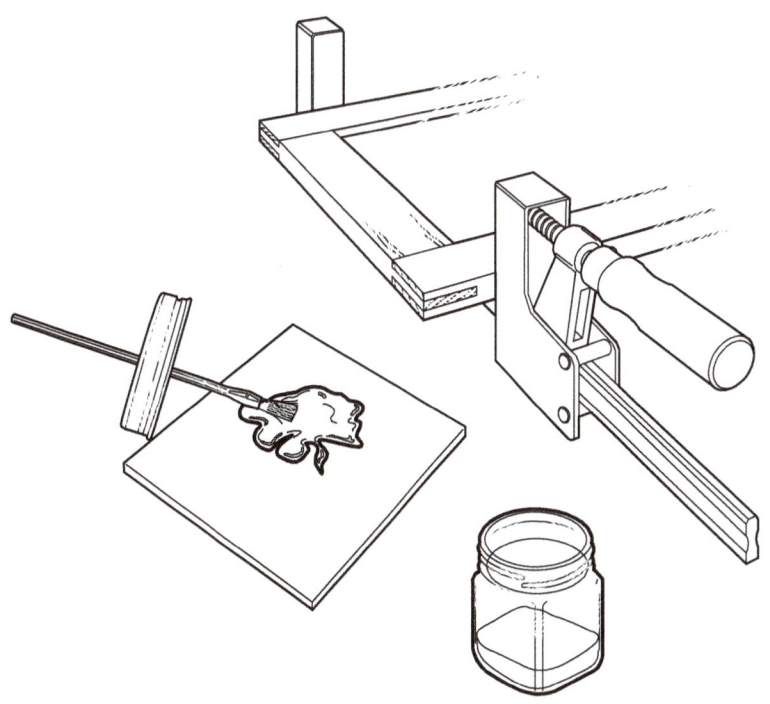

Another twist on glue bottles

For easy glue storage and application, I use a bottle with a slanted snout. Bottles like this one are available at women's beauty supply stores for cheap. The design allows the bottle to be held in a horizontal position that's comfortable to the hand and keeps the bottle out of your line of sight to the glue. The snout's tip allows very accurate placement of the glue bead on the wood.

The snouts can be cut back to provide various thicknesses for the glue bead. Sometimes, you want a lot of glue; other times, a little. The caps to seal the bottle are electrician's twist caps that come in many diameters to fit various snout tip sizes. I have used these bottles for years without their contents drying out.

As for cleaning, very little glue builds up on the snout's tip during application because the tip is in direct contact with the wood. I always have a damp cloth when gluing, so I use it to clean what little glue gets on the tip.

—Charles Thompson, Fairhope, AL

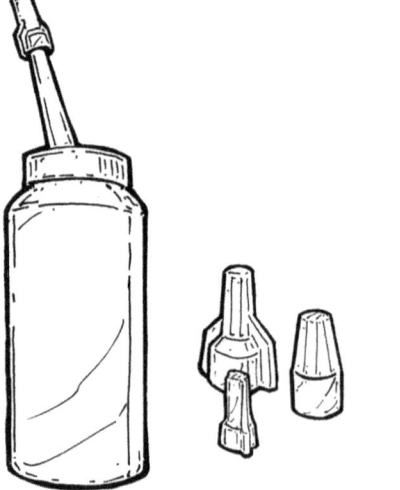

Bottle up

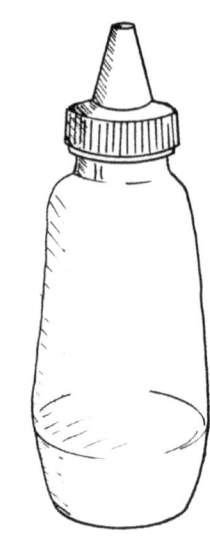

Having tired of constantly cleaning the nozzles and searching for lost caps on various glue bottles, I came up with the idea of using a self-cleaning plugged nozzle to solve the problem. Many food bottles, such as mustard and other condiments, use the self-cleaning plugged nozzle.

I simply wash the bottles and make sure that they are thoroughly dry. I then pour my glue of choice into the bottle, and the problem is solved. This has proven to be a great time-saver in the shop and eliminates wasted and spilled glue which is all too common. I keep a separate bottle for each type of glue.

—Tom Hill, Van Buren, AR

Flying disc mixing bowl

Next time you're at a ballgame or auto show, grab a promotional flying disc for your shop. The shallow plastic bowls are perfect for mixing epoxy or filler. The wide surface area prevents heat build-up that accelerates the curing process, giving you more time to use the batch. (And in most cases, the dried glue will pop out of the soft, slick plastic.)

—Travis Collier, Minneapolis, MN

Spread glue quickly

If you ever build projects with laminated components, you know how difficult it can be to lay glue over a large surface quickly and evenly. Here are two strategies that will give you great results.

When you're spreading glue on really large surfaces, pour glue directly out of the bottle and spread it on the surface with a plastic trowel having 1/8" notches. Next, smooth out the application with a small-diameter foam paint roller. If you're working with narrow strips, squeeze most of the glue out of the roller. Wash out the remainder with soap and water, and you can re-use the cover on your next laminating job.

—Kate Logan, San Diego, CA

Stabilize with super glue

Turners have long used thick and thin cyanoacrylate glue to stabilize workpieces, especially bowls. I have found that super glue is also good for stabilizing knots, cracks, and flaws in regular milled lumber. I simply fill cracks in lumber and loose knots with regular super glue, then give it a shot of spray-type rapid cure before I begin working with it. I have saved quite a few pieces of lumber that might otherwise have been discarded as unworkable.

—Lee Mothershead, San Marino, CA

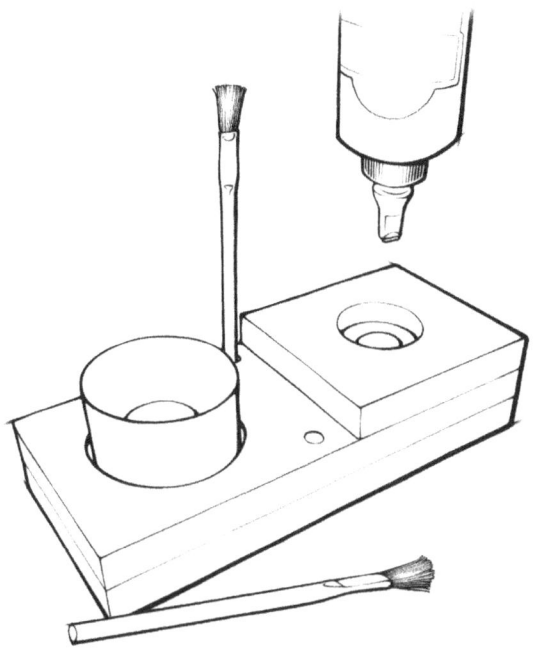

Put glue materials within easy reach

For small glue jobs, I made this handy support to store my glue, glue brushes, and water. Storing the bottle upside down ensures that the glue is always ready at the first squeeze.

The scrapwood project requires two 3/4" × 4" × 9" blocks and one 3/4" × 4" × 4-1/2" piece. To make a 2-5/8" hole for the spray paint lid water reservoir, I used my scrollsaw and cleaned up the cut with my spindle sander. After gluing the blocks together, I made the two-step hole for the glue. Drill a 1-3/4"-diameter × 3/4"-deep hole through the top board, and second 1"-diameter × 1-1/4"-deep hole through the middle and into the bottom block. Finally, I made two 3/8"-diameter × 3/4"-deep holes for the glue brushes. Now my glue, glue brushes, and water are all at my fingertips.

—Melvin Rhodes, Jackson, MO

TECHNIQUES > GLUING

Warm box for chilly glue-ups

During cold weather, it's impractical to heat my whole shop so that a glued-up project can cure properly. Instead, I made a "warm box" using inexpensive, 1/2"-thick rigid foam insulation panels. To heat the box, I use a 150-watt heat lamp, placing it a safe distance from the work and the box walls. Monitor the temperature with a thermometer, shutting off the lamp occasionally if necessary to maintain a temperature between 60 and 80° F.

The panels can be cut and taped together to make a large box. The foil-faced variety can simply be scored on one side and snapped to create several sides of a smaller box. Leave the edge of one wall untaped for access. For the top, simply lay a piece on the box. When not in use, you can store the panels flat.

—Chuck Chinaski, Memphis, TN

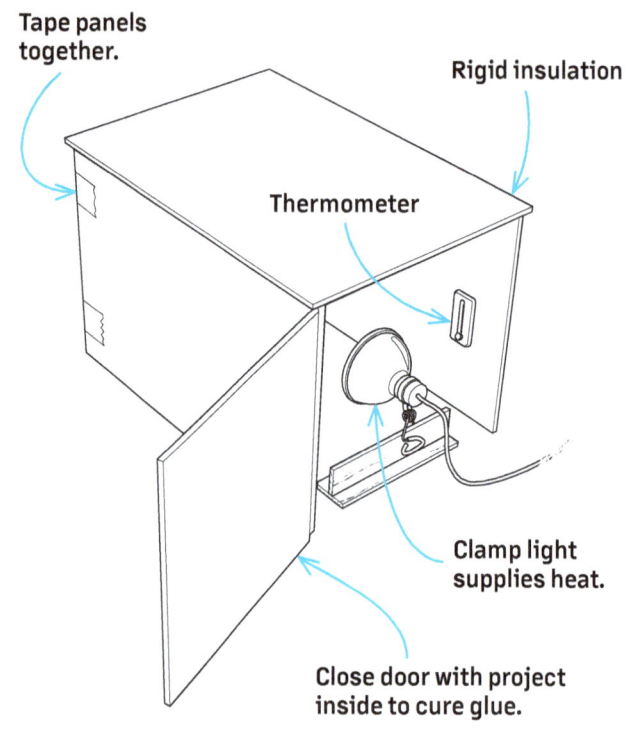

Pipettes hit the target

I find that when I need to neatly apply a thin glue or solvent, a plastic pipette is just the tool for the job. These squeezable lab dispensers, with their tiny tips, work great for targeted applications of thin or medium viscosity cyanoacrylate (CA) glue when filling cracks or making repairs. They're also perfect for discharging a small stream of naphtha between a template and workpiece to release double-faced tape securing the two. And if I need to concoct a dye stain recipe, I can use them to add carefully controlled drops of this and that color to a sample mix.

—Bil Mitchell, Riegelsville, PA

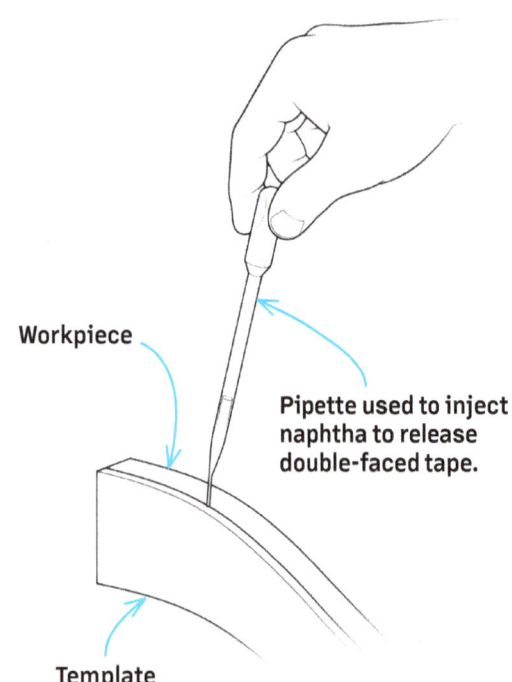

Cool glue

It occurred to me one day, as I was preparing to glue up 15 pieces of red oak for a tabletop, that I would perhaps not be able to get the glue spread on all the edges and have time to clamp all the pieces together before the glue set up. I thought about buying a slower-setting glue to do the job, but then it dawned on me that the lower the temperature, the more slowly a chemical reaction takes place.

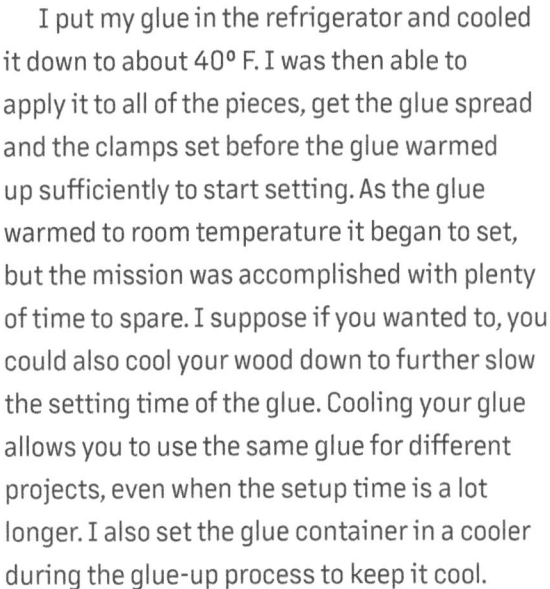

I put my glue in the refrigerator and cooled it down to about 40° F. I was then able to apply it to all of the pieces, get the glue spread and the clamps set before the glue warmed up sufficiently to start setting. As the glue warmed to room temperature it began to set, but the mission was accomplished with plenty of time to spare. I suppose if you wanted to, you could also cool your wood down to further slow the setting time of the glue. Cooling your glue allows you to use the same glue for different projects, even when the setup time is a lot longer. I also set the glue container in a cooler during the glue-up process to keep it cool.

—Dan Zinda, Alexandria, MN

Glue storage

For longest shelf life and best performance, keep liquid glues in temperature-controlled storage. Freezing degrades proteins, compromising adhesion. Ideal working temperatures—listed on the container—typically range from 50 to 75° F.

—Larissa Huff, Schwenksville, PA

Cozy winter glue-ups

During cold weather, I rely on space heaters to keep my garage shop comfortable. When I turn off the heat, the temperature quickly drops to outdoor levels. Since many glue-ups fail when done in temperatures below 50°F, I cover end-of-day assemblies with an old electric blanket. Running the blanket is safer and much cheaper than heating the whole shop overnight for the sake of a few boards.

—Jeff Day, Perkasie, PA

Fresh cleanup water

Constantly refresh glue cleanup water to prevent wiping diluted glue into wood pores, where it will impede finish.

—Paul Anthony, Riegelsville, PA

Don't monkey around

I had some gaps between pieces of my last inlay project (there were a lot of odd contours and radii). I used polyurethane glue in the joints, knowing that it would just foam out during cure and could be trimmed later.

What I found was that after trimming, all of the little foam-out pockets leave a very nice catch for sanding dust. I did normal finish sanding, the pockets filled with dust, and I was able to apply my lacquer with no need for additional filler. The color match was perfect, since the dust came directly from the finished piece. You could not do this with normal yellow wood glue, which leaves a fully filled, smooth surface after trimming that is difficult to hide.

—Ken Bedel, Vandalia, OH

Techniques > Gluing

Ironing in the shop

Although I'm not one for ironing my clothes, I do own an electric iron. It lives in my shop, where it helps me perform chores like removing old veneer or plastic laminate for repair jobs. Just set it to "medium," and slowly push it across the surface as you peel up the material. It will release contact cement, white glue, hide glue, and other adhesives. (Cover finished surfaces with paper to prevent contaminating the iron with softened finish.) Similarly, you can use it to remove PSA sandpaper from its metal backing disc, to flatten rolled patterns, to apply edge banding, or partner it with a wet rag to raise minor dents.

—Marvin Gatlin, Birmingham, AL

Ink brayer as spreader

An ink brayer—available at art supply stores—is a great glue applicator. It works much better than a finger when it comes to spreading glue evenly, efficiently, and economically.

—Ken Burton, New Tripoli, PA

Instant glue shield

When using instant glue, it can be frustrating to align parts without gluing your fingers to the project. A simple solution is to put sandwich bags on your hands. The glue will not stick to the bags or your hands.

—Frank LaRoque, The Dalles, OR

Getting glue-ready

In preparing for complicated glue-ups, you need every efficiency, so make sure your glue bottle is nearly full for quick dispensing. Either that, or drill a hole in a thick block to create a holder for an inverted glue bottle.

—Paul Anthony, Riegelsville, PA

Blister package tray

When fighting your way into stiff blister packaging, try not to bust it up too badly. The plastic makes a good disposable tray for glue or epoxy.

—Ken Burton, New Tripoli, PA

Release hot-melt glue

To remove hot glue from small jigs or workpieces, put them in the freezer. Once frozen, the glue will pop off cleanly.

—Rob Spiece, Berea, KY

JOINERY

Easy offset biscuits

When applying wide, solid-wood facing to plywood, it's wise to offset the facing a little bit to allow trimming it flush to the plywood surface afterward. I like to attach facing with biscuits, but creating the offset requires first slotting all the shelves, then resetting the fence to cut the edging slots. Instead, for more efficiency, I begin by cutting the slots in the shelf edges with the biscuit joiner resting on the bench, then I simply slip a piece of notepad cardboard under the tool when slotting the mating edging, which is inverted for the job.

—Chad McClung, Vienna, WV

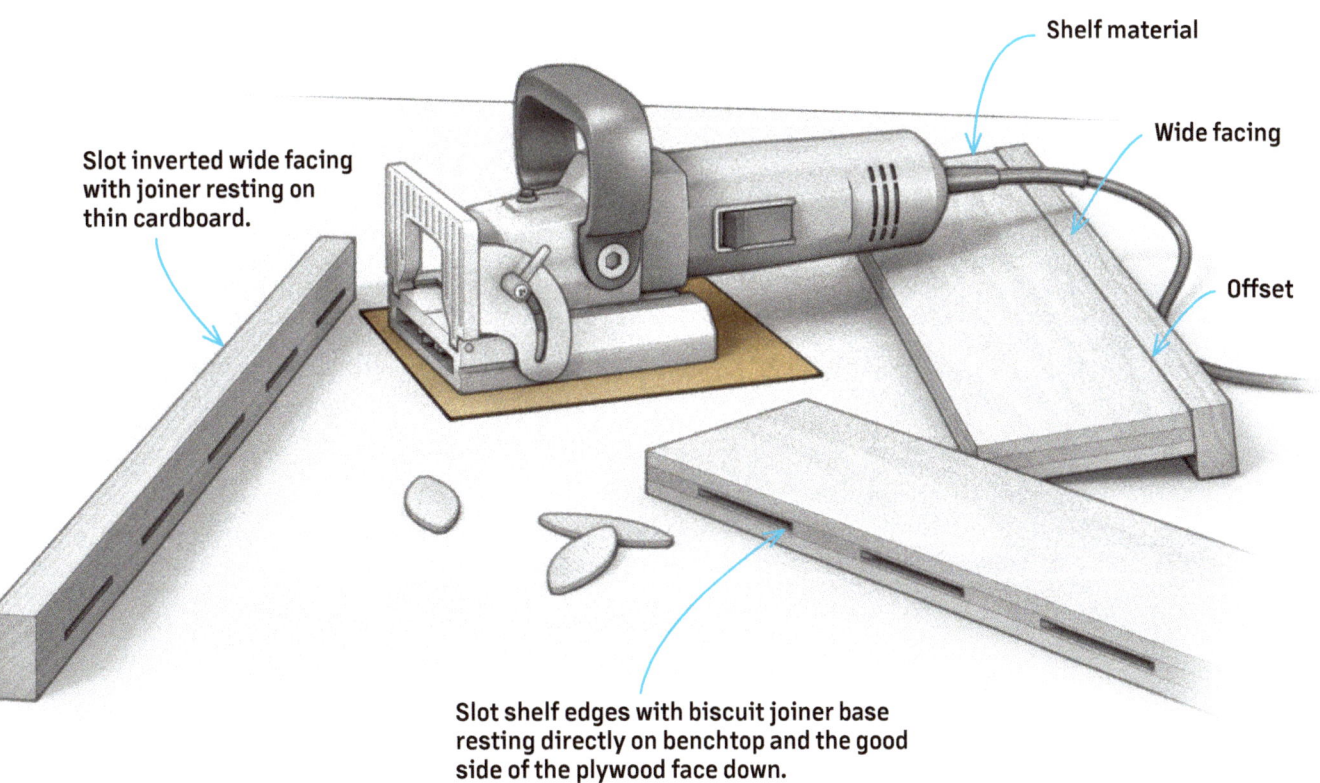

Slot inverted wide facing with joiner resting on thin cardboard.

Shelf material

Wide facing

Offset

Slot shelf edges with biscuit joiner base resting directly on benchtop and the good side of the plywood face down.

TECHNIQUES > JOINERY

Drilling the ends of long boards

I recently built a project that required drilling a couple of 1/4"-diameter holes 2-1/2" deep into the ends of several 6'-long boards. It was crucial that the holes were drilled square to the ends of the boards. I knew I couldn't accurately drill freehand, and the boards were obviously too long for the drill press.

After some head scratching, I realized that the solution was to bore out a drill guide block on the drill press, then glue it to a backer block that would allow clamping the guide to the workpiece, as shown in the drawing. Making the guide block about 1-1/2" long allowed me to drill deep enough into the board to create good starter holes. After removing the jig, I drilled them to final depth. A doweling jig would also work, but the beauty of my setup is that, by aligning the edge of the jig with the edge of the board, the holes are self-registering.

—Guy Weiss, San Diego, CA

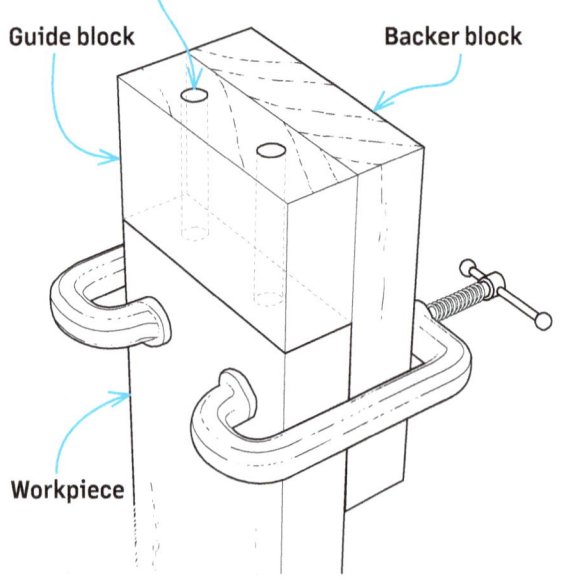

Bore holes on drill press, then glue guide block to backer block.

Guide block — Backer block — Workpiece

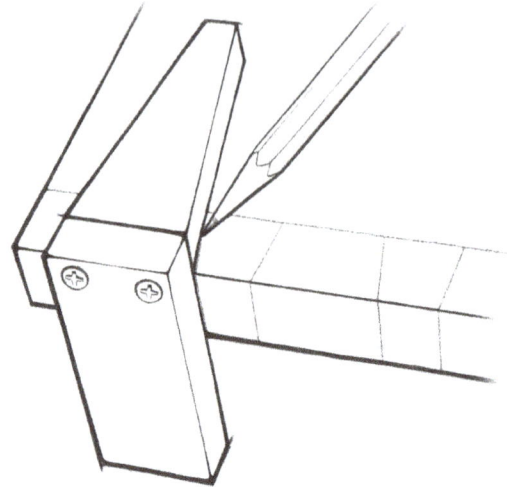

A formula for perfect dovetails

Though a sliding bevel can be used to mark dovetails, a dovetail marker is easier to use and more accurate. You can buy one of many varieties, but shop-made markers are cheaper and customizable. I made my marker out of a small piece of red oak from my scrap pile. It measures about 2" × 2-1/4" × 3/4" wide, with a 1:6 slope, and took less than half an hour to make, using only hand tools.

Find a piece of scrap 3/4" or 1" wide and about 7" long. Find the midpoint on the end of the piece and mark it, then mark across the piece the proportional distance of the slope. For example, a 1"-wide piece would be marked 1/2" in from each edge, so for a 1:6 ratio the length is calculated 6" × 1/2" (3"). For a 1:8 ratio on a 3/4"-wide piece, make your mark at 8" × 3/8" (also 3"). Draw your slope lines from the center point to the place where this mark meets the edge of the piece, and cut the piece. Saw and plane down exactly to the lines. Cut another piece from your scrap approximately the same length and join them perfectly square to each other.

—Isaac Stafstrom, Madison, WI

Can't-miss biscuit guide

Cutting biscuits in a frame-and-panel side proves trickier than in a solid-panel side. The problem lies not only in making matching sets of slots in the sides, shelves, top and bottom, but also in laying out the slots so that they don't accidentally cut through the narrow stiles. This scrapwood support board addresses both issues quickly and easily. To make this jig, simply cut the support board to match the width of your frame and carefully mark out the biscuit slot locations.

Now, align the front edge of the support board flush with the front edge of the side, clamp it securely in place, and use it to guide the biscuit joiner as you slot the solid ends for the top and bottom panels. To slot the stiles for the shelves, bridge it over the panel section and slot at the marked pencil lines, as shown. To cut matching edge slots, simply clamp the support board on top of your panel and align your biscuit joiner with the layout lines. Again, make sure to register the board with the front edge of the panels.

—Jamie McLoughlin, Keene, NH

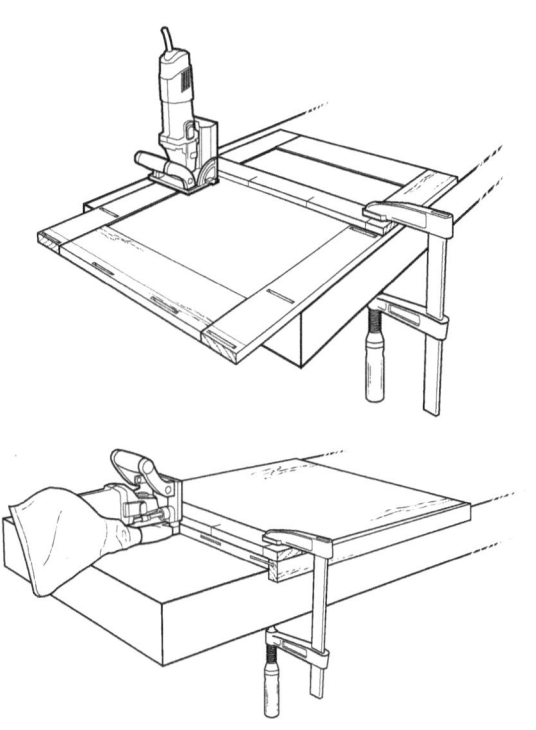

Squaring mortises with a hollow chisel

Although I own a hollow-chisel mortiser, I often find that routing mortises is faster and cleaner. Of course, the rounded ends of routed mortises then have to be squared to accommodate square-edged tenons. This is where I bring my mortiser into play. I mount the appropriately sized hollow chisel in the machine—omitting the internal drill bit—and adjust the fence to suit the mortise location. With the machine powered off and the workpiece located, a simple pull on the handle is all it takes to quietly and cleanly cut the end of a mortise. I find this approach is much less trouble than rounding the edges of tenons to fit the ends of routed mortises.

—Ray Dewey, Chattanooga, TN

TECHNIQUES > JOINERY

Dovetailing platform

When making hand-cut dovetail joints, it's common to use a completed tail board as a template to lay out the pins. However, I've found it difficult to keep the tail board and pin board accurately and securely aligned for the process, especially while bending uncomfortably low over my workbench. This small clamping platform solves the problem nicely. The simple open-sided box is made from five pieces of 3/4" plywood, which I cut to length from a single 6"-wide ripping. Just glue and screw the pieces together, taking particular care to align the front panel with the front edges of the top and bottom. In addition to having a fast, foolproof way to keep boards aligned for joint layout, you can clamp a tail board against the front panel for cutting the tails. Just extend the top end up above the platform.

—*Tim Snyder, Sandy Hook, CT*

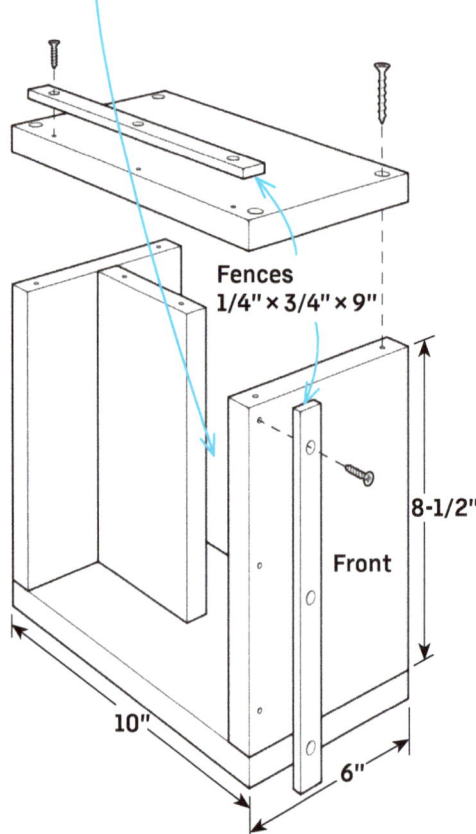

Center gap allows access for clamping wide pin boards to platform front.

Fences 1/4" × 3/4" × 9"

Front

8-1/2"

10"

6"

Attach fences flush with platform edges.

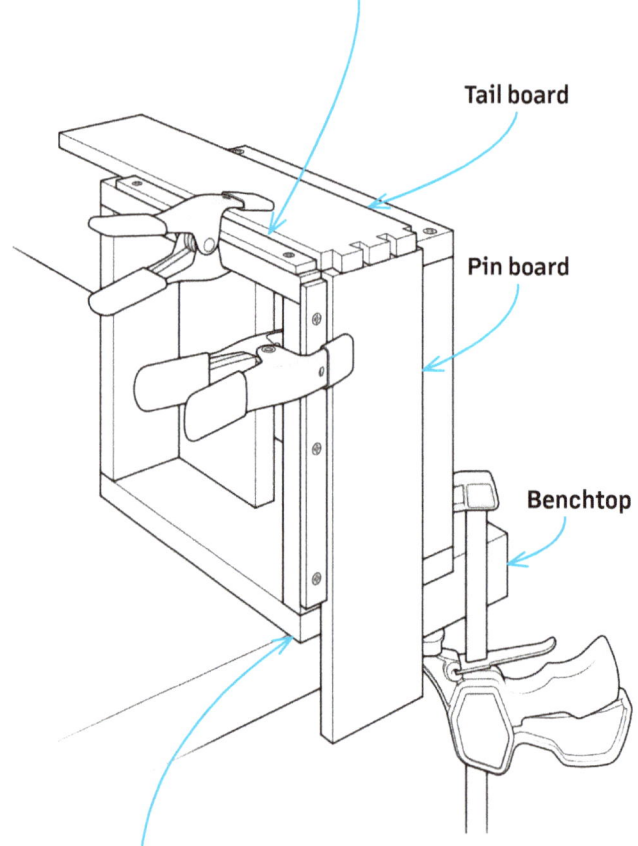

Register workpieces against fences, aligning them for scribing the tail profile onto the end of the pin board.

Tail board

Pin board

Benchtop

Clamp platform to bench with front overhanging slightly.

JOINERY < TECHNIQUES

Breadboard epiphany

I never had any formal woodworking training—not even a high school shop class—so most of my knowledge comes from publications like this one. I've read about making breadboard ends for tabletops, and the illustrations always show the boards that make up the field of the table cut with intermittent tenons—but without explanation.

Until recently, I didn't understand why this was necessary; it seemed to me a continuous tenon was easier to make and served the same purpose. Several years ago, I made a breakfast table with breadboard ends out of cherry (4" wide and more than 1" thick) with this simpler method. As I expected, the field expands slightly beyond the end boards in the summer, but the tabletop as a whole has remained perfectly flat. After several seasons, I concluded that the intermittent tenon design was just an unnecessary, fussy detail.

But recently, I built an oak desk with breadboard ends (1-1/2" wide and 3/4" thick), sticking with the continuous tenon. In the summer, the field of the desktop moved just like the table, but a slight crown developed at the inside center of the breadboards, up to about 1/16". Using a straightedge, it was easy to see the end boards had opened up in the middle.

Now I understand the purpose of the intermittent tenon; it has nothing to do with the field of the tabletop, but rather keeps the end boards flat. Obviously, the thick cross section and closed grain of the cherry tabletop did not move like the thicker cross section and open grain of the oak top.

—Ken Bayer, Pittsburgh, PA

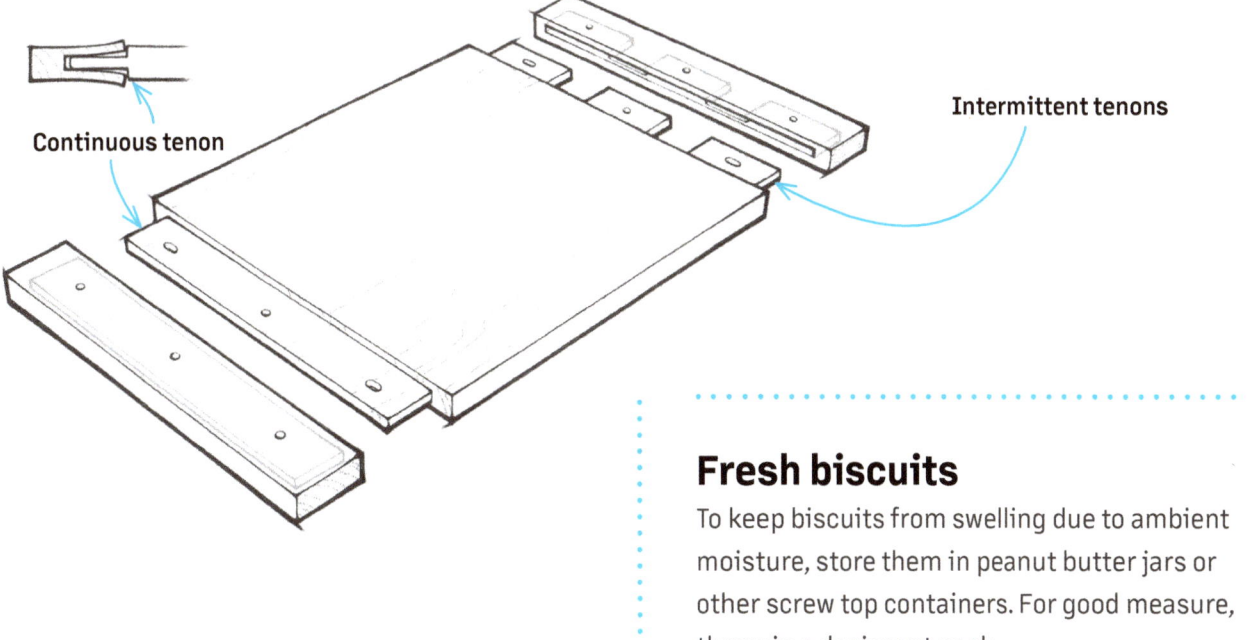

Fresh biscuits

To keep biscuits from swelling due to ambient moisture, store them in peanut butter jars or other screw top containers. For good measure, throw in a desiccant pack.

—Ken Burton, New Tripoli, PA

TECHNIQUES > JOINERY

Extracting blind dowels

When restoring antique doors, cabinets, and other projects, I often need to disassemble a joint that was secured with either half-blind dowels or with through-dowels that can only be accessed from one end. Here's a technique that I've found works very well on most older joints (although new joints with some modern adhesives may prove problematic).

To extract the dowel, I first drill a hole through its axis, leaving some wood at the perimeter. I then cut a length of threaded rod (or section of machine screw), whose diameter is slightly less than the hole's diameter. Next, I fix the rod into the hole using quick-set epoxy, taping off the area around the hole to protect it from epoxy spillage.

After the epoxy has cured fully, I center a flat washer over the dowel, surrounding it as closely as possible without overlaying it. Atop that, I place a short length of schedule 40 or 80 PVC pipe that has an outside diameter that's slightly less than that of the washer, and top that off with another washer. All that's left to do is thread on a nut and tighten it to pull the dowel out of its hole.

—Alan Bowes, Alna, ME

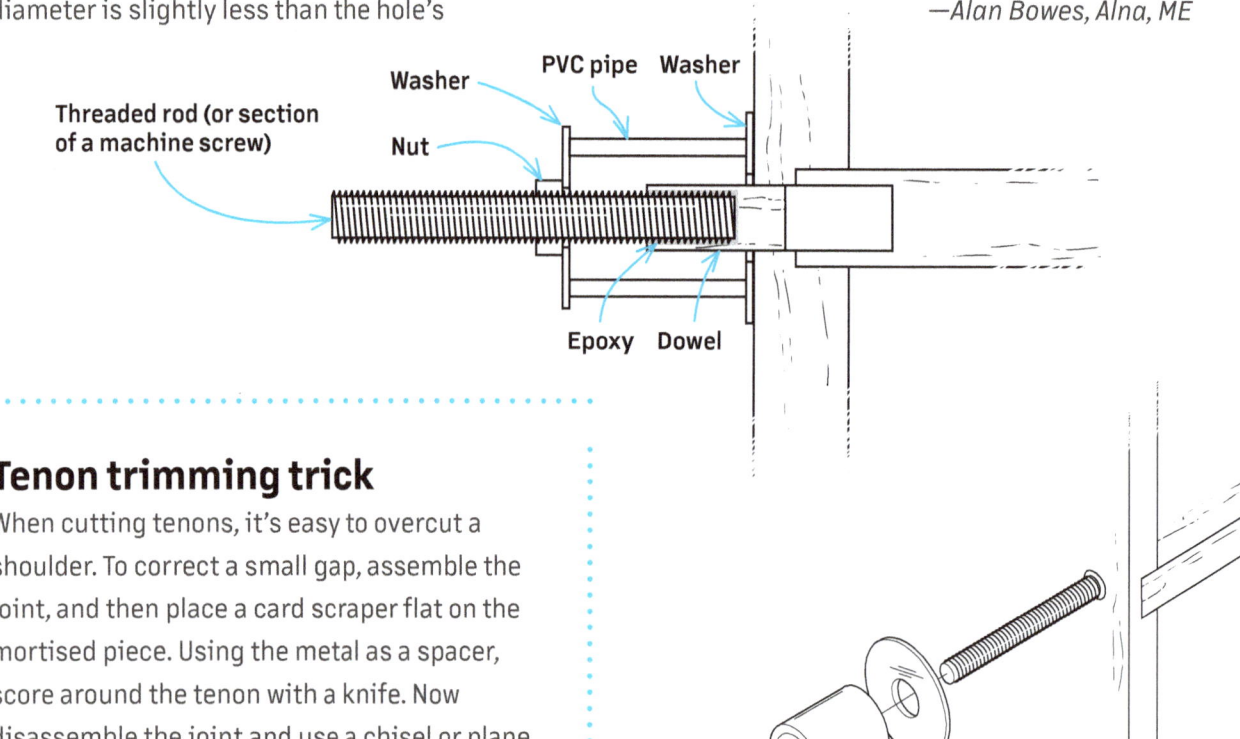

Tenon trimming trick

When cutting tenons, it's easy to overcut a shoulder. To correct a small gap, assemble the joint, and then place a card scraper flat on the mortised piece. Using the metal as a spacer, score around the tenon with a knife. Now disassemble the joint and use a chisel or plane to pare up to your scored line.

When the joint's reassembled, the shaving or two removed from the fat edge should allow the shoulder to sit seamlessly on the joining piece without affecting the fit of any other parts.

—Mark Hall, Seneca, NY

Miter-biscuiting bench hook

Cutting biscuit slots in the ends of mitered pieces can be a hassle because of the setup time required to clamp every piece for safe, accurate cutting. As a solution, I came up with this production hold-down jig to quickly secure mitered pieces for slotting. It works with stock up to 1-3/8" thick.

Because the base is constructed like a bench hook, it doesn't need to be clamped to the bench. The business end consists of a V-block to which I screwed two half-discs that serve as cams to hold the mitered end of the workpiece. (I used a bandsaw to bisect a 3-3/8"-diameter disc cut with a holesaw.) These are each wrapped with wide rubber bands or PSA sandpaper to grip the work when it's forced backward underneath a cam. Locate the pivot holes where shown in the drawing. To allow the cams to spin freely, attach them using screws with unthreaded upper sections of the shanks. When using the jig, position the workpiece miter close to the V-block for stability.

—*Serge Duclos, Delson, Québec*

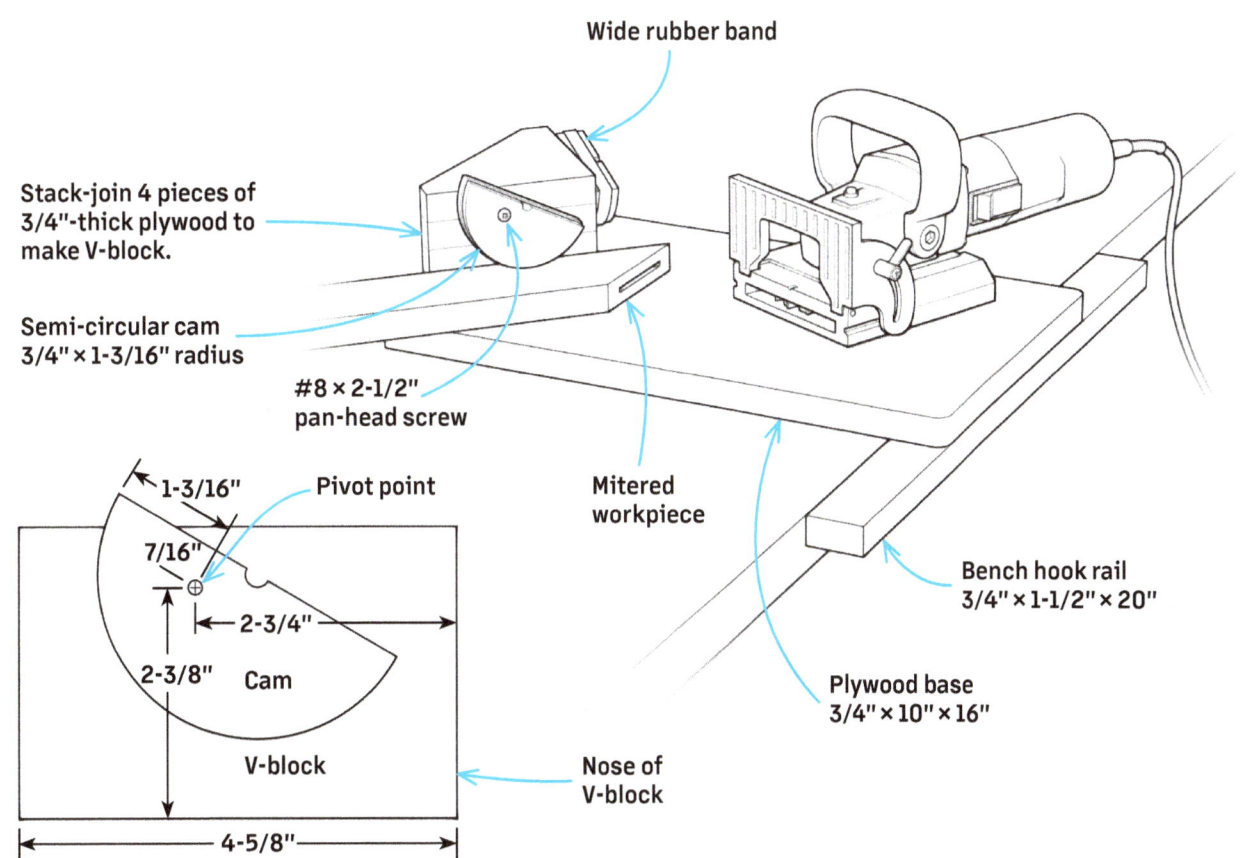

TECHNIQUES > JOINERY

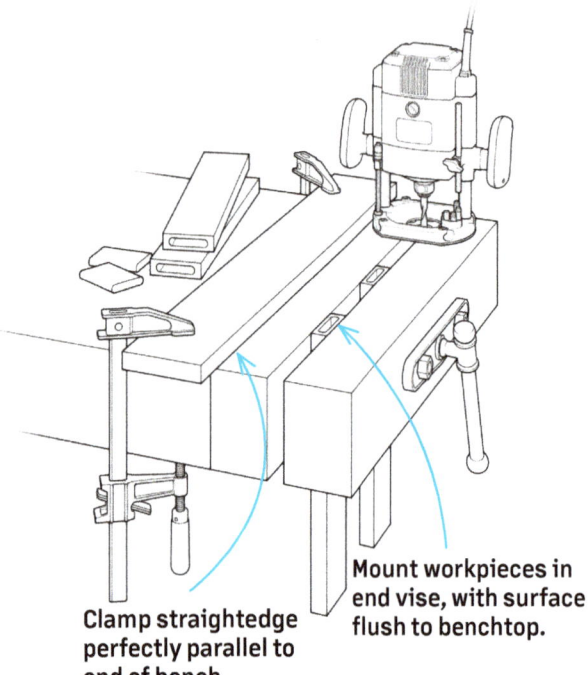

Clamp straightedge perfectly parallel to end of bench.

Mount workpieces in end vise, with surface flush to benchtop.

Dead-simple mortising setup

Loose-tenon joinery is a great way to join pieces. For ease, efficiency, and dead-on accuracy, making the joint requires using a jig that secures the workpiece on end while guiding the router. However, in a pinch, you can get away with using just your workbench, its end vise, and a simple plywood or MDF straightedge. First, clamp your workpiece into your vise with the end of the work flush to the benchtop. Lay out the ends of the mortise, and outfit your router with an upcut spiral bit. Then secure a straightedge at the proper distance away from the cut and parallel to the end of your bench. To restrict router travel to the length of the mortise, you can set up stops, or simply begin the cut by plunging to full depth at the beginning and end of the mortise, and then removing the waste between in subsequently deeper passes. You can rout the mating edge mortises in the same manner.

—Andy Rae, Asheville, NC

Tail-cutting bandsaw fence

Using my bandsaw and a tapered sliding fence, I can saw variably spaced tails that look hand-cut more consistently than I can with my dovetail saw, and in about the same time that it would take to set up a router jig. To make this tail-cutting jig, saw a 7° to 9° taper along one edge of a 6"×24" board and attach a stop to the back end.

After laying out and marking the tail board, position it against the tapered fence, line the blade up with your cutline, and saw up to your shoulder line. Flip your board to cut the opposing angle. To minimize chisel work, you can also use the bandsaw to nibble out the remaining waste between the tails.

—Buzz Kelly, Indian Springs, AL

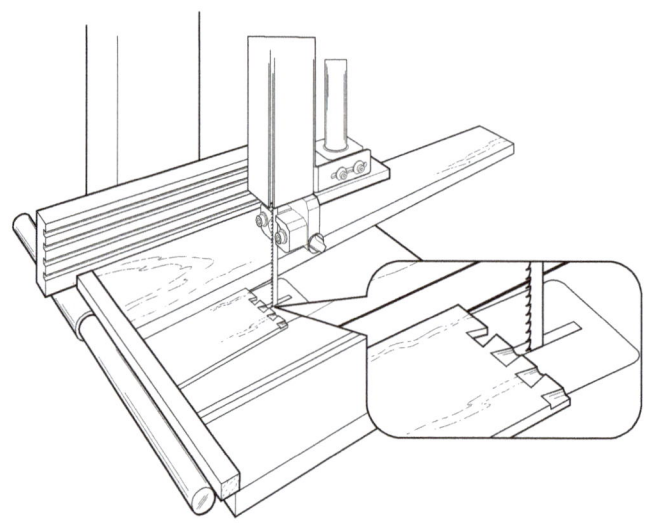

Stale biscuits

If ambient moisture has swollen a biscuit too much to fit in its slot, you can often squash it back to size in a vise with metal jaws.

—Ken Burton, New Tripoli, PA

Dowel-grooving collar

I've used this approach for years to groove dowels up to 1/2" in diameter. My trick is to use a "collar jig" that has a feed hole through the axis, with nails projecting into the hole to create the grooves as the dowel is fed through the jig. I have several of these, each one suiting a particular dowel diameter.

To make a collar, drill through the axis of a 1-1/4"-long section of 1-1/4"-diameter dowel, using a bit that matches the diameter of the desired dowel size. Next, lay the collar on its side and use a 1/16"-diameter bit to drill a hole completely through, intersecting the main hole at its center, and exiting the opposite side of the collar. Insert a 4d finish nail through each side hole, far enough for the tip to project into the center hole about 1/32". Slide the collar down a length of dowel to create two opposing grooves, then reorient it 90°, and take a second pass to create a total of four grooves in a dowel. That'll do it.

—Gary Rohs, Cincinnati, OH

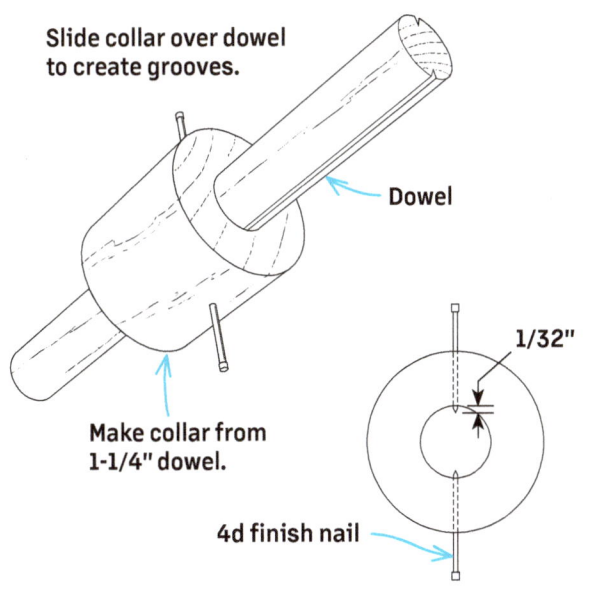

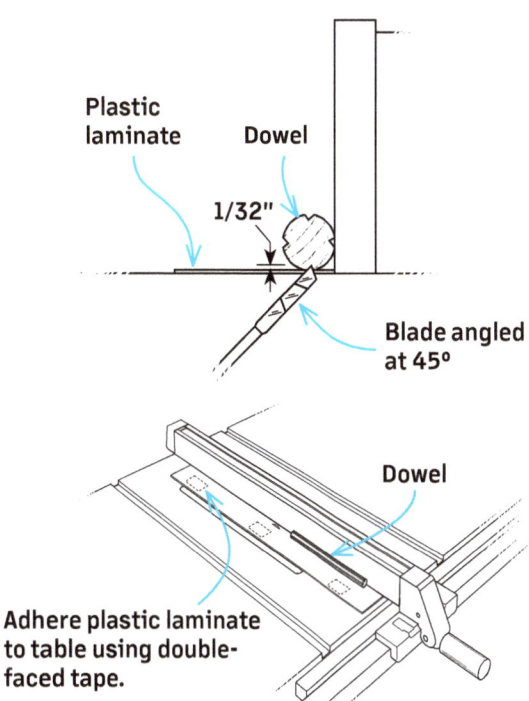

Grooving dowels

When used in joinery, dowels work better if they're grooved to let glue and air escape during installation. Commercially grooved dowels are available, but you can easily saw the grooves yourself on the table saw. To set up the saw, crank the blade over to 45° and raise it level to the tabletop. Locate the rip fence so that a dowel placed against it is centered over the teeth tips, and then lock the fence in place. Fasten a strip of plastic laminate to the saw table against the fence, using double-faced tape. Hold the laminate down with a block of wood, while raising the blade until it projects about 1/32". To cut the groove, feed your dowel past the running blade, holding it down firmly and rotating it after each pass to cut three or four grooves. The plastic laminate will prevent it from diving into the throat plate opening.

—Frank Crutchfield, Newark, DE

TECHNIQUES > JOINERY

Wedges for tenons

A while back, I made a desk that had 36 tenons, each slotted for two 3/4" × 1"-long wedges. Here's how I managed to make so many efficiently and safely: Begin with a piece of squared stock that's 1-1/4" thick by at least 6" wide (for feed stability). Also for safe feeding, it should be at least 8" long. To set up the cut, first make a wedge-length cutline on the face 1-1/4" up from one end. Lean your blade over 8°, and then outfit your rip fence with an auxiliary tall fence. Locate the fence for a cut that will slice to your line, then saw a wedge from each opposing face. Invert the workpiece and perform the same two cuts at the other end. The four wide wedges you just cut can now be knifed or bandsawn to their desired width (trimming them flush to final length after installation). If you need yet more wedges, tilt the blade back to vertical and adjust the fence to cut a new wedge adjacent to each of the first cuts, as shown. Then crosscut these wedges free of the stock.

—Richard Libera, Newark, DE

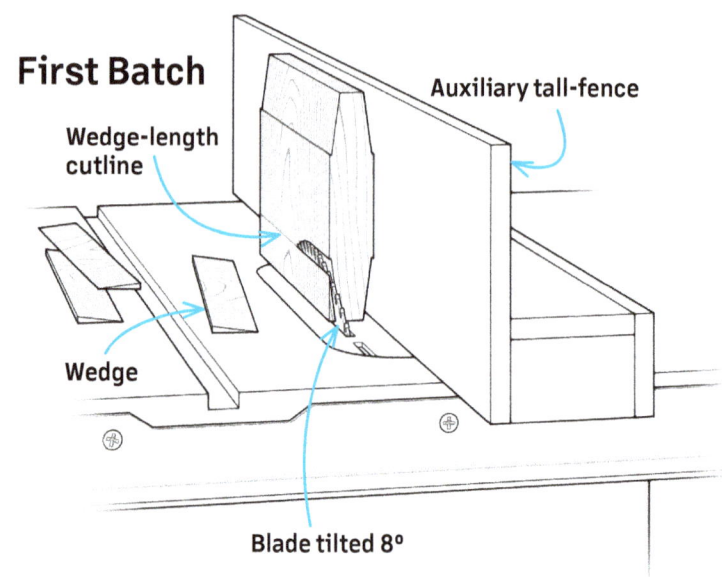

First Batch

Auxiliary tall-fence
Wedge-length cutline
Wedge
Blade tilted 8°

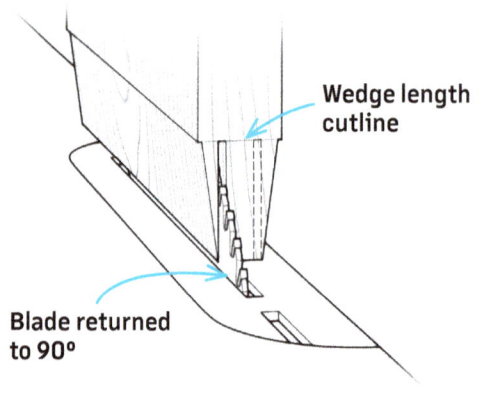

Second Batch

Wedge length cutline
Blade returned to 90°

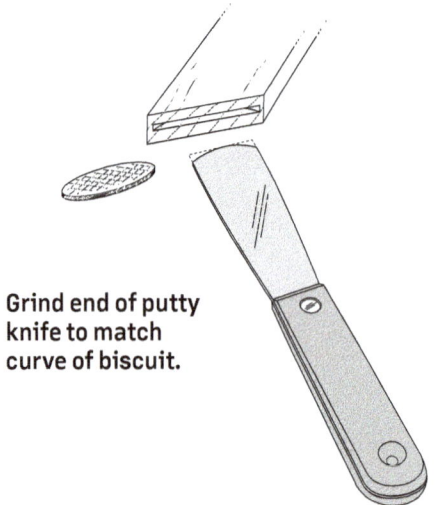

Grind end of putty knife to match curve of biscuit.

Biscuit slot glue spreader

The quickest way to spread glue in biscuit slots is using a tool tailored for the job. I made my own by grinding the end of a putty knife to match the contour of a biscuit. Squeeze glue into the slot, smear it against the sides of the slot with the knife, and you're done. Putty knives are cheap enough that I've actually made several of these spreaders to suit different sized biscuit slots.

—Alice Wallace, San Mateo, CA

MEASURING & MARKING

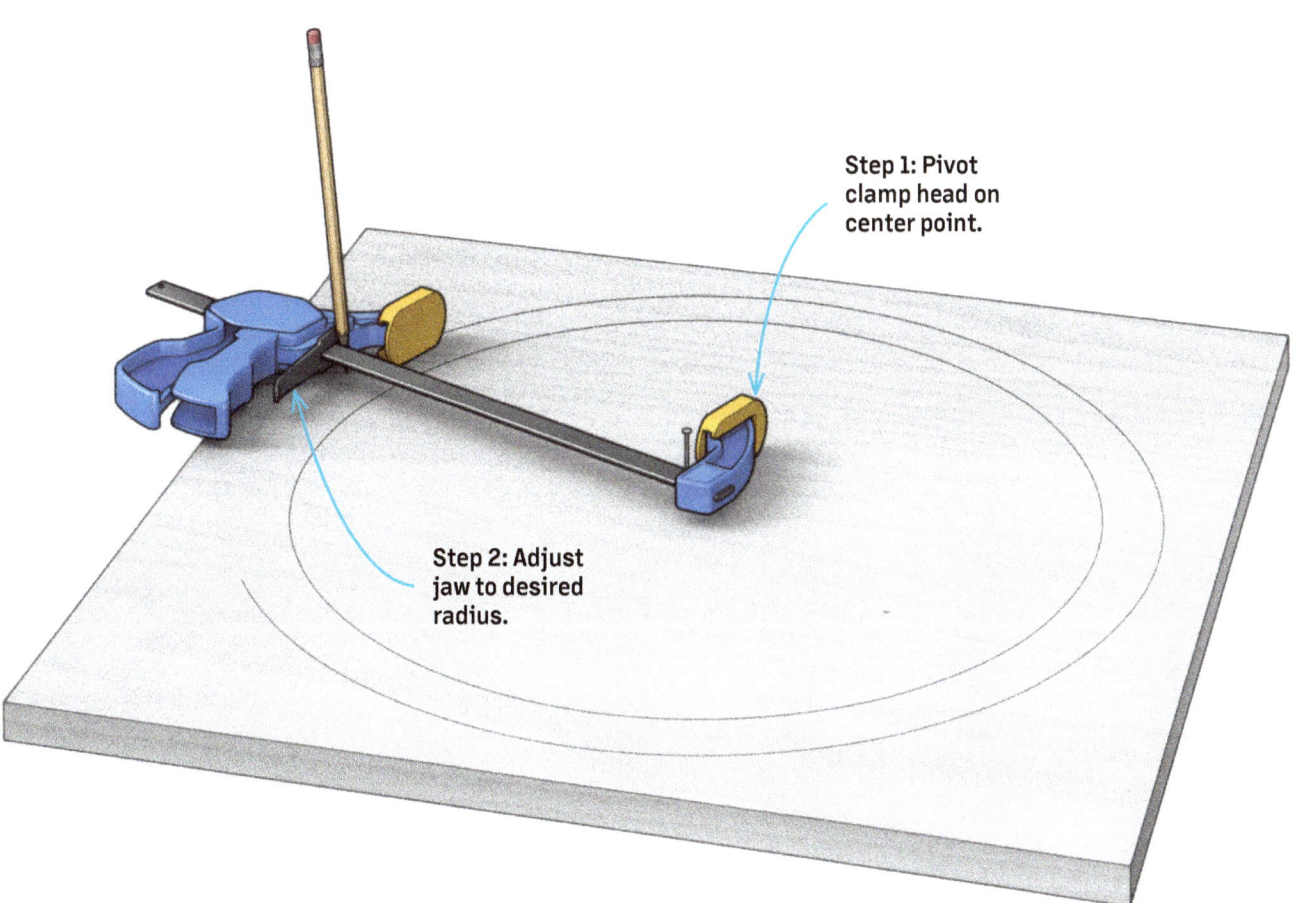

Step 1: Pivot clamp head on center point.

Step 2: Adjust jaw to desired radius.

Bar clamp compass

When a project requires you to draw a large circle, you don't necessarily need a trammel. Instead, try using a quick-set bar clamp. Hook the fixed jaw over a nail driven at the center point and hold your pencil at the intersection of the movable jaw and bar. Squeeze the handle to precisely adjust the pencil's location to match the radius you need.

—*Richard Entwistle, Highland Lakes, NJ*

TECHNIQUES > MEASURING & MARKING

Angle calculator

Here is a list of angles that can be easily formed with a straight board across a carpenter's square. For the desired angle, set the board at the length and height marks listed and clamp into place. All the angles shown in the table are accurate within 1/4°. For angles larger than 45°, just exchange the height and length. For example, a 30° angle would be formed when setting your board at 19" long and 11" high, so 60° would be measured at 11" long and 19" high.

—Dave Van Ess, Arlington, WA

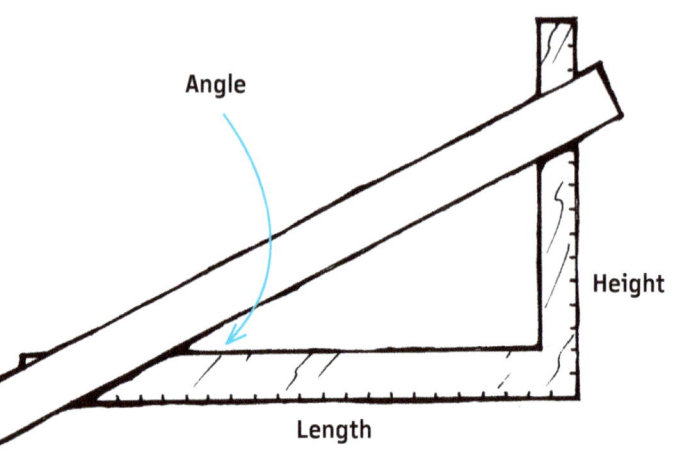

Angle	Length	Height	Angle	Length	Height
3°	19"	1"	23°	19"	8"
4°	14"	1"	24°	9"	4"
5°	23"	2"	25°	15"	7"
6°	19"	2"	28°	15"	8"
7°	8"	1"	29°	9"	5"
8°	7"	1"	30°	19"	11"
9°	19"	3"	31°	5"	3"
10°	17"	3"	32°	8"	5"
11°	21"	4"	33°	20"	13"
12°	14"	3"	35°	10"	7"
13°	13"	3"	36°	11"	8"
14°	4"	1"	37°	4"	3"
15°	15"	4"	38°	9"	7"
16°	7"	2"	39°	16"	13"
17°	23"	7"	40°	19"	16"
19°	23"	8"	41°	15"	13"
20°	11"	4"	42°	10"	9"
21°	13"	5"	43°	15"	14"
22°	5"	2"	45°	1"	1"
22.5°	17"	7"			

Chalk talk for dark lumber

Pencil lines barely show up on dark wood species and tempered hardboard, which can lead to mistakes when you're breaking lumber into manageable pieces for your projects. Putting tape on so you can write down joint-matching information is a real time waster.

Avoid these problems by using chalk instead of pencil. In fact, you can choose from several types of chalk to suit the level of accuracy required. For bold marks, reach for a jumbo piece of sidewalk chalk, which is available in several colors. For joint identification and notes, downsize to regular blackboard chalk, which also comes in several shades so you can color-code project components. Use a light touch with both of these types, and you'll be able to erase lines with a soft cloth. For the finest lines, switch to tailor's chalk. You can buy all these types of chalk at a hobby center.

—Andrew Allen, Tucson, AZ

MEASURING & MARKING < TECHNIQUES

Tape rule trammel

Trammel heads—the kind that clamp onto a strip of wood—are the tool of choice when laying out circles and arcs. Unfortunately, they can be expensive, and require a suitable strip of wood for the job, which may not be available when you need it. A handier alternative may be sitting in your kitchen junk drawer: an old tape rule.

All it takes to convert a tape rule into a trammel is a few minutes on the drill press. I drilled a row of 1/8"-diameter holes (roughly the diameter of a #4 finish nail) at 1" increments in the tape blade. For a custom-sized arc, it's easy enough to drill or punch another hole where needed.

—*Walt Summers, Miami, FL*

Cheap tape measure

Use finish nail as pivot point.

Start by drilling holes at 1" increments for rough layout, then as needed for custom arcs.

Do not drill into riveted section.

Check square corners with repurposed antenna

Measuring corner to diagonal corner is a common check for squareness in projects such as boxes and frames. Using an antenna from an old radio, I created a device to quickly check the diagonal dimensions of a project to ensure all 90° corners.

My antenna extends from 7-1/2" to 30". One end has a flat screw mount, while the other had a protective button. I removed the plastic button and found a brass end, which I filed to a point for more precise checking. On the screw-mount end, I fashioned a small corner attachment that allows it to be placed inside a corner or outside of a corner. A single screw attaches it to the antenna.

To check dimensions, extend the antenna to the opposite corner. The antenna will pivot in the fashioned attachment while the extended total length remains the same. This allows you to move to another corner, pivot the fixed length and check for uniformity.

—*Mark Thiel, Coral Springs, FL*

Tape rule accuracy

For best accuracy when measuring with a tape rule, don't bring the hook into play. Instead, align the 1" increment with the starting location, and then subtract an inch from the reading on the tape rule.

—*Paul Anthony, Riegelsville, PA*

TECHNIQUES > MEASURING & MARKING

Perfect alcove-fit countertops

In my finish carpentry work, it's not uncommon to have to fit a countertop into an alcove that's badly out-of-square. That's when I turn to a pattern-transfer trick that I learned from an old carpenter.

First, screw temporary ledger strips to the alcove walls 3/4" below the height of the desired countertop. Then cut a piece of 3/4"-thick plywood to the depth of the alcove and somewhat shy of the three walls. Place the plywood on the ledger strips, and tape a large piece of paper to it. Next, cut a point on the end of a stick of wood and mark one face as "up." Place the point of this transfer stick against each corner of the alcove in turn, and trace the outline of the stick onto the paper.

Remove the paper and tape it to your oversized countertop material. Position the stick inside each set of traced lines, and make a mark at the point onto your material. Connect the points with a straightedge, and you've got the shape of your top. If a wall isn't flat, scribe and fit a cardboard template against it, then use the template instead of a straightedge to connect the points.

—Sam Williamson, Birmingham, AL

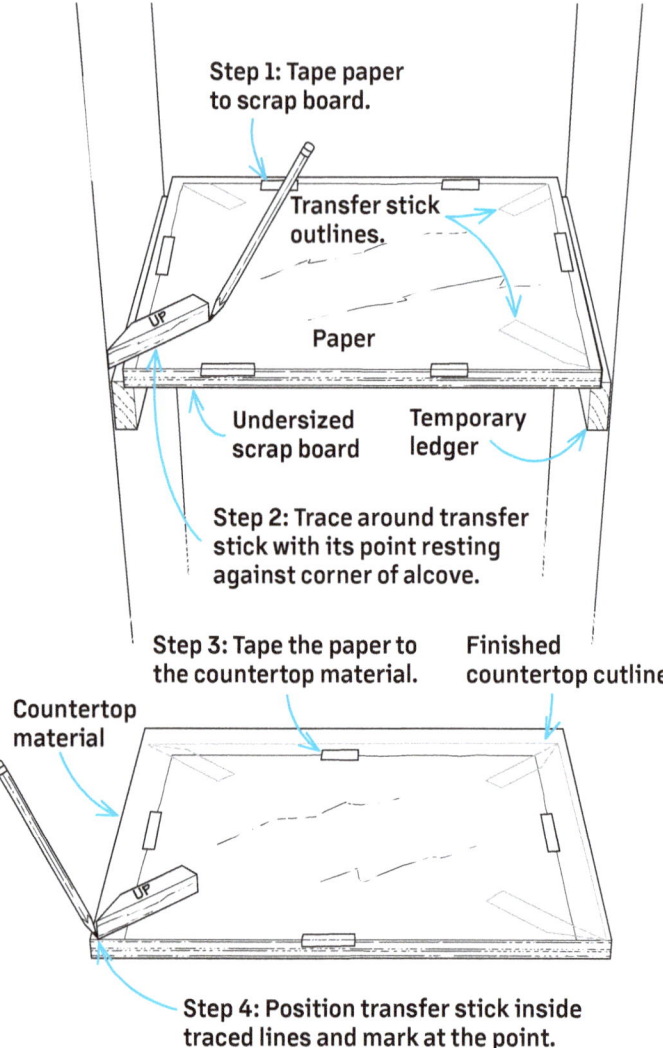

Step 1: Tape paper to scrap board.

Transfer stick outlines.

Paper

Undersized scrap board

Temporary ledger

Step 2: Trace around transfer stick with its point resting against corner of alcove.

Step 3: Tape the paper to the countertop material.

Finished countertop cutline

Countertop material

Step 4: Position transfer stick inside traced lines and mark at the point.

Angling for center

Fractions got you down? To divide a piece in two, simply angle your ruler to two major increments, and mark the halfway point. The same principle applies when dividing a board into multiple pieces of consistent width.

—Rob Spiece, Berea, KY

Shop-made squaring sticks

One of the best ways to check assemblies for square during glue-ups is to compare opposing diagonal measurements to make sure they match. One of the best ways to do that is to use squaring sticks, also called "pinch rods." I like to make my own using any straight-grained stock. The tongue-and-groove joint keeps the sticks aligned in use, while a spring clamp pinches them together to register the distance for comparison. You could also make a hardwood collar with a thumbscrew to fit around the sticks instead of the clamp. Marking increments on the sticks provides easy reference while adjusting them in use.

—Bruce Robertson, Raleigh, NC

Roundabout scribing

When installing wall cabinets some time back, I needed to scribe a face frame to fit against an irregular wall surface, but couldn't find the compass I normally use for the job. Fortunately, I remembered that an old finish carpenter once showed me how to scribe using regular flat washers, which I happened to have in my toolbox. Here's how it works: With the cabinet braced plumb and level, and with the face frame abutting the wall as closely as possible, select a washer whose ring width approximates the widest section of the remaining gap. Pressing the washer against the face frame and the wall, insert a pencil tip in the washer hole as shown, and drag it the length of the area to be trimmed to create your scribe line. Cut to the line, check your fit, and repeat if necessary, using a smaller washer to refine the fit.

—Mark Latimer, Florissant, MO

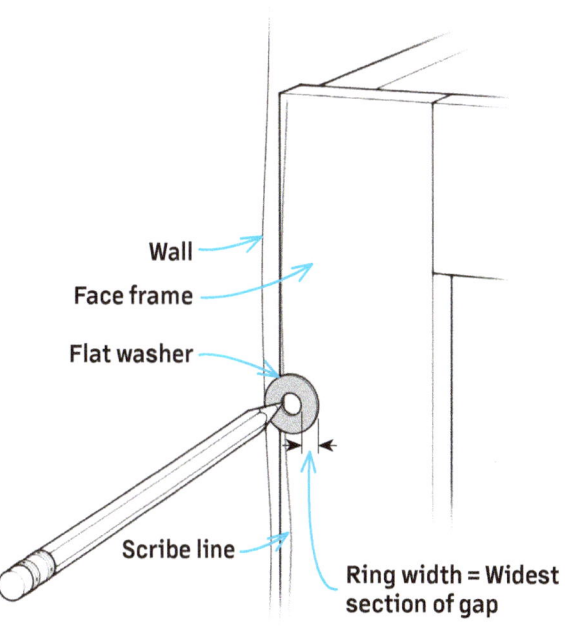

TECHNIQUES > MEASURING & MARKING

Accurate inside measurements

I find that taking inside measurements of a cabinet using a common tape rule can be iffy because the tape won't bend completely into a corner for a dead-on read. To get an accurate measurement, I incorporate a stick of wood cut precisely to an easy-to-add length, such as 10". Holding one end of the stick against one cabinet side, I extend the tape to the opposite cabinet side and note the measurement at the extended end of the stick. Adding 10" to that measurement gives me the precise interior width of the cabinet.

—Paul Kellam, Visalia, CA

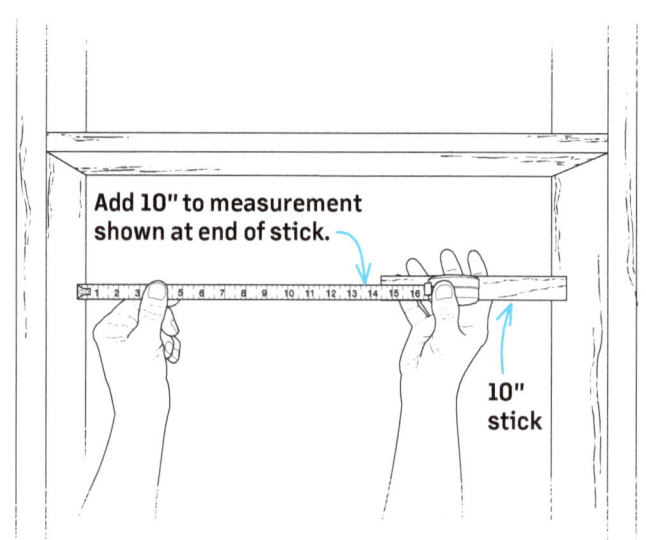

Add 10" to measurement shown at end of stick.

10" stick

Give a framing square the edge

A framing square can be useful for laying out large panels, but its lack of a shoulder makes it difficult to register a leg accurately against the edge of the workpiece. Sure, you can retract the square enough to drop the inside edge of the lower leg against the workpiece edge, but that raises one edge of the other leg off the workpiece, compromising layout accuracy. It also shortens the reach of the square.

My simple fix is to pinch the stock (i.e., the body) of a try square against the framing square leg as I'm placing both against the workpiece edge. Obviously, the longer the try square stock, the better, but even the head on a 12" combination square provides plenty of registration as long as you pinch the two squares together tightly.

—Alejandro Balbis, Longueuil, Quebec

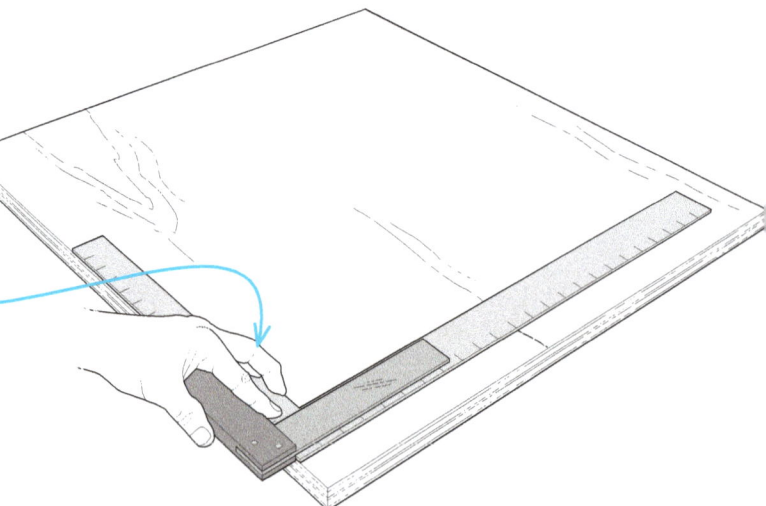

Pinch try square and framing square together while registering shoulder of try square against workpiece.

MEASURING & MARKING < TECHNIQUES

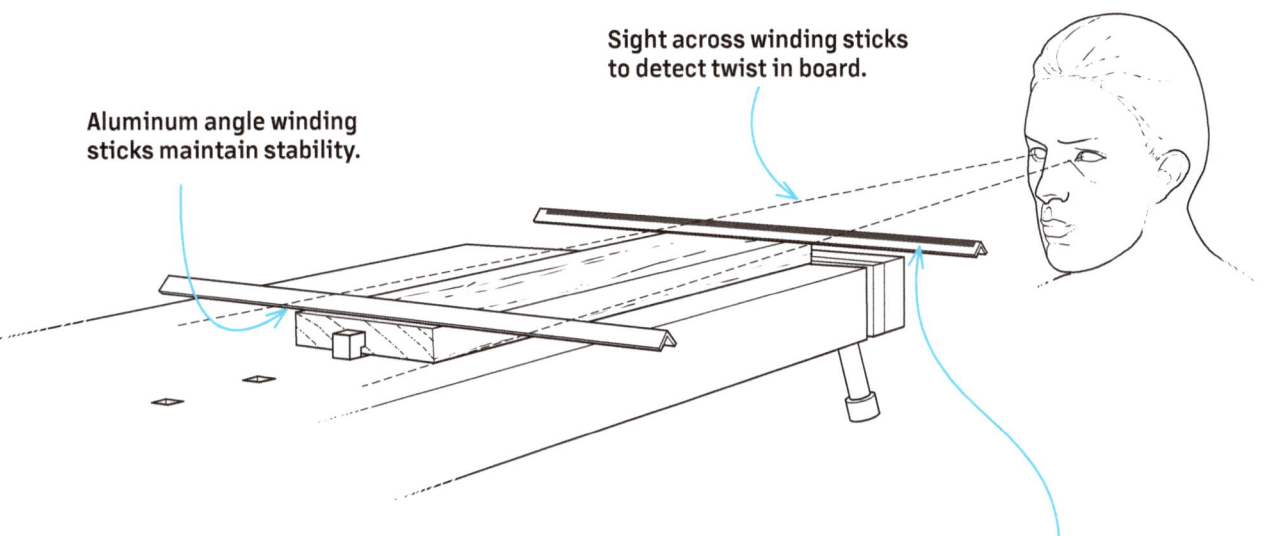

Aluminum angle winding sticks maintain stability.

Sight across winding sticks to detect twist in board.

Electrical tape creates visual contrast between sticks.

Aluminum angle winding sticks

Winding sticks provide a time-honored way to check the flatness of workpieces or assemblies. Used in pairs, winding sticks are placed parallel to each other at opposite ends of, for example, a board being handplaned. To check for twist, or "wind," crouch so that your eyes are level with the top edges of the sticks, and then sight across them with both eyes open. Any deviation in the flatness of the surface will be immediately apparent. Traditionally, winding sticks are made from straight-grained, identically sized pieces of hardwood—often of strongly contrasting colors for easy sighting. The problem with wood is that it can warp over time, requiring occasional redressing. Instead, I use aluminum angle from my local home supply store. For straightness and rigidity, get the 1/8"-thick stock. To provide contrast, crown one with black electrical tape.

—*Will Murphy, San Francisco, CA*

Tape overlay sketch pad

Whether it's a wooden handle for a small box, or the shape of a cutting board, it's amazing how hard it can be to make a curve appear simple, especially when you're working with unusual grain. Truth be told, most of my "organic" curves are carefully planned. To do this, I cover the face of the workpiece with a few strips of packing tape, or a clear plastic page protector, and then draw the shape on it using a grease pencil. Unlike an errant cut, mistakes can be wiped away with a rag.

—*Joe Hurst-Wajszczuk, Birmingham, AL*

WOODCRAFT MAGAZINE TIPS & TRICKS FOR WOODWORKING

TECHNIQUES > MEASURING & MARKING

Easy offset marking

To mark a consistent offset from a template, trace the outline using a washer as a spacer.

—Ken Burton, New Tripoli, PA

Knife line accuracy

For pinpoint accuracy when knifing a cutline, poke the tip of the blade into your layout mark, and then slide your try square against the knife edge before knifing the cutline.

—Paul Anthony, Riegelsville, PA

Ruler widths

Note the widths of various rulers, squares, and straightedges. They are often manufactured to precise sizes such as 1/2", 3/4", 1", 1-1/2", and 2", which makes for quick, easy layouts of common measurements.

—Paul Anthony, Riegelsville, PA

Center finder as saddle square

You can use the accessory center finder of a combination square as a saddle square. Because its faces are at a 90º angle, you need only position one leg of the center finder against a cutline drawn on one face of your stock, and then carry the line onto the adjacent face. Simple. Sweet. Accurate.

—Don Wood, Galena, OH

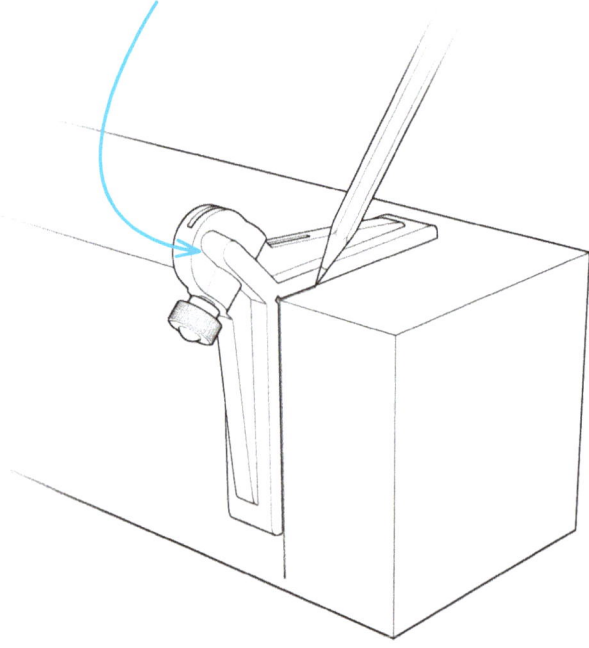

Combination square center finder serves as a saddle square for marking adjacent surfaces.

Pre-shimming for wall cabinets

When installing a run of cabinets on a badly bowed wall, I find it easier and more accurate to pre-shim the wall instead of shimming individual cabinets straight and plumb as I go. Here's the approach: Begin by drawing a level reference line that indicates the cabinet bottom locations. Then, at the height of the cabinet upper screw cleats, stretch a string taut between #8 nails driven into studs outside each end of the cabinet run. Do the same at the lower cleat location. Finally, stretch two strings diagonally from the nails, as shown.

Using a level, roughly plumb the two horizontal strings to each other. Adjust the diagonal strings in or out on their nails until they touch each other and the horizontal strings, with the web as close to the wall as possible without bending the strings. You have created a flat plane reference, and can now stack shims out to the string at the stud locations. Believe me, your cabinet installation will go fast and look great!

—Paul Anthony, Riegelsville, PA

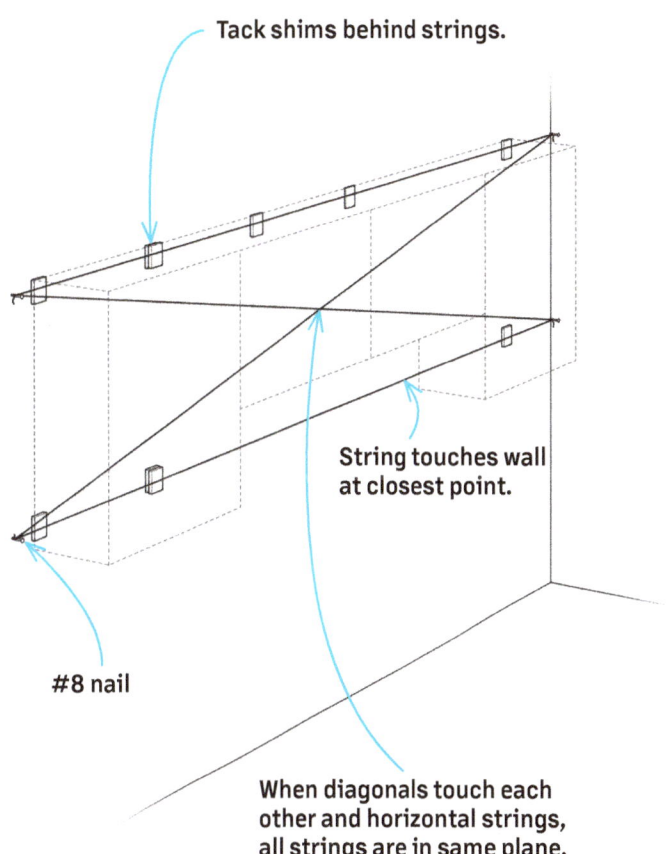

Square check

To check the accuracy of a combo square, register its beam (or stock) against the straight edge of a piece of scrap, strike a line, and then flip the square over (against the same edge), and compare the lines.

—Larissa Huff, Schwenksville, PA

TECHNIQUES > MEASURING & MARKING

Clamp-and-rule curve layout

One traditional way to lay out fair curves is to trace against a thin strip of wood bent to the desired shape, with the ends of the strip clamped or tacked in place to the workpiece. This approach works okay, but it can be a bit fussy to get the curve just right, and wood doesn't always bend as perfectly as you might like. I find that a much better approach is to use a thin steel rule. Squeeze it into the desired bow between the jaws of a bar clamp whose pads have been notched to prevent the rule from twisting. This allows great control of the curve shape, and holds the rule very firmly for use as a tracing guide.
—Alejandro Balbis, Longueuil, Quebec

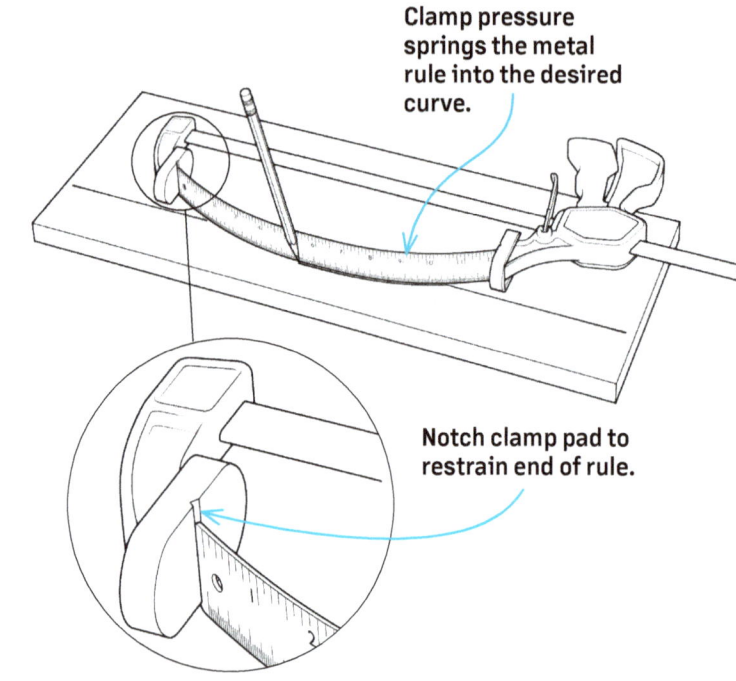

Clamp pressure springs the metal rule into the desired curve.

Notch clamp pad to restrain end of rule.

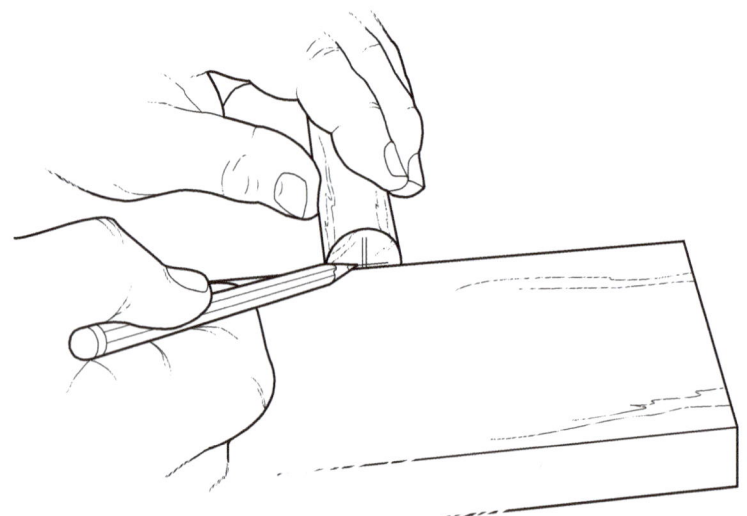

No-cost center finder

Here's a no-cost trick for finding the center of a dowel using a scrap of wood with a thickness that's approximately the radius of the dowel. Position the cylinder's end against the board, then run the tip of a sharp pencil along the end and mark the edge. Rotate the cylinder approximately 90°, and make another line. Repeat two more times. The intersecting lines should create a tiny square on the end of the dowel; from there, you can judge the center by eye.
—Robert J. Settich, Gladstone, MO

Rule depth gauge as mini square

When it comes to hand-cutting dovetails, precision matters. For the joint to fit well, the baseline shoulders and the tail cheeks must be square to the faces of the boards, and the pin cheeks must be square to the ends of the boards. Unfortunately, it can be difficult to maneuver a regular square into place to check those surfaces, especially with closely spaced dovetails. However, you can repurpose a rule depth gauge to do the job. Designed to measure the depth of dadoes, mortises, and other recesses, its narrow blade also easily slips into pin sockets to allow checking of dovetail cheeks and baseline shoulders. Likewise, you can retract the blade and place the tool's stock against the end of a pinboard to check pin cheeks.

—Ric Hanisch, Quakertown, PA

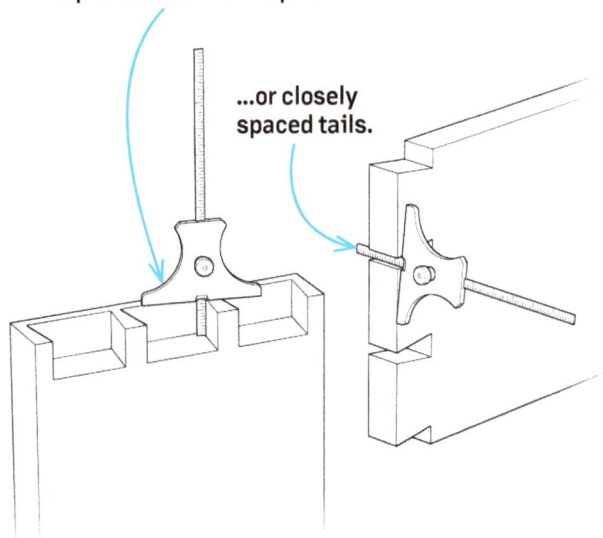

Use a rule depth gauge to check for square on half-blind pins...

...or closely spaced tails.

Tape rule gauge

For accurate work, you need accurate measuring tools, and that includes your tape rule. Unfortunately, the sliding tang on a tape rule—which allows for taking inside and outside measurements—is often the tool's Achilles' heel. Inexpensive tape rules are particularly prone to inaccurate measurements taken from the end of the tape.

When buying a new tape rule, make sure that both the inside and outside measurements made using the tang are accurate. To check this, I bring to the store a very accurate gauge block I made for the purpose. To avoid parallax when gauging the tape, roll it over slightly so the edge of the tape actually lays on the workpiece. The gauge is also useful for checking the accuracy of your tape rule after dropping it and possibly bending the tang. A bent tang can easily be corrected with a pair of pliers.

—Paul Anthony, Riegelsville, PA

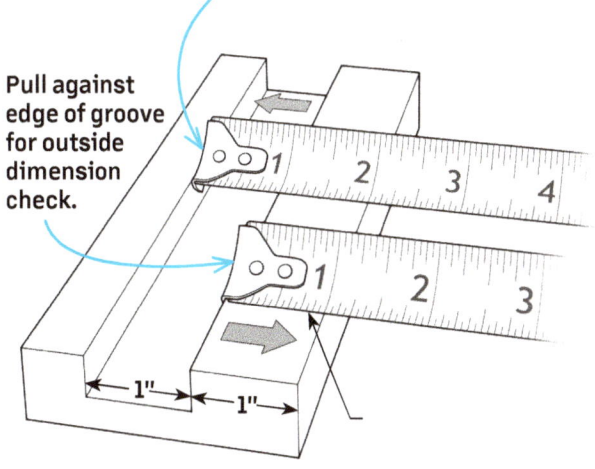

Press tang against side of groove to check accuracy for taking inside dimensions.

Pull against edge of groove for outside dimension check.

For best read, roll edge of tape against gauge block.

TECHNIQUES > MEASURING & MARKING

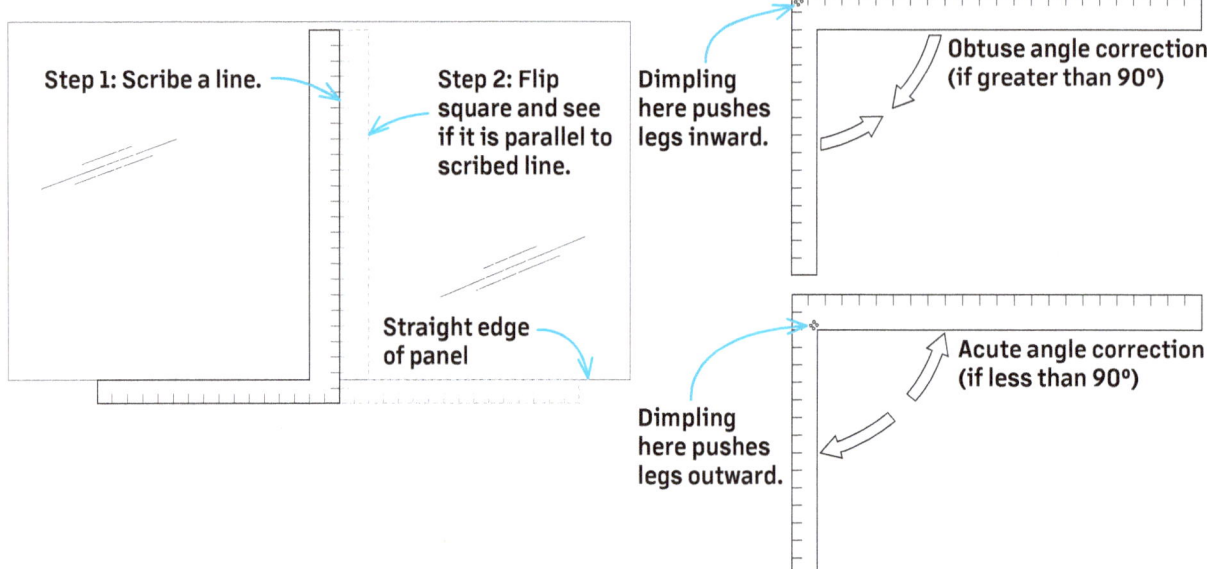

Yardstick compass for tabletops

Easily make round tops of various sizes for your furniture projects. Take a wood yardstick and drill a nail hole at the 1" mark, making sure it is located in the center of the rule. For a 6" radius, drill a larger hole (to accommodate a pencil) at the 7" mark, again centering the hole on the ruler. Tap the nail into the center of your board blank (preferably into the underside) and push the pencil to form the 12" circle. The only trick is to make sure the pencil fits tightly in the hole and is held straight when making the circle. After that, it is a simple matter of bandsawing the blank and sanding down to the pencil mark for a perfect edge.

You can use the same ruler for any radius up to 34". If you have too many holes in the ruler or if they are too close together, simply get a new yardstick. They are available at most home supply centers.

—Jim Wolff, Berlin, WI

Squaring a square

If you have a framing square that's not square, don't toss it—yet. If the error is small, there's a good chance it can be fixed. If the edges are straight and the legs are uniform in width (not tapered), give this old trick a try. If the square is obtuse (greater than 90°), dimple the outer corner area a couple times using a center punch and a hammer, and check your results. If the square is severely off, you may need to do this several times. What you're doing is stretching the metal on the outer corner to push the legs toward each other. Conversely, if the square is acute (less than 90°), you'll need to dimple the area near the inside corner of the square.

—Craig W. Bentzley, Chalfont, PA

Offset and depth gauge block

When laying out screw-hole locations offset from the edge of a workpiece, I used to set a combination square to do the job. But then I remembered that I saw a carpenter once using a rabbeted block to mark the offset for his door and window trim reveals. I decided to make my block do quadruple duty by rabbeting all four edges to different commonly used offsets. When I found that the block also served as a great table saw and router depth gauge, I made a couple more to create a total of 12 rabbets, ranging through 3/4" in 1/16" increments.

—Serge Duclos, Delson, Québec

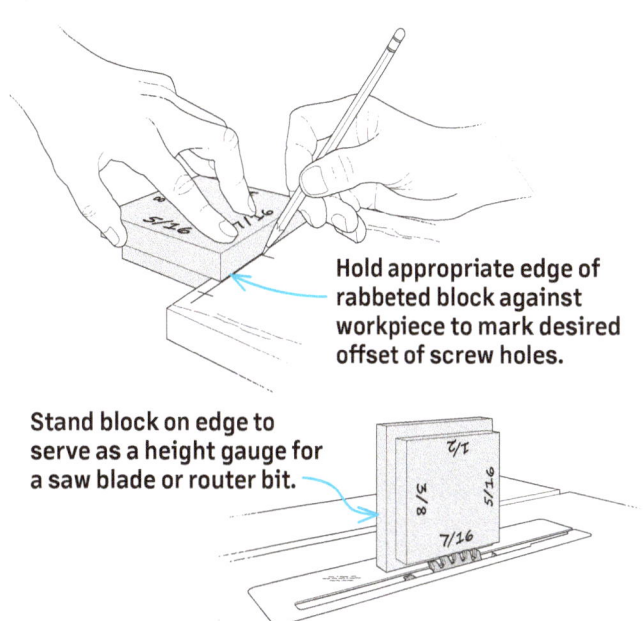

Hold appropriate edge of rabbeted block against workpiece to mark desired offset of screw holes.

Stand block on edge to serve as a height gauge for a saw blade or router bit.

Improvised center finder

A recent project required installing 3/8"-diameter dowels centered into the ends of a length of 1-3/8"-diameter dowel. Not being a turner, I didn't own a proper center finder for locating the dowel holes. Instead, I made do with my combination square. I found that, by clamping a small piece of square scrap to the tool's blade, I created a perfectly usable center finder. To use it, I place the end of the dowel against the square's body and the wood scrap, and strike a line across the dowel. Striking a similar line at about 90° to the first locates the center at the intersection of the lines.

—Brad Mumford, Boise, ID

Combination square

Align corner of scrap with intersection of blade and square head.

TECHNIQUES > MEASURING & MARKING

Tracing mouse

In my furniture restoration work, I often have to reproduce missing or broken parts, tracing their shapes from the originals. Tracing around flat work is easy, but sculptural parts like cabriole legs present a problem that I solved by devising this tracing "mouse." To make one, start with a 1" × 4" × 5-1/2" hardwood block. Next, drill a 5/16"-diameter hole through the block to fit a commonly available straight-sided ballpoint pen. Center the hole across the thickness, about 1-3/4" back from one end. Then, make the profile cuts as shown in the drawing. Use a disc sander to form a 60° point on the nose—tweaking and sanding until the point aligns with the tip of the inserted pen. Sand a comfortable radius for a hand on the opposite end of the block. Finally, tap a 1/4"- 20 hole in the middle of the body, and install a thumbscrew to secure the pen. To use the mouse, push the pen down until it contacts the paper, lock the thumbscrew, butt the knife-edge against the part, and trace your pattern.

—Craig W. Bentzley, Chalfont, PA

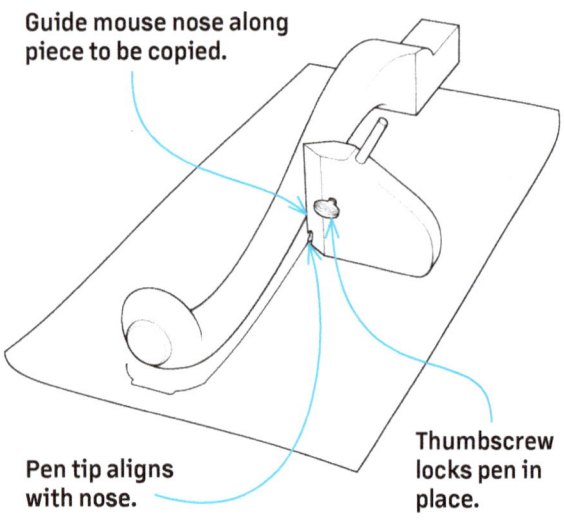
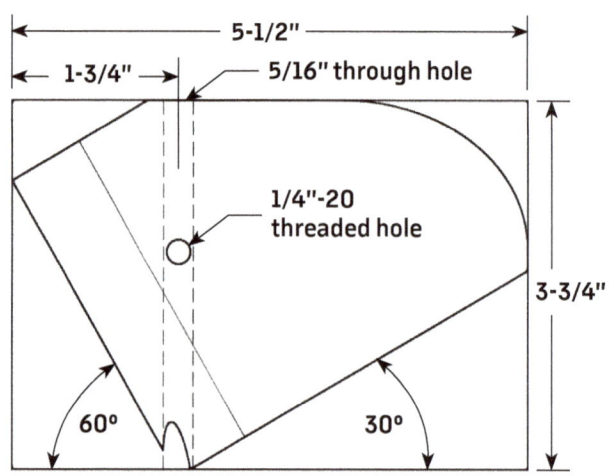

Chalk for layout

Use white chalk to lay out rough-sized parts on roughsawn lumber. It shows up well and wipes away easily as you change your mind about the layout.

—Larissa Huff, Schwenksville, PA

SANDING & SHAPING

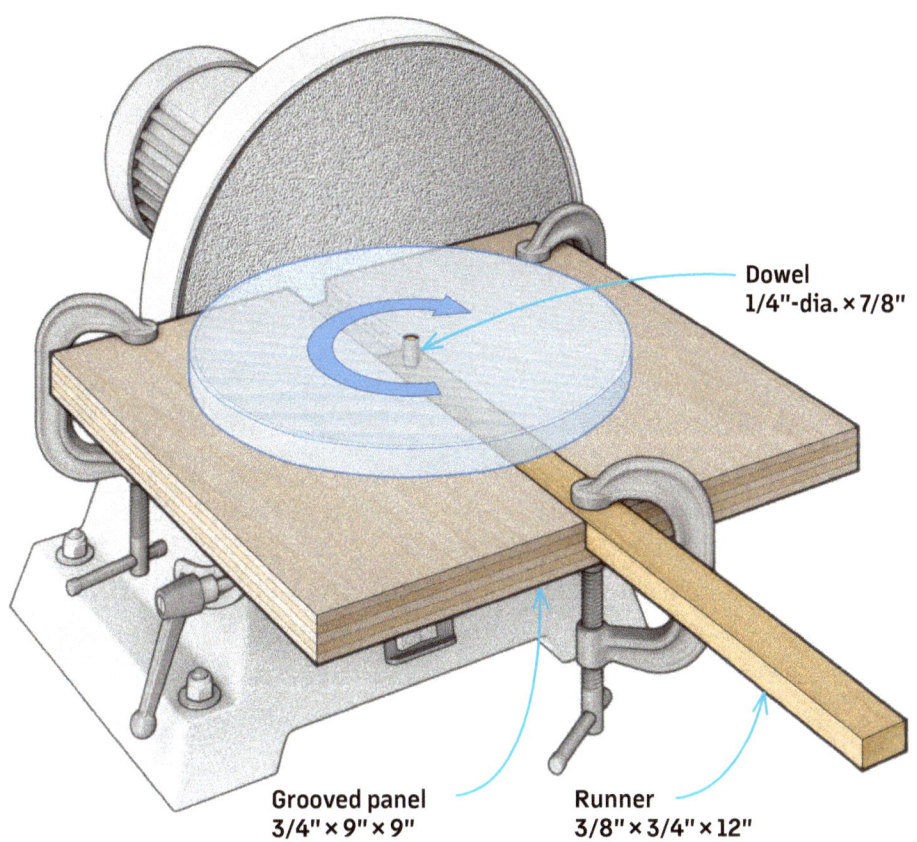

Dowel
1/4"-dia. × 7/8"

Grooved panel
3/4" × 9" × 9"

Runner
3/8" × 3/4" × 12"

Simple circle-sanding jig

I needed a jig to sand some small round discs to an accurate diameter after bandsawing them to rough shape. I cobbled together a quick jig to do the job using my disc sander. The jig is simply a grooved panel that houses a runner with a 1/4" dowel at one end. The dowel inserts in a hole in the workpiece to serve as a pivot point that can be set to the desired distance from the sanding disc.

To use the jig, first drill a 1/4"-diameter center hole in your workpiece. Clamp the grooved panel to your sander table. Insert the runner in its groove; mount the workpiece on the dowel. With the sander running, slide the runner forward until you've sanded to your layout line. Then, stop the tool and clamp the runner to the panel. Restart the sander and slowly rotate the workpiece to complete the job.

—*Derek Richmond, Easton, PA*

TECHNIQUES > SANDING & SHAPING

Circle-sanding jig

I cobbled up this disc sander jig to clean up the edges of small circular workpieces. It consists of a sled that rides on a base fixed to the table. To build the jig, first make the base and sled from 3/4"-thick plywood about 5" wide. To determine the length for both pieces, measure the distance between your sanding disc and the front edge of the tool's table, and add an inch or so. Saw a dado lengthwise down the center of each piece. Size a 1/2"-thick runner to fit the dado, terminating it 2" from the outer end of the base, and then glue it in place where shown. Glue a 2"-long stop into the outermost end of the sled dado. Size a "registration bar" to fit your table slot, and glue and screw it to the underside of the base, so that the base and sled both rest against the sander disc.

To use the jig, drive a 4d finish nail into the sled at the centerline, setting it back from the inner edge of the sled a distance equal to the desired circle radius. Clip off the head of the nail. Drill a 5/64"-diameter hole in the backside of your workpiece, and set it on the nail. Place the sled on the jig base, and slowly push it inward while rotating the workpiece. Continue until the stop hits the end of the sled runner, creating a smooth-edged, perfect circle.

—*Bil Mitchell, Hellertown, PA*

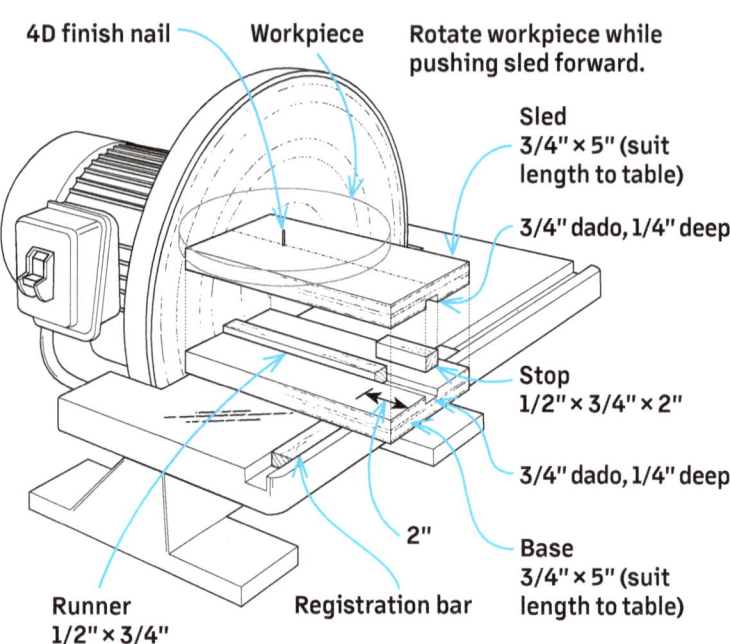

Combo sanding disc

Sometimes it would be an advantage to be able to fine-sand a bunch of small parts on a disc sander and not have to change out the discs from coarse or medium to fine. One solution to the problem is to cut out the center of a large disc of coarse paper to accommodate a smaller-diameter disc of fine sandpaper. Cut out the proper-sized area from the back of the large disc (possibly the size of a small disc—depending on the small disc available), and attach the small disc to the middle of the sander with the large disc around the outside. This, in effect, gives you two grades of paper on the same sanding disc. Be really frugal and save the center of the large disc that you cut out for the same sort of setup on some other job.

—*Janice Farver, San Clemente, CA*

SANDING & SHAPING < TECHNIQUES

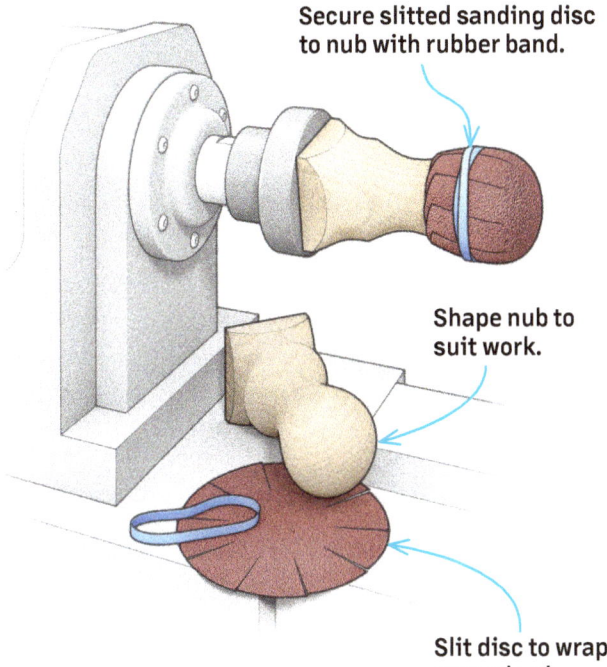

Secure slitted sanding disc to nub with rubber band.

Shape nub to suit work.

Slit disc to wrap around nub.

Sanding nub

In need of a cheap but effective way for students to smooth the inside faces of their carved spoons, I hit upon this shop-made, lathe-mounted "sanding nub." It is simply a block of hardwood turned to a small dome shape and covered with a disc of coarse sanding paper held in place with a rubber band. Strategically placed radial slices allow the abrasive to conform well enough to the curved surface of the block. The sanding nub does a great job of smoothing out carving tracks, and prepares the surface for easier hand-sanding with finer papers. Obviously, you can turn a nub with a wider face for broader surfaces like bowls, using adhesive to attach the paper if necessary.

—Ken Burton, New Tripoli, PA

Cleaner sanding for a better finish

Successfully smoothing a finish depends on keeping your sandpaper clean by frequently brushing or blowing it off. Paper loaded with dust won't cut properly. Worse yet, some finishes—particularly those that haven't cured a long time—can cause "corns," tiny blobs of partially cured finish that accumulate on your sandpaper and can mar the surface, defeating the very purpose of sanding. To ward off these problems, I keep the proper weapon at hand: a file card and brush. This combination tool, which is designed to clean files and rasps, sports a soft-bristle brush on one side and wire brush on the other. I keep it in my free hand while using the other hand to sand with paper wrapped around a felt block. When the paper loads up with dust, a quick swipe or two with the brush does the trick. I attack corns with the file card.

—Andy Rae, Asheville, NC

Use brush face to remove dust from sandpaper.

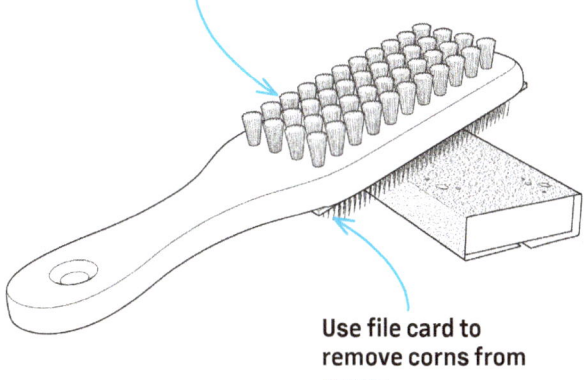

Use file card to remove corns from paper.

TECHNIQUES > SANDING & SHAPING

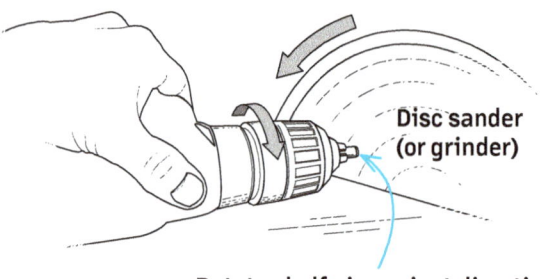

Rotate shelf pin against direction of disc (or grinder wheel).

Disc sander (or grinder)

Shaping shelf-support pins

I like to use a 1/4"-diameter brass rod (available at hardware stores) to make classy-looking shelf supports, cutting them to length with a hacksaw. I round the ends for easy insertion and a finished appearance. The best way to do this is to chuck a pin in a handheld drill and then round the end against a grinder or disc sander, making sure the rotation of the drill opposes the rotation of the wheel as you move the drill in an arc. You can also round wooden dowels in this fashion for use with utility cabinets.

—Sam Strickland, Portland, OR

A makeshift drum sander

Sometimes I make little turned vessels with drilled-out interiors, and need to clean up the relatively deep openings. I've found that the best tool for the job is a 1/2"-diameter dowel that I use as a drum sander of sorts. I bandsaw a slot in the end of the dowel to accept a strip of sandpaper that automatically wraps itself around the dowel as it spins inside the hole. Refreshing the paper occasionally is a simple matter of tearing off the used section. This technique actually works well for sanding the edges of pierced scrollwork too. On large workpieces, you can chuck the sander into a hand-held drill for better maneuverability.

—Stu McPherson, Truth or Consequences, NM

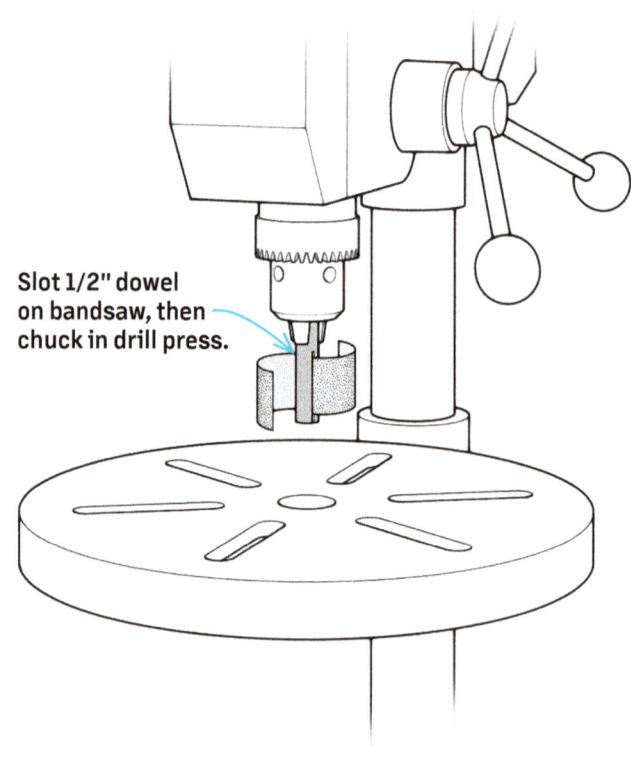

Slot 1/2" dowel on bandsaw, then chuck in drill press.

Emery boards in the shop

I keep a cup of emery boards within easy reach in the shop. Thin, flat, strong, and with different grits on each side, they can fit into and sand places not normally accessible. Cleaning out mortises, dovetails, and dadoes is a snap, as is sanding into tight corners and crevices.

A whole package of emery boards doesn't cost much, so you'll be far better off buying your own supply than raiding your wife's stash. Don't ask me how I know this.

—Terry Hinzman, San Mateo, CA

Zero-clearance sanding table

The problem with sanding small parts on a disc sander is the gap between the table and spinning disc. Should the piece tip or your grip slip, the disc will wrench the wood out of your hand. In an instant, you'll find yourself with a ruined part and sometimes a really bad case of road rash.

To prevent this, I cut a piece of 1/4"-thick hardboard a few inches wider than the table and positioned it against the sanding wheel, neatly bridging that finger-eating gap. Use clamps to keep the auxiliary table in place. Consider screwing a stop to the bottom of the hardboard to keep the table from creeping into the sander and disappearing in a cloud of dust.

—Tom Goltry, Platteville, WI

Narrow belt sander gap filler

When I tilt the table on my stationary narrow belt sander for beveled work, the gap in front of the belt grows wider to the point where smaller parts can drop through. To close this void, I made a reducer from a piece of stiff sheet metal with a length of self-adhesive magnetic strip adhered to its back side. The magnet holds the reducer firmly to the sander's table as shown. When not in use, I simply store it on the back of the machine.

—Dave Black, Holdrege, NE

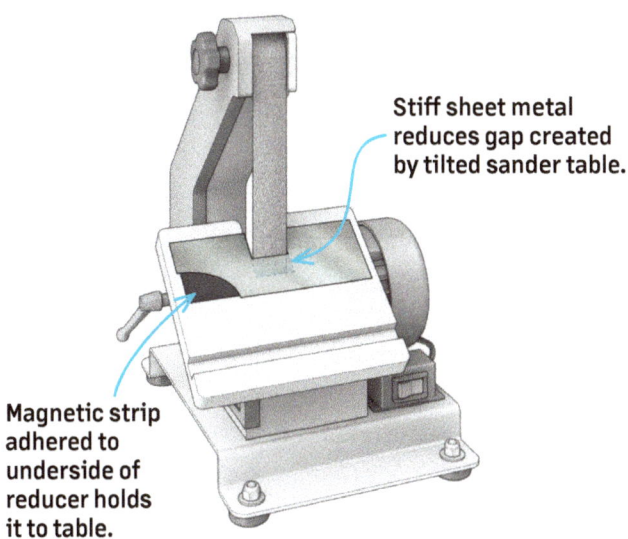

Stiff sheet metal reduces gap created by tilted sander table.

Magnetic strip adhered to underside of reducer holds it to table.

Yoga mats as sanding pads

Is someone in your home upgrading their old yoga mat? Put it to work as a sanding pad. The non-slip surface will grab both your workpiece and your bench for tasks such as routing edge profiles. It will also protect your workpieces from dents and dings.

—Rob Spiece, Berea, KY

Keep your card scraper cool

In use, a card scraper can generate enough heat to hurt. Try attaching an advertising sheet magnet that's cut to an appropriate size. It will serve as a heat sink to prevent burning your fingers.

—Craig W. Bentzley, Chalfont, PA

TECHNIQUES > SANDING & SHAPING

Chamfer-sanding jig

A recent project called for making a lot of small square pegs in which both ends needed to be encircled with small chamfers. I tried to create the chamfers by touching the angled pegs lightly against the belt sander, but the results were inconsistent at best. In frustration, I improvised this simple jig, which works great with a stationary belt sander. The jig is essentially a chute that holds the workpiece at the desired angle and distance from the sanding belt. As shown, the workpiece rests on a spacer that's sandwiched between two angled supports. A finish nail driven into the base near the bottom of the spacer serves as a stop to limit the amount of sanding, to ensure consistent chamfers.

Build the jig to suit the size of your sander table and pegs. The only dimension that's critical is the thickness of the spacer, which should match the thickness of your peg stock. Lay out the slope of the supports to suit the chamfer angle, and then bandsaw to your cutline. Apply double-faced tape to both sides of the spacer before nailing it between the supports to widen the channel for an easy sliding fit for the workpiece. Tack or screw the support/spacer sandwich to a base that's sized to your sander table. Finally, install a finish nail near the front of the base. Adjust its height and angle to contact the center section of the workpiece end. Clamp the base to your sander table, load a test workpiece into the chute, and adjust the location of the base to create the desired chamfer. Then get to quick work chamfering your pegs.

—Cliff Charron, Baker, FL

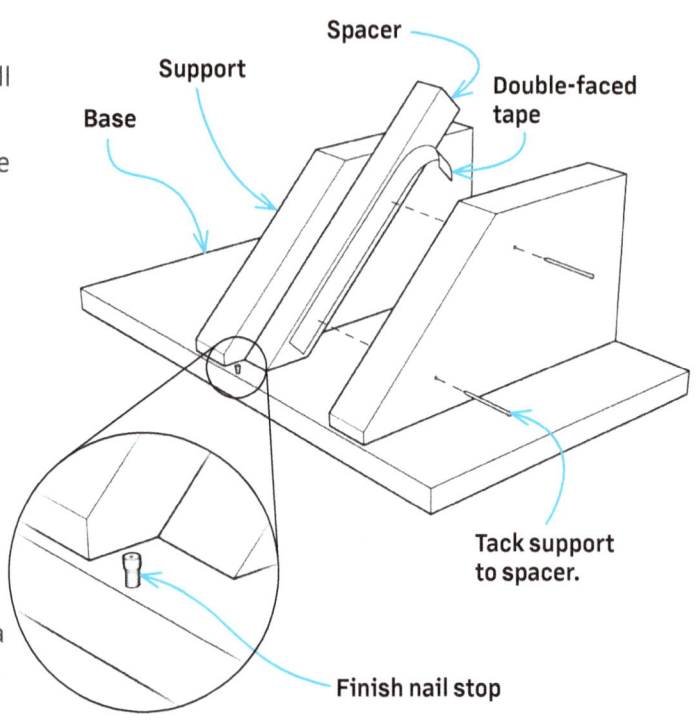

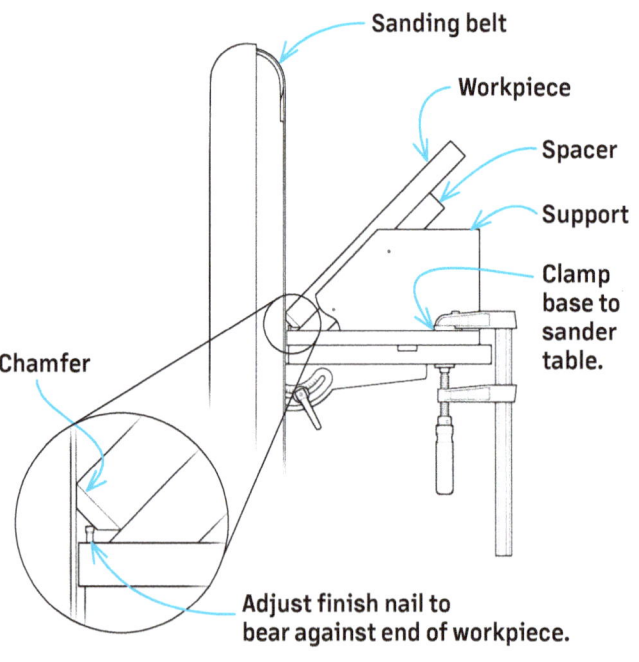

Side view of setup

Dowel as mini drum sander

When smoothing concave edges, particularly in confined areas, I find that a dowel wrapped in sandpaper and chucked in a drill serves as a great mini drum sander of sorts. To make one, bisect one end of a short length of stout dowel using a bandsaw or handsaw, and insert a strip of sandpaper into the kerf. Then chuck the other end in a drill. The rotation of the drill as you work causes the paper to wrap around the dowel, creating the drum sander effect. The real beauty of this is that, when the paper wears, you simply tear off the used section to expose new grit and quickly get back to work.

—*Bob Howard, Saint Louis, MO*

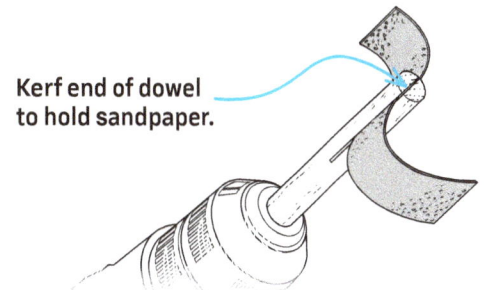

Kerf end of dowel to hold sandpaper.

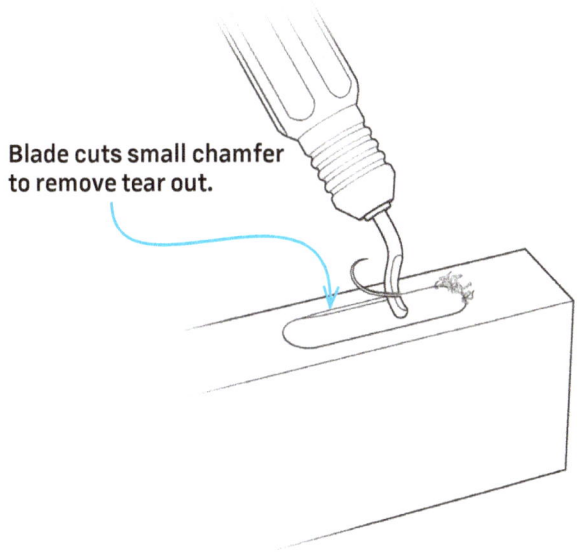

Blade cuts small chamfer to remove tear out.

Deburring tool

Sometimes a tool from one craft works well for another. I've found that a hand deburring tool, used to clean up rough edges in metalwork, has great applications in the woodshop. The tool's sharp cutter rotates freely in its handle and cuts a small chamfer on edges and corners. In metalworking, it's used to remove burrs caused by the cutting tool, and can serve essentially the same purpose in woodworking, removing exit tear out from mortises or holes, and quickly scraping away rough edges on shop plastics and metals. Hand deburring tools can be purchased online.

—*Dan Martin, Galena, OH*

Adhesive-backed sandpaper

PSA-backed sandpaper wrapped around dowels or other shaped backers works great for sanding moldings and other curved surfaces. The pressure-sensitive adhesive also allows folding the paper tightly over the edge of a credit card to sand into tight spaces.

—*Craig W. Bentzley, Chalfont, PA*

TECHNIQUES > SANDING & SHAPING

Complementary sanding backer

It's easy to make a sanding block that perfectly matches many coves. Just adhere fine sandpaper to the face of the target surface, and then rub a piece of packing styrene against the paper as shown. You now have a perfectly complementary styrene backer that you can wrap with sandpaper.

—Paul Anthony, Riegelsville, PA

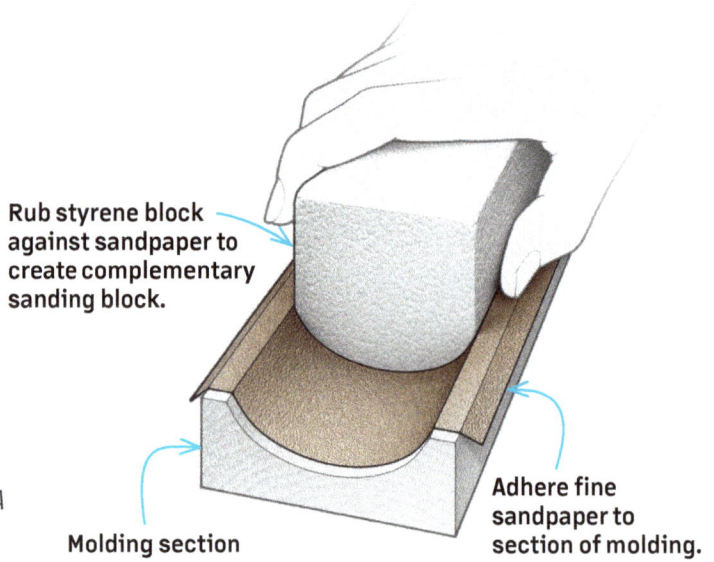

Rub styrene block against sandpaper to create complementary sanding block.

Molding section

Adhere fine sandpaper to section of molding.

Sanding in tight spots

To sand a narrow slot, you can use sandpaper attached to a putty knife. You simply cut the sandpaper slightly oversize for a 1-1/2" × 3" blade and attach it with spray adhesive, then trim to fit. I keep two versions handy: one with 80-grit on one side and 120-grit on the other side, and the second equipped with 150- and 180-grit.

—John S. Wilson, Redwood City, CA

Blackboard eraser sanding block

Sanding blocks can be just plain blocks of wood, or blocks padded with cork, felt, or another material. I have used all of the above, but I have found that a blackboard eraser with sandpaper wrapped around it works the best for fine sanding and sanding before recoating.

—Alex K. Nadler, Swansea, IL

A safety razor scraper

Over the years, I've often used a single-edge razor blade to scrape dried finish drips and runs flush to the adjacent surface. To scrape heavy runs or particularly hard finish, I often turn a hook on the blade, in the same manner I do with a card scraper, but to one side only. To target the area of concern and to keep the corners of the blade from digging in, I would do my best to flex it into a downward curve, again, as with a card scraper. But a luthier friend recently showed me a better way to control the cut. Simply wrap a piece of regular cellophane tape around each end of the blade, leaving the space between the two pieces wide enough to do the requisite scraping. This way, you don't have to flex the blade, the corners won't dig in, and the cutting will stop when only about .002" of finish remains raised to sand level with very fine abrasives. Brilliant!

—Jesse Roberts, St. Louis, MO

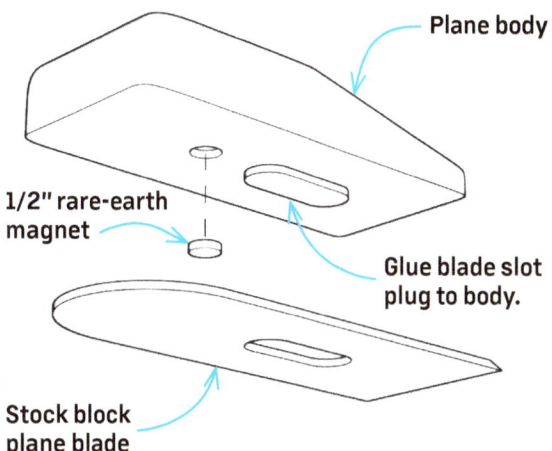

Shop-made flush-cut plane

Over the years, I have replaced many of the thin stock blades in my vintage handplanes with modern aftermarket blades. Looking for a way to put an old blade to good use, I combined it with a few scraps of wood to make a flush-cut plane—a handy tool for various trimming chores and for removing dried glue at intersecting project parts.

To make a plane like this, begin with a block of wood about 1" thick, exactly as wide as the blade, and about 1/2" shorter. Bevel the front half of the block down to about 3/8" for a good grip, and ease the edges for comfort. Shape a bit of hardwood to make a plug that snugly fits the blade slot, glue the plug in place to the underside of the body, and then trim it flush to the surface of the blade. Finish up by epoxying a 1/2"-diameter rare-earth magnet into a blind hole in the bottom, insetting it so it's flush with the surface of the block to hold the blade in place.

—Alejandro Balbis, Longueuil, Quebec

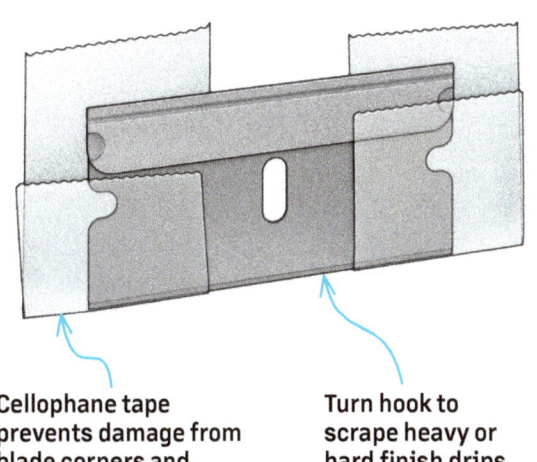

TECHNIQUES > SANDING & SHAPING

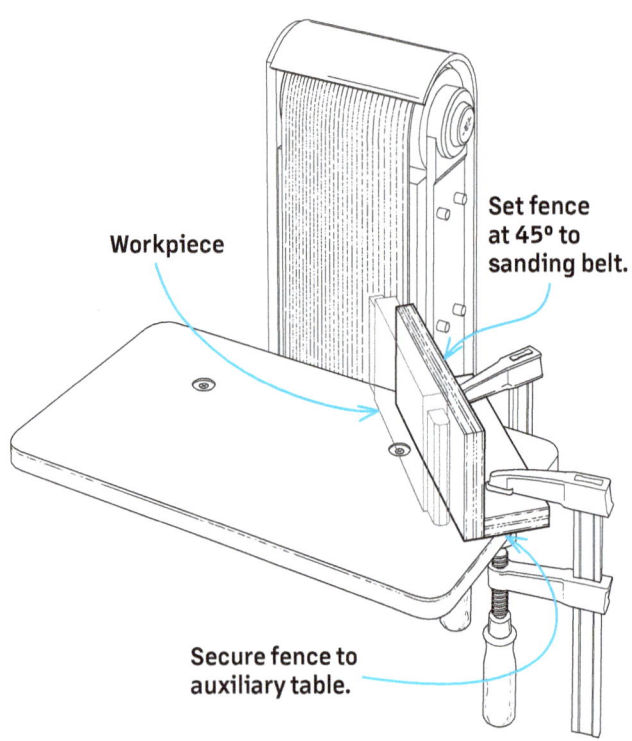

Workpiece

Set fence at 45° to sanding belt.

Secure fence to auxiliary table.

Sander chamfering

The problem with router chamfering bits is that they tend to tear out end grain, so when chamfering the end of a board, I prefer to do the job by sanding. To guide the workpiece, I employ a scrap wood jig with a tall fence clamped at a 45° angle to the face of my stationary belt sander. After marking the desired chamfer on the board's end, I then place the workpiece on edge against the fence. With the tool running, I ease the end against the belt, chamfering the long edge to the line. I then flip the workpiece and chamfer the opposite edge.

Next, I lay the board facedown with its edge against the fence and chamfer a short edge, flipping it to do the remaining short edge.

—Tom Svec, Lockhaven, PA

Sandpaper file folders

A standard A–Z or 1–31 day folder is great to hold sandpaper, divided by grit size.

I print labels for all my existing sandpaper showing grit, paper weight, and other descriptors. I start with 50-grit and end with 2,000-grit, leaving spaces between existing papers for additional papers to be added in the future, allowing similar grits to stay in the same relative area. When leaving for a job, a hook-and-loop band tightly wraps the folder, and all my sandpaper follows me to the job.

—Fred Callus, Seanet, WV

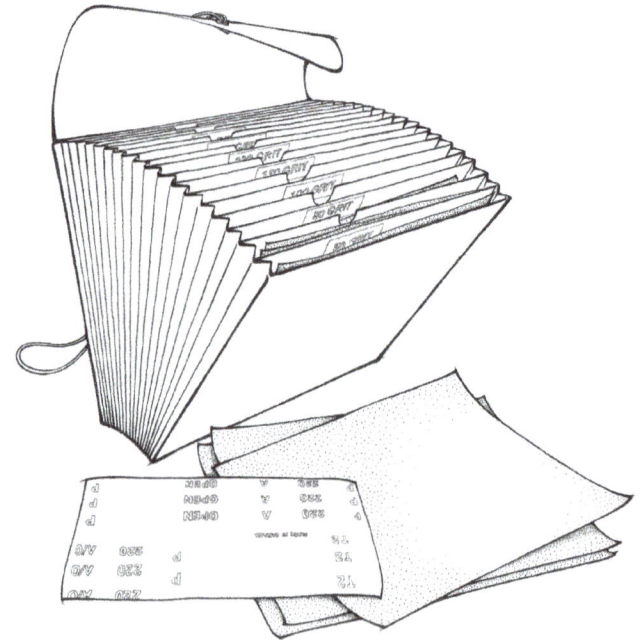

Goodbye to sandpaper gunk

All sandpaper—whether on belt sanders, orbital disc sanders, or drum sanders—will eventually collect glue, varnish, or other gunk, making these machines nearly unusable. Sandpaper cleaning sticks work great to remove this unwanted buildup, but if you don't have any, here's a tip. Since most cleaning sticks are made of some type of rubber compound, I liberally spread contact cement on a piece of scrap plywood, let it dry, and then sanded it off. Within a few minutes, the sanding belt was like new.

—Ryan W. Hager, Hickory, NC

Clean sandpaper tearing

Whenever I need a piece of sandpaper of a specific size, I used to simply tear it on the edge of my workbench. As the edge of the bench became worn and rounded over the years, I couldn't tear the sandpaper cleanly. I then screwed an old metal bench rule to the front of my workbench; whenever I need to tear sandpaper, I just slip the sheet behind the rule and give a sharp tug on the sandpaper to tear the sheet to size with a clean-cut edge. As an extra benefit, I'm never at a loss when it comes to measuring short workpieces—I just hold them up to the rule attached to the front of the bench.

—Rick Blaine, Cincinnati, OH

Sandpaper sizer

This is a speed machine that will net you a lot of sized sandpaper in a hurry. It's nothing more than a platform, outfitted with two adjacent fences and a piece of standard-thickness plastic laminate as wide as your desired paper size and at least as long. You can stack your sandpaper in this jig to tear several sheets at a time, depending on the grit and weight of the particular paper.

To use it, place your paper grit-side down and against both fences with the laminate on top and against the fences. Press down on the laminate while tearing off two or more sheets with your other hand. As you proceed, remove some of the sized sheets and continue tearing. When the first stack is done, butt the remaining sheets against the fences and repeat until you have all the sized paper you need.

—Andy Rae, Asheville, NC

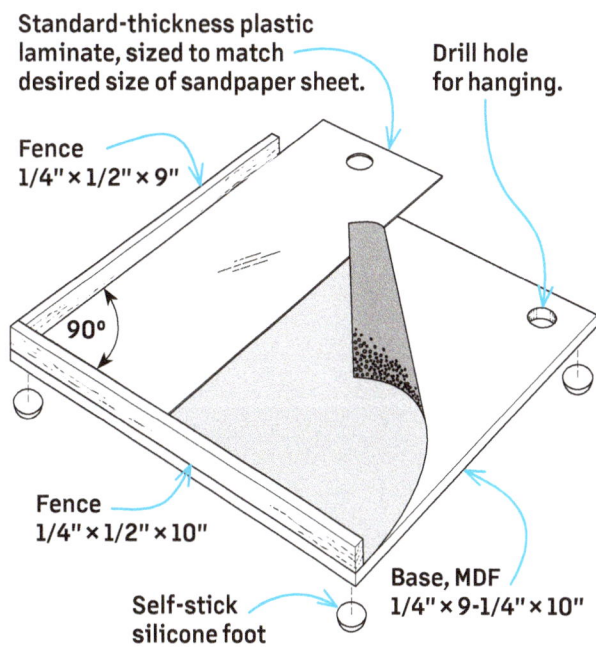

TECHNIQUES > SHARPENING

SHARPENING

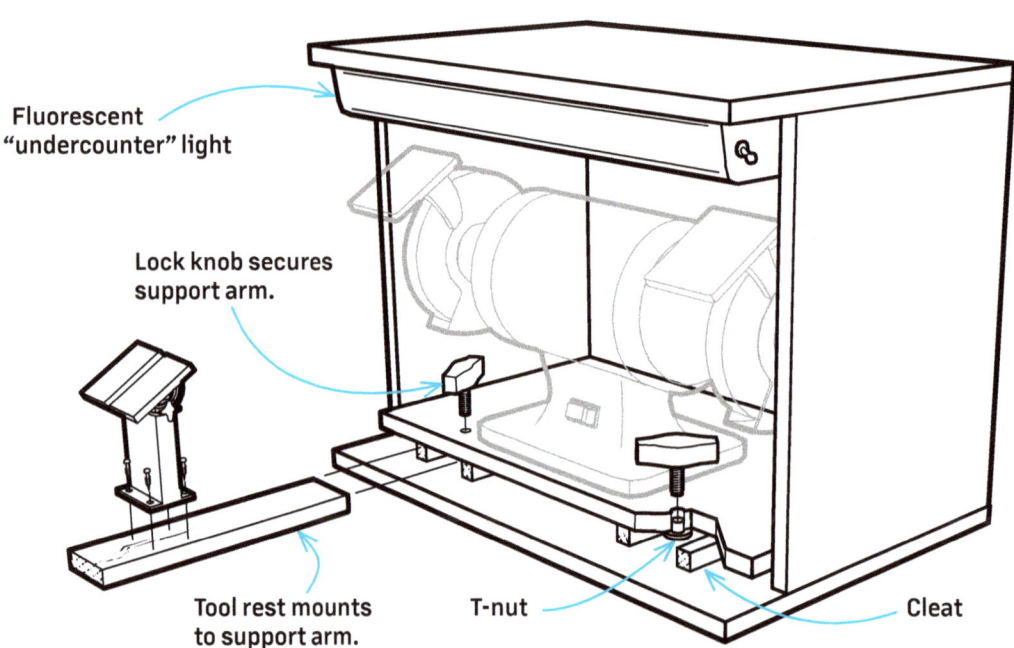

Self-contained grinding station

Fed up with the metal particles and wheel grit strewn all over my sharpening station, I decided to house my bench grinder in a simple plywood box. The box corrals the detritus and provides a mounting place for a task light overhead for good grinding visibility. An undercounter fluorescent light was easy to attach and serves the job well.

    I also wanted to accommodate a variety of grinding jigs and tool rests to suit my turning tools, chisels, and plane irons. The solution: Attach the grinder to a plywood panel that mounts atop two pairs of solid wood cleats centered under the grinding wheels. The resulting channels accept support arms for mounting my various jigs and tool rests. I can secure each arm in its channel at any location with a stud-lock knob that threads into a T-nut attached to the underside of the panel.

—*Louis Lovas, Hollis, NH*

Waterstone holder

I have a designated sharpening station, but there are times when I like having a sharpening stone within arm's reach. To keep my waterstone from wandering across my bench, I made a simple holder from a piece of scrap. Size the wedge and notched ends so that they sit below the top of the stone's top face.

Secure the base in a vise, rest the stone in place, and tap the wedge to lock in the stone. You're now set to sharpen.

—*Tommy MacDonald, Boston, MA*

Honing guide jig

I found sharpening planes and chisels somewhat intimidating and tedious until I started using a honing guide (mine grips the sides of the blade) and the jig shown. The jig helps me to clamp the blade in the guide in a repeatable manner; the cutting edge always projects the same distance from, and at a right angle to, the edge of the guide. As a result, it takes just a few seconds to set up the guide and the bevel is maintained at exactly the same angle every time I sharpen the tool; thus, the least amount of metal is removed to bring the edge to perfection.

The jig is made from three pieces of hardboard. C is glued to A at a right angle to the edge of A. The blade projection for 30° and 25° bevels is, on my guide, given on the side of the device. If you do not have this information, or if you prefer non-standard bevel angles, first clamp the blade in the guide and adjust it as if you were to sharpen the blade at the required angle, than hold the blade flat against A with the guide's edge butting the edge of A, and glue B to A so that its edge touches the cutting edge. Of course, separate jigs have to be made for each bevel angle.

To use the jig, hold the plane blade in the jig against the L formed by B and C and clamp the guide to the blade so that it touches the edge of A.

—*Frank Penicka, Mount Pearl, Newfoundland*

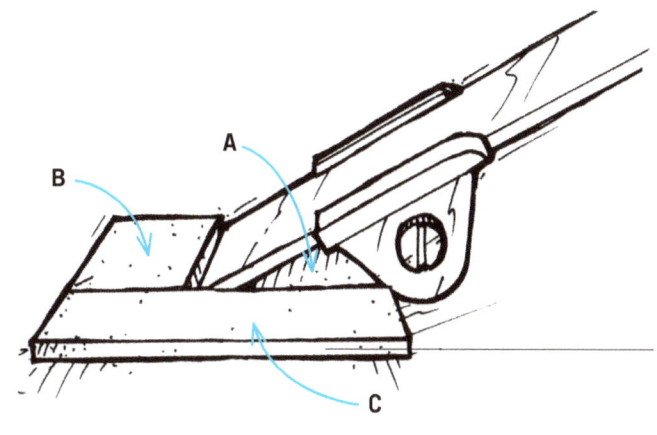

TECHNIQUES > SHARPENING

Sharpen short blades with ease

I was once given an old metal spokeshave by a friend. For a time, it worked beautifully (he had sharpened the blade), until the blade became dull. At first I experimented with freehand honing, but because the blade is so short, I achieved only mediocre results. Next, I set my mind to the task of making a jig that could hold the blade securely in my honing guide. The following is what I came up with.

The body of the jig is a piece of hardwood, 3/16" thick, as wide as your spokeshave blade (2-1/8" for me), and about 6" long. At the front, a 1" rabbet about half the thickness of the body is cut to hold the blade. Make sure one edge is square; glue on the hardwood piece that is 3/16" × 3/16" × the length of the body, making sure that it is square to the rabbet. Once the glue has dried, clean up the excess glue and drill a hole in the middle of the rabbet. Insert a bolt head down through the hole with a nut and washer. The bolt should be 1/4" in diameter or slightly larger.

To use, put the blade on the step with the bolt through the slot in the blade and square it to the fence. Put the jig in your honing guide or use it freehand. Either way, you'll receive a square, sharp edge.

—Isaac Stafstrom, Madison, WI

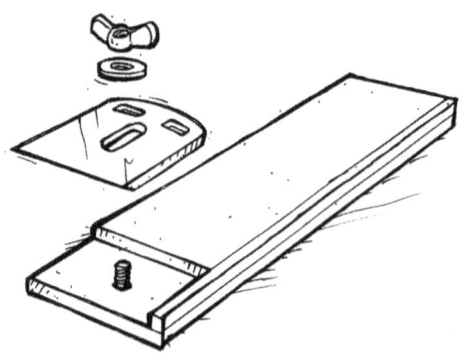

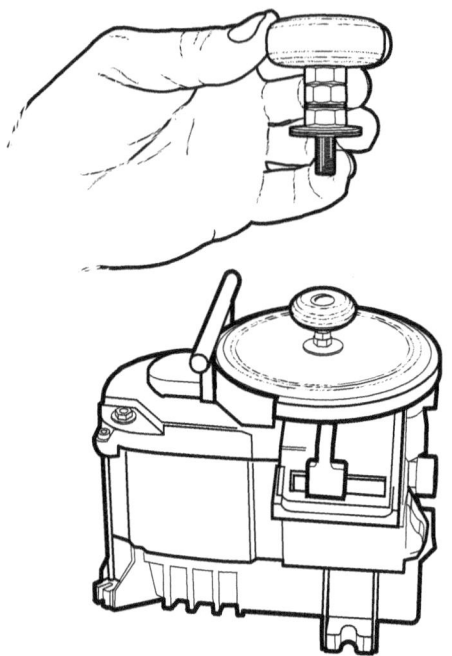

Double-headed honer

Needing a way to hone the inner bevels of my carving gouges, I made a custom top knob strop. The knob/strop is effective, easy to make, and does not interfere with access to the flat plate.

To make the strop, cut a 1"-thick stack of 2"-diameter discs from scrap cowhide, drill center holes in each one, and then thread onto a 1/4"-20 × 4" carriage bolt. Secure the discs to the bolt with a washer and nut, and then add a few extra nuts so that the exposed end of the bolt is the same length as the original top nut. Finally, round the edges of the leather on a belt or disc sander. (You can also shape the disc to strop V-shaped tools.)

Screw the strop onto the top of the wheel, charge it with your favorite honing compound, and you're set to hone outside and inside bevels at the same station.

—David Dabercoe, Sarasota, FL

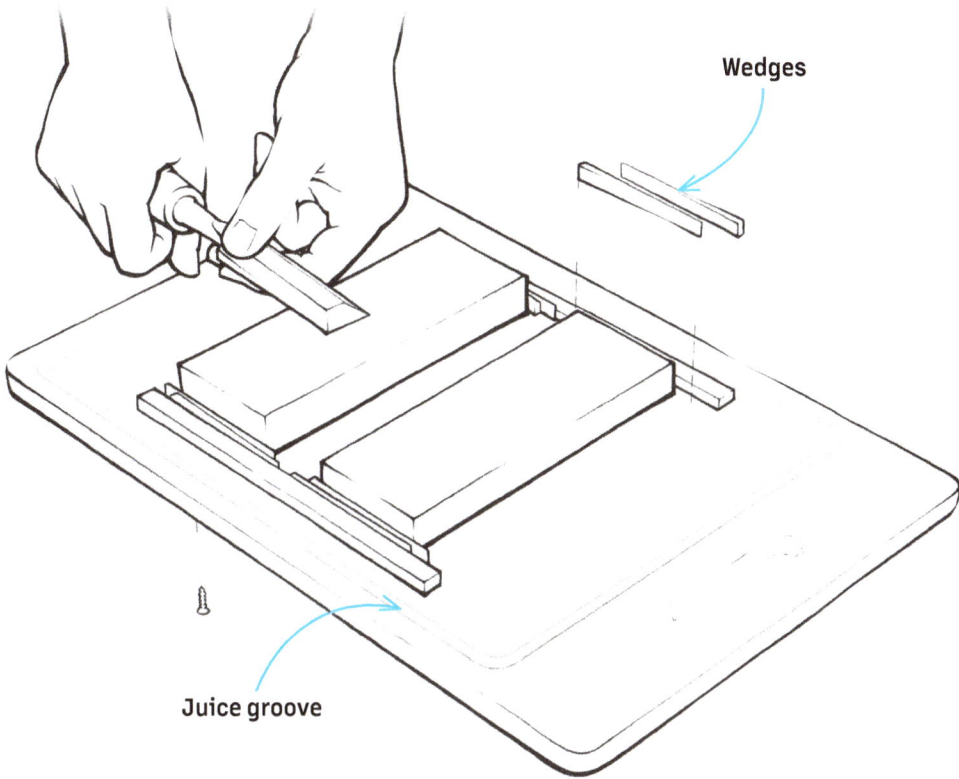

Wedges

Juice groove

Sharpen anywhere with a portable station

Too often my workbench pulls duty for a variety of tasks, forcing me to find another shop location to sharpen my tools. I also teach woodworking classes, taking my hand tools on the road. For both reasons, I needed a portable solution for sharpening with waterstones.

What I came up with is basic and compact, and keeps my benchtop clean. It's just a 7/16" × 12" × 18" polypropylene cutting board with a juice groove around the perimeter and two pieces of 1/4" × 1/4" × 9" UHMW (ultra high molecular weight) plastic attached with ten 6-32 × 5/8" stainless steel flat-head machine screws (five screws per strip).

I drilled through-holes, countersunk the underside of the cutting board, and drilled and tapped the UHMW. I spaced the UHMW bars about 1/4" farther apart than my longest 8" stone. I cut a bunch of cherry wedges of varying thicknesses so I can accommodate all of the stones I currently use. The wedges are placed opposing each other and are used to lock the stones in place. The juice groove keeps water off the bench, and the board easily cleans up when I'm done.

I set the whole apparatus on a piece of non-slip shelf liner, which secures everything nicely. I can apply as much pressure as I want and nothing moves. The handle hole makes it easy to pull out from under my bench and can also be used to hang it on the wall.

—*Craig W. Bentzley, Chalfont, PA*

TECHNIQUES > SHARPENING

Simple scraper sharpener

This tip may not convince you to snip the cord on your belt sander, but should shatter the myth that cabinet scrapers are some lost art.

The only trick to using a scraper is making the burr. Dozens of different jigs and techniques can help you get that metal micro-hook, but my filing jig is fast and cheap. When the burr fails, I can renew an edge and resume scraping in a few seconds.

To make the jig, all you need is a fine mill file and a scrap of wood. Using your table saw, groove the board to fit the file. (Aim for a snug fit. If it's loose, shim the file with masking tape.) Insert the file into the groove; draw the edge of the file against the face of the scraper. Within two or three passes, you'll have a somewhat rough, but surprisingly serviceable, hook.

This jig can also be used to hone a square edge to create a burnished hook for finer scraping. After filing, place the scraper bottom facedown on your sharpening stone to knock off the rough burr; then use the edge of the jig as shown to hone a square edge. Flatten both faces one last time before drawing and turning the burr with a burnisher (or as I do, with an old screwdriver).

—Brian Hurst, Portland, OR

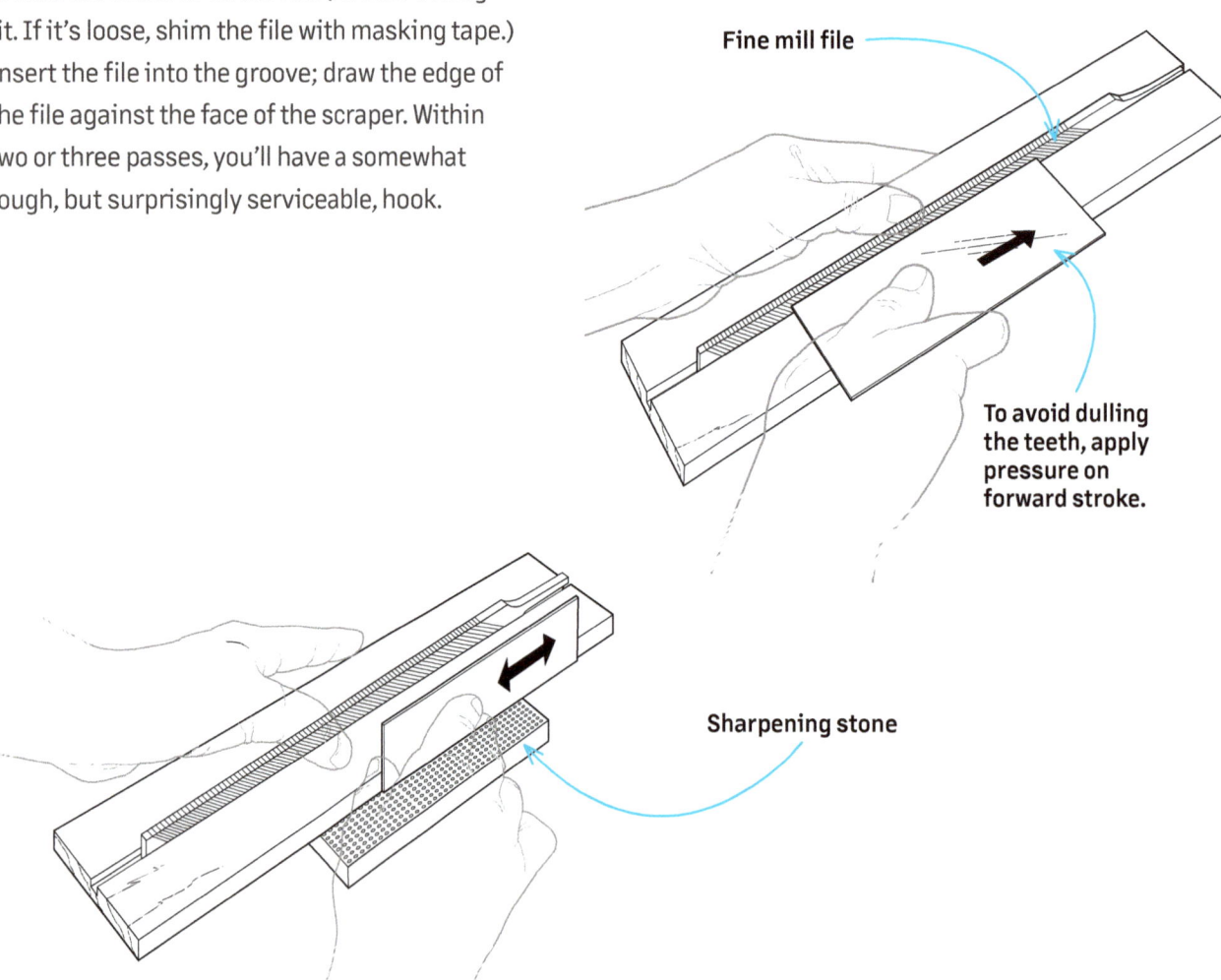

Fine mill file

To avoid dulling the teeth, apply pressure on forward stroke.

Sharpening stone

76 *WOODCRAFT MAGAZINE* TIPS & TRICKS FOR WOODWORKING

Sander-grinder for cool sharpening

I prefer using my 1" × 42" sander-grinder to grind plane blades and chisels. My low-tech method provides the same results as a regular-wheeled grinder, minus any expensive attachments. The belt also seems to run cooler than a wheel. This reduces the risk of accidentally overheating the edge and ruining the tool. This method can be easily adapted to fit a disc sander.

Starting with a 1" to 1-1/4" thick piece of scrap, miter one end to 25°. Next, adjust the sander's top so that it's perfectly perpendicular to the belt. Clamp the block to the table to match your sharpening needs.

To grind a fresh 25° bevel, use a square to make sure that the guide block's edges are perpendicular to the front the table. Alternately, you can rotate the block to match a completely different angle. To do this, simply touch the bevel

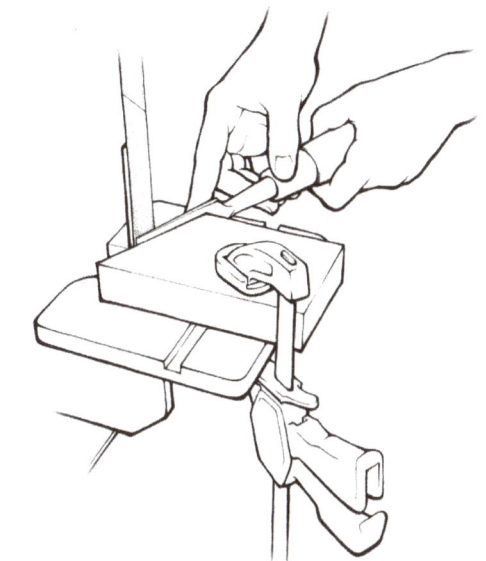

against your belt before clamping your guide block.

Be aware that grinding does produce some sparks. If you use your sander for wood, be sure to clean out any sawdust before doing any metalwork.

—*Richard J. Libera, Newark, DE*

Marking gauge wheel sharpening

I love my wheeled marking gauge but, like any other cutting tool, it needs occasional sharpening to work effectively. The darned wheel is so small, though, that it can be hard to hone. After abrading my fingertips, I discovered that a standard wooden pencil with eraser works great to scrub the wheel on my honing stones.

—*Mark Hassleblad, Los Angeles, CA*

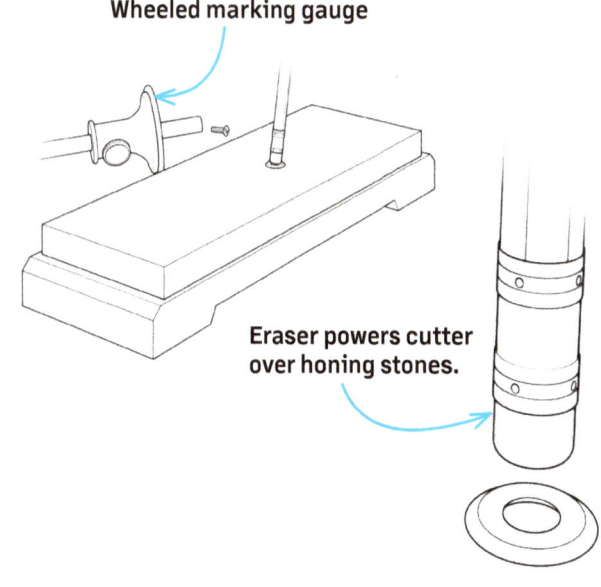

Scraper sharpening jig

Years ago, I discovered the capabilities of a cabinet scraper. This steel-bodied tool, with its "gull wing" handles and 45º beveled blade, is great for smoothing large surfaces without dishing them as a card scraper might. It will also make fine cuts if the blade is sharpened well. Unfortunately, the short blade doesn't suit most commercial honing jigs, so I made my own from hardwood scraps.

The head of the jig is mounted at 45º to the body, matching the blade's bevel angle. A clamping strap made of 1/8"-thick scrap steel holds the blade to the head, secured by thumbscrews. A lag screw at the base of the jig can be adjusted in or out to fine-tune the sharpening angle. To use the jig, I simply clamp the blade in place, projecting out a bit from the edge of the head, and then sight the angle of the blade on the stone using a 45º triangle. A bit of work on a 1,000-grit stone, followed by an 8,000-grit stone, produces amazing results once the burr is turned.

—Philip Houck, Boston, MA

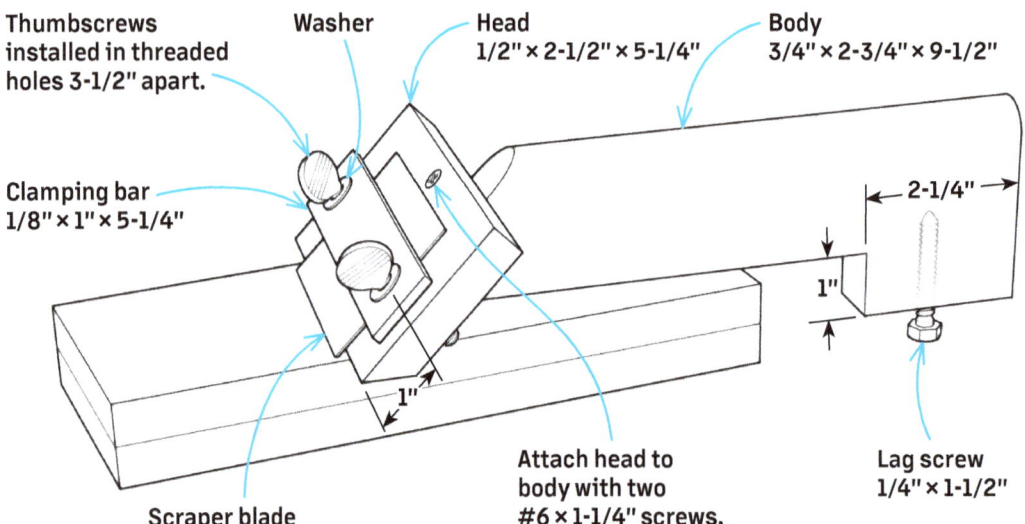

Find the grind

When grinding a chisel or plane iron, it's easy to lose track of your landing spot among the various facets you've created along the way. When that happens, just swipe the bevel face with a wide-tip marker. Now when you touch the wheel again, the fresh grind will be apparent.

—Paul Anthony, Riegelsville, PA

Avoid rust after waterstone use

Wipe down your tools with a rust-preventer, like WD-40, after honing them with waterstones. This is especially important with planes because moisture can get trapped between adjoining metal surfaces.

—Ken Burton, New Tripoli, PA

Heat sink for sharpening

Grinding a chisel or plane iron generates a lot of heat, and quenching the blade in water can create minute fractures that can affect the quality of the cutting edge. Oil will cool the metal more slowly and safely, but it's messy. Instead, try a passive heat sink scavenged from a computer motherboard. This small square of metal (typically aluminum alloy) is deeply grooved on one face, creating fins that help disperse heat quickly. Before your tool gets uncomfortably hot to hold, cool it down by pressing the flat face against the heat sink, which will dissipate the heat in short order without damaging the steel.

—Hunter Clyde, Lancaster, KY

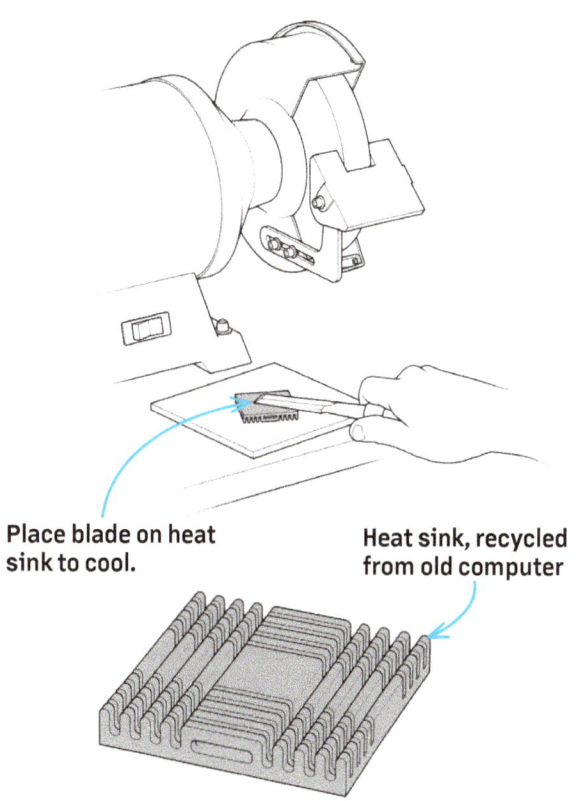

Place blade on heat sink to cool.

Heat sink, recycled from old computer

Chipbreaker grinding guide

When grinding a plane blade, you need a guide to ensure a straight edge. Some aftermarket tool rests include blade-holding jigs that run in a groove in the rest. Alternatively, you can clamp a short wood or metal "fence" to the blade that runs along the front edge of the tool rest. However, many metal-bodied planes have their own built-in guide of sorts. Simply switch the chipbreaker to the opposite side of the blade, and rotate it 90°. You can then slide the chipbreaker up or down as necessary to create the proper orientation to the grinding wheel, and then lock the chipbreaker in place using its own screw.

—Joe Hurst-Wajszczuk, Birmingham, AL

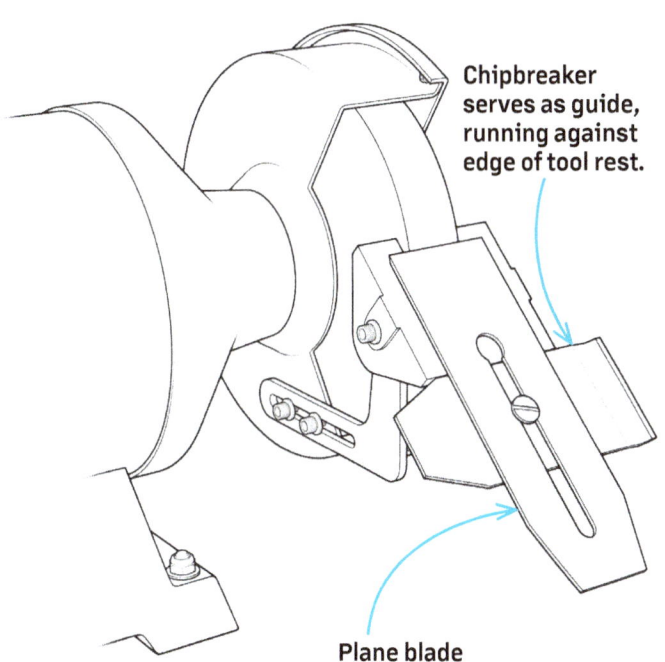

Chipbreaker serves as guide, running against edge of tool rest.

Plane blade

TOOLS

BANDSAW 82

DRILL & DRILL PRESS 90

JOINTER 113

LATHE 116

MITERSAW 125

OTHER POWER TOOLS 129

PLANER 135

ROUTER 138

TABLE SAW 151

TOOLS > BANDSAW

BANDSAW

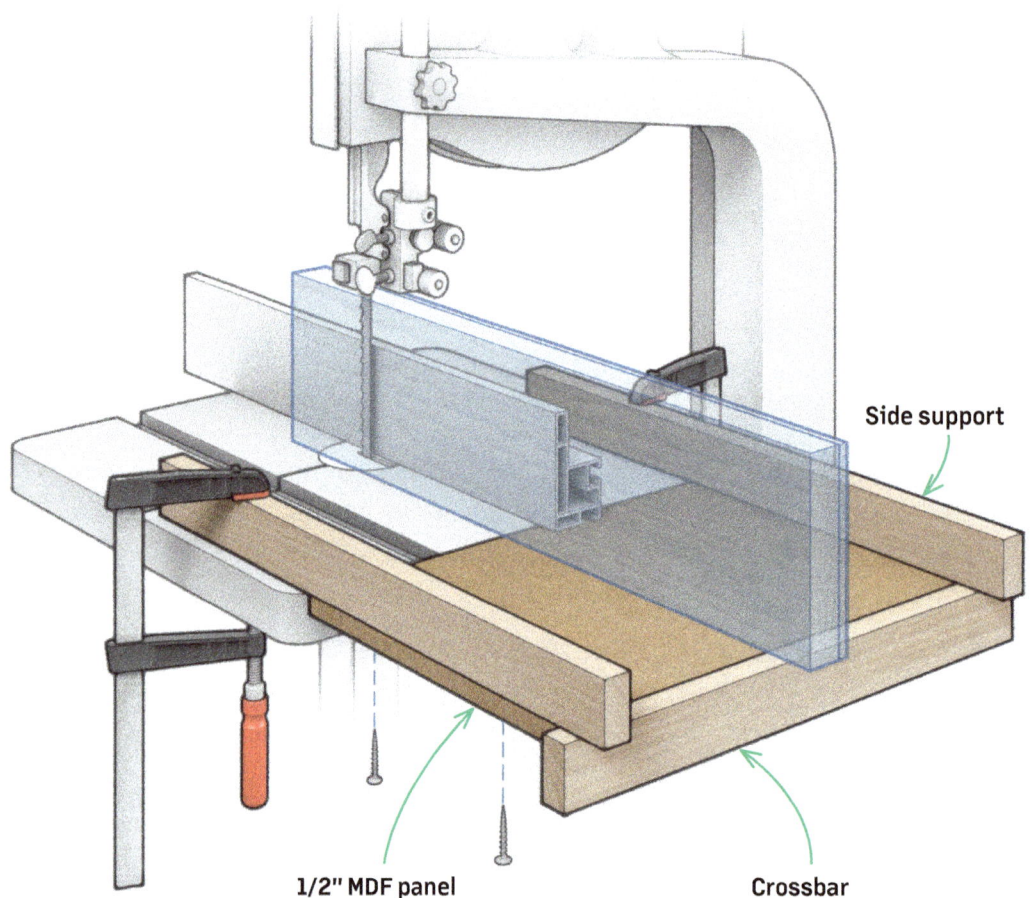

Easy outfeed support

I developed this simple outfeed extension for my bandsaw to provide extra support while resawing. The fixture consists of a 1/2" MDF panel screwed to two dressed hardwood side supports that clamp to the saw's table. A hardwood crossbar provides added support and helps to keep the panel flat. Unlike outfeed rollers, my system automatically aligns with the table, reducing setup time. And having the workpiece glide over the flat surface means I don't have to worry about a roller leading it astray.

—Dwayne Smyth, West Springfield, MA

Segmented rings on the bandsaw

The segmented bowls I make sometimes have veneer accent layers that need to be cut and glued up with several segmented rings that make up the bowl. Since the veneer rings I use are frequently about 1/16" thick, it can be difficult to get tight glue joints because there is very little to clamp against.

My solution was to make segmented rings out of 3/4" dimensioned stock, and then use my bandsaw to cut the veneer as a completed ring. However, it can be dangerous to crosscut large-diameter round pieces on the bandsaw, because most of the cut is unsupported and can twist on the blade. So, I created a vertical sledding jig specifically for cutting these rings safely and efficiently.

My sled is made of 3/4" plywood and measures about 8" tall by 12" long, but the size of your jig should be determined by the size of the rings you want to cut. It should be tall enough to hold the ring stable so it doesn't roll into the blade. A matching 3" × 12" base is screwed to the bottom of the sled to create a right angle. (You can use triangular braces on the back of the sled, as I did, to ensure that squareness is maintained.)

I attach the ring to a vertical sled with double-sided woodturner's tape and adjust the bandsaw's fence for drift, then use the sled to slide the ring along the fence to create several thin veneer rings. As a bonus, the jig doubles as an auxiliary fence for the bandsaw by simply clamping it to the saw table.

—Larry Marley, Mission Viejo, CA

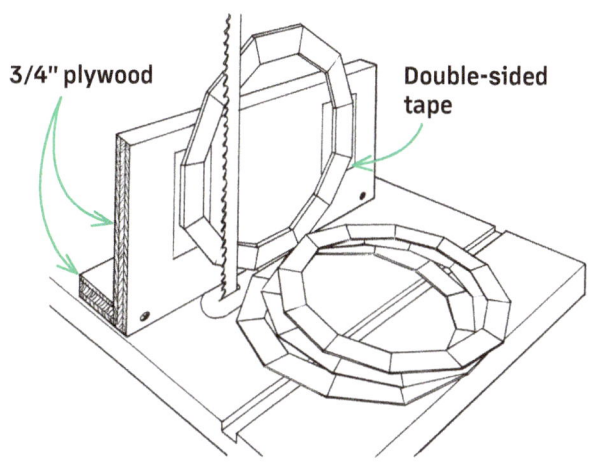

Homemade bandsaw blocks

The metal guideblocks that come standard with most bandsaws can create blade-damaging heat and friction or can damage the teeth. Aftermarket graphite and ceramic guide blocks work well, but before you buy, consider making your own blocks from any dense hardwood, such as maple. Like the blade-friendly graphite, hardwood guides can be set against the blade without risk of damaging the teeth or tooth set. When worn, hardwood blocks can be sanded or trimmed true.

After cutting the blocks to fit, I stand them in a small container with some WD-40 to allow the end grain to absorb extra lubricant.

—Tim Feirer, Fairfield, CT

Dressing bandsaw guide blocks

I replaced my bandsaw's steel guide blocks with graphite-impregnated phenolic blocks. For accurate operation, the blocks' faces should be routinely dressed to remove regular wear. I tried freehand filing and sanding, but had a hard time keeping the ends square with the edges.

To solve the problem, I made this simple jig. It's a 3/4" × 2" × 6" scrap of hardwood, with a notch sawn in the end to snugly accommodate a guide block. A 1/8"-thick end-strip screwed to the scrap secures the guide block in place. (If necessary for a snug fit, wrap the block with masking tape.) To smooth and square the blocks, position them in the jig so that they project just a bit from the bottom and rub the whole thing over 150-grit and 220-grit sandpaper until the ends are flush with the bottom of the jig. It's best to do this on a dead-flat surface, like a saw or jointer table. To dress guide blocks with a 45° face, I bevel-cut the opposite end of the jig before notching it.

—*Bob Howard, St. Louis, MO*

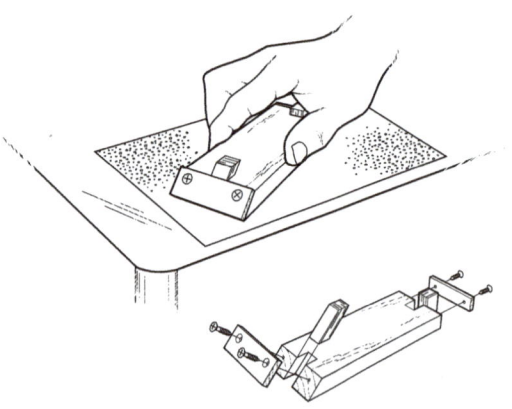

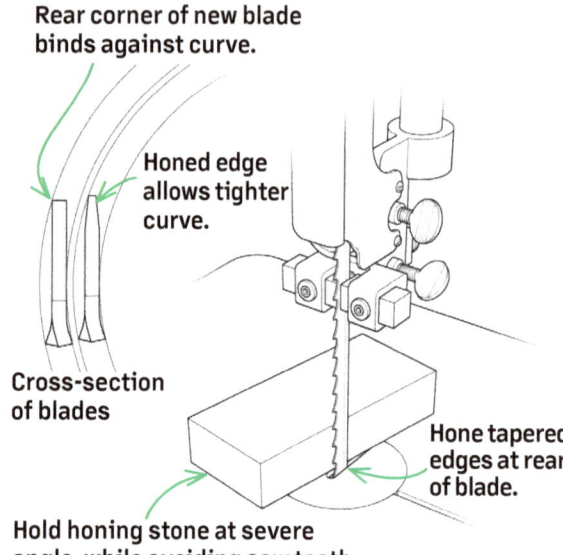

Tighter turns from a bandsaw blade

Demanding the tightest turn from a bandsaw blade can cause it to bind and burn. One way to provide more maneuverability is to make relief cuts in the waste, so that those outer parts can fall away to give the rear of the blade wiggle room.

However, sometimes you want to keep the entire workpiece intact. In those cases, tapering the trailing edge of the blade will give it more clearance in the curved kerf, allowing a tighter turn, as shown in the drawing. To create the taper, slowly slide an 80-grit carborundum honing stone back and forth against each side of the running blade. Hold the edge of the stone at a low angle to the blade, avoiding the teeth and keeping your fingers a safe distance from the blade. Be patient, and make sure to leave a flat on the rear edge of the blade because a knife edge would be hard on the thrust bearing. For fire safety, vacuum the saw interior before honing to prevent sparks from igniting sawdust.

—*Ric Hanisch, Quakertown, PA*

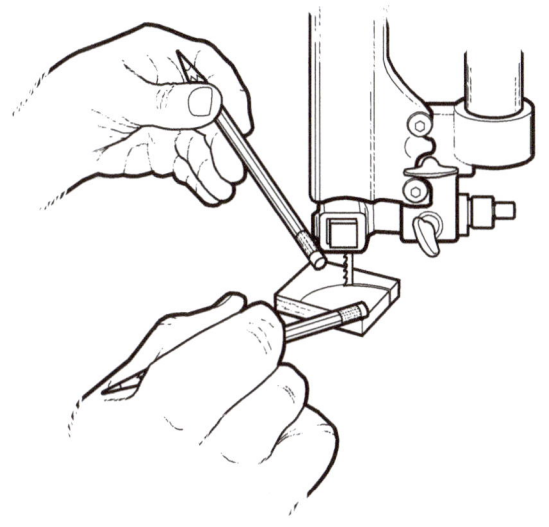

Safe bandsawing of small pieces

Equipped with a narrow blade, the bandsaw can easily cut small parts. The only problem is safely handling the pieces. It's best to saw them from larger pieces that can be gripped at a safe distance from the blade. When that's not possible, I find that the next best thing is to steer the piece using erasers at the ends of full-length pencils. Stick with new pencils with soft, fresh erasers that haven't hardened over time.

—*Mark Bentley, Napa, CA*

Small strip ripping tips

My instrument making often involves ripping very narrow strips of wood for use as bindings and inlay, among other things. I find that the safest way to cut these tiny strips is on the bandsaw, using a low profile fence. This allows setting the blade guides very low to keep the blade on track and prevent deflection. For a fence, I use a self-clamping aluminum straightedge, which is quick to set up, and which can be angled as much as 5° or so if necessary to accommodate blade drift. Using a 6 TPI blade, I can accurately rip strips as narrow as 1/32". When doing this, just make sure to tape a thin underlying piece of wood to the saw table to serve as a zero-clearance throat to prevent your rippings from disappearing down the saw's throat.

—*Bil Mitchell, Riegelsville, PA*

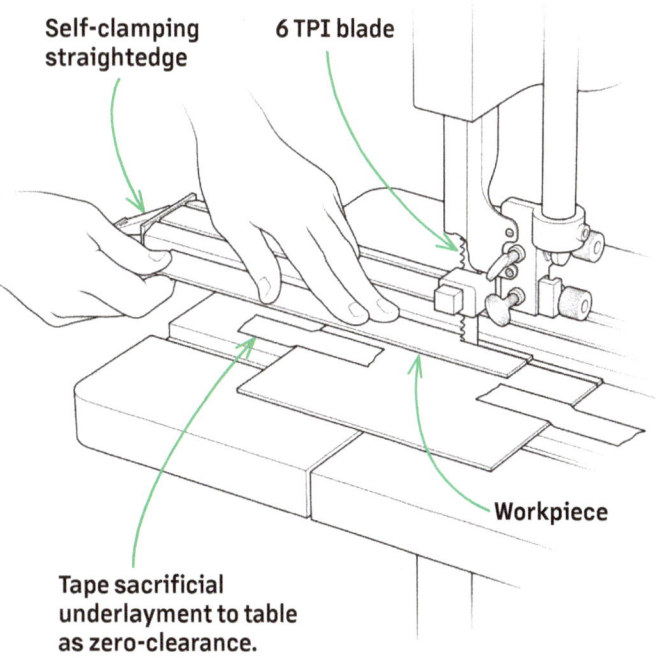

Setting bandsaw thrust guides

When adjusting the thrust guides on a bandsaw, the aim is to set them just a few thousandths of an inch behind the blade. The principle is that the back of the blade should touch the guides only when the blade is cutting—not when it's freewheeling. The typical approach is to hold a dollar bill against the rear of the blade and then move the bearing up against the bill. This is great in theory and would work fine if the back edge of the blade was dead-straight, but it very often isn't, and wavers fore and aft during the cut.

I find that a much better approach is to first bring the bearing up lightly against the blade while slowly rotating the bandsaw wheels by hand (with the saw unplugged). Then, while observing the bearing, back it off until it stops spinning and then continue to back it off just a hair more. If it's hard to detect the rotation of a bearing, simply strike a few lines across its edge with a thick marker. After locking in the bearing's location, double-check that the locking screw didn't shift the bearing forward.

—Paul Anthony, Riegelsville, PA

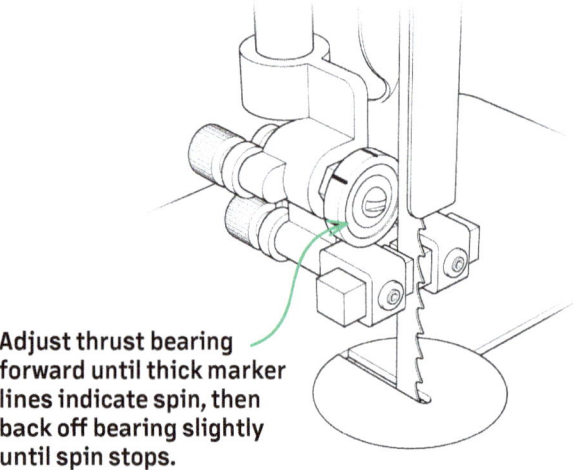

Adjust thrust bearing forward until thick marker lines indicate spin, then back off bearing slightly until spin stops.

Temporarily adhere patterns

When I need to temporarily adhere a pattern to a piece of wood to cut on a bandsaw, I rub a removable glue stick onto the back of the pattern. There are several brands; they all hold patterns to the wood well and peel off easily. It's not as messy as a spray-on adhesive. It only needs to be applied to the edges of small patterns, and on the edges and maybe several places in the center of a larger pattern.

—Randy L. Wolfe, Owensboro, KY

Lignum vitae bandsaw blocks

Lignum vitae is a great wood for making your own bandsaw guide blocks. It's dense and durable, and its resin is a natural lubricant. The wood can also be dressed easily when necessary to smooth worn faces. The only problem is that it's not cheap, and I hate to have to buy big pieces of it since I don't use it for much else. That dilemma was solved recently when I discovered that affordable wooden pen turning blanks are available in lignum vitae. A 3/4" × 3/4" × 6-1/4" pen blank is big enough to make several years' worth of guides for my bandsaw.

—Bruce Robertson, Raleigh, NC

A personal blade buyer's guide

In order to gauge the trial performance and longevity of a new bandsaw blade, I cut the relevant info (type, make, etc.) from the product box and affix it to the column of my bandsaw with a strong rare-earth magnet. That way, when I notice that a blade cuts exceptionally well, gives me problems, or seems to dull prematurely, I can quickly note the manufacturer, as well as blade characteristics. (When switching out blades, it's easy enough to switch out the product label at the same time.) It's a great way to inform future blade purchases.

—Steven Baxter, Indianapolis, IN

Secure clamping at the bandsaw

When I tried to clamp a resaw fence to my bandsaw, I found it very difficult to find a flat section to apply the clamp jaw on the underside of the table because the table has a series of cast iron ribs on the underside for stiffness. To solve the problem, I cut several pieces of scrap lumber of the appropriate size and thickness to fit between the ribs on the underside. A bit of hot-melt glue easily keeps the wood parts adhered in place. Now, there are sufficient "flat" areas for the clamp jaw to rest against when mounting my guide to the top of the table. The same process works equally well for drill press tables.

—Marty Tusim, Midland, MI

Bandsaw dust collection

I own two 14" bandsaws that work well except for dust collection. The older saw has no dust port at all, while the newer model has a port that's too small to be very effective. I found that the solution was to attach a length of 4"-diameter metal duct to a dust-collection hose, and then place 1"-diameter rare-earth magnets in a vertical row along the edge of the saw's lower blade cover. (Four or five will do the job.) Placing the open end of the duct directly under the saw table provides remarkably good dust collection. As an added benefit, the metal duct serves as a quick-connect fitting onto the 4"-diameter dust ports on most of my other machines.

—Paul Anthony, Riegelsville, PA

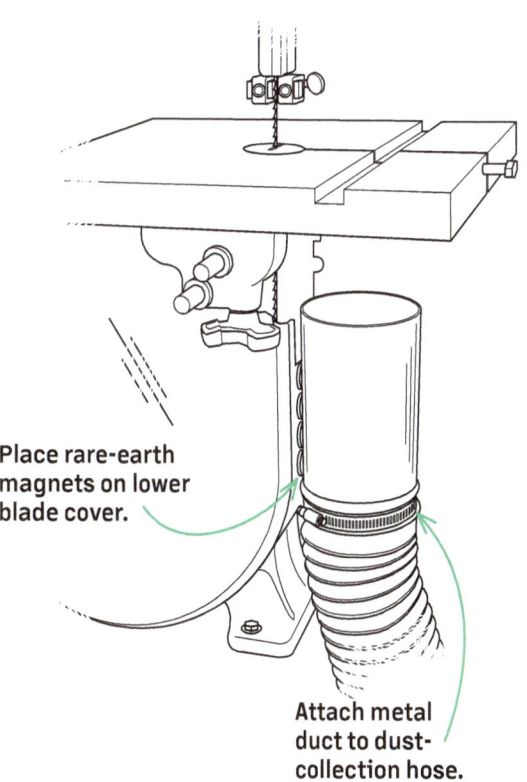

Place rare-earth magnets on lower blade cover.

Attach metal duct to dust-collection hose.

TOOLS > BANDSAW

Wedge cutting jig

When making wedged through mortise-and-tenon joints, I need the wedges to be spot-on, and I often require lots of them. To quickly and accurately bandsaw multiple wedges, I use a thick block of wood with wedge-shaped notches cut into its side. To make a jig like this, begin with a squared chunk of 8/4 or 12/4 scrap about 7" wide by 9" long, adding a handle for safety. Notch the edge to match the angle of your desired wedge. (My jig includes 3°, 4°, and 5° notches.)

To make your wedges, first prepare your wedge blank by thicknessing a board to the desired width of your wedges. Then crosscut away a piece that equals the desired length of the wedges. Next, offset the bandsaw fence from the blade a distance equal to the width of the jig. Nestle the end of the wedge blank in the notch, and then slice off a wedge. Test-fit it in your joint, readjusting the fence if necessary to adjust the thickness of the wedge to create a sharper or blunter point.

When your fence is set properly, cut a few inches into a piece of plywood, and clamp or tape it to the table surrounding the blade as a zero-clearance base. Now cut a wedge as before. Then rotate the stock 180° and reinsert the same end in the notch to make the next cut. Repeat to make all subsequent wedges.

—Alan Turner, Philadelphia, PA

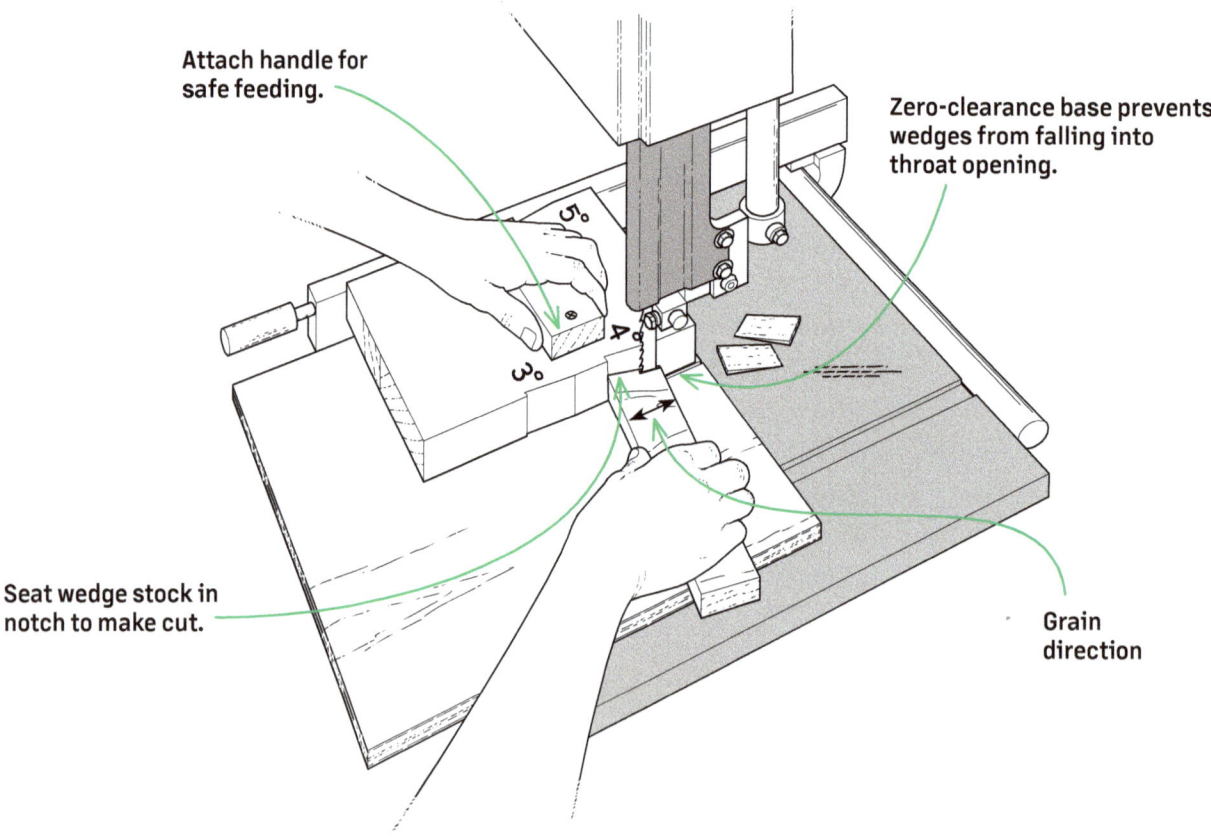

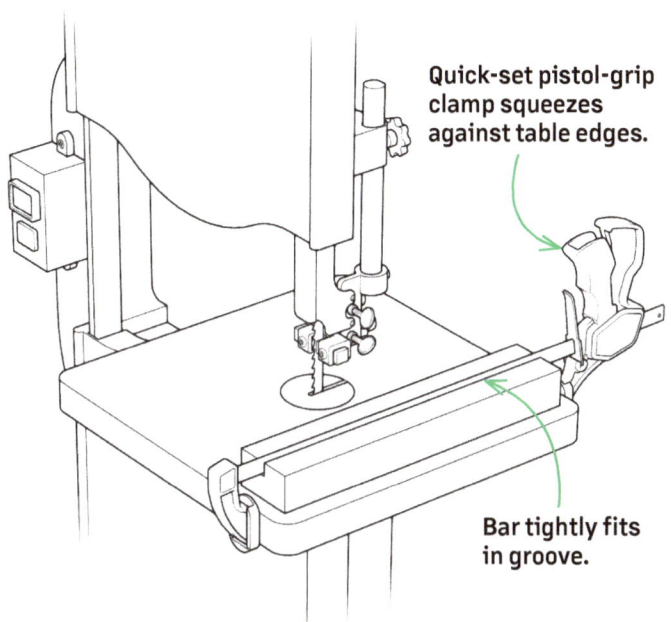

Quick-set pistol-grip clamp squeezes against table edges.

Bar tightly fits in groove.

Quick-set bandsaw fence

The bandsaw I inherited from my dad came to me without a fence, so I made a wooden one. But rather than clamp it down to the table at each end, which can be problematic due to the cavity on the table underside, I decided to use a quick-set pistol-grip bar clamp to span the table, clamping to its sides instead. The length of the fence is just a tad shorter than the width of my saw table, and the groove in the top of the fence precisely matches the thickness of the clamp bar. The fence works great and couldn't be faster to set up.

—Austin Zach, Omaha, NE

Magnet-assisted resawing

The magnetic base that comes with most dial indicators is good for a lot more than just setting jointer knives and table saws. Used with a metal socket, it can be used as a clamp-free point fence for bandsaw resawing. When switched to "on," the base grabs hold of the base and socket, providing you with a reliable guide that also allows the flexibility to shift the stock to account for blade drift. To reposition or remove the base, simply flick the switch to "off." Should your base require extra grip, affix a small sandpaper patch to the base's bottom.

—David Arnold, New Albany, IN

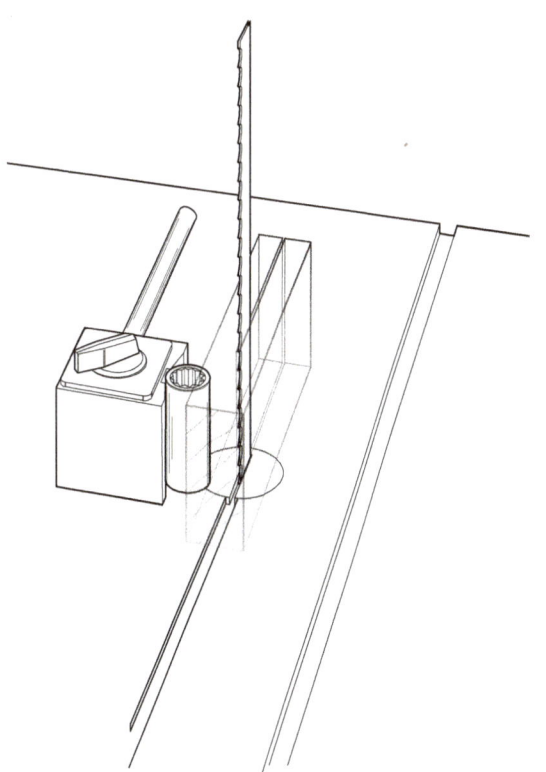

DRILL & DRILL PRESS

Drill press V-fence

While making a decorative disc, I needed to drill a series of holes near its perimeter, insetting them a consistent distance from the disc's edge. Normally, I might create a jig by installing a pin of some sort in a scrap panel that would allow the disc to rotate on the drill press table. But I didn't want to drill into the underside of the disc to create the center pivot point. Instead, I bandsawed a V-cut in a board that I then clamped to the drill press table. This custom fence provided perfect support for the job.

—*Geoff Epstein, Marlborough, MA*

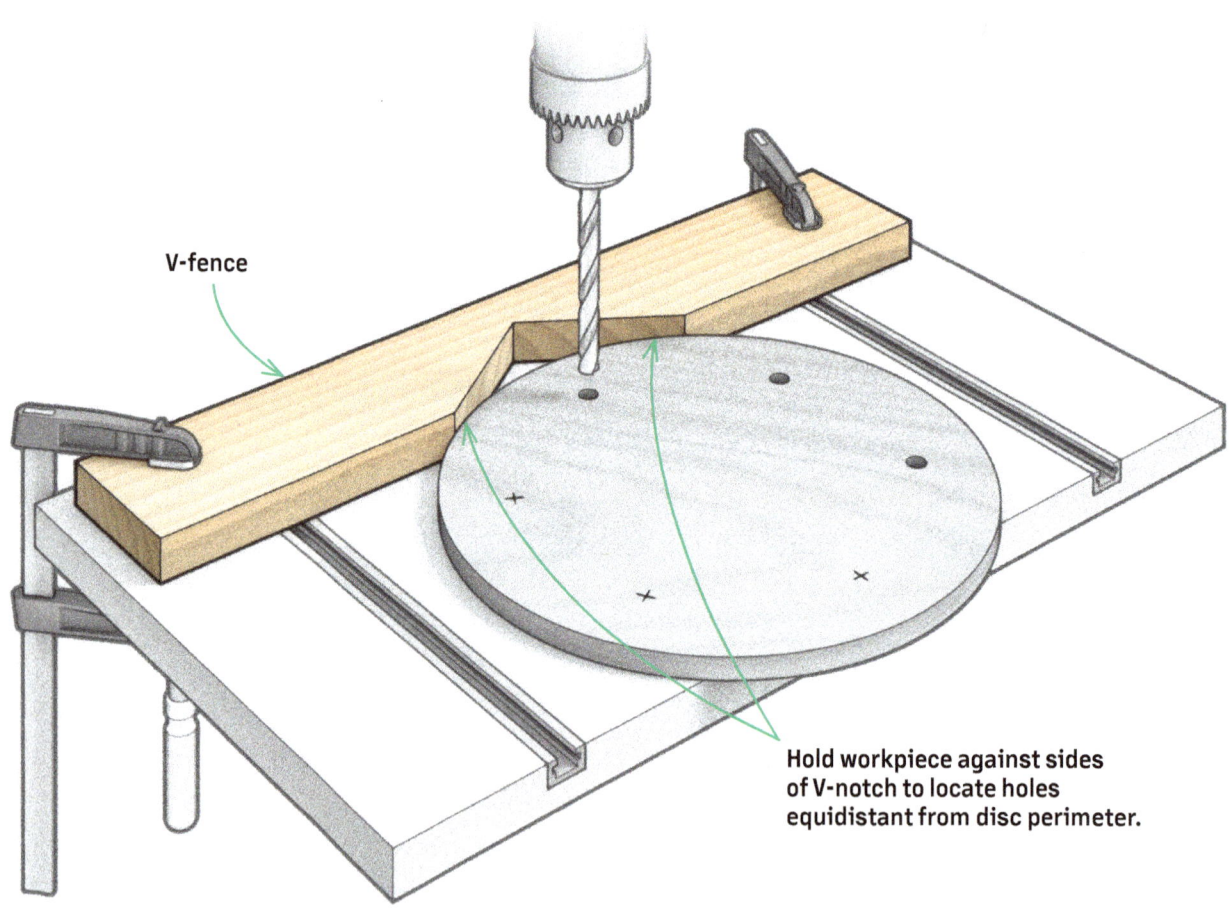

V-fence

Hold workpiece against sides of V-notch to locate holes equidistant from disc perimeter.

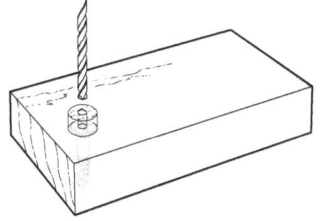 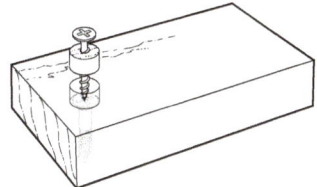

Drywall screw fixes wooden plug coverup

Sometimes the best tricks come from the most frustrating situations. One of my passions is refinishing old furniture and that means sometimes dealing with someone else's "quick fixes." One day while trying to refinish a dresser for my sister, I came across a stubborn wooden plug that covered a screw head. Completely fed up, I drilled a 1/8" pilot hole through the center of the plug and then drilled a drywall screw through the hole. The drywall screw bottomed on the hidden screw head and forced the plug up and out of the hole. A well-bonded plug may need to be drilled out.

—Linda Rowe, Washington, WV

Boring dowels

Faced with the prospect of having to drill a 1/4"-diameter hole through the center of four dozen short lengths of 3/4"-diameter dowel, I needed to come up with a way to quickly position the pieces without having to find the center of each one. To do so, I clamped a piece of 1-1/2"-thick scrap to my drill press table, and drilled a 3/4"-diameter hole about half way through it. Then I swapped out the 3/4" bit for a 1/4" bit, and popped each of the dowels in turn into the hole for drilling. No layout was required as the hole was already perfectly centered under the bit.

—Kelly Burns, Minneapolis, MN

Spare bits

Keep a set of spare drill bits on hand (especially those under 3/16") so that a broken bit doesn't interrupt your work. Put the broken one in your wallet to remind you to replace it the next time you go to town.

—Ken Burton, New Tripoli, PA

Magnetic drill press key

Epoxy a rare-earth magnet to the rear end of your chuck key; that way, you can always find it attached to the underside of the cast iron table or other dedicated location. You don't even have to take your eye off the work to grab it or put it back.

—Richard Lewis, Port St. Lucie, FL

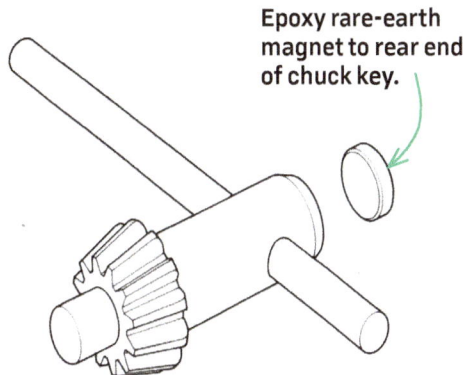

Epoxy rare-earth magnet to rear end of chuck key.

TOOLS > DRILL & DRILL PRESS

Drill press accessory board

Like most woodworkers, I've accumulated a large collection of bits, sanding drums, and other accessories that are used primarily at my drill press. For convenience and efficiency, I devised this wall-mounted rack so that the items are where they're needed most.

My system is nothing more than a plywood backboard outfitted with a bottom shelf and a few solid wood shelf blocks that have a series of drill holes suited to my collection of Forstner and brad-point bits. You can adjust the hole spacing, or add an extra shelf, to match your collection. The remaining free space provides room for hanging additional items.

—*Tommy MacDonald, Boston, MA*

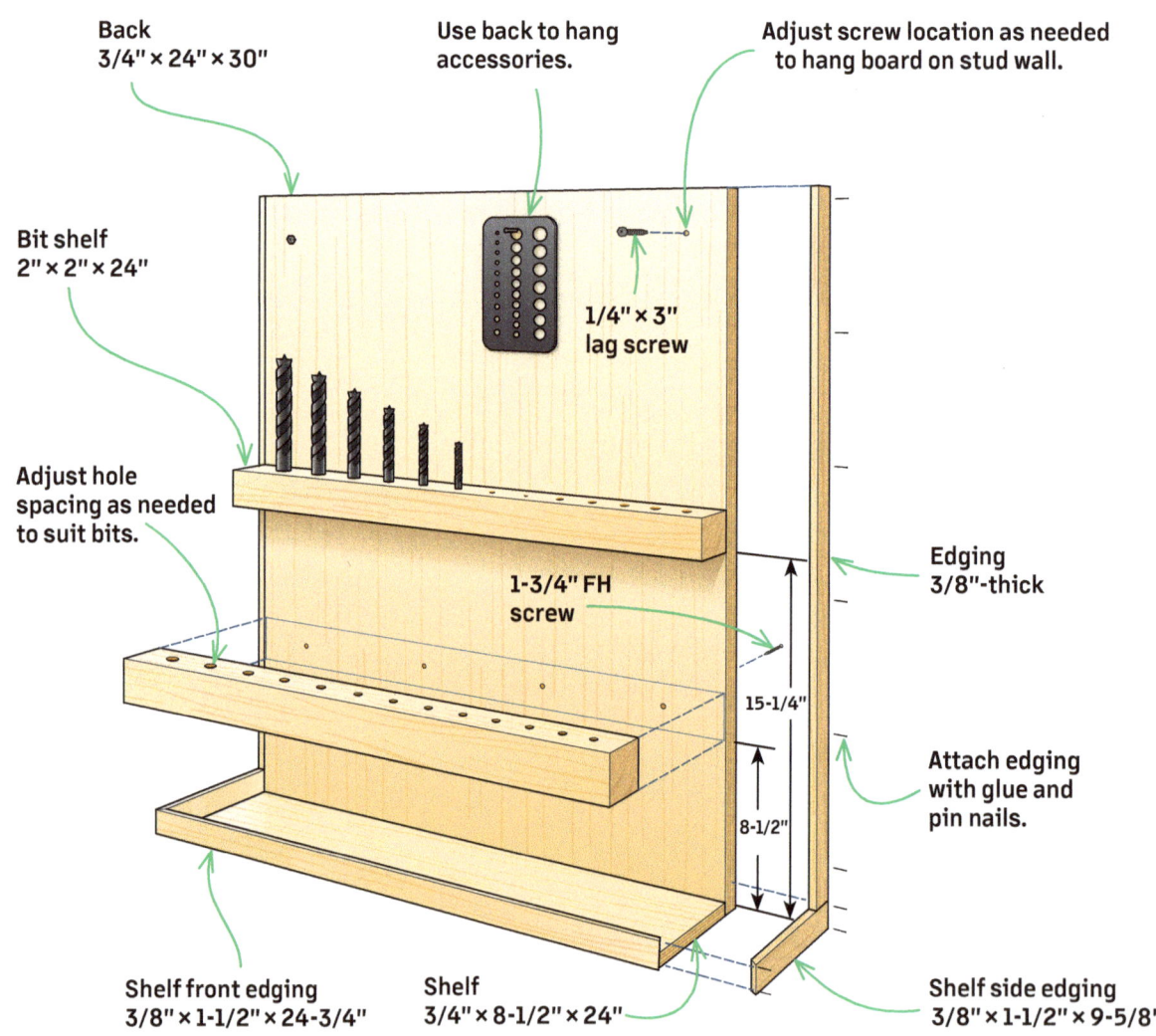

Drill press height gauge

To set the press, start by cutting a spacer block equal in width to the depth of the hole you want to drill. To use the spacer, simply set the bit so that the tip is touching the wood, insert the block as shown, and then lower and lock the drill press's stop. Remove the block and you're ready to drill.

—Issac Andrews, Erie, CO

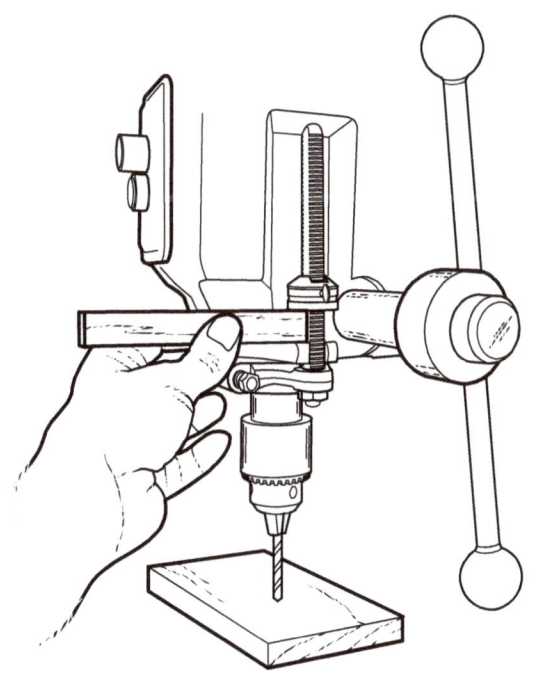

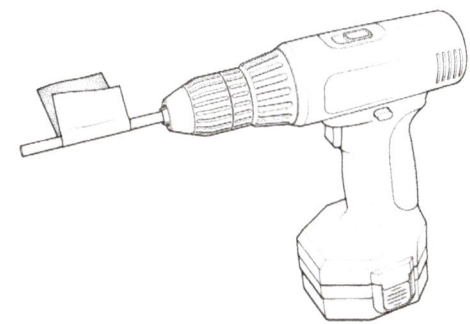

Slimming down dowels

Anyone who uses dowels knows that they seldom match their stated diameter. They're almost always slightly oversized and have to be sanded down a bit to fit their holes. Unfortunately, this can be pretty tedious work to do by hand. I've found that a great way to speed it up is to chuck a short length of dowel stock into a drill, and then wrap a sheet of coarse sandpaper around the spinning dowel. After a bit of testing and fitting, you have a perfectly sized dowel. This technique also works great when you need to undersize a dowel enough to create a freewheeling axle in a wooden vehicle or other toy.

—John Hutchinson, Delaware, OH

Drill press step switch

I have a switch on the side of the drill press cabinet that turns the motor on and off. With the switch off, I plug in a step switch in the outlet under the switch, which allows me to turn the motor on or off by stepping on it. It works very well when using large drill bits.

—Robert H. Hays, Chicago, IL

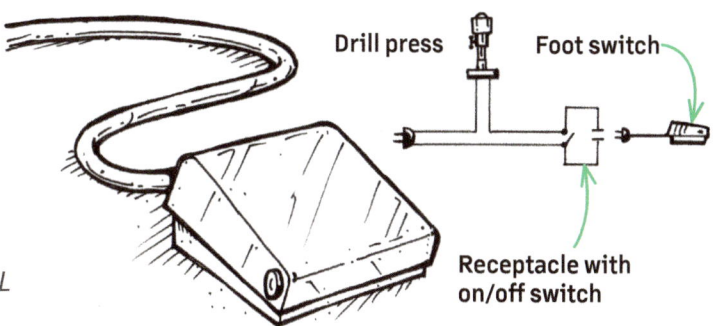

TOOLS > DRILL & DRILL PRESS

Magnetic tip holder

My new cordless drill came with everything I needed except for a driver tip holder. I solved this problem by attaching a small rare-earth magnet to the body of the drill using epoxy. While you're driving screws, the magnet provides a great parking place for a bit. If you find yourself switching out several different bits for drilling pilot holes, clearance holes, and countersinks in sequence, consider attaching two or even three magnets to your drill to accommodate everything.

—Bill Wells, Olympia, WA

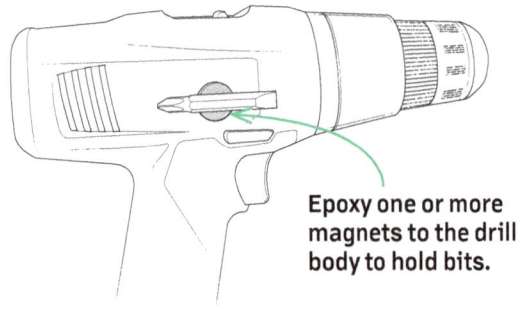

Epoxy one or more magnets to the drill body to hold bits.

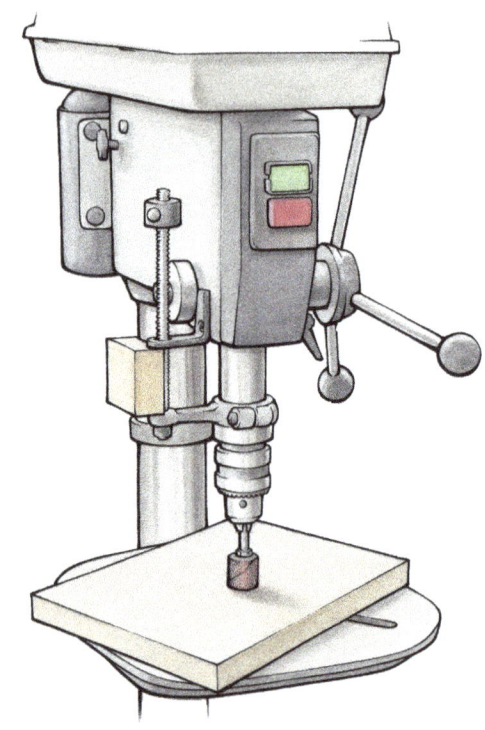

Keep hands free with drill press "lock"

I use sanding drums with my drill press to sand the full edge of a workpiece. However, while lowering the head and holding the feed handle steady, I found it difficult to sand edges with only one hand, especially for small pieces where both hands are needed to hold the work safely.

To free my hands, I figured out how to "lock" the chuck on the spindle once it's set at the right location. I lower the chuck steadily until the sanding drum is in position. Then I insert a small block that is cut to fit between the depth stop lug and the chuck set ring and release the feed handle. The block keeps the chuck fixed, freeing both of my hands to work on the piece.

—Charles Mak, Calgary, Alberta

Perfect circles

Whenever I have a project that calls for a number of arced cuts on either a bandsaw or scroll saw, I use a circle template to match up any circular cuts. Then I use the appropriate size Forstner bit to make that arc. This process avoids the need for sanding, improves accuracy, and gives a more aesthetically pleasing appearance. It's wonderful for something like a Chippendale mirror that has many small arcs.

—Kevin Martin, Cincinnati, OH

Brush up your bits

At the drill press, old toothbrushes can prove handy for cleaning out chips before they become packed enough to clog bits. The brushes contain small, stiff bristles that you can press against the spinning bit. A minor time-saver perhaps, but if you've had to repeatedly stop and start your drill press in order to pick out chip buildup, you'll recognize the convenience.

To keep the brush within reach but also out of the way, I trimmed the handle and fastened it to the long arm of my chuck key. The retractable chain keeps both in easy reach.

—Len Dorsett, Orange, CT

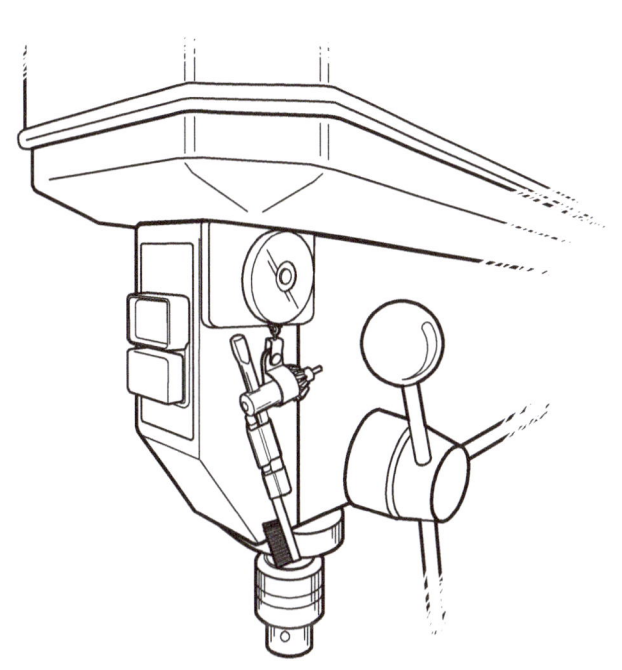

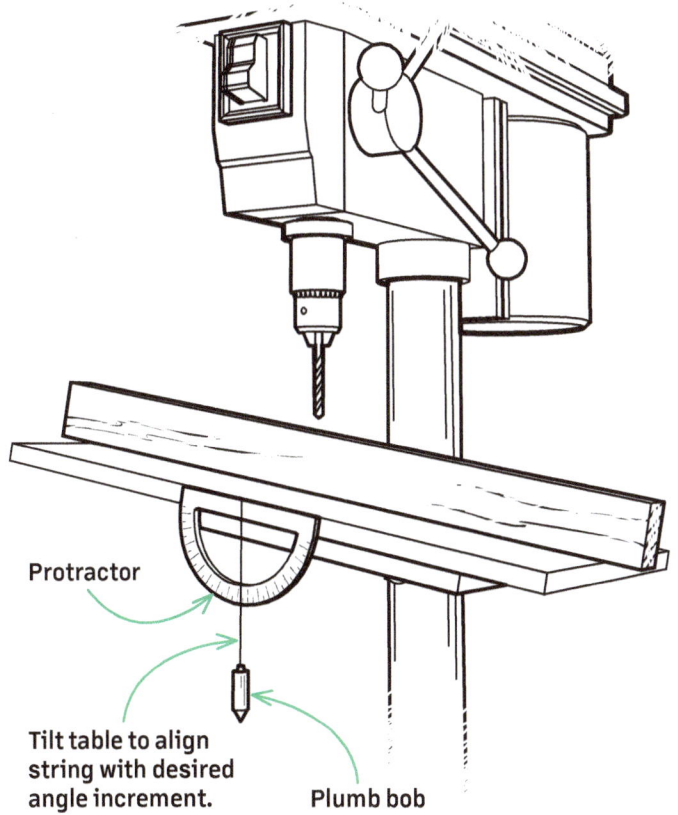

Protractor

Tilt table to align string with desired angle increment.

Plumb bob

Shop-made table-tilt gauge

After installing an auxiliary table on my drill press, I found that the machine's angle gauge (located at its rear) was all but impossible to read. To effectively shift the readout to the front, I attached a plastic protractor and plumb bob to the front edge of the table as shown. Using the gauge is a simple matter of setting the table level and square to the bit, adjusting the protractor to align its 0° increment with the string, and then tilting the table to align the string with the desired angle. No, the gauge isn't perfect, but it homes in closely on the correct angle. For best precision, use a large protractor and a thin string.

—Jim Wurst, Omaha, NE

TOOLS > DRILL & DRILL PRESS

Dowel depth stop

A recent project required hand-drilling a lot of 1/4"-diameter holes exactly 5/16" deep. After some thought, I realized that I could make an accurate depth stop from a length of dowel. First, I fully seated a 1/4" bit in my hand drill to calculate the stop's length. I cut a 1/2"-diameter dowel to that length and marked center on one end with an awl. I chucked the 1/4" bit in my drill press and bored a hole through the axis of the dowel, which I held vertically in a notched handscrew. I then chucked the dowel in a 1/2"-capacity hand drill and chamfered the end by rotating it against the spin of my disc sander. I rechucked the 1/4" bit in my hand drill and slipped the dowel over it. The inner end of the dowel that pressed against the end of the chuck provided solid registration, while the chamfer at the business end allowed better visibility at the contact area.

—*Jim Kelly, Trappe, PA*

Color-coded pilot drill bits

Drilling pilot holes used to involve finding the screw chart to remember the right size, then squinting at the bits until I found the right size.

Now I use a simple color-coding system so I can instantly grab the right bit and get to work. I borrowed three shades of nail polish, and painted the tip of my bits. Don't glop it on too heavily or you could clog the flutes of the bit. One color identifies each size I use most: 3/32" for #6 screws, 7/64" for #8, and 1/8" for #10.

Tape a piece of white paper with the color key to the inside lid of your drill bit box so you'll remember the code.

—*Jack McGraw, Tampa, FL*

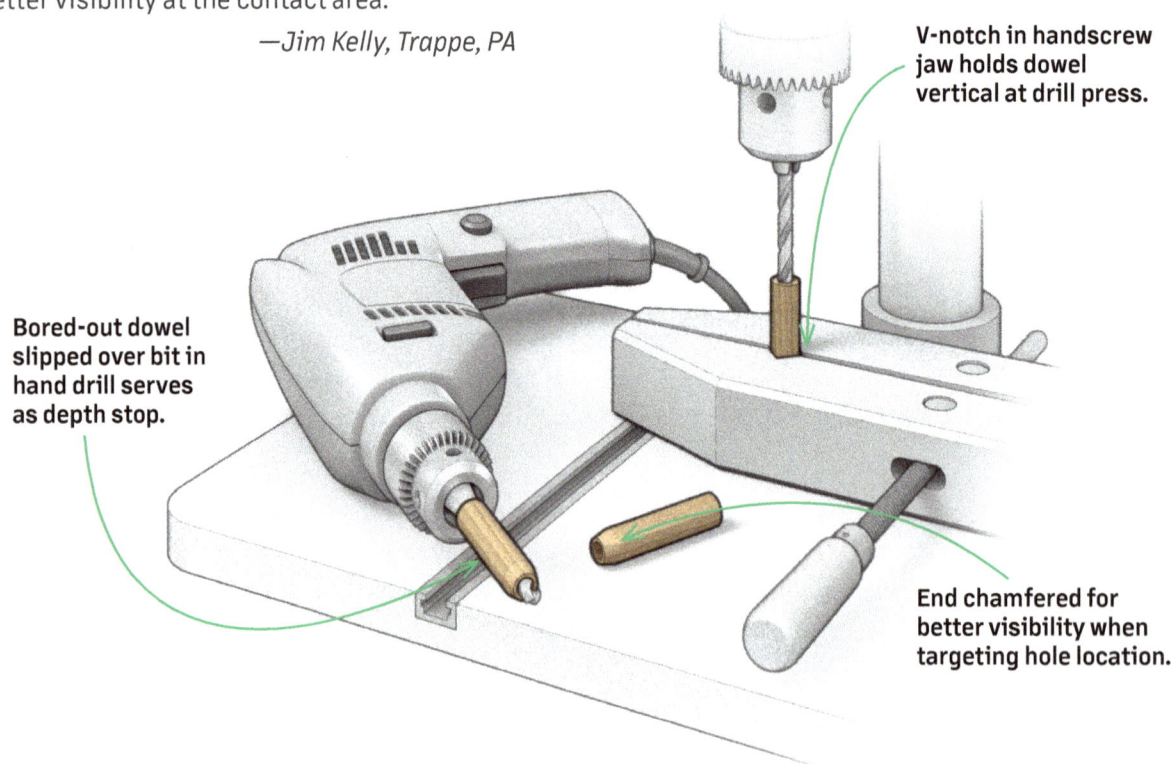

Bored-out dowel slipped over bit in hand drill serves as depth stop.

V-notch in handscrew jaw holds dowel vertical at drill press.

End chamfered for better visibility when targeting hole location.

Drill press key upgrade

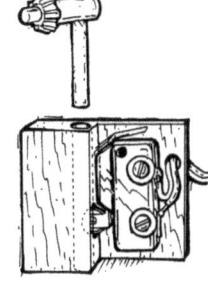

There have always been two things that bothered me about a drill press key. One, if you forget to remove it from the chuck, it'll be launched like a missile when you start the motor; and, two, when you do remember to remove it from the chuck, there's no convenient place to store it. I felt there had to be a solution to both problems. What was needed is a storage place for the key that will not permit the motor to run if the key is removed from storage.

My solution was built from parts I had on hand: a microswitch and a 1-1/2" square by 3" long maple block. The block is drilled lengthwise to accept the handle of the key. Drill through top to bottom, so that dust and wood chips can fall through and not get trapped as they would in a blind hole. That hole is centered 1/4" from one face. About halfway down that face (the actual position for the cross-hole is determined by the dimensions of the switch) a 1/2" hole was drilled to intersect the first hole. This is for the switch actuator.

To keep fingers away from the live electrical connection, I fashioned an enclosure from 1/8" fiberboard. I attached the holder to the drill press next to the existing on/off toggle switch and I wired the new switch in series with the existing switch.

—Abe Litman, Lincoln, NE

Twin-flip hinge gauge

Two hinges and four boards are all you need to make an easy-to-use, easily repeatable Euro-hinge drilling jig. Simply attach a fence to a scrapwood or plywood base, draw a reference line halfway across the fence, and then attach the two hinged stops the same distance from that line. (Depending on your doors and hardware, this distance can be anywhere from 3" to 6".)

To use the jig, mark out your first door so that you can adjust the base to set the necessary edge clearance, and then set the bit depth. Flip down the first stop, butt one corner of the door against it, and drill your first hole. Next, flip the first stop up, and lower the second stop. Drill the cup hinge hole on the adjacent corner.

—Paul Mueller, Chantilly, VA

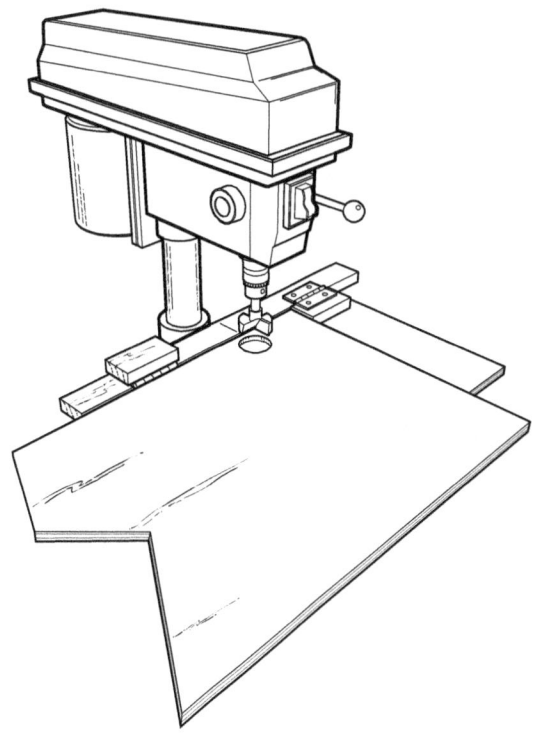

V-jig centers dowel hole

It's hard to drill a dowel through its side by hand, but comparatively easy to do with a wooden V-jig. Cut a symmetrical V-shaped notch in one face of a piece of 1-1/4" or heavier stock. Square a line from the point of the V and drill a vertical hole through the apex. Place the notch over the dowel and drill as shown.

—Javan Franklin, Cedar Rapids, IA

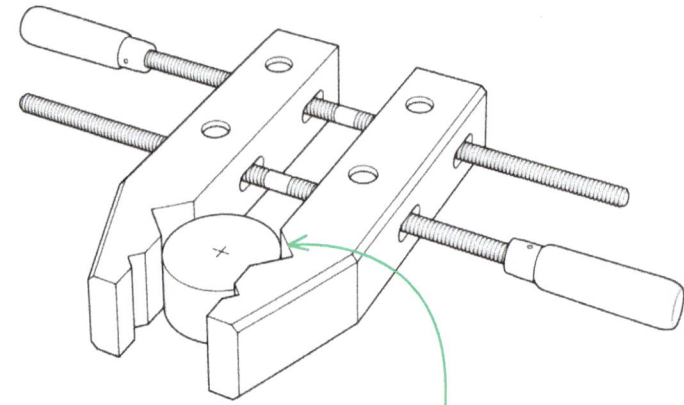

Notches hold short pieces on end for boring on drill press.

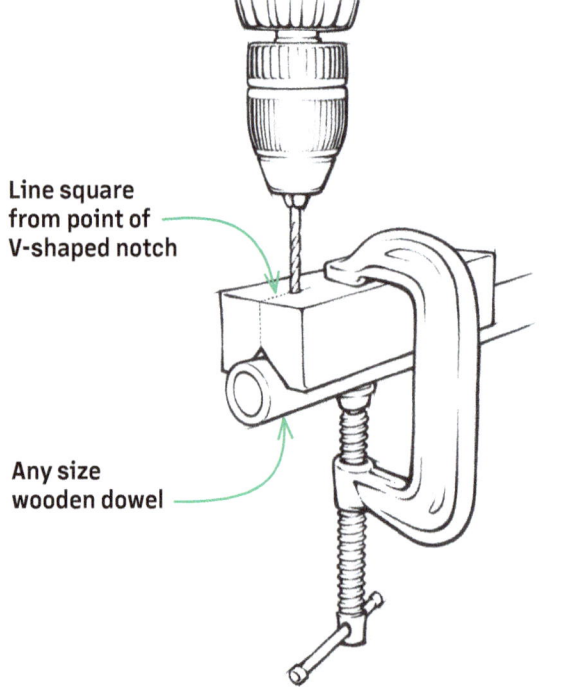

Line square from point of V-shaped notch

Any size wooden dowel

Handscrew headstand

Standing short pieces at the drill press can be challenging if you don't have the right kind of vise. But there's a perfectly good way to get by with no vise at all by using a notched handscrew. For safety and accuracy when holding both round and square pieces, the notches must be cut at 90°, and their walls must be perfectly square to the sides of the wooden jaws. For best results and greatest versatility, use a bandsaw to cut a small and a large notch.

—Marge Fillmore, San Diego, CA

Wax for screws

I love my cordless drill, but I'm reluctant to use it for finer finish work for fear of getting careless and overdoing it. When I do have to resort to elbow (or wrist) grease, I will lubricate my screws with wax to make driving them easier. To keep a supply handy, I drill a hole in my old screwdriver handle (this can be tricky, so make sure it is secure) and fill it with wax. Watch the kind of material you're drilling, keep the hole under 3/8", and avoid getting the wax on unfinished wood. A little goes a long way.

—Oliver Wayne, Columbus, OH

A better handscrew drill press vise

Many woodworkers know that you can pull a wooden handscrew into service as a drill press vise. However, I've found that it can be difficult to set up the workpiece and hold the clamp in place, especially when drilling large holes—an operation that can wrest the setup from your grip. I've found that a much better solution is to screw one jaw of the handscrew to a plywood panel from below. This fixes everything in place for easier setup and allows you to clamp the panel to the machine table for rock-solid security when drilling.

—Bill Wells, Olympia, WA

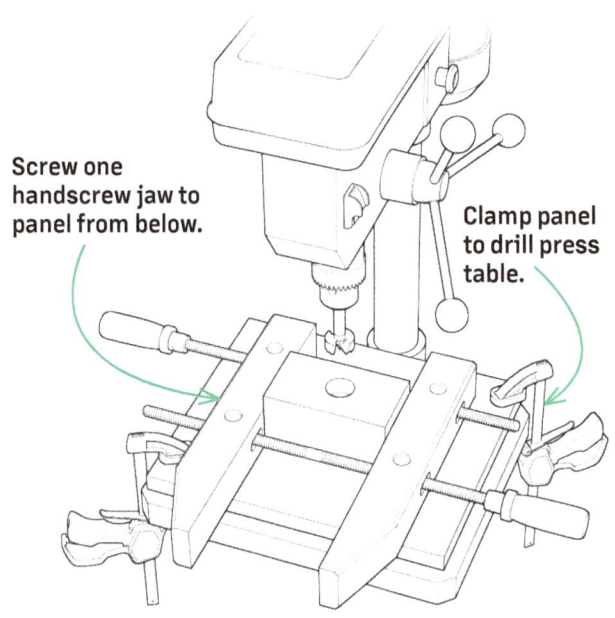

Screw one handscrew jaw to panel from below.

Clamp panel to drill press table.

End-boring at the drill press

Drilling into the end of a pen blank, dowel, or long workpiece at the drill press can be challenging, especially if your machine table doesn't rotate easily or accurately. Rather than hassling with that setup, I clamp the work in a small hobbyist bench vise that's bolted to a plywood panel for easy clamping to my drill press table. The vise adjusts easily, holds the work very securely, and can be used just as conveniently at a bench or other workstation when not in use at the drill press.

—Serge Duclos, Delson, Québec

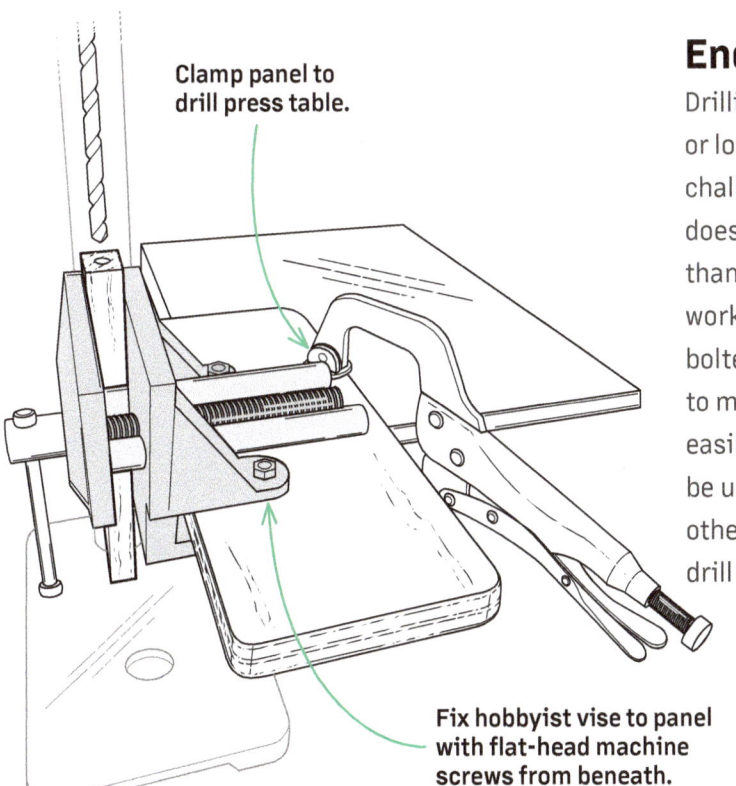

Clamp panel to drill press table.

Fix hobbyist vise to panel with flat-head machine screws from beneath.

TOOLS > DRILL & DRILL PRESS

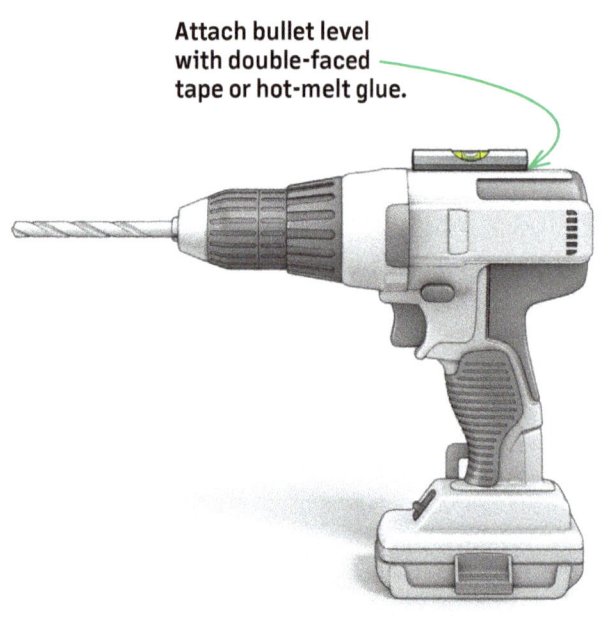

Attach bullet level with double-faced tape or hot-melt glue.

Drilling on the level

Whenever I have to drill a hole in a cabinet wall or other vertical surface, it's often important to make sure the hole is square to the surface. When maneuvering the drill for this, it's pretty easy to sight square side-to-side. However, sighting for up-and-down is awkward at best. To help, I attach a small spirit level vial, often sold as a bullet, torpedo, or line level to the top of my drill using hot-melt glue or double-faced tape. Just make sure to locate the vial so that it reads level when the bit is level.

—Joe Pestana, Stoneham, MA

Drill guide for flat-bottom bits

Occasionally, I need to drill blind holes in a completed project using a Forstner or multi-spur bit to install round magnets as cabinet catches. The problem is that it's tricky to guide a bit like this freehand. I've found that the solution is to use a guide block that I first bore on the drill press using the desired bit. Make the block long enough to allow clamping it to your cabinet case, panel, or other project part. When laying out the hole, extend the centerlines beyond the perimeter of the hole diameter to help you position the block in use by aligning it with crosshairs on the workpiece. After boring through the block, clamp it in place and use the same bit to drill your blind hole freehand.

—Sara Ducklin, St. Paul, MN

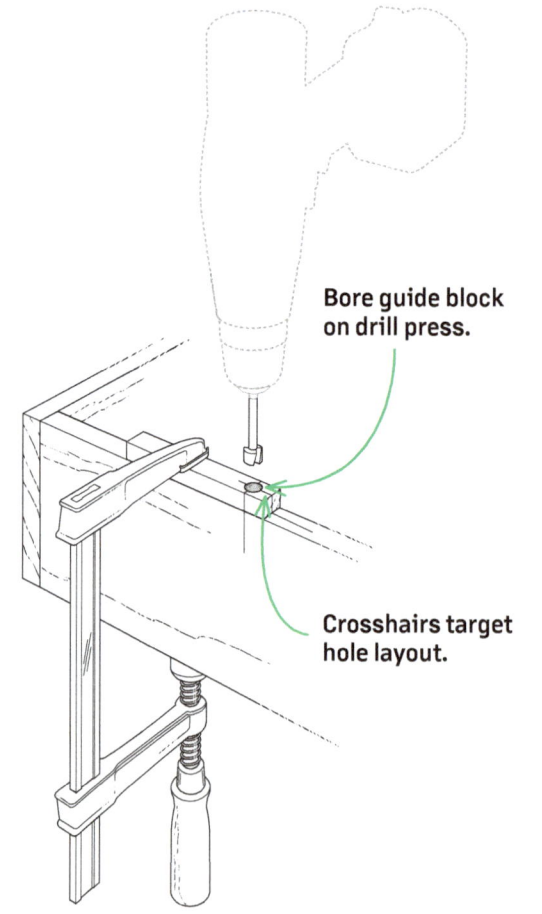

Bore guide block on drill press.

Crosshairs target hole layout.

Straight and easy

Drilling a perfect 90° hole on the drill press is a piece of cake, but using a hand drill can be more daunting. Here's a jig that's easy to make from available scrap that can help keep your hand drill perpendicular to the work surface. Cut a rabbet into the corner of a rectangular block of hardwood sized to easily fit your hand while working. Line up your mark in the corner of the rabbet, using the sides to support the shaft of the drill bit as a guide. Once your hole is started, just pull the block away and finish drilling the hole to the desired depth.

Here's an additional tip: If you frequently have to drill a lot of holes of the same depth, you may want to make several blocks of differing thicknesses. Just match the thickness of the block to your drill bit so that it stops the drill chuck at the precise depth you need. The block will not only help make perfect 90° holes, but will also act as a drill stop to make each hole the exact depth.

—Nate Common, Mystic, CT

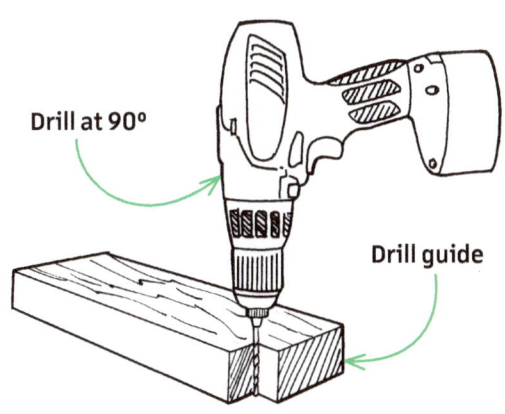

Drill at 90°

Drill guide

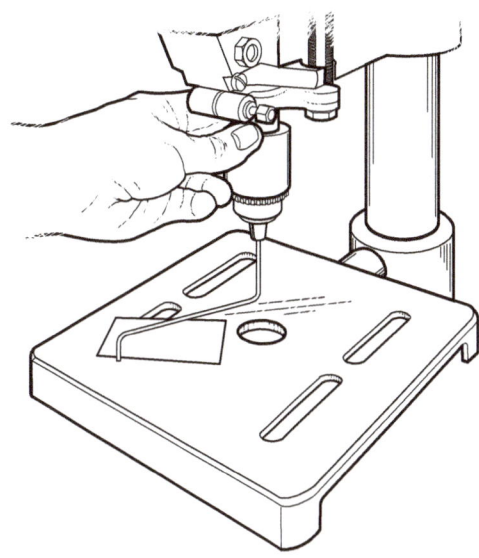

Two-piece drill press table setter

Using a bent piece of stiff wire (a piece of wire hanger works) to check that a drill press chuck is perpendicular to the table isn't entirely new, but adding a business card to this familiar tip adds near micrometer-like precision without the hassle of squinting to read a dial. To quickly set the table, bend the wire so that its bottom end sits just above the surface. If the wire can push a business card across the top without skipping over the card or touching the table, it means that you're only a few thousandths of an inch from perfect. (Most cards are printed on .010"-thick, 10-point stock.)

This go/no-go gauge may not be accurate enough for machining rocket parts, but I find it more than adequate for most woodworking applications and easy enough to repeat every time I adjust the height or tilt-angle on my table.

—Brian Anderson, McLean, VA

Just the right angle

There are times when you have to drill a piece of wood that just won't fit in a drill press, such as when drilling into the ends of long boards. Guiding a drill in at exactly 90° is tricky, and I usually get one of the holes at a bit of an angle by accident. So, I came up with this simple horizontal boring jig, which consists of a piece of wood precisely aligned with the shaft of the drill and mounted on top. With the piece to be drilled clamped next to it, this allows precise guiding of the upside-down drill at a right angle into the wood.

A lot of drills have a cylindrical section just behind the chuck that serves as a good primary attachment point for the jig. Measure this area (both my drills measure 43 mm) and see if you have a matching Forstner bit to cut a hole in a block of wood for the front attachment. I had to use a slightly smaller bit (1-3/8") and graze a little off on the bandsaw (after cutting it in half) for a good fit. Attach the bottom half to the board with two long screws.

When you attach the top half to hold the drill in place, you want the screws to engage only in the bottom piece. Therefore, expand the holes in the top with a larger drill bit. Permanently attach a rear block near the handle, cut to fit the drill. Repeatedly test the setup for straightness and rigidity as you go.

Here's another tip for using your jig: When drilling multiple holes into the same piece, place spacers between the guide piece and the drill jig to avoid reclamping the workpiece, especially if you are drilling multiple pieces.

—Matthias Wandel, Waterloo, Ontario

Easily tighten keyless chucks

I have a keyless chuck on my cordless and corded drills, and I could never get them tight enough to prevent my drill bits from slipping. Then, one day, I thought about my wife's hand-held jar lid opener, and my problem was solved. I cut two strips of insulation off a piece of old tool cord, removed the wires, and slipped the insulation over the arms of the opener (to protect the plastic-coated chucks).

I grip the narrow section of the chuck with the opener and the larger end with my hand. I get it so tight now that I even have to use the opener to loosen the chuck when I am finished.

—Wayne Johnson, Grand Ledge, MI

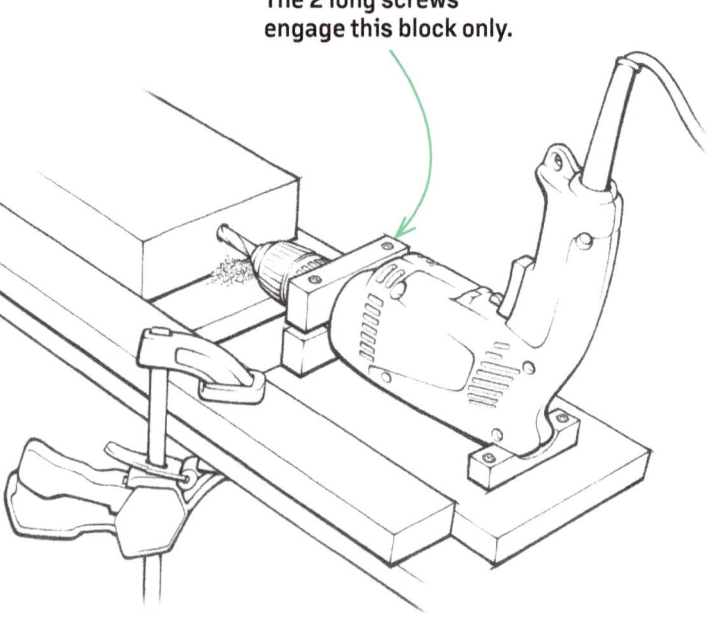

The 2 long screws engage this block only.

Drilling for stem casters

When boring out furniture legs to accept stem casters, the holes must be drilled perpendicular to the axis of the legs for aesthetics and proper operation. Unfortunately, it can be difficult to do this freehand, and setting up a drill press for the operation can be a hassle. I find that it's best to use a 1-1/4"-long drill guide block cut from the end of a leg that was made oversized in length for the purpose. After crosscutting the ends of the block square, drill through its axis on the drill press using a bit that suits the diameter of the caster stem. Then, attach a couple of plywood flanges to opposing sides of the block to allow clamping to the end of each leg for drilling its hole. If your bit is too short for the job, simply drill as far as you can, then remove the block to complete the job.

—Arlo Boyd, Wheeling, WV

Magnetizing a screwdriver

In my work, I often need to maneuver screws into recesses and tight places. A magnetized screwdriver that holds the screw really helps a lot. But rather than invest in a set of expensive drivers, I simply affix a small, powerful rare-earth magnet to the shank. I can adjust the magnetic strength by moving the magnet up or down on the shank. When working in tight spots, I'll reinforce the magnet's connection with double-faced tape or heat-shrink tubing to prevent it from shifting.

—Tracy Longo, Ventura, CA

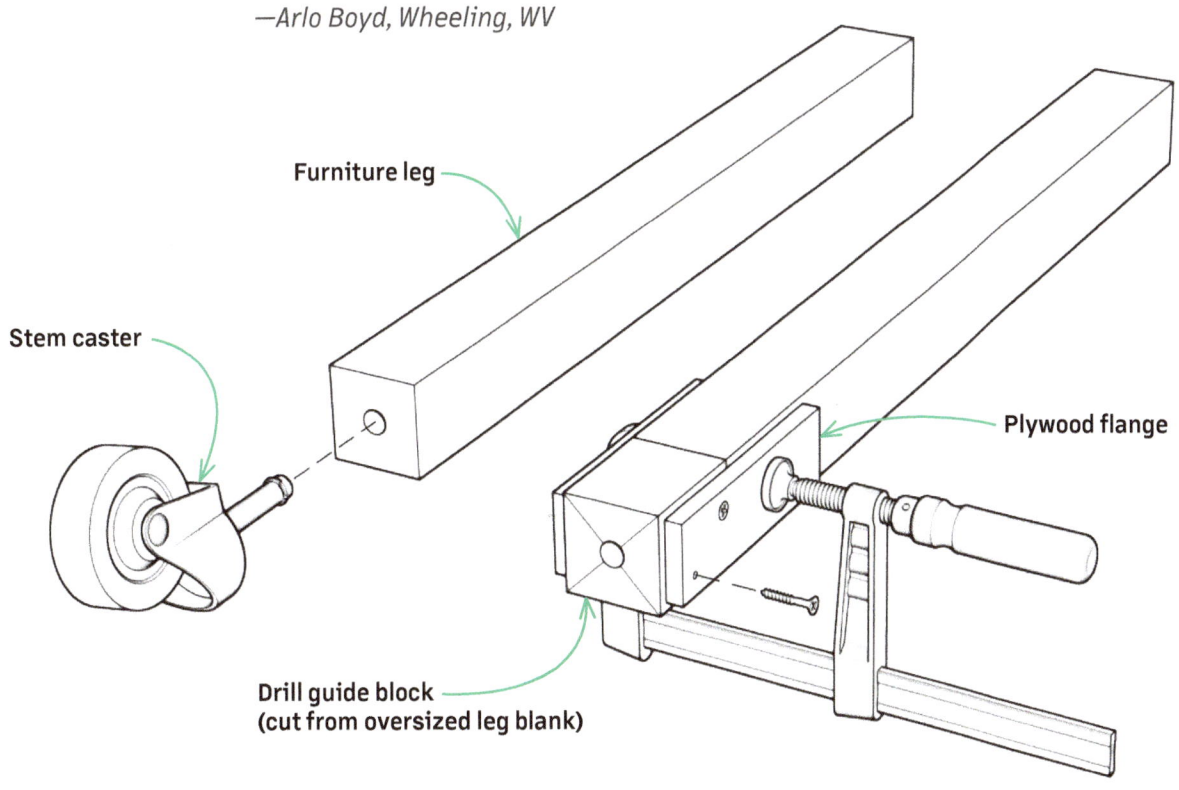

Furniture leg

Stem caster

Plywood flange

Drill guide block (cut from oversized leg blank)

Give a jig base a magnetic personality

This fast and handy jig holds a pen makers' center-drilling vise in place on a cast-iron drill-press table using two switchable magnets, such as Mag Jigs. We first attached the vise to a piece of 3/4" MDF. Then we added two 30mm Mag Jigs to the MDF, one on each side of the vise (Note: the illustration has been modified for clarity). The one-piece jig becomes magnetic with the turn of the knob and holds the vise in place during the machining process. With the drilling complete, we turn the knob the other direction to switch off the magnets, freeing the jig to easily remove it. No more klutzy clamps! Could be this idea will work with other jigs and cast-iron tools.

—Dan Domzalski, Mobile, AL

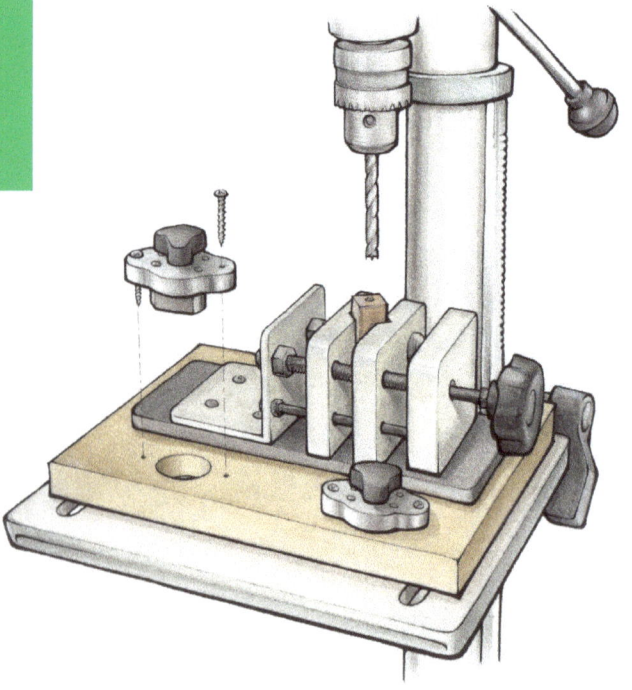

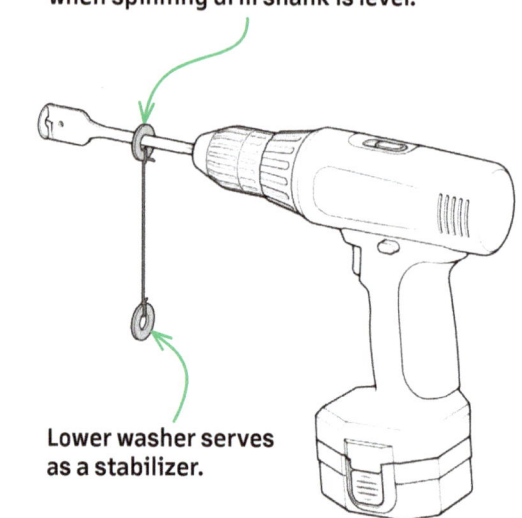

Large flat washer will remain in place when spinning drill shank is level.

Lower washer serves as a stabilizer.

Washers for level drilling

A recent job required drilling a couple of large holes in the walls of an installed cabinet to accept the ends of a large dowel rod. For the rod to span the two holes, they both needed to be horizontal in order to align with each other. Unfortunately, it's hard to gauge level with a spade bit, which is the tool I had for the job. After some head-scratching, I realized that I could employ the same sort of balancing principle used by a toy I had as a child. I strung together a couple of washers, which I then hung from the shank of the bit as shown. When drilling, the shank-hung washer would "walk" as a result of any drill tilt, providing a great leveling gauge. The side-to-side perpendicularity wasn't too difficult to maintain, gauging it by eye with the help of a small square placed nearby.

—Bill Shapwell, Fargo, ND

Leveling a drill press table

When leveling my drill press table, I've tried the old trick of mounting a bent coat hanger in the chuck and rotating it as a reference. However, I found that the hanger flexed too much for reliability. Instead, I use a sturdier gauge made from a 3/4" × 3/4" stick and two 16d common nails. Make the stick long enough to reach from the chuck to the edge of the table, and drill slightly undersized pilot holes to firmly hold the nails without splitting the wood. Install the nails as shown, mount the gauge in the chuck, and adjust your table to barely graze the head of the nail when rotating the chuck by hand.

—John Worst, Orlando, FL

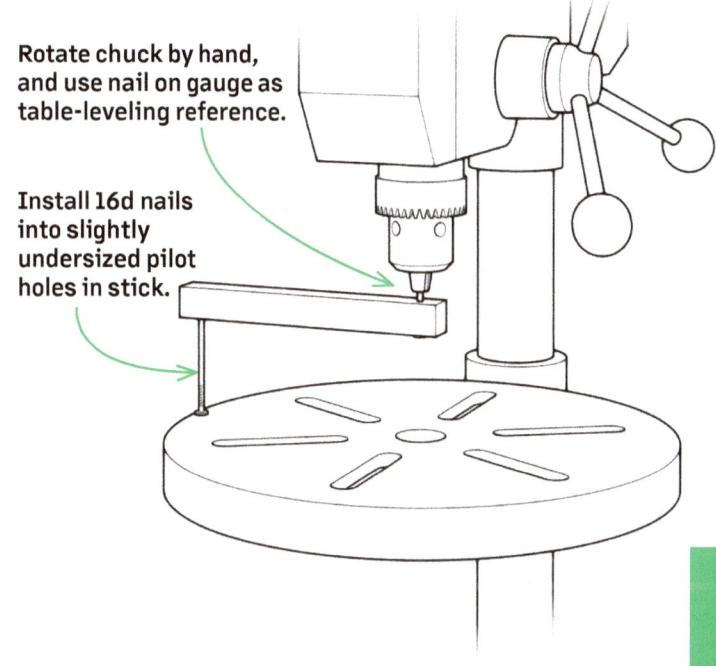

Rotate chuck by hand, and use nail on gauge as table-leveling reference.

Install 16d nails into slightly undersized pilot holes in stick.

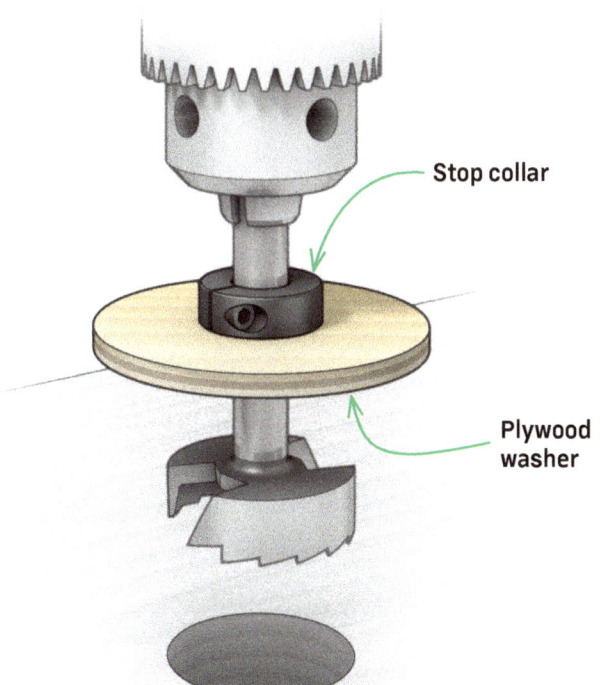

Stop collar

Plywood washer

Stop collar for Forstner bits

For projects requiring several different-sized holes drilled to precise depths, I like to set up stop collars on the bits required rather than constantly changing the depth stop on my drill press. The collars work well on regular drill bits, but their outer diameter is often too small to work with a Forstner bit. I've found that drilling a hole in a 1/4" plywood "washer" and sliding it to the desired depth between the collar and the bit's cutting end works with even the biggest of my collection. This trick also works well when using Forstner bits on the lathe.

—Jeff Peters, Redgranite, WI

Drilling out broken screws

When installing hinges or other hardware with brass screws, I first bore pilot holes and pre-thread them by driving in a steel screw of a similar size. I then lubricate the brass screws with wax for easier insertion. In spite of these precautions, I still manage to snap off the occasional screw head. To remove the embedded screw body, I use the same self-centering drill bit (also called a "Vix bit") that I used to drill the pilot holes. With the intended hinge or other hardware secured by screws in the remaining holes, I simply redrill with the self-centering bit, feeding it slowly with a low rpm to bore out the metal.

—*Richard Libera, Newark, DE*

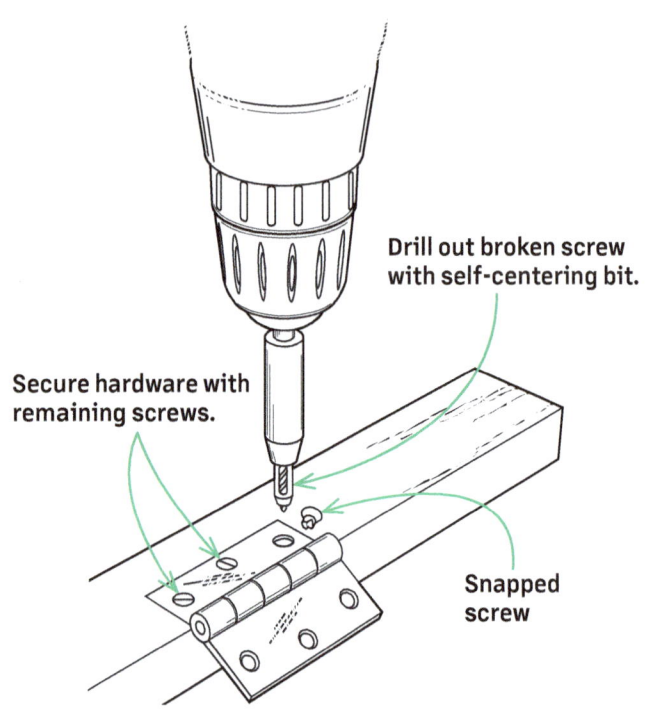

Drill out broken screw with self-centering bit.

Secure hardware with remaining screws.

Snapped screw

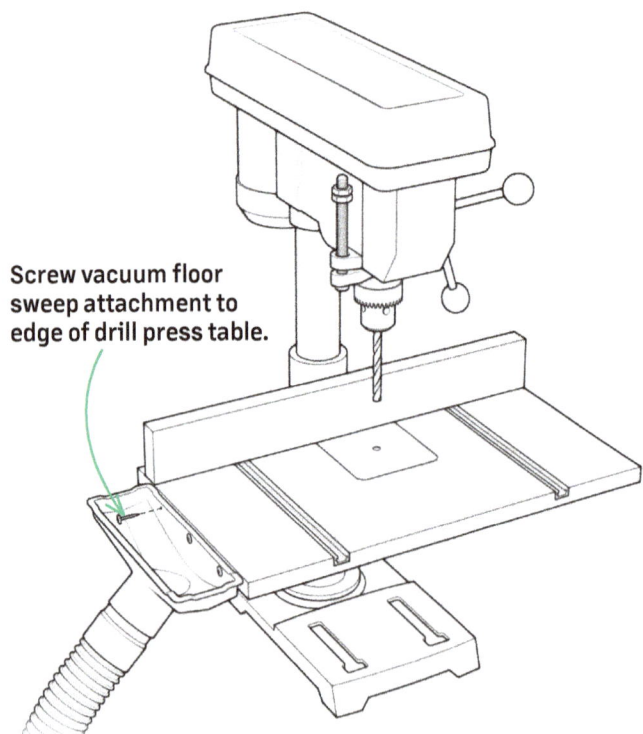

Screw vacuum floor sweep attachment to edge of drill press table.

Drill press chip collection

The area around my drill press sure gets messy from the wood chips that I'm always brushing off the table. I finally realized that, rather than vacuuming the chips from the floor afterward, it made more sense to mount the vacuum's floor sweep attachment to the edge of the table with a few screws. I leave it there permanently since I don't use the attachment for much else, but you could hang it using keyhole slots for easy removal if you like. To avoid the chance of losing the chuck key, a bit, or some small part, try attaching a piece of metal mesh over the sweep's opening.

—*Russ Svendsen, Olean, NY*

Self-supporting vertical drilling jig

Here's a simple jig for your drill press that will come in handy the next time you need to bore a vertical hole in the end of a pen blank, post, or any other long workpiece. Unlike other versions that simply clamp to the table, my jig bolts to it. This allows the jig's support bar to pivot easily for repositioning without risking a fall to the floor.

Use these dimensions as a starting point. If you have a large auxiliary table, lengthen the bar to suit. (If your table has T-slots, replace the hex head bolt with a T-bolt.) To use the jig, swing the drill press table clear of the bit, bolt the jig in place, and then clamp the workpiece to the fence and base as shown. When the workpiece is in position, use an F-clamp to lock the bar to the table, and then drill your hole.

—Joe Hurst-Wajszczuk, Birmingham, AL

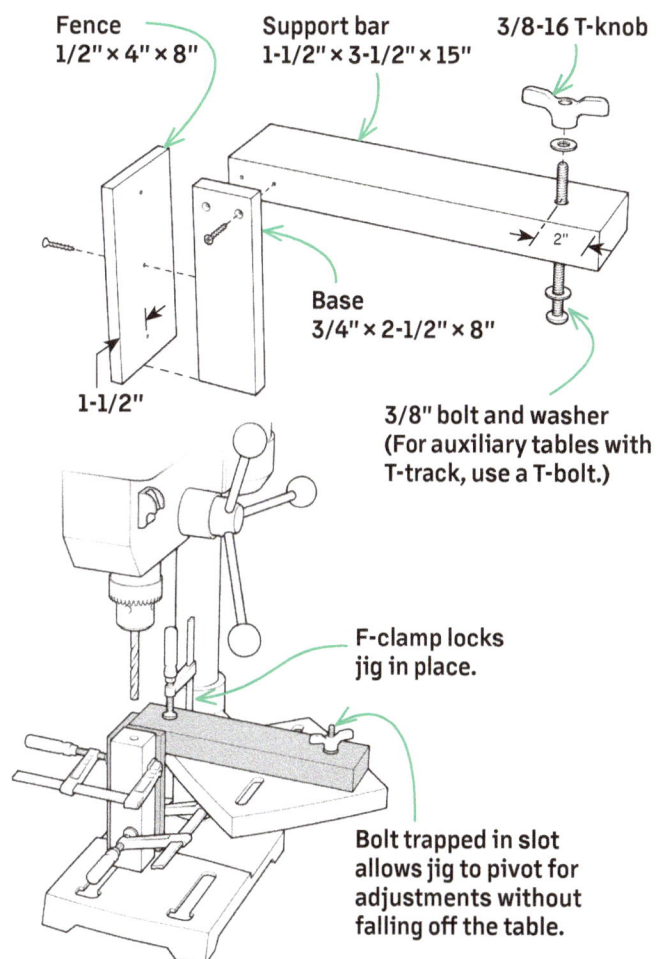

Preventing runaway plugs

I often use wooden plugs to fill counterbores in my screw-assembled projects, making the plugs on my drill press with a plug-cutter. I used to saw the plugs free of the drilled stock after running a strip of tape across a row of them to prevent them from being thrown by the saw blade. All the same, I found myself digging around in the sawdust on the shop floor to retrieve wayward plugs. Then my old dad showed me a better way. Now, I drill the plugs with the cutter slightly tangent to the edge of the stock and use a chisel to pop each one free as needed. Thanks, Pop.

—Mark Breyer, Tucson, AZ

Drill press base platform

I prefer a benchtop drill press because of the storage capacity and mobility a wheeled cabinet beneath it provides. However, it annoys me that the area under the machine tends to be such an unusable mess, especially when every bit of staging space in my small shop is precious. The awkwardly shaped machine base doesn't serve well as a platform, and just attracts shop detritus. My solution was to outfit the cabinet top with a platform that covers the machine base and provides a useful surface. To create it, I simply screwed together a frame of the appropriate height around the edges of the cabinet, and then topped the frame with twin panels, scribing and sawing out a cutaway to accommodate the machine post. Do not glue the parts in place, as you'll want to remove them someday. (P.S. The platform makes a great hiding place. Shh.)

—Anthony Fisher, Sebastopol, CA

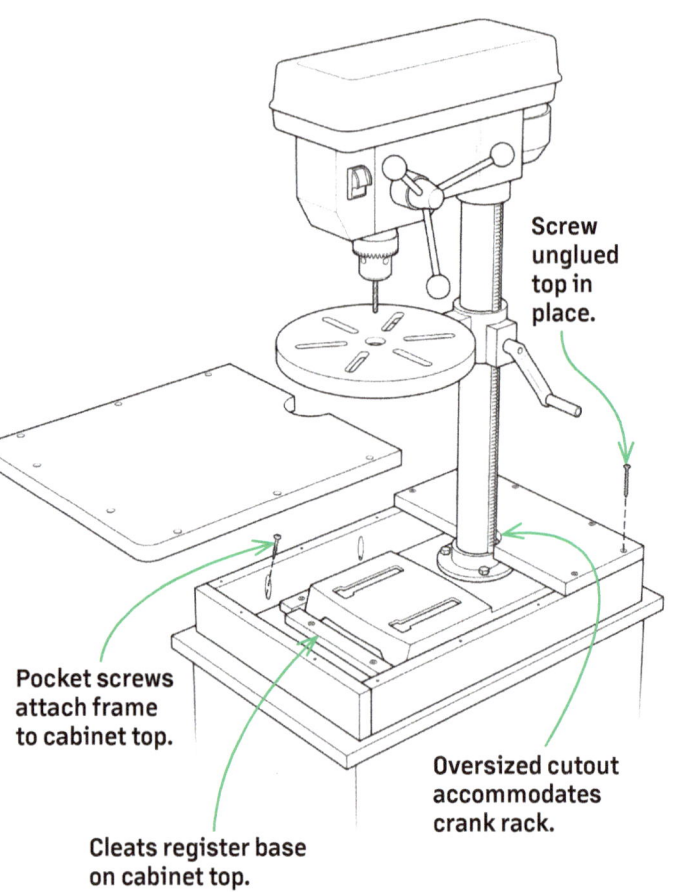

Screw unglued top in place.

Pocket screws attach frame to cabinet top.

Cleats register base on cabinet top.

Oversized cutout accommodates crank rack.

Shelf bracket as workpiece support

I regularly use my drill press to bore holes in the ends of long workpieces. Rather than setting up a freestanding, height-adjustable work support, I simply screwed a typical metal shelf standard to a nearby cabinet. When working with long pieces, I just attach a shelf support bracket to the standard at the proper height to carry the workpiece.

—Fred Frommelt, Janesville, WI

Drilling tiny parts

I do a lot of miniature woodworking, and have had to learn how to handle tiny workpieces. One problem I regularly face is safely holding small parts at the drill press. When they're too little to hold firmly in a vise or handscrew, I simply press them firmly down onto a piece of double-faced tape attached to a backup panel, which holds the piece in place for drilling. I use the same trick when I need to shape a small piece on a disc sander or belt sander.

—Charles Mak, Calgary, Alberta, Canada

Piloting for continuous hinges

Self-centering drill bits (also called "Vix bits") are great for quick, accurate drilling of pilot holes for hinges. Unfortunately, they don't work very well for continuous ("piano") hinges. That's because the leaves on continuous hinges are too thin to allow the beveled nose of the spring-loaded bit housing to fully seat in the countersunk hinge holes.

When faced with installing about 10 feet of continuous hinges for my tool cabinet doors, I came up with a great solution. I went to my refrigerator door and pulled off a couple of business card sheet magnets to use as risers. I knifed them into small pieces that I stuck on the underside of a hinge leaf between each pair of screw holes. After clamping the hinge to the cabinet, it was now raised enough to allow the nose of the bit housing to seat fully in each hinge hole. When done drilling the pilot holes for one hinge leaf, I switched the magnets to the next one. It really sped up the work and ensured perfect alignment of the hinges.

—Paul Anthony, Riegelsville, PA

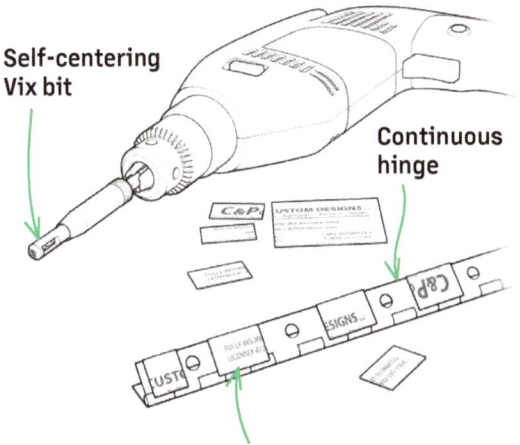

Sheet magnets on underside of leaf raise it enough to allow a Vix-bit nose to seat fully in countersunk screw holes.

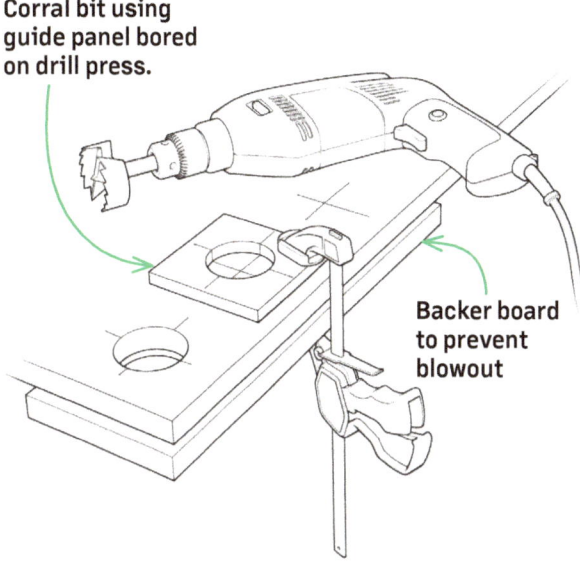

Precision drilling with a large-diameter bit

Handheld drilling with a Forstner or multi-spur bit can be a skittish operation. However, sometimes it's necessary when a panel is just too big or cumbersome to place on the drill press table. In those cases, simply make a small guide panel at the drill press, using the desired diameter bit to drill the hole. Then clamp or screw the guide panel to your workpiece.

The guide panel doesn't need to be much thicker than 1/2" or so. To allow precise targeting of a centerpoint, extend long crosshairs outward from the initial guide panel centerpoint, and then carry those lines down across the edges of the hole afterward. That way, you can align them with long crosshairs laid out on your workpiece.

—Mike Johns, St. Louis, MO

TOOLS > DRILL & DRILL PRESS

Ball-drilling jig

For a recent project, I needed to drill accurately centered holes into some wooden balls I had purchased, so I came up with this jig to hold them securely on the drill press. To make the jig, first make the upper "clothespin" board from a short piece of stock whose thickness approaches the radius of the ball to be drilled. Cut a 1/4" slot in it and screw it to a baseboard that's long enough to span your drill press table. Then drill a hole through the upper board using an adjustable-diameter holesaw, which allows slight upsizing to accommodate the typical variance of wooden balls from their nominal diameters.

To use the jig, first outfit your drill press with a standard twist bit whose diameter matches that of your holesaw's pilot bit. Lower the bit into the pilot hole in the baseboard to center the jig under the drill chuck. After clamping the baseboard to the table in this position, switch out the bit with the one you'll use to drill the ball, and pinch a ball in the jig by clamping across the slot. Now you're ready to drill a perfectly centered hole.

—John Hutchinson, Delaware, OH

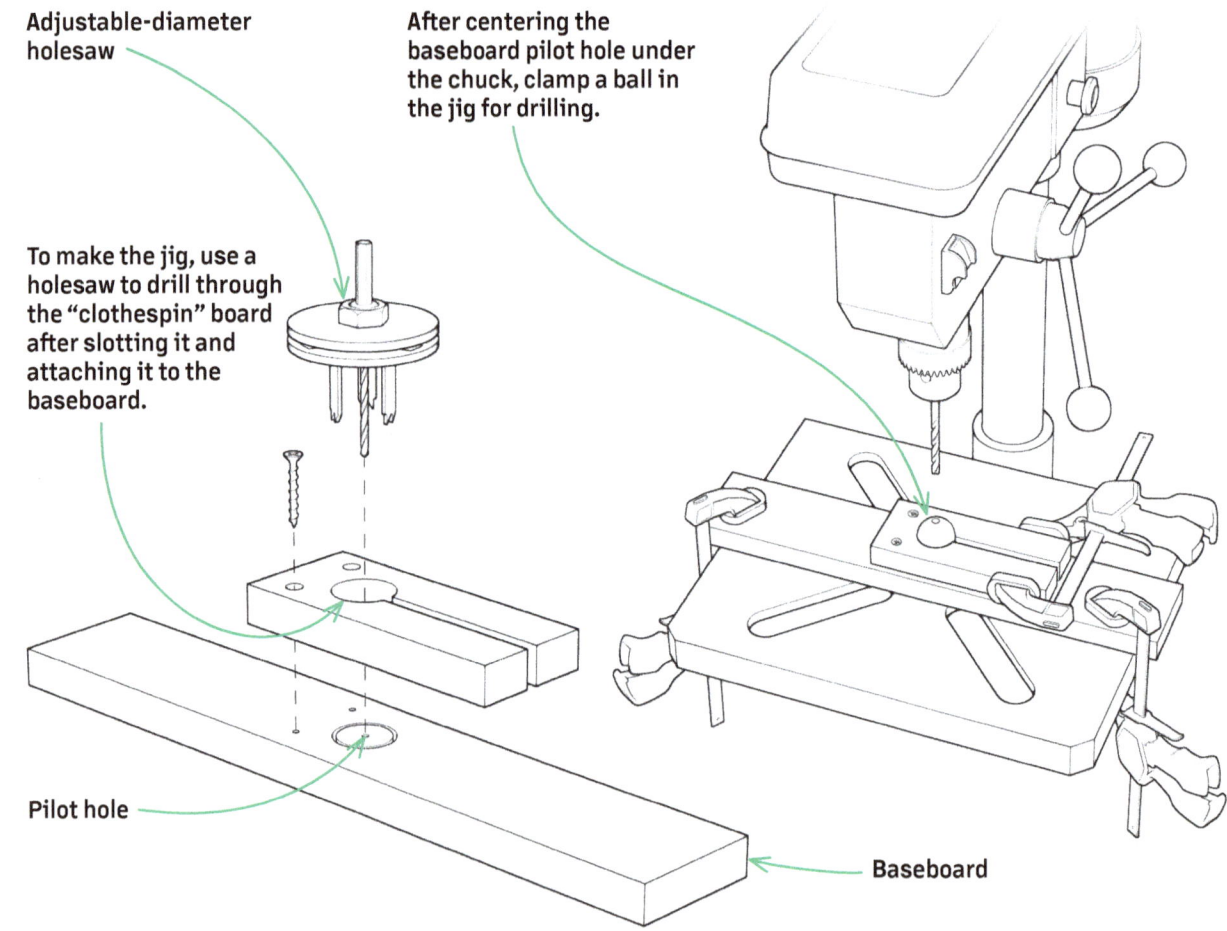

Drill press hold-down

Like many woodworkers, I outfitted my drill press with an auxiliary table that includes two T-tracks for mounting the fence and/or hold-downs. Unfortunately, hold-downs mounted in the tracks were often out of the reach of small parts. As a solution, I devised this hold-down bar that spans the T-tracks and allows me to position a hold-down at any point with great force. I drilled the hard maple bar to accept T-bolts and knobs that connect it to the table T-tracks. Then I routed a 12"-long through-slot (recessing it on the underside) to connect the hold-down. (I replaced the hold-down's hex head bolt with a T-bolt for smoother sliding operation.)

The unit is simple to make. Just get T-bolts and knobs to fit the size of your table T-tracks, and then rout the slot to suit your chosen hold-down. I offset the slot as needed to allow the short leg good footing.

—Vic Danart, Wacissa, FL

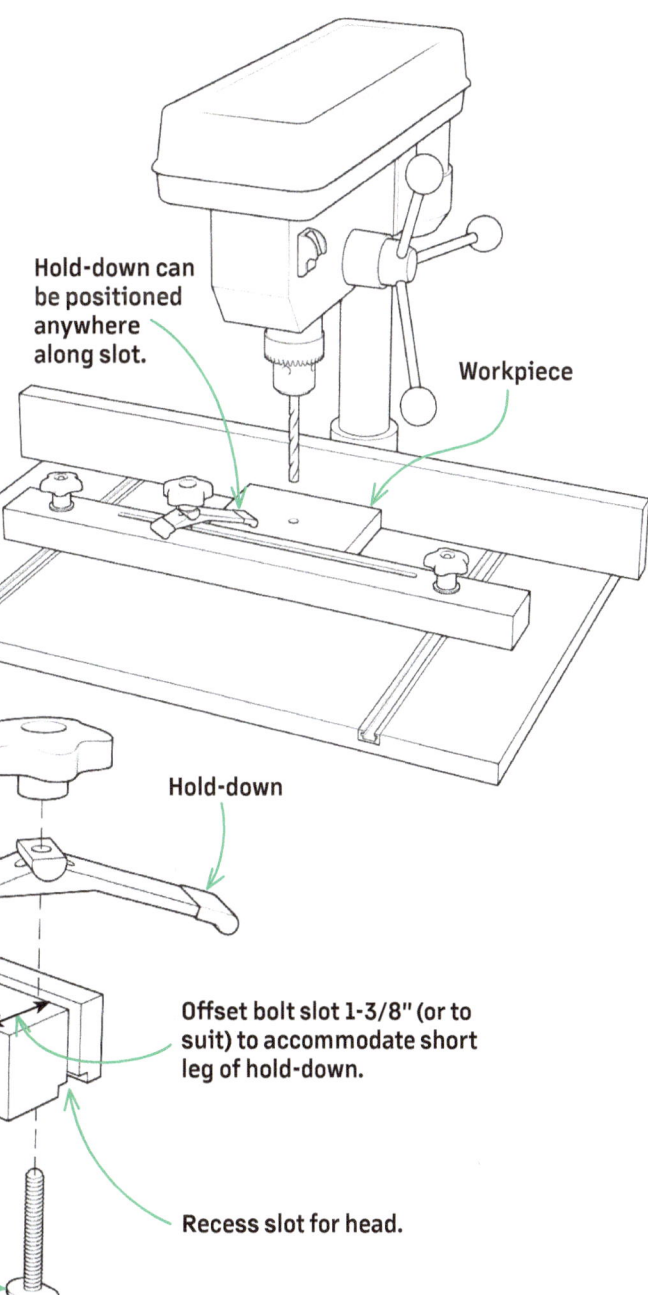

Drill press angle platform

It's a hassle to tilt my drill press table for boring angled holes, so I devised this workpiece platform to do the job instead. It's nothing more than a couple of plywood panels hinged together, with a T-track installed in the bottom panel. A bolt and cap nut in the T-track hold the panels apart at the desired angle, with the bolt locked in place with a wing nut. A cleat along the hinged edge of the top panel registers a workpiece to hold it in place for drilling. The jig is easy to make, simple to use, and allows infinite adjustment within a 5º to 45º angle range. Simply slide the bolt assembly to whatever location holds the top panel at the desired angle. For quick setup, I mark the bolt locations for commonly used angles.

—Don Winslow, Indian Trail, NC

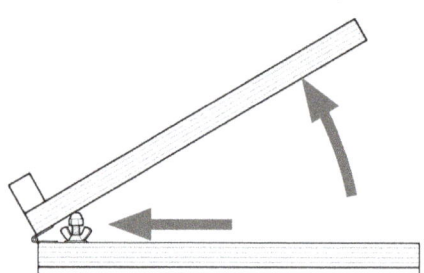

Position bolt mechanism to create desired platform angle.

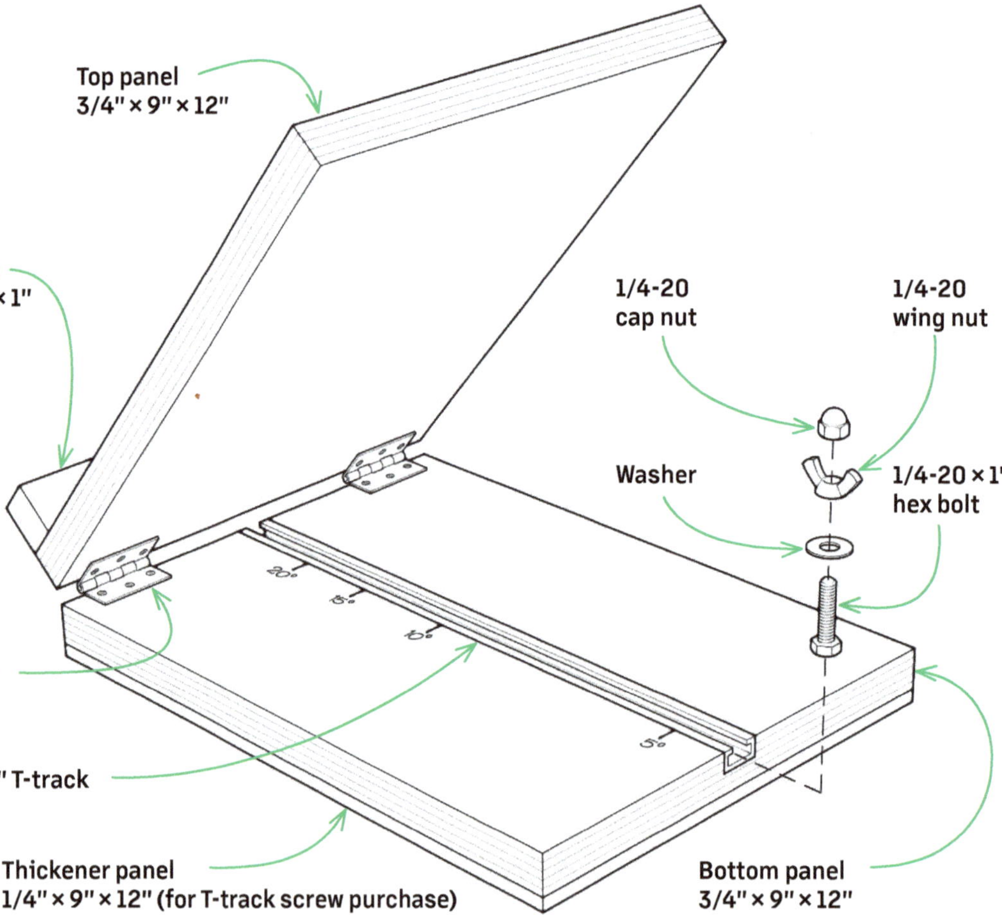

JOINTER

Jointing veneer

Over the years, I've tried about every method for jointing the edges of veneers. Ultimately, I've found that the best way is also the simplest. Here's how it works.

Begin by laying out your veneer sheets in a way that suits your project. Then, stack together similarly sized sheets, taping these packets together at their ends. Next, lay a long, thick board across your jointer tables, bringing the jointer fence up against the board to ensure that the two are parallel. Clamp the board to the tables.

Sandwich a veneer packet between the board and the fence, adjusting the fence to allow the packet to slide easily but with just a bit of friction. This creates a chute that compresses and stabilizes the stacked veneers to allow easy, accurate jointing of their edges. After jointing the first packet, readjust the fence if necessary to suit the thickness of the next packet, and continue in the same manner.

—Thomas Starbuck Stockton, Montgomery Creek, CA

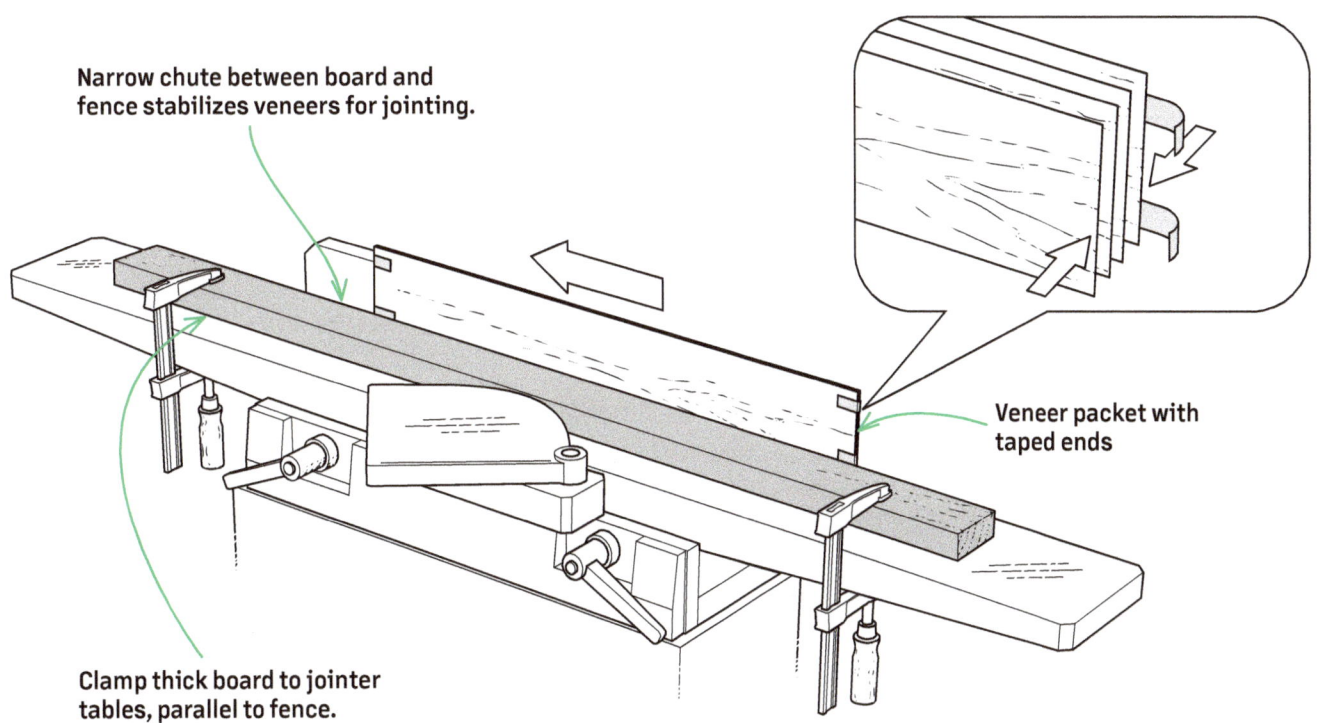

Narrow chute between board and fence stabilizes veneers for jointing.

Veneer packet with taped ends

Clamp thick board to jointer tables, parallel to fence.

TOOLS > JOINTER

Curved tapers on the jointer

I recently had to replace a broken leg on a Duncan Phyfe–style candlestand table. These legs are curved, so you can't taper them on the table saw. They are also tapered fully end-to-end, so you can't shape them on the jointer the way you can a stop-tapered leg. Here's how to pull off the job: After planing the leg stock to the thickest dimension at the head and cutting the curved shape, mark the desired thickness at the toe. Prepare a piece of sacrificial support stock that's wider than the head end by an amount equal to twice the desired taper, and longer than the length of the head by a couple inches. Center the support across the thickness of the head, attaching it with two screws. Run the piece over a jointer from head to foot in successive passes until the support is flush with the leg, at which point it should be down to the thickness marks you made at the toe.

—Russ Svendsen, Olean, NY

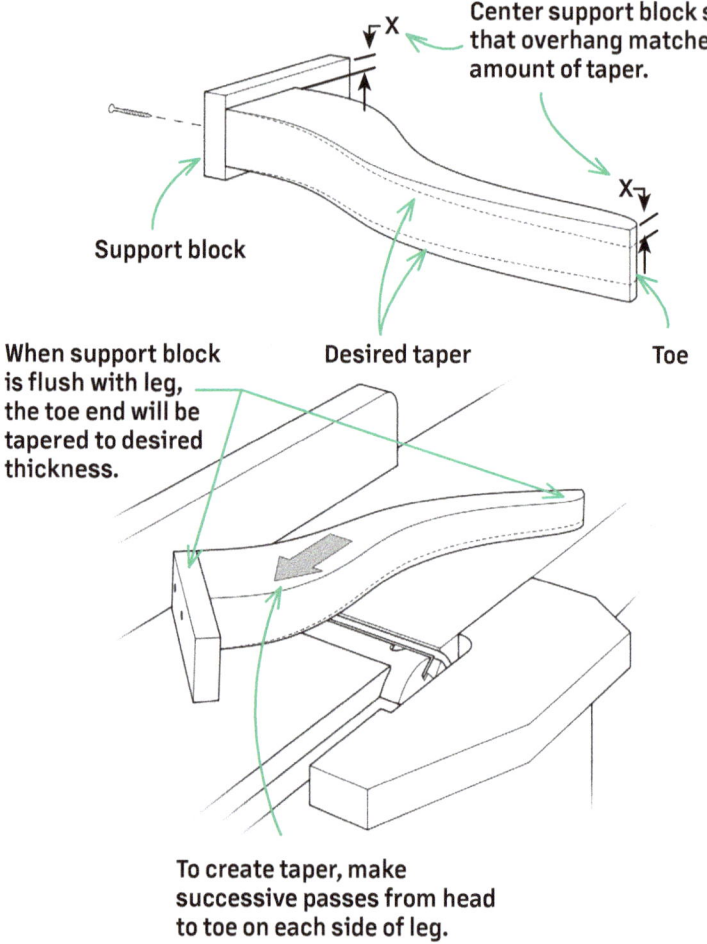

Center support block so that overhang matches amount of taper.

Support block   Desired taper   Toe

When support block is flush with leg, the toe end will be tapered to desired thickness.

To create taper, make successive passes from head to toe on each side of leg.

A perfect jointer angle

I've often found it difficult to adjust the fence on my jointer to achieve exact angles of 90º and 45º. To make adjustment easier and faster, I took a 6" length of 4×4 stock and cut it lengthwise from corner to corner to make an equilateral prism with a perfect 90º angle on one side, and 45º angles on the other two. (I measured the block carefully to be sure the angles were exact.) Now, whenever I need to adjust the fence, I just loosen it, place the side of the block against the fence at either 90º or 45º, then lock the fence down.

—Arthur Tappem, Jacksonville, FL

Jointer knife "stretcher"

Want to push a few more boards through your jointer before sharpening the knives? Try my two-step honing process. It's simple, safe, and easy. Once you know how to set the cutterhead, you'll find honing a secondary bevel on a knife like touching up a plane blade. I can hone my knives three times before they need to be pulled and reground.

First, unplug your jointer and lower the outfeed table so that it's just below the knives. Rotate the cutterhead so the tip of the first knife points approximately to one o'clock and then lock it in place with a few wooden wedges. To repeat the same exact angle for the remaining two knives, make a reference mark on the outfeed table and two marks on the ruler—at the reference mark and where the tip of the knife touches the blade. Now wrap a piece of paper around your finest stone and take about a dozen passes along the knife. (At this point, you should see a shiny microbevel running along the edge.)

Remove the wedges and use the marked straightedge to position the tip of the next knife to the same angle, wedge, and hone. Repeat the process with the third knife. Finally, reset the outfeed table so that it's level with the tip of the knives at the highest point of rotation.

—Joe Whitmore, San Destin, FL

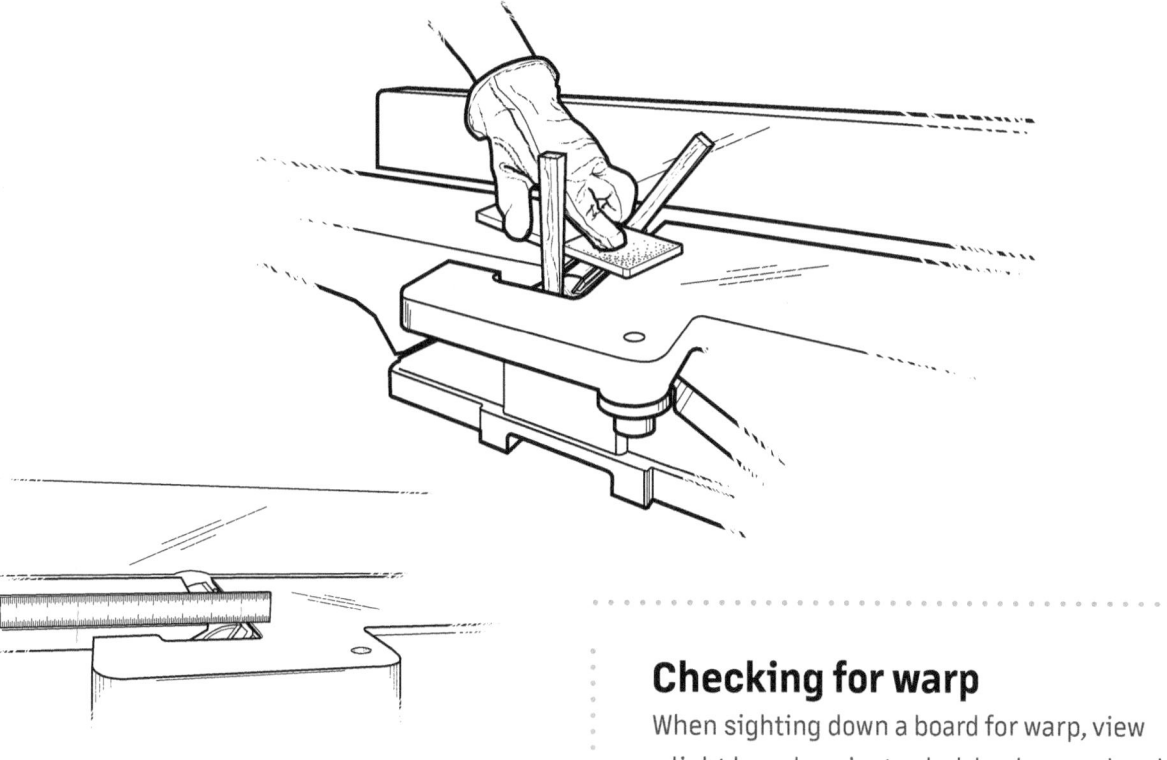

Checking for warp

When sighting down a board for warp, view a light board against a dark background and vise-versa.

—Paul Anthony, Riegelsville, PA

TOOLS > LATHE

LATHE

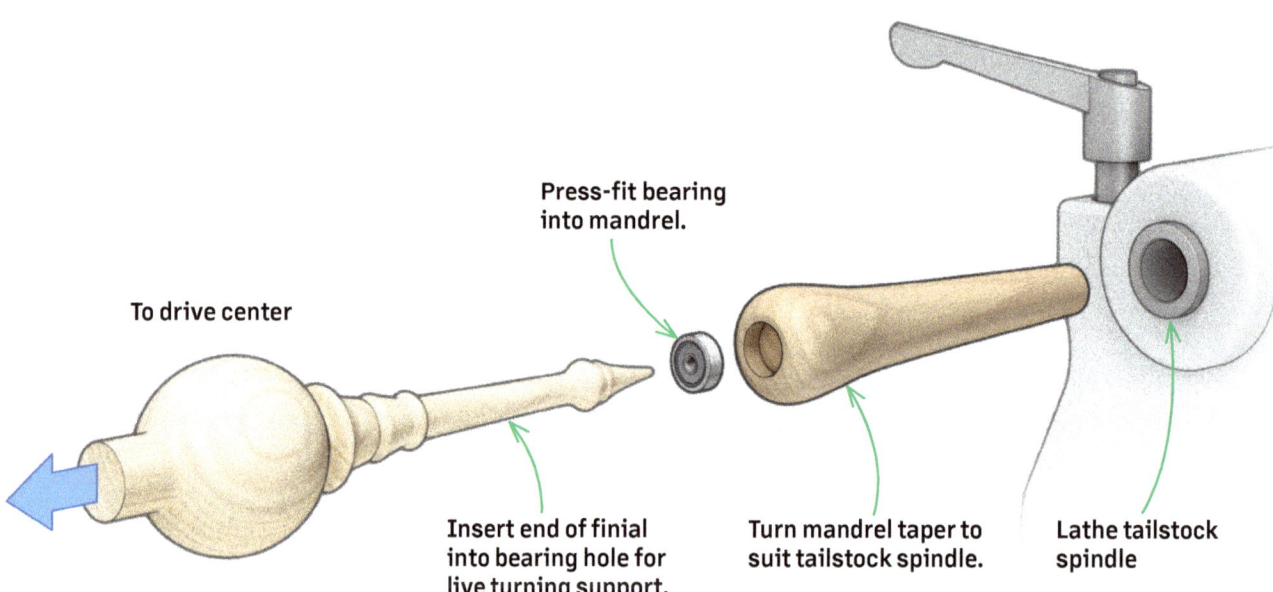

Live tail center for finials

I enjoy turning finials, ornaments, and other pieces with long, slender tips. However, supporting those delicate ends can be tricky, and a standard live center with a pointed end won't do the job. Instead, I made up a live center with a hole to accept the finial tip. It consists of a standard ball or roller bearing inset into a wooden mandrel made from a 1-1/2" square × 6" long blank. First turn one end of the blank to match the Morse taper in your tail stock, making it long enough to self-eject when the spindle is fully retracted. Then pop the tapered end in the headstock, turn the bulb shape, and drill a shallow hole that is a snug fit for a machine bearing whose hole size suits the diameter of the work you typically turn. I used a 1/2" O.D., 3/16" I.D. bearing from a dead router, but you could use a router bit bearing or order any size you like from an online bearing dealer. Press the bearing into the hole and you're done.

—*Jeff Peters, Redgranite, WI*

Caliper gauge block

Since most of my woodworking involves the lathe, I was constantly setting up my calipers to different dimensions using a ruler. This was always time-consuming and it was easy to make mistakes. To speed the process, I made this simple gauge from a piece of 3/4" scrap hardwood with incremental steps matching my most commonly used dimensions. Mounted to one of the support legs of my lathe, it takes only a moment to set the calipers perfectly every time.

You can make your gauge any size you want, with as many steps and dimensions as you need. Depending on how you mount it, mark the steps either vertically or horizontally to make the measurements easy to read. Initially, you'll need to measure very carefully when making the gauge to give you the highest accuracy possible, but you'll only need to make those measurements once.

—*Carl Lepley, Fort Worth, TX*

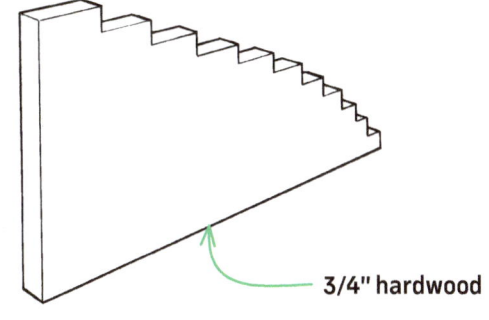
3/4" hardwood

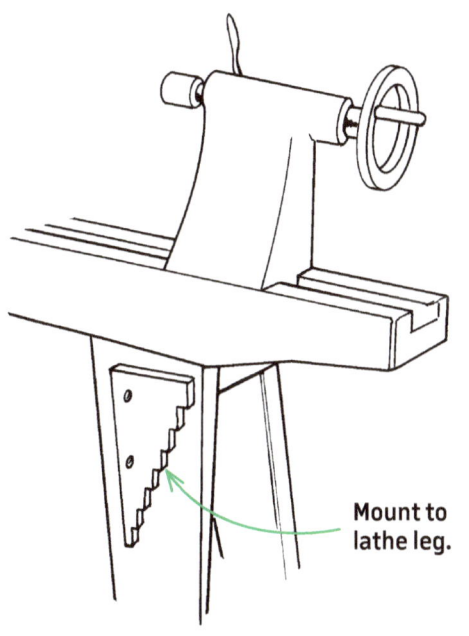
Mount to lathe leg.

Non-catch calipers

I use Vernier calipers to measure my progress when turning tenons. I set the caliper jaws to the desired diameter of the tenon, and then hold the jaws against the turning in progress until they slip over the tenon section. To prevent the tips of the caliper jaws from catching on the spinning workpiece, I grind a slight radius on them. This also allows them to easily slide onto the tenon once it reaches the proper diameter.

—*Judy Silfer, Tucson, AZ*

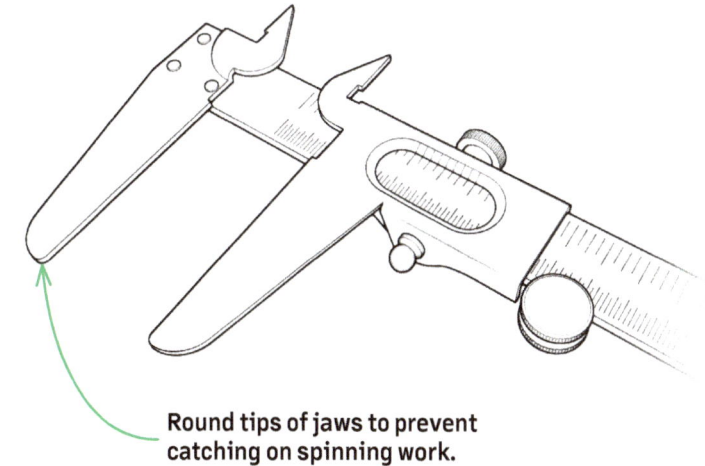
Round tips of jaws to prevent catching on spinning work.

TOOLS > LATHE

Banjo holder for a chuck

Sometimes when I'm adding carved or burned details to my turned bowls, I find it easier to hold the work upright. To facilitate this, I've found that I can use my lathe's banjo as a sort of bracket to hold work that's still secured to a chuck or faceplate. To create the setup, first cut the head off a large bolt whose threads match those on your lathe spindle, and install a nut to serve as a shoulder. Now, when you want to hold work-in-process horizontally, just unscrew the chuck or faceplate from your headstock spindle, thread it onto the headless bolt, adjust the nut against the chuck, and slip the assembly into the banjo hole. (If your spindle diameter doesn't match your banjo hole, buy an adapter that will connect two appropriately sized bolts.) As an added benefit, I find that switching out different-sized chuck jaws is much more easily done when the chuck is held horizontally.

—Jeff Peters, Redgranite, WI

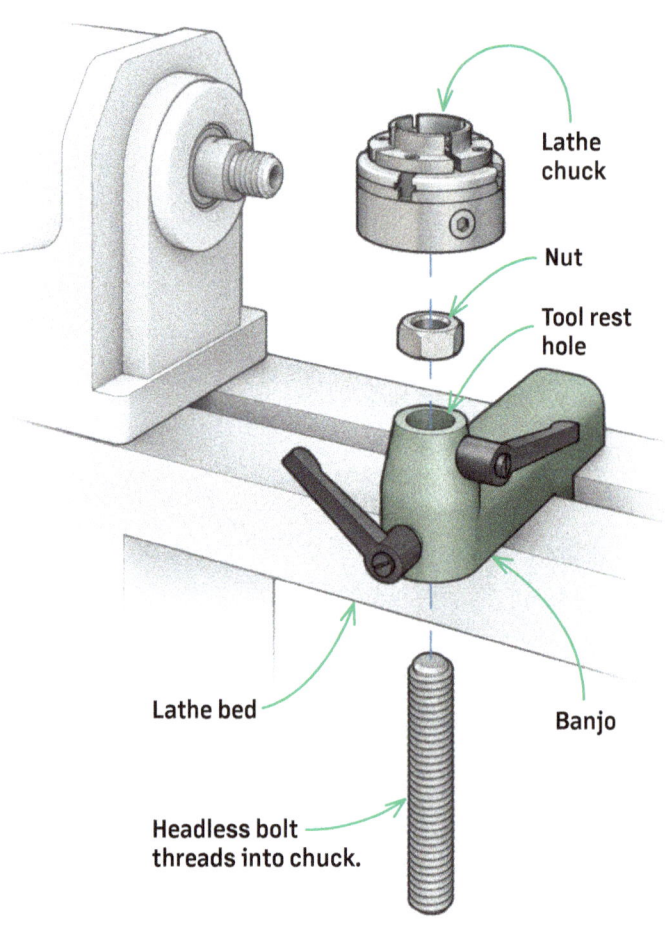

Dogwood uses

What do you do with that dogwood tree in the front yard that has to come down for one reason or another? Even a mature dogwood is generally too small to yield any usable lumber. However, dogwood is a very hard wood that turns cleanly on the lathe and comes out silky smooth. My answer is to save the trunk and large branches to turn wooden mallets (heads and handles) and bench chisel handles. Why not make a set of premium turning or carving tools all with dogwood handles? Guaranteed, they would look beautiful and work great.

—Don Guillard, Parkersburg, WV

Easy faceplate centering

I recently discovered a simple way to locate a faceplate precisely over a center point on the end of a turning blank. I find that a 7/8" Forstner bit fits exactly inside the threads of my 1"- 8 TPI faceplate. With the center point of the bit just protruding from the faceplate, I can position it into a center-punched divot on the end of the blank. Then it's just a matter of holding the faceplate securely at this location while drilling the screw pilot holes. Remove the bit, attach the faceplate, and you're ready to go.
—Bill Wells, Olympia, WA

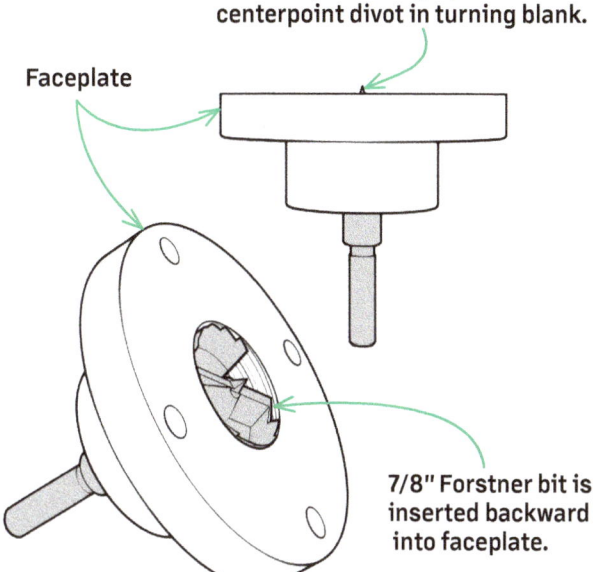

Jumbo Jaw standoffs

Like many turners, I use adjustable, flat-plate Jumbo Jaws to hold a bowl inverted for the final turning of its foot. However, I find that if the rim of a bowl tapers inward, the grip of the rubber buttons against the work can be compromised. My solution is to mount the buttons on "standoffs" I make from 5/8"-diameter dowel rod. The increased reach makes all the difference.

The standoffs can be made to any suitable length, and bored through their axis using a drill chuck on the lathe. For stability, make sure the ends are cut perfectly perpendicular to the length of the dowel. Replace the stock button machine screws with longer versions from the hardware store.

—Eugene H. Schlaman, Charlotte, NC

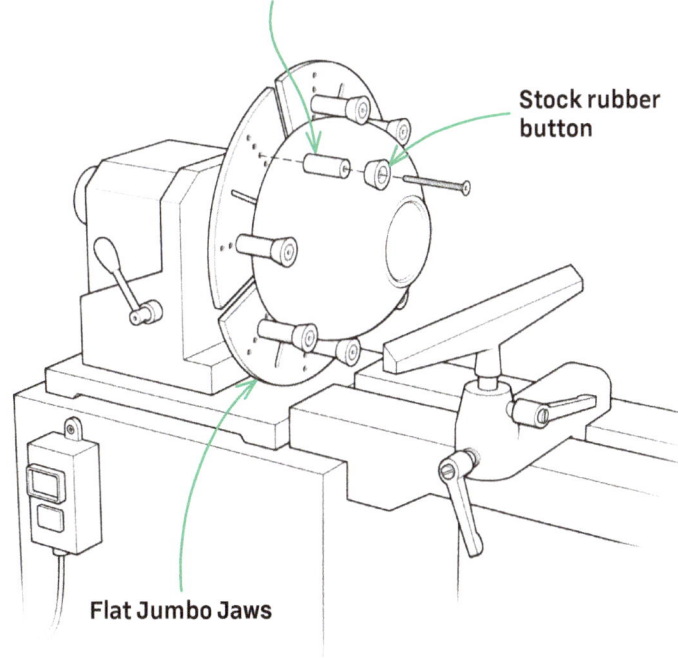

TOOLS > LATHE

Turning with a block plane

As far as turning goes, I'm closer to terrible than terrific. Trying to make eight identical, rather thin spindles for a Shaker stool, I found that I just couldn't get the surface finish and precise diameters that I wanted without resorting to a lot of tedious hand-sanding. About halfway through, I tried using my block plane. With the lathe spinning slowly, I rested the skewed plane on the rough-turned spindle, and moved the tool slowly forward. After a few bumpy passes, it began producing wispy shavings. The resulting finish was super-smooth, and the control afforded by the plane enabled me to turn the spindle diameters that I wanted.

—*Bob Joseph, Birmingham, AL*

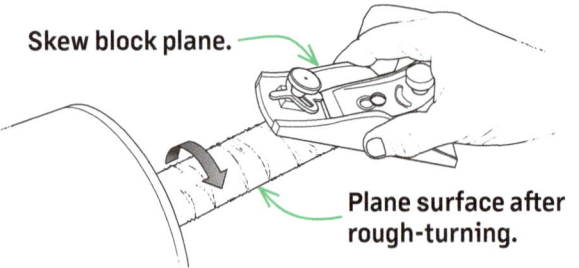

Skew block plane.

Plane surface after rough-turning.

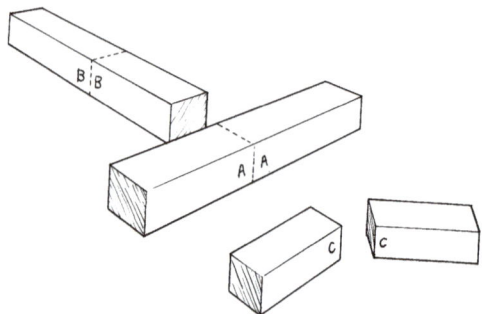

Making a perfect match

I turn a lot of pens as gifts for family and friends, and use a lot of nicely grained woods such as olive and zebrawood. To me, it shows far better craftsmanship if the woodgrain matches on each pen piece. Before I cut the blank in half, I will always mark the center of the blank with a pair of numbers or letters, then cut right between the marks. That way, it's easy to keep the two matched pieces of blanks together until they're securely mounted on the lathe. After turning, the two halves will meet in the middle and match with a perfect grain pattern.

—*Tom Hill, Van Buren, AR*

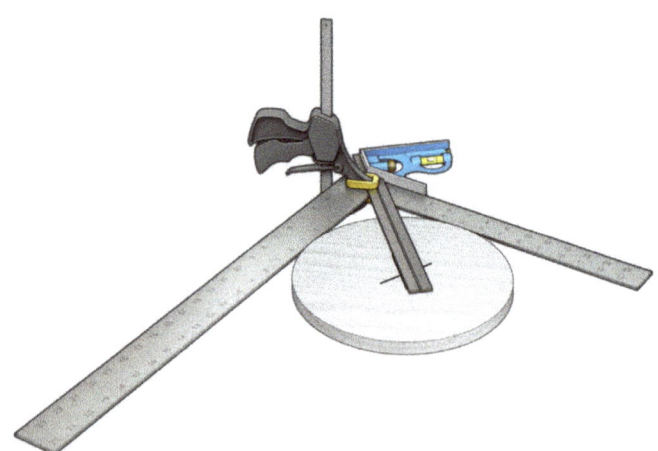

Large-scale center finder

Plastic center finders are great for spindle turnings and smaller bowl blanks, but won't work for larger blanks such as those for platters. For those, I make a bigger version by clamping a combination square to a framing square with the combo square's blade aligned with the vertex of the framing square, as shown. Draw two intersecting lines along the combo-square's blade to mark the center.

—*Richard Entwistle, Highland Lakes, NJ*

LATHE < TOOLS

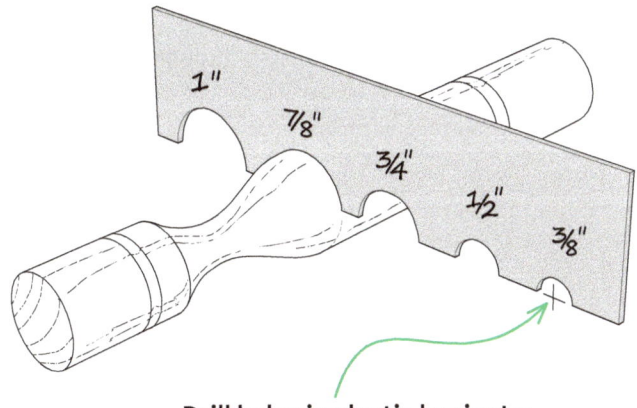

Drill holes in plastic laminate; bisect on saw.

A shop-made lathe gauge

I do a lot of spindle-turning at the lathe, and find myself turning sections and details to the same common diameters time and again. Rather than constantly resetting my calipers, I devised a gauge for these diameters, making it from plastic laminate, which is thin enough to slip into parted areas and in between beads.

Making a gauge like this is easy. Begin with an oversized scrap of plastic laminate for safe handling. Lay out the centers for the desired diameters along a line drawn parallel to one edge. Bore out the holes on the drill press, and then saw through the centerline. Finish up by trimming the gauge to a convenient size.

—Mark Pilsner, Milwaukee, WI

Keeping cool at the lathe

When sanding turnings on a spinning lathe, I often use my fingers instead of a pad to back up the sandpaper, especially for coves, beads, and other detailed surfaces. But, as any turner knows, it's a hot operation. When I spied a package of "rubber fingertips" at my local office supply store, I knew that I'd found a solution to the problem. Designed for nimble handling of money and paper, these nibbed thimbles proved to provide heat protection for lathe sanding. They're also effective when using a cabinet scraper, providing a good grip while keeping your fingertips cool.

—Charles Mak, Calgary, Alberta

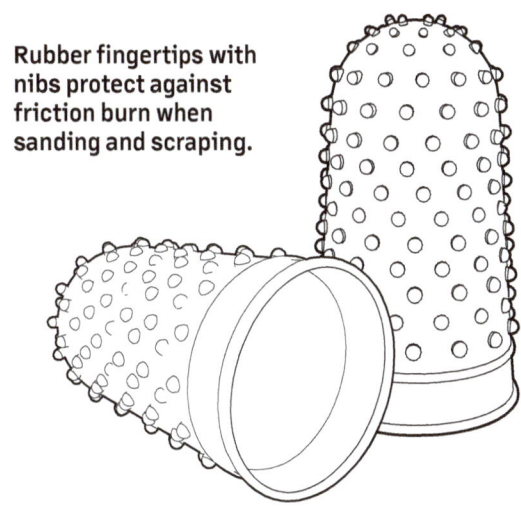

Rubber fingertips with nibs protect against friction burn when sanding and scraping.

Morse taper as jam chuck

Here's an easy way to make custom-sized dowels on a lathe using squared stock that's too small to hold with a spur or jawed drive chuck. Just remove the chuck, and use the Morse taper in the drive spindle as a jam chuck of sorts. (A #2 Morse taper will snugly accommodate a 5/8"-square blank.) Push one end of a wannabe dowel into the tapered recess, center other end on the tailstock, and turn.

—Mikey Panicky, Ventura, CA

WOODCRAFT MAGAZINE TIPS & TRICKS FOR WOODWORKING

TOOLS > LATHE

See-through bowl blank template

I use a round 3/8"-thick acrylic template with lines scribed on it at 1/2" intervals to lay out bowl blanks. It helps me see and avoid checks and knots while including areas of attractive grain. (The template's diameter matches my lathe's capacity.) To make the disc, I marked the center, the perimeter, and the 1/2" increments, and then cut the shape on the bandsaw. I drilled a pilot hole in the center and mounted the disc on a faceplate on my lathe, using the tailstock to center the piece. With the lathe running slowly, I lightly scribed the incremental circles with a parting tool.

To lay out a bowl blank, I position the template strategically on the stock, mark the center through the template, and note the desired diameter. After removing the template, I mark out the circle using a layout stick made for that purpose. The stick has a screw at the pivoting end and a row of holes spaced 1/2" apart, sized to accept the tip of a marker.

—Chris McKee, Landisville, PA

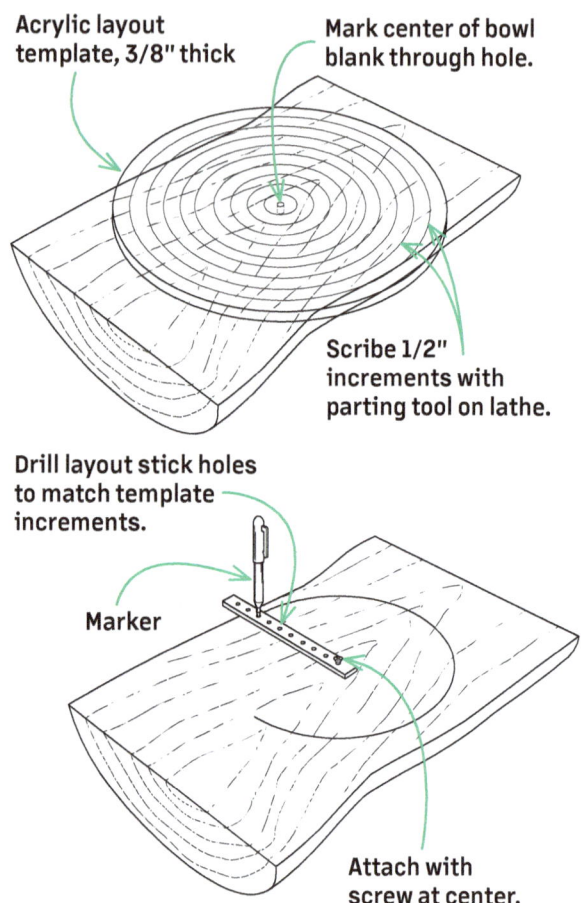

Piloting a Forstner bit

When drilling out a salt shaker interior on the lathe recently, I was having trouble keeping the Forstner bit traveling on center. I wondered if the old metal-working trick of drilling a large hole by starting with a smaller one might help. Sure enough, a 1/8"-diameter hole drilled though the axis of my shaker blank was enough to guide the tip on the Forstner bit to keep it on track.

—Ben Kerr, Minneapolis, MN

No-marks faceplate

To prevent marring of workpieces when using faceplates on the lathe, use a bit of hot melt glue to attach wood false faceplates to bowls and plates for turning. The false faceplates can be removed from the workpiece more easily and cleanly if you place the two in the freezer for 30 minutes. If some glue still adheres to the turned project, it is easy to remove with a little mineral spirits or paint thinner. It also comes off more cleanly if the bottom of the turning has been fine-sanded.

—John Williams, Kingston, Ontario

Spindle splint

Turners of all experience levels know how quickly and easily a skew chisel can dig into a bead, ruining the entire workpiece. For that reason, I'll factor in a little "catch insurance" when doing complex turnings or making a set of legs. To do this, all you need is a blank that's a little long. Before mounting it to your lathe, use a mitersaw to square an end, and then trim off a small slice, about 1" long.

When a catch happens (and sooner or later, it will), drill a hole though the center of the offcut; then break the piece in half along the grain line. Next, turn down the damaged section with a parting tool so that the offcut can wrap the spindle. Glue the patch to the spindle, and then turn the section when the patch has dried.

Since the offcut is from the same piece, the patch should be a perfect match.

—Tommy MacDonald, Boston, MA

Ruined bead

Replacement bead

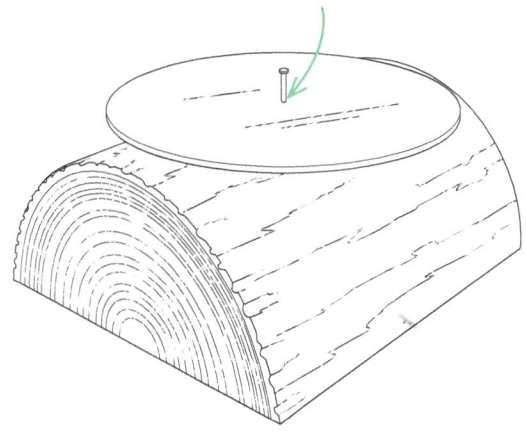

Nail template to half-round blank; then bandsaw around perimeter to create round bowl blank.

Bowl blank templates

When turning bowls, I like to rough out the round shape on the bandsaw first. The problem is that it's difficult to mark out the shape on a half-round blank that must be fed flat side down for safety on the saw. My approach is to first create a circular pattern from 1/8"-thick hardboard, with a 1/8"-diameter hole at its center. I nail the pattern to my blank through the center hole, and then bandsaw just outside the edges of the pattern to create the round blank. (Leave the nail proud for easy removal.) Afterward, I place the pattern onto the flat side of the blank, and mark through the hole to establish the center on that face for quick, accurate mounting on the lathe.

For convenience, I made a series of these patterns in 1"-diameter increments from 4" to 24", which is the limit of my lathe capacity. I just draw them out and bandsaw them to shape. They don't have to be terrifically accurate since they're just a rough guide.

—Mike Kehs, Quakertown, PA

Better faceplate mounting

When I started turning years ago, I learned to glue a piece of standard paper (about .004" thick) between my bowl blank and the mounting block for easy separation of the finished piece. Unfortunately, I found that the technique worked a little too well, often releasing the bowl before I was ready to dismount it. I soon realized that the solution was to cut the paper discs about 1-1/4" smaller in diameter than the mounting block. This leaves a solid band of glued wood-to-wood contact at the perimeter of the block to keep the bowl solidly attached during turning. When I'm ready to remove it, I use a parting tool to cut into the seam down to the paper. At that point, a bump with the heel of a hand will pop the bowl free.

—Ken Burton, New Tripoli, PA

Tighter threads for smoother turnings

After some detective work, I discovered that the minor vibration issues that I was having with my lathe were because the 1" × 8 TPI threaded headstock wasn't providing adequate metal-to-metal contact with screw-on chucks and faceplates. Consequently, they tended to wiggle a bit in use. To correct this problem, I now wrap the headstock's threads with plumber's Teflon tape. In addition to making a more solid fit, the tape lubricates the threads, easing removal of the chuck when I'm done.

—Craig Borgman, Plymouth, MN

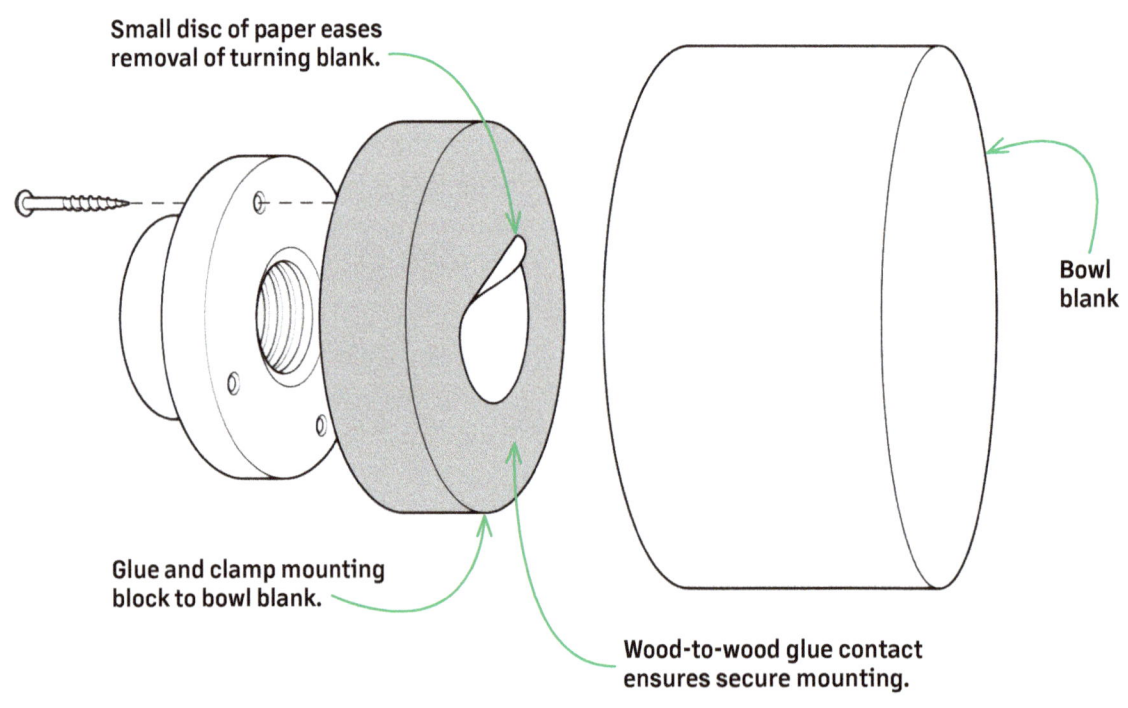

Small disc of paper eases removal of turning blank.

Glue and clamp mounting block to bowl blank.

Wood-to-wood glue contact ensures secure mounting.

Bowl blank

MITERSAW

No-fuzz mitersaw cuts

The mitersaw can do a great job of precision cutting, but the blade can tear out wood fibers where it exits the wood. This often gives a fuzzy appearance to the stock face resting on the table and the edge on the fence. Fortunately, you can solve this problem by attaching an auxiliary fence and table surface with double-sided tape.

Make the auxiliary fence from a piece of 1/2"-thick scrap plywood. It can be longer than your saw's metal fence, but make sure that its height doesn't interfere with your saw's blade or guard. Use a piece of 1/4" plywood or hardboard for the table.

After you've attached the fence and table, your first saw cut makes a kerf that keeps your workpiece supported right up to the cutline, minimizing tear out. As an added benefit, the kerf shows the cutline exactly, enabling you to quickly position your stock for line-splitting accuracy.

—*David Smithson, Syracuse, NY*

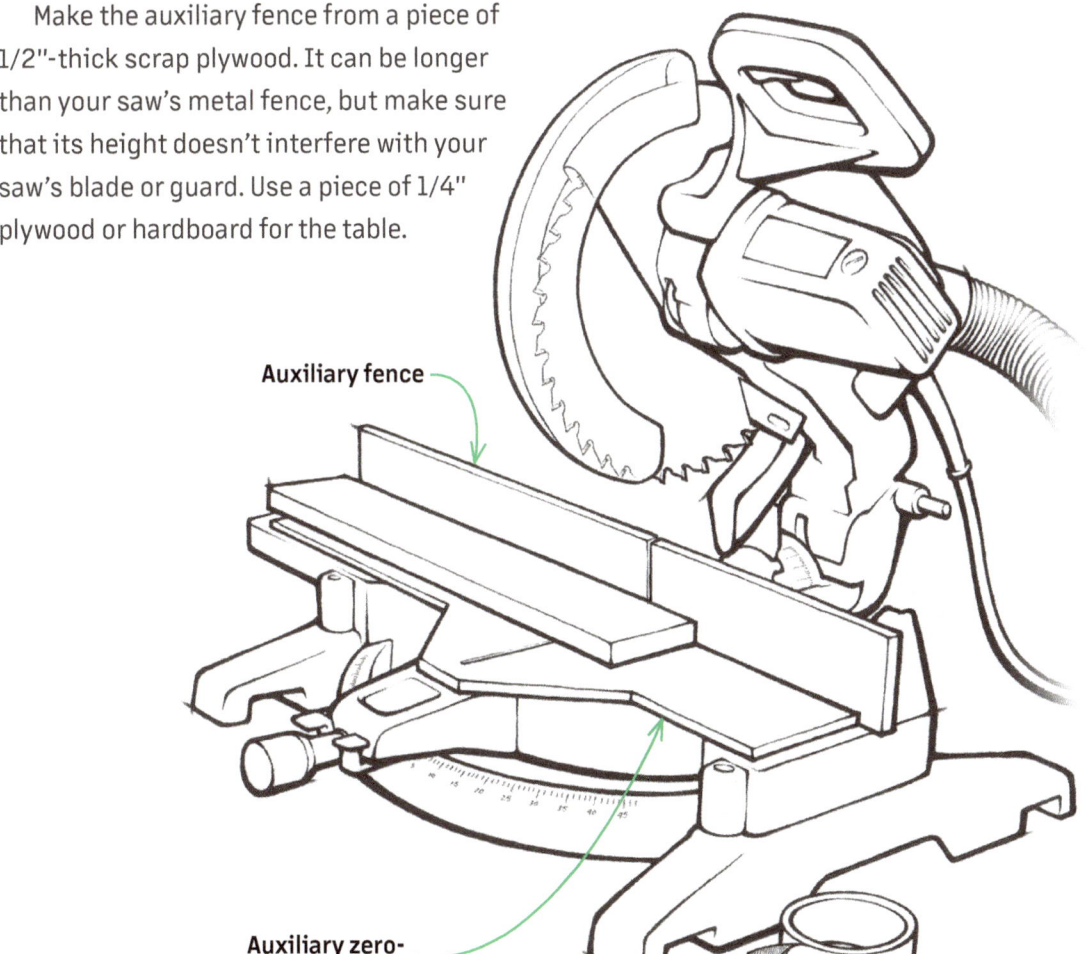

No-spin dowel mitersawing

Most woodworkers know that crosscutting dowels on a miter saw can be dicey because the blade can grab the piece and spin it out of your hands. To prevent this, you can secure the piece in a sandpaper-lined wooden V-cradle, or temporarily affix self-adhesive sandpaper to your fence and table. However, I've found that the quickest approach is to simply press the dowel in place against a scrap of nonslip bench padding like that used for routing and sanding.

—Charles Mak, Calgary, Alberta

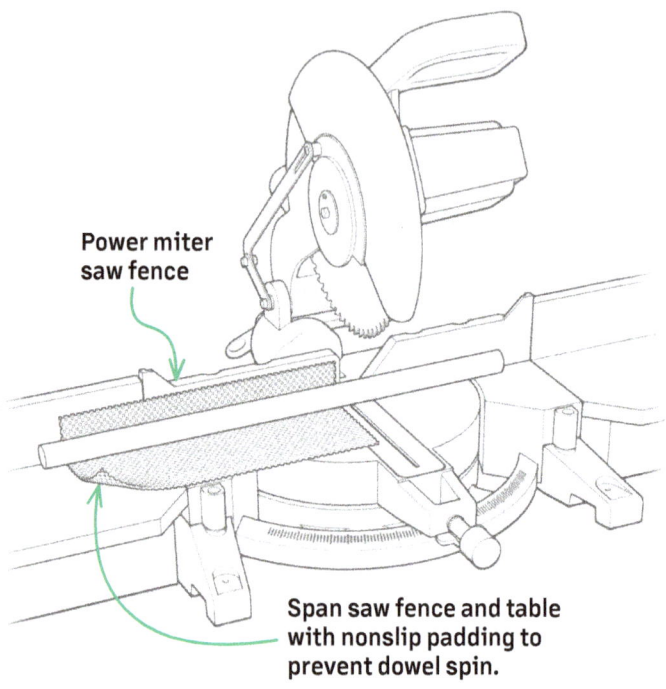

Power miter saw fence

Span saw fence and table with nonslip padding to prevent dowel spin.

Crosscutting short pieces

Over the years, I've seen a variety of jigs for holding short pieces to be crosscut on a power mitersaw. Some incorporate toggle clamps and other hold-downs to secure the work while keeping your hands a safe distance from the blade.

These setups are fine for guys who love to make jigs. Me, I like to keep things simple. I usually crosscut small pieces using a technique I call "bridge-clamping." All you need is a short piece of wood the same width as the one you're cutting and a stout stick at least 12" long. Position your workpiece for the cut; firmly hold it in place by bridging over from the fulcrum scrap as shown, keeping your hand a safe distance from the blade. This same technique works on a crosscut sled or miter gauge extension fence.

—Peter Ashton, Sacramento, CA

"Fulcrum" scrap matches width of workpiece.

"Bridge" scrap holds workpiece against fence, with hands at safe distance.

Short workpiece

Crosscutting short multiples

A while ago, I was making wooden tabletop clips and needed to crosscut multiple short pieces to identical lengths. Marking individual cutlines would have taken too much time, so I decided to set up a stopblock on my power mitersaw. Unfortunately, at the end of the cut, the saw would jettison (and often ruin) the freed piece, which had been trapped between the blade and the stopblock.

After a bit of head scratching, I realized that the fix was to set up the cut with a removable spacer between the stopblock and the end of the workpiece. Hold the workpiece firmly against the fence and stopblock while removing the spacer. Now the sawn piece has room to fall freely away from the blade at the end of the cut. To further minimize the chance of kickback, allow the blade to stop fully before raising it out of the cut.

—Ralph Burns, Montgomery, AL

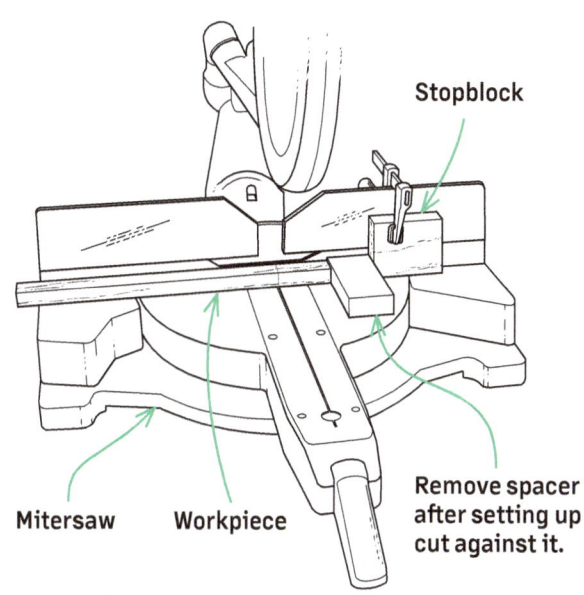

Long-arm miter stop

I came up with this long-arm stop on a job site in order to cut deck balusters, but found that it was just as useful in my small garage workshop. Held in place by the saw's hold-down clamp, the jig provides a reliable stop (for accuracy) and support (the workpiece can't tip and split at the end of the cut). The auxiliary fence also enables you to install a toggle clamp closer to the saw blade for better stock control.

The stopblock is glued to the end of the auxiliary fence. To adjust the cutting length, slide the jig fence along your saw and reclamp. Adjust the saw's depth of cut so that the blade doesn't slice through the fence, and you can use the stop for a long time before it needs to be replaced.

—Patrick Breen, Providence, RI

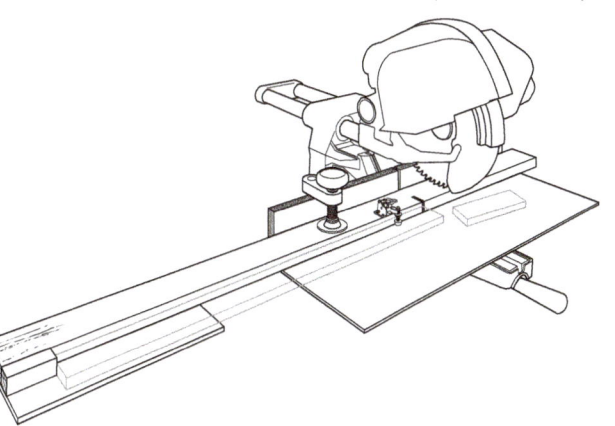

TOOLS > MITERSAW

Mitersaw flip-stop

Clamping a stopblock to the right-hand side of a power mitersaw blade to register short multiple workpieces can be dicey. That's because the freed workpiece becomes trapped between the blade and the block, inviting kickback. Although you could set up the cut by placing a removable spacer against the stopblock, I find it more efficient to use a flip-stop.

Here's a very effective flip-stop made from two blocks of wood connected with a shutter hinge. To use it, simply locate the stop where desired, and then clamp the fixed block to your saw fence. Set up the cut by butting your workpiece against the flip-stop, and then lift it up out of the way before making the cut.

The wraparound shutter hinge, also known as an interior shutter hinge with L-leaf, is crucial to the jig's operation. This hinge's low pivot point produces an arc that allows the stop to swing clear without pushing against and shifting the workpiece—almost. To create the needed clearance, simply cut a 1/16" chamfer on the bottom corner of the block.

—*John Cusimano, Lansdale, PA*

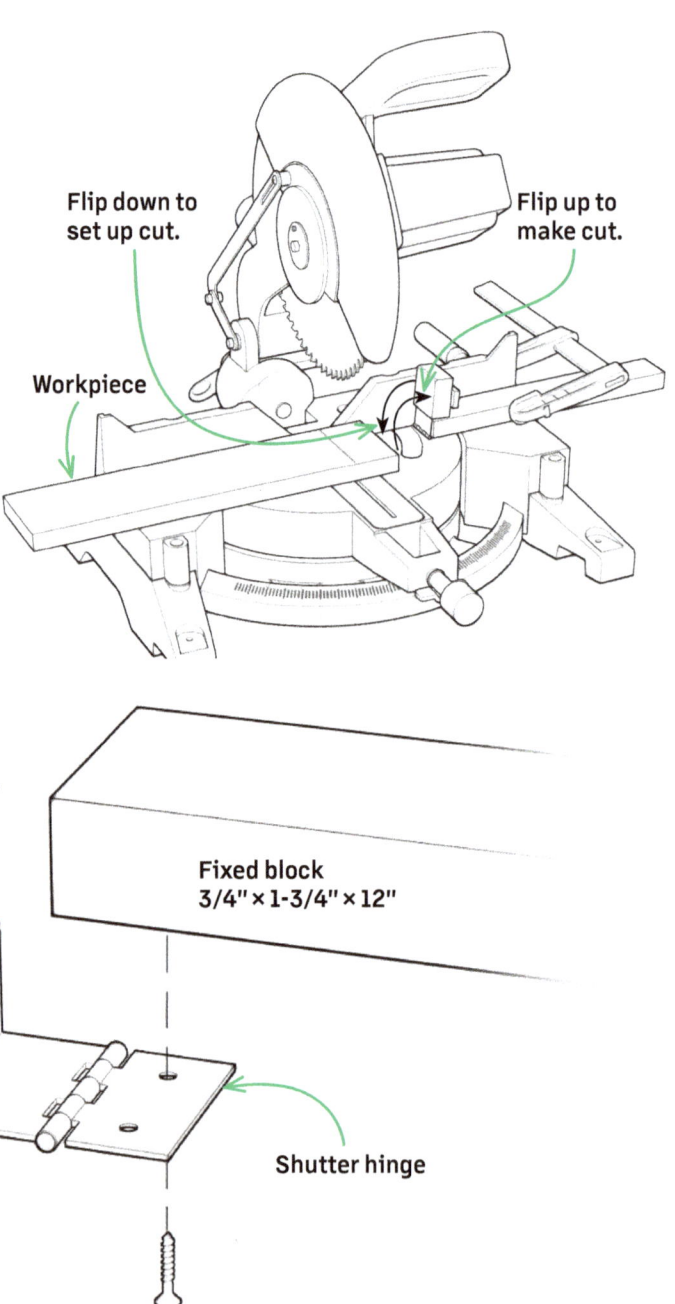

128 *WOODCRAFT MAGAZINE* TIPS & TRICKS FOR WOODWORKING

OTHER POWER TOOLS

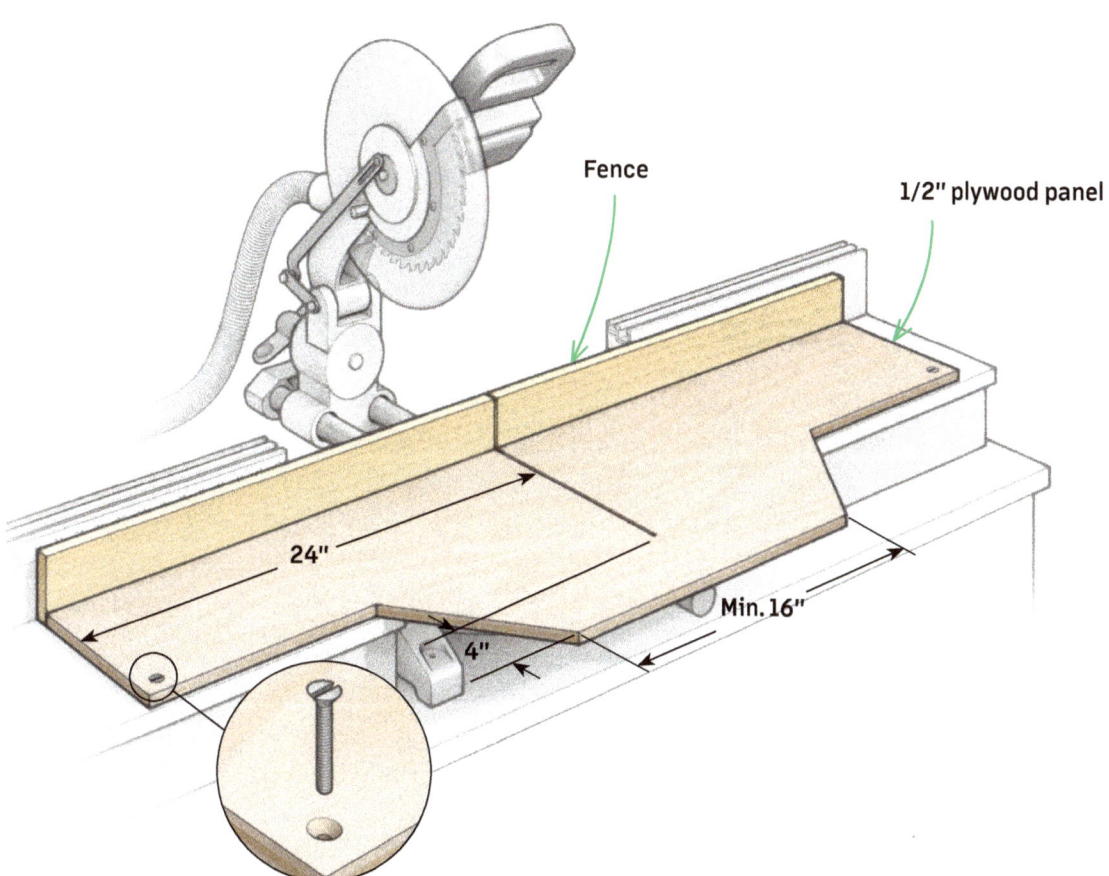

Zero-clearance chop saw overlay

Here's a great accessory for minimizing tear out when making 90° cuts on your power miter saw. Start with a 48" length of 1/2" hardwood plywood with one dead-straight edge. Make its overall width about 4" more than the crosscut capacity of your saw. Leave the center section of this platform 16" wide, but taper the ends back to form wings as shown. Glue a fence to the panel's rear edge, making sure its face is square to the surface of the panel. Center the completed overlay on the saw and clamp it in place. Next, drill and countersink a 1/4"-diameter hole through each end of the platform into the saw's fixed extension tables. Drop a 1/4" flat-head machine screw into each hole to secure and locate the platform. Done. I remove the overlay when making angled cuts, which would chew up the fence. To reinstall it, I just slip the machine screws in place—no nuts or clamps needed.

—*Mark Spurn, Indianapolis, IN*

TOOLS > OTHER POWER TOOLS

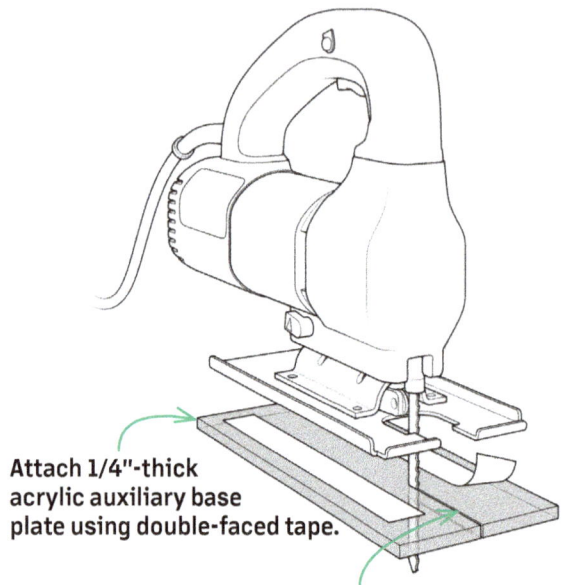

Attach 1/4"-thick acrylic auxiliary base plate using double-faced tape.

Zero-clearance blade slot holds down wood fibers for splinter-free cuts.

Zero-clearance jigsaw base

Some jigsaw manufacturers offer zero-clearance inserts that pop into place in a saw's base to hug the blade, minimizing tear out by holding down wood fibers at the edge of the saw kerf. If a commercial version isn't available for your particular saw model, you can make an auxiliary base plate with a zero-clearance blade slot to do the same job. Begin by cutting a piece of 1/4"-thick clear acrylic or polycarbonate to roughly the size of your tool's base plate. Lay out and saw a blade slot using the bandsaw or your jigsaw, lightly sanding away any melted plastic burrs at the edges afterward. Attach the new plate to the bottom of your saw with double-faced tape, and you're good to go for splinter-free cuts. When making my base plate, I took the opportunity to extend it 1/2" forward of the existing base to provide more workpiece contact when starting a cut.

—Andy Rae, Asheville, NC

Quick circular saw track setup for multiples

In my crowded, cramped shop, it can be difficult to rip long pieces from full-sized sheet goods using the table saw. That's when I turn to my track-guided portable circular saw. Although this eliminates the hassle of wrangling work onto the table saw, I don't have the convenience of using its rip fence for quickly sawing multiple pieces to the same precise width. When faced with sawing a bunch of identical cabinet sides recently, I cobbled up a pair of T-shaped spacers that allowed for quick, accurate, repetitive track setup. Registered against the edge of the stock, the spacers ensured that the track is parallel to the edge, and that all resulting cuts were the same width. The spacers are simple to make; just ensure that their length includes the width of the saw kerf and that they're wide enough to provide a solid, reliable reference when setting the track.

—Joe Hurst-Wajszczuk, Birmingham, AL

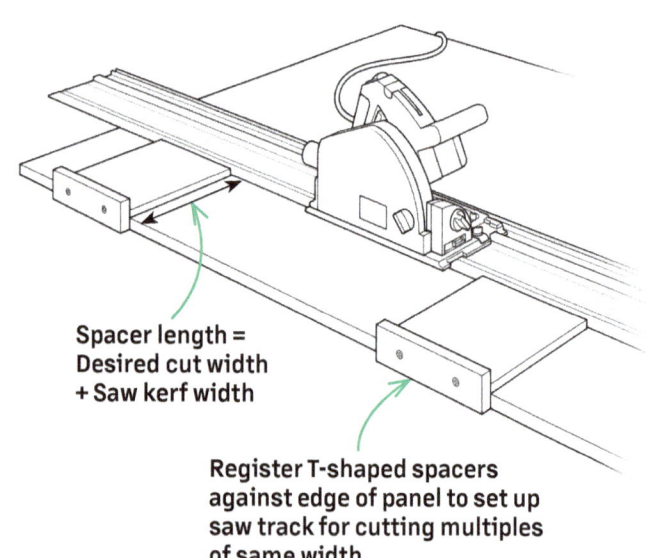

Spacer length = Desired cut width + Saw kerf width

Register T-shaped spacers against edge of panel to set up saw track for cutting multiples of same width.

Dead-setting a hollow chisel mortiser

When setting up a hollow chisel mortiser, it's crucial that the chisel is perfectly aligned to the fence to ensure straight, smooth mortise walls for a strong glue bond. Using a square to do the job hasn't always yielded consistent results, especially with small chisels. To solve this issue, I made a simple hardwood gauge that effectively multiplies the width of the chisel wall facing the fence. To use the gauge, place it against the lowered chisel, and bring the fence forward, rotating the chisel until the gauge contacts the fence at both ends. Tighten the chisel-locking screw to ensure perfect chisel-to-fence alignment, and offset the fence as necessary for the cut.

—*Gerald Welf, Fridley, MN*

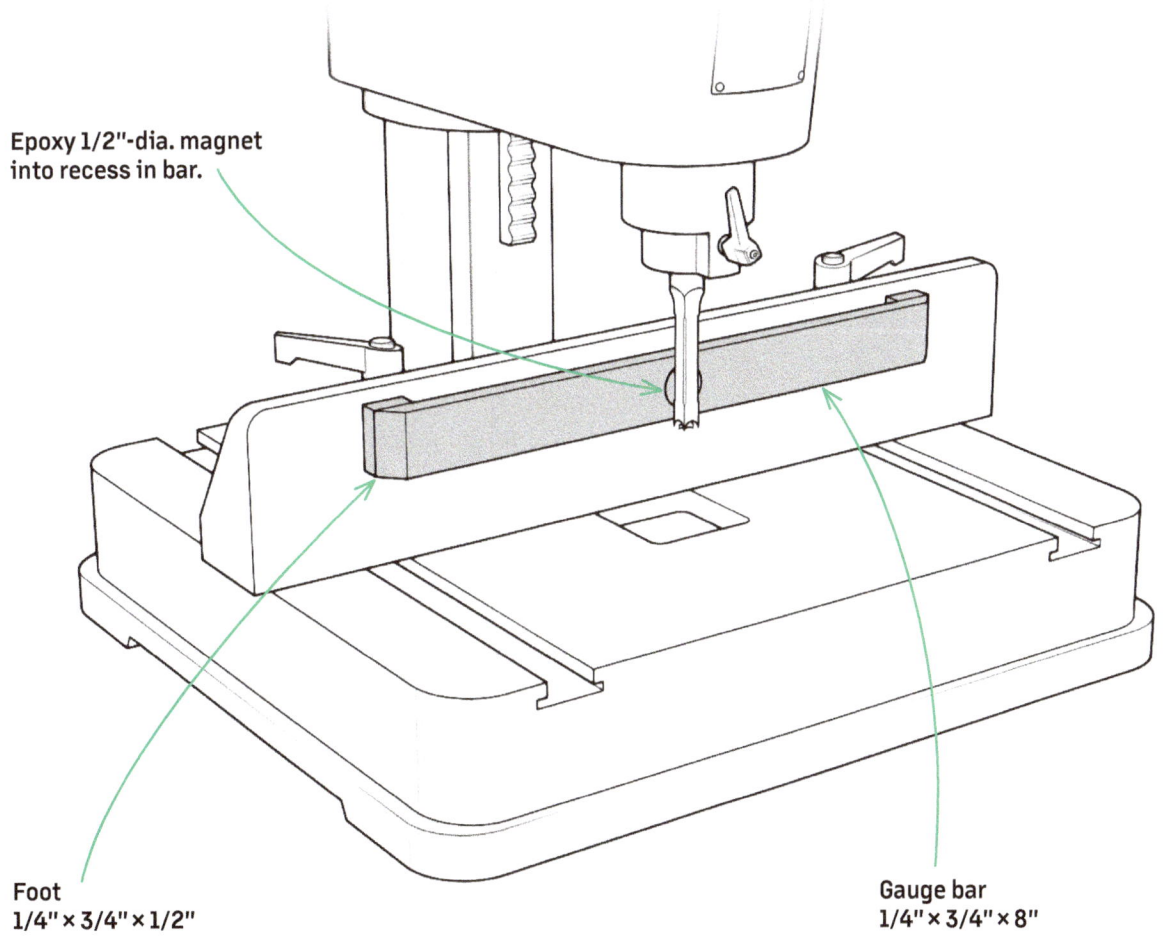

Epoxy 1/2"-dia. magnet into recess in bar.

Foot
1/4" × 3/4" × 1/2"

Gauge bar
1/4" × 3/4" × 8"

Keep nail gun pins pointed in the right direction

The pins used with 21- and 23-gauge guns are so small that it's very difficult to determine the angled tip end from the non-existent head end. Knowing this, some nail manufacturers print directional arrows on the side of the strip. These arrows work well, until you've fired through that section.

To provide a can't-miss reference, use a permanent pen to draw arrows on each strip to indicate which end goes down. Doing this will not only prevent an upside-down clip, but will encourage you to use up those partially-used strips that litter the bottom of your toolbox because you can't see which end to shoot into the wood.

—Joe Schambow, Montclair, NJ

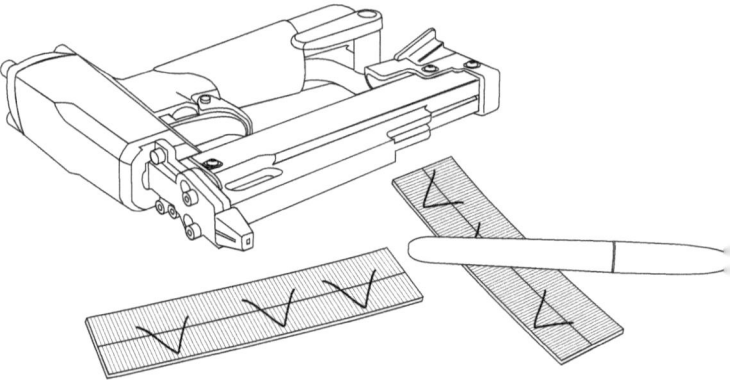

Scrollsaw vac attachment

While many scrollsaws have accessories that blow dust away from the cut, doing so only means future cleanup. My solution solves the sawdust problem. I positioned the end of an extra crevice tool for my shop vac as close as possible to the throat opening (the end of the nozzle may be modified to suit the purpose if necessary) and attached it to the trunnion of the saw with a 1/4"-20 U bolt, washers, and two four-prong plastic knobs. It does not interfere with blade changing or minor tilting of the table, and gets 99% of the dust. (Your particular scrollsaw may require slightly different hardware.)

—Craig W. Bentzley, Chalfont, PA

Perfect height on the shaper

I've found a way to save setup time and improve accuracy when switching between stile and rail cutters on my 3-horsepower shaper for specific projects. I simply have each set of cutters on its own spindle. After initial setup with shims, all I need to do is replace one spindle with the other, and the cutting heights match perfectly.

—Paul Daigle, Cohasset, MN

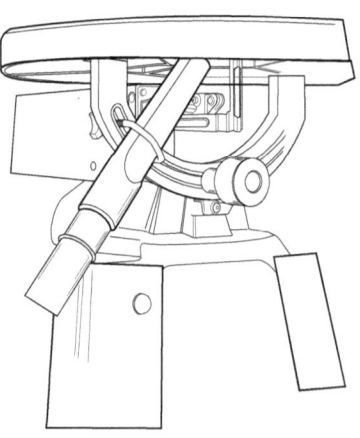

Clamp-free circular saw guide

When it comes to shop-made guides for portable circular saws, there are two important criteria: The guide must track the saw accurately, and the edge of the guide must align perfectly with the blade so that no offset needs to be calculated when setting up a cut. For tracking purposes, my 3/4"-thick guide includes a 3/4"-wide, 3/8"-deep slot, which guides a wooden runner that screws to my saw base. (When affixing the runner, make sure it's perfectly parallel to the blade.) I made the base oversized initially and then trimmed it to final width with the saw running in its slot. That aligned the edge of the guide with the blade for easy positioning against a cutline. I made the track about 54" long so it generously spans a 4×8' sheet of plywood crosswise.

The real trick here, though, is that this guide does not require clamps to hold its position. Instead, I attached a sheet of rubber nonslip padding to the underside of the base, keeping it back from the edges 1/4" or so. The padding—designed to hold workpieces in place for routing, sanding, and other maneuvers—is simply stapled in a few places along its perimeter. It holds the guide in place remarkably well with no slippage whatsoever that could compromise cut accuracy.

—*Russ Svendsen, Olean, NY*

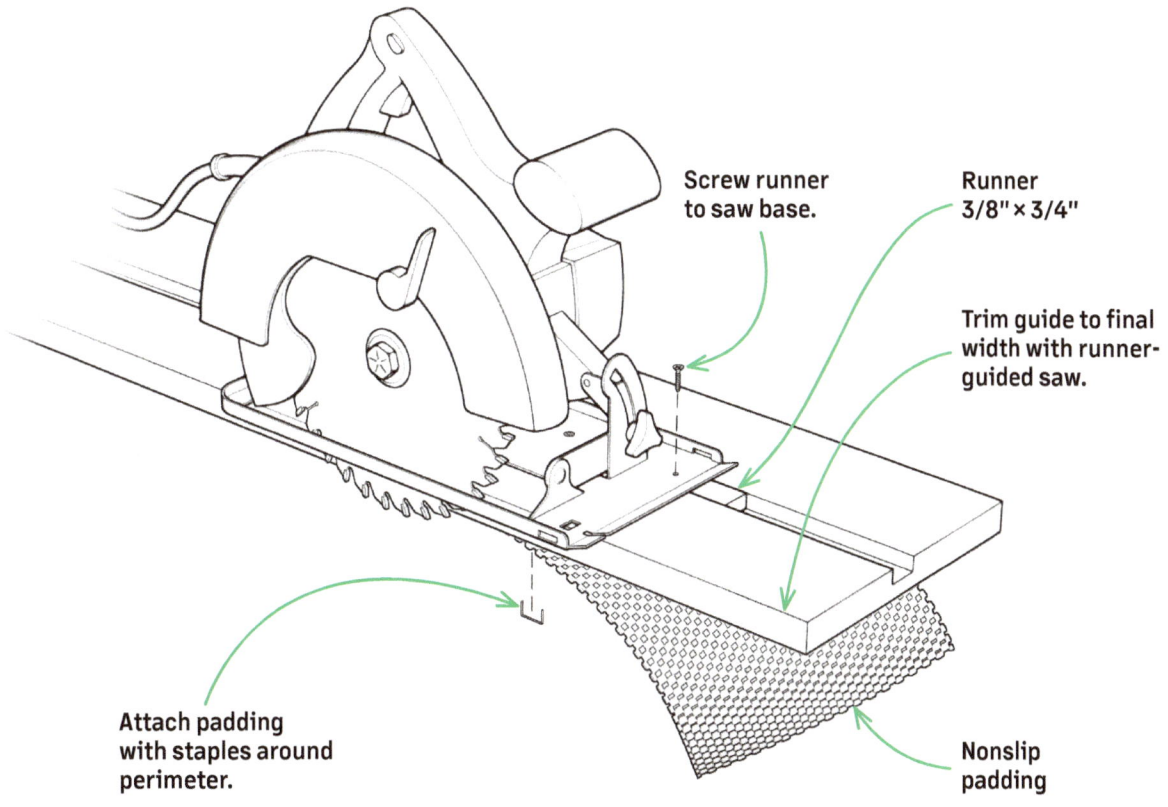

Squaring up a hollow chisel

When setting up a hollow chisel mortiser to make a cut, it's important that the chisel be set square to the machine fence. If it's cocked, your mortise wall won't be flat and smooth, compromising the strength of the joint. To set larger chisels, it's easy enough to press a small machinist's square against the fence and chisel to check the angle. However, getting a read on a smaller chisel this way can be difficult, especially for weak or mature eyes.

Instead, try this: First, secure your fence at the desired distance from the chisel, and place a small rare-earth magnet against the outward face of the chisel. Place a steel 6" rule against the inward face. The ruler serves as a long reference surface for gauging parallelism (and thus square) to the fence. Simply measure to the fence from each end of the ruler, rotating your chisel as necessary to bring the rule and fence into perfect alignment.

—Paul Anthony, Riegelsville, PA

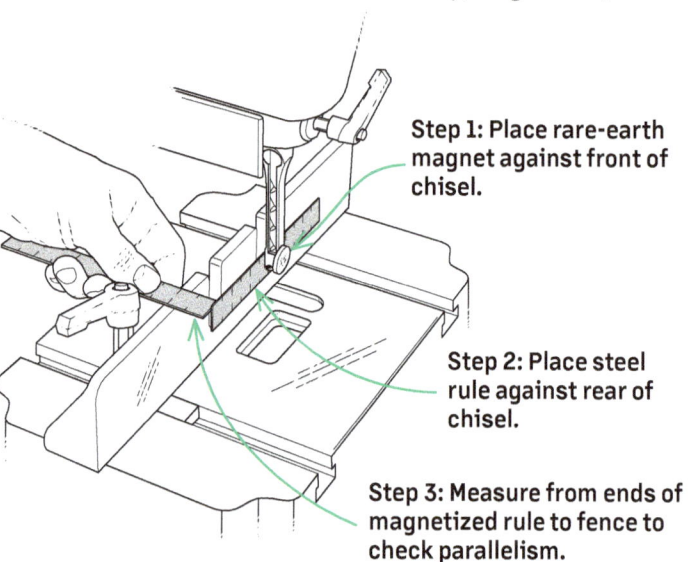

Step 1: Place rare-earth magnet against front of chisel.

Step 2: Place steel rule against rear of chisel.

Step 3: Measure from ends of magnetized rule to fence to check parallelism.

Repurposing a narrow bandsaw blade

You just installed a brand-new 1/8" blade on your bandsaw and are cruising along in the cut when all of a sudden you hear a "snap!" Yep, your blade has broken. If you don't have a welder, that expensive blade would usually go to waste. Not with me. I turn it into scrollsaw blades by using heavy-duty snippers to create lengths that fit my scrollsaw. All that's left is to file down a few teeth at each end to fit between my scrollsaw's blade clamps.

—Danny Lash, Magnolia, TX

Simplify scrollsaw sanding

My co-worker and I found an inexpensive way to make sanding with a scrollsaw easier. Cut 1/4" × 7" strips of emery cloth in varied grits. The length allows an inch at each end to be folded over a nail (we use 5/8" #18 brads) and glued, using wood glue or contact cement. I prefer the wood glue because it does not stick to the nail, allowing easy removal for sanding inside scrollsaw cuts.

The thickness of the doubled-over cloth and nail combined make just the right size to fit in the side slot of your scrollsaw head. They work great together and are so flexible, it is easy to sand both inside and outside radiuses. And you can make several at a time for almost nothing.

—Sydney Geovonti, Rosharon, TX

PLANER

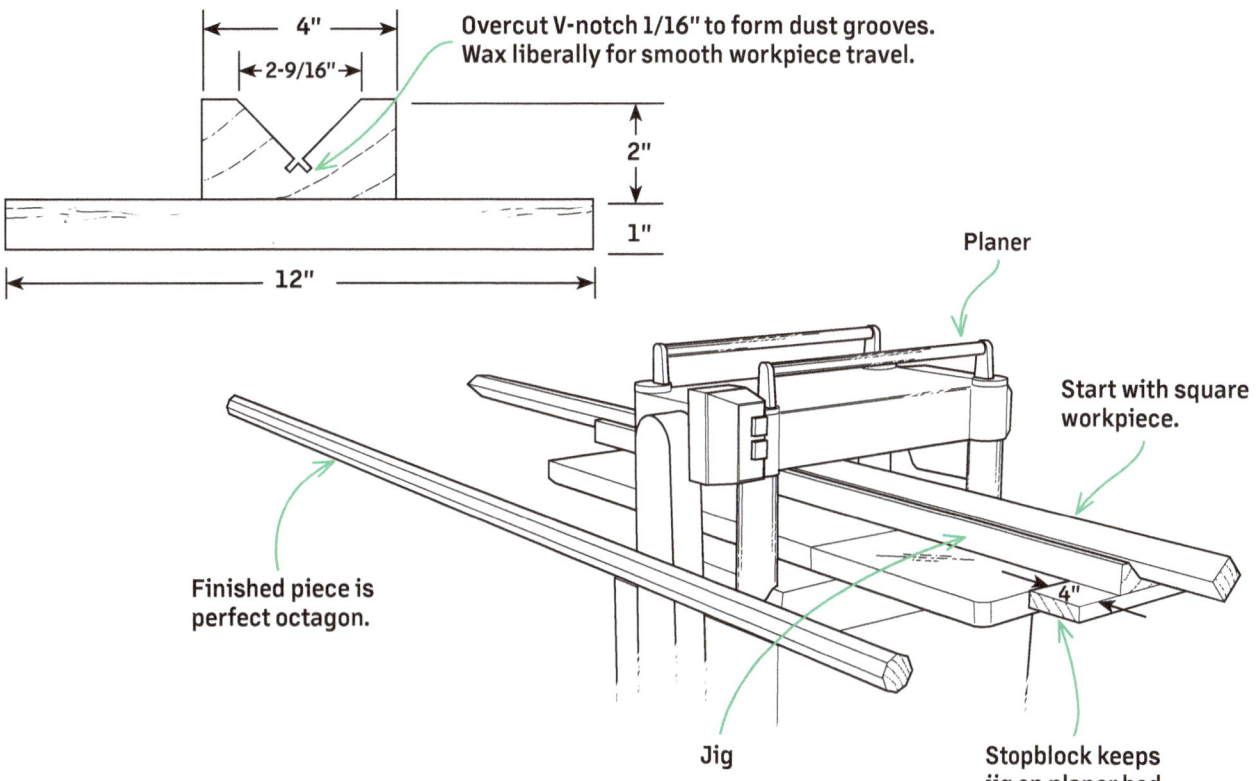

Chamfering on the planer

I needed to make 10'-long tent poles for our Boy Scout troop, and decided to chamfer square stock to create octagonal posts. To do this, I devised a planer jig for the job. It's a 2×4 board with a V-notch to carry the workpiece at 45° to the planer bed. I made the board a bit longer than my planer bed and screwed a stopblock to the trailing end to resist feed roller pull. Waxing the notch ensures smooth workpiece travel, and shallow kerfs at the bottom serve for dust clearance. The jig is also useful for "octoplaning" parts for all sorts of projects, including shelf clocks, trophy stands, and candlesticks.

—Ernie Conover, Parkman, OH

Planing boards short and sweet

Here is technique I use for safe planing of short boards. As any thickness planer manual notes, it's unsafe to feed boards shorter than about 12" through the machine. But there's a simple solution: Use double-faced tape to attach long scrap runners to the workpiece edges, making sure that the runners start off at least as thick as the stock so that the whole assembly will be pulled safely through the planer.

—Adam Swinton, Baltimore, MD

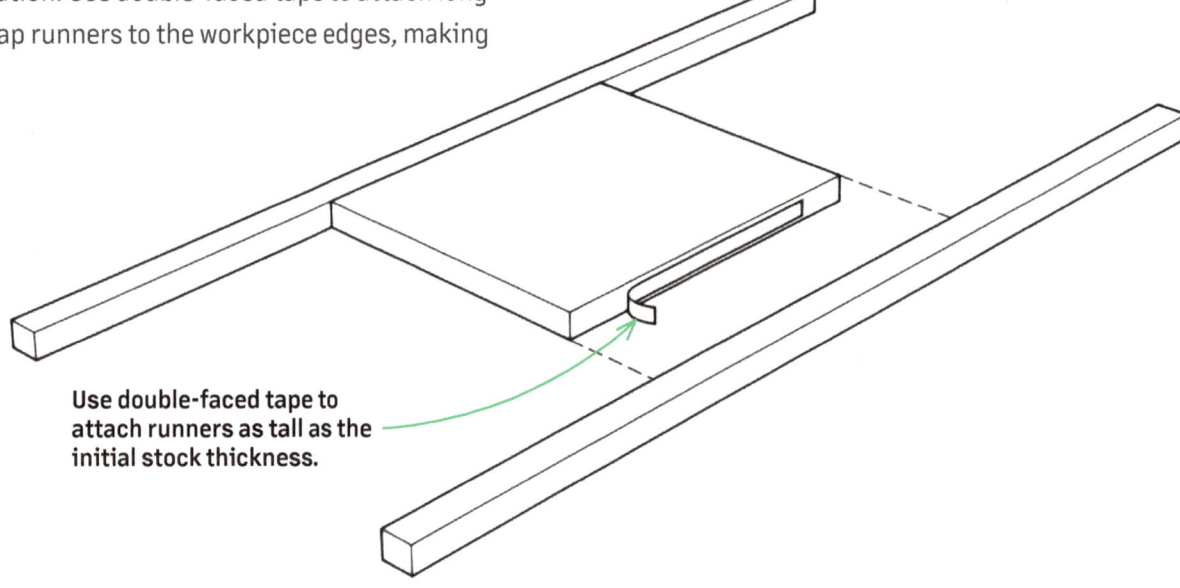

Use double-faced tape to attach runners as tall as the initial stock thickness.

Snipe-free planing

Planer snipe is hard to avoid. Sure, you can cut away the sniped ends, but that's not a good approach with expensive woods. Or you can precede and follow the board with scrap of the same thickness, but that can make for clumsy feeding. Here's a better approach: Joint one face and both edges of the board, and make up four lengths of straight scrap about 10" long and just a bit taller than the desired finished thickness of the board. Working on a dead-flat surface, attach the strips to the edges of the board at both ends using double-faced tape, extending the scraps about 4". (Clamp them for a few moments to ensure a good bond.)

Now, when you feed the board through the planer, the scrap will take the snipe instead of your stock.

—Paul Anthony, Riegelsville, PA

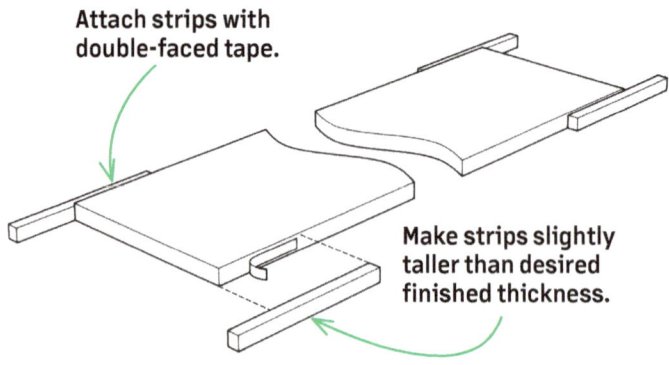

Attach strips with double-faced tape.

Make strips slightly taller than desired finished thickness.

Microfiber grain detector

With certain woods that lack distinct graining, it can be difficult to gauge in which direction to plane to prevent tear out. In these cases, I've found that dragging a microfiber cloth on the surface is very helpful. With most woods, there's a noticeable resistance when the cloth is pulled against the slope of the grain. So, whichever way the cloth moves easiest, that's the direction you want to move the cutter.

—Thomas Moss, Bradenton, FL

Mill some extra

Mill plenty of extra material every time you make parts. Having same-thickness material is great for receiving any planer snipe by feeding them first and last. Extra parts are also key to facilitate easy setup throughout the process and inevitable repairs.

—Larissa Huff, Schwenksville, PA

Planer riser for thin stock

Feeding thin stock through a thickness planer can be problematic for a couple reasons: First of all, the cutterhead on many planers will only lower to within 1/4" of the table, preventing the planing of stock thinner than that. Secondly, some planers have bed rollers—with gaps around them—that can deflect the work upward into the spinning knives, cracking and splintering the stock. This planer riser solves both problems. By elevating the stock, you can plane it as thin as you can get away with (depending on how stiff and mild the wood is). At the same time, the riser covers over any bed rollers.

To ensure flatness, make the riser from 3/4" MDF (medium density fiberboard) or MCP (melamine-coated particleboard). Although they're not strictly necessary, I attach hardwood fences to restrain wayward stock, cutting them out at the feed roller locations. Glue and nail the stop to the infeed end of the platform to prevent it from being pulled into the planer. Finally, apply paste wax to minimize friction when in use.

—Andy Rae, Asheville, NC

Riser panel (3/4" × length of bed × width of planer bed minus 1/2")

Hardwood fence (1/4" × 1" × length of planer bed)

Feed direction

Hardwood stop (1/4" × 1-1/2" × width of planer bed)

Relieve fences to accommodate feed rollers.

ROUTER

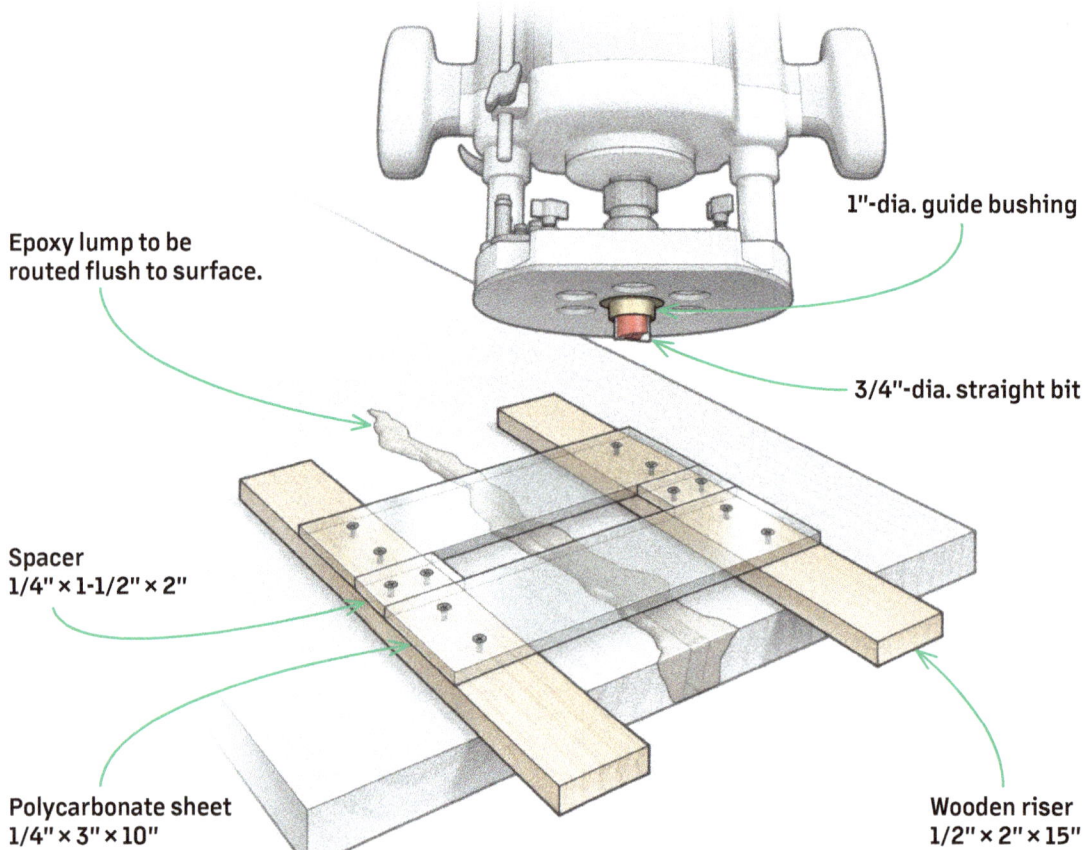

1"-dia. guide bushing

Epoxy lump to be routed flush to surface.

3/4"-dia. straight bit

Spacer
1/4" × 1-1/2" × 2"

Polycarbonate sheet
1/4" × 3" × 10"

Wooden riser
1/2" × 2" × 15"

Flush-routing risers

I recently built a large slab table that required a lot of epoxy filling. I devised this router jig to help with the leveling of the hardened epoxy. The jig consists of four polycarbonate pieces screwed to a couple of maple risers as shown, creating a 1-1/2" × 6" opening in the center. To use the jig, I first outfit my router with a 3/4" -diameter straight bit and a 1"-diameter guide bushing. Then, I position the jig over a lump of hardened epoxy and place the router atop the jig with the bushing corralled by the polycarbonate. After adjusting the bit to just skirt the surface of the work, leveling the epoxy is a simple matter of pushing the router back and forth, moving the jig, and repeating.

—David Diaman, Bel Air, MD

Space Ball is a down-to-earth router fix

I learned early on that you should never let a bit bottom out in the router. That's because tightening the collet nut tends to force the bit deeper, so you need to provide some room for the bit to move or you won't be able to snug it properly.

When you can lay a router on its side, the procedure is fairly easy. But when you're changing bits in a router table, it's easy to run out of hands.

I solve the problem by dropping a single Space Ball down the router's collet. (You usually use these .026"-diameter resilient spheres along the edge of solid-wood door panels to prevent rattling and to accommodate seasonal wood movement without cracking.) I can then drop the end of the bit right onto the ball and tighten the nut. The rubber easily compresses under the pressure, allowing the collet to fully tighten.

—Phil Thiemann, Wilmington, DE

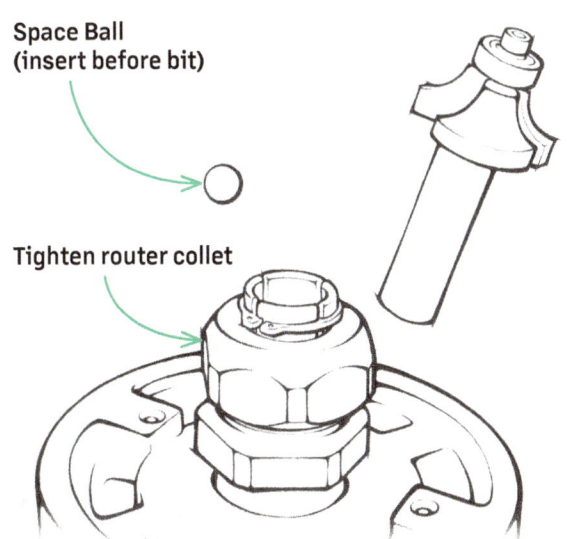

Space Ball (insert before bit)

Tighten router collet

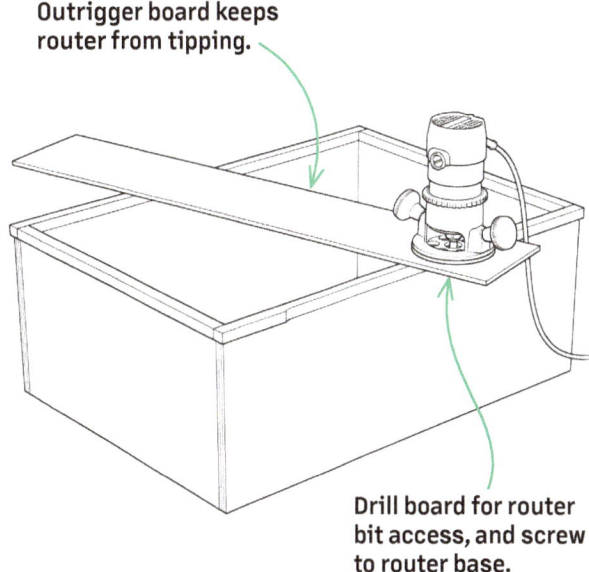

Outrigger board keeps router from tipping.

Drill board for router bit access, and screw to router base.

Router edge stabilizer

When I was outfitting my shop some years ago, I built a bunch of frameless cabinets from 3/4"-thick hardwood plywood, gluing strips of solid wood to the edges to hide the plies. I made the strips about 7/8"-wide so I could use a flush-trim bit to rout their edges flush with the faces of the plywood after attachment. The only difficulty with this approach is that even a small router gets tipsy when riding on the edge of 3/4"-thick stock.

To solve the problem, I mounted my router to a stiff solid-wood board (about 5/16" thick) that was wide enough to accommodate the router and long enough to span the openings of the cabinets. The board then serves as a stabilizing outrigger that rides atop multiple cabinet edges to keep the router from tipping. This makes the whole operation fast, accurate, and free of white knuckles.

—Philip Houck, Boston, MA

TOOLS > ROUTER

Dowel tenoning jig

A recent project that required multiple tenons in 1" oak dowels prompted me to build a jig to machine them on my router table. The jig allows you to feed the dowels through a pair of 1" holes and cut the tenon in much the same way as you'd sharpen a pencil. The two holes provide for a straight alignment while providing support against kickback. The 1/4" dowel pin provides a positive stop so that all tenons are the same length. (I didn't glue the 1/4" dowel in place, so it can be replaced if I adjusted it too close to the router bit and it became damaged.) The "wings" in the back can easily be clamped to the router table to hold the jig securely.

For a finer cut, twist the dowel as you slowly feed it into the bit. Some wax in the holes will reduce friction.

When machining the 1-1/4" × 3" parts, work with longer stock and drill them simultaneously by clamping or taping them together. The parts can then be crosscut to length at the same time if a short scrap of 1" dowel is placed through the holes to keep them aligned. It's also important to mark the top corners of both pieces so that the parts are assembled in the same orientation as they were cut. That way, even if the holes are slightly off-center, you'll still maintain alignment.

You can adjust the size of the holes and all parts to match your needs.

—*Keith Wheeler, Frankfort, IN*

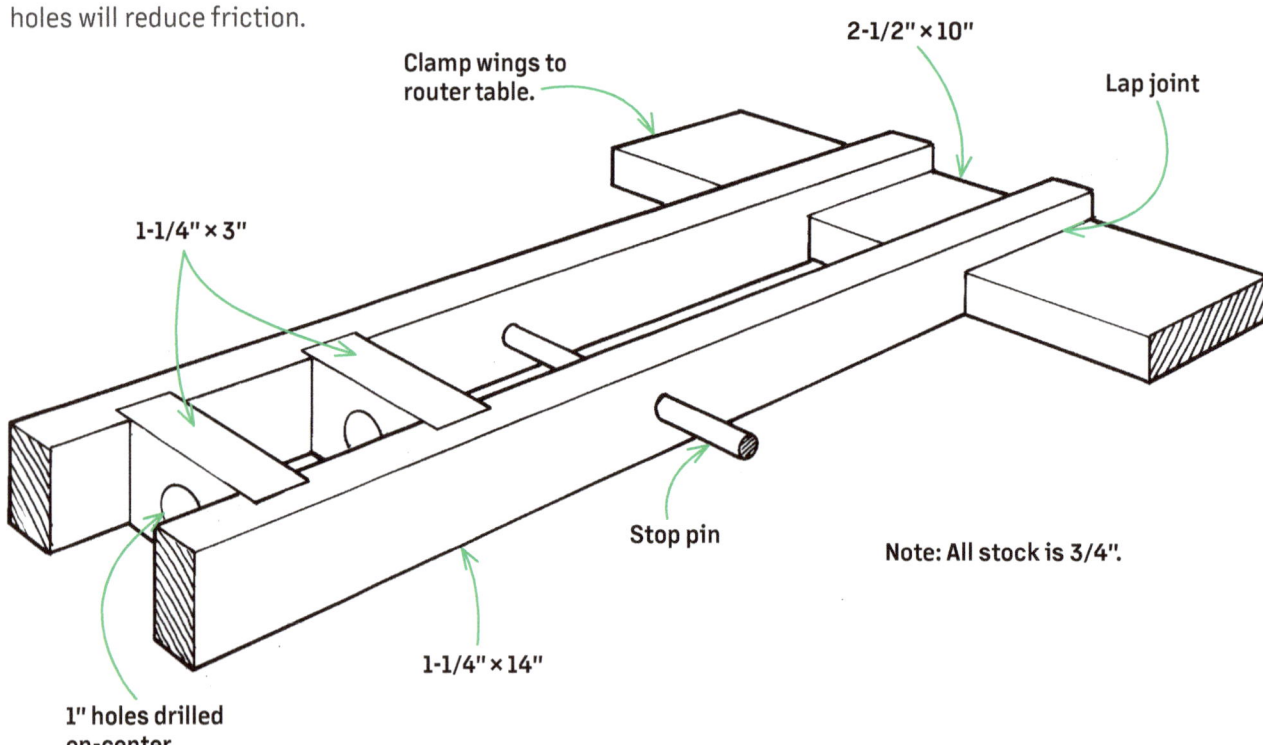

Clamp wings to router table.
2-1/2" × 10"
Lap joint
1-1/4" × 3"
Stop pin
1-1/4" × 14"
1" holes drilled on-center.
Note: All stock is 3/4".

Precision plunging

I've found that the depth gauges on some plunge routers are tricky to read. For the kind of precision needed when routing inlay recesses, for example, I use as a depth gauge a drill bit whose diameter matches my desired depth of cut. With the router bit zeroed out on the workpiece surface, I trap the drill bit between the router's turret and its adjustable depth rod, and then lock the rod. Remove the drill bit and go to work, plunging with precision.

—*William Keith, San Diego, CA*

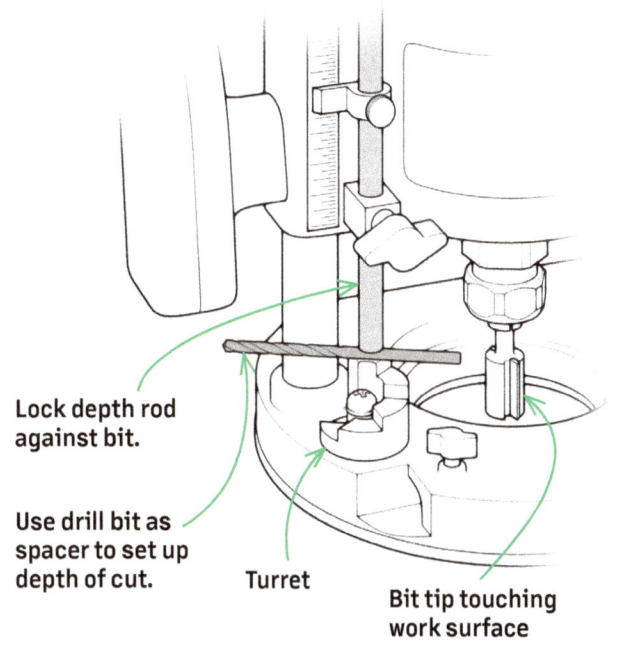

Lock depth rod against bit.

Use drill bit as spacer to set up depth of cut.

Turret

Bit tip touching work surface

Router parking pad

I designed this fixture as a place to park a router in use. It protects the installed bit and provides easy access to collet wrenches and additional bits. Built to the dimensions shown, the larger pad will accommodate most mid-size and large routers, but size your unit to suit your machines. The smaller pad accepts trim routers and other small machines with bases up to about 5" in diameter. Make the two-tier pad assembly first, joining the parts with dadoes. Position the smallest router you'll use in each section in turn, and mark the location of each bit centerpoint. Drill a 1"-diameter hole at each of those points, and cut out the pads where shown using a jigsaw. After kerfing and drilling the base for the wrenches and bits, screw it to the pad assembly.

—*Joe Hurst-Wajszczuk, Birmingham, AL*

Note: All dadoes 1/2" W × 1/4" D

Full-sized pad 1/2" × 6-1/2" × 9"

3/4" × 3" × 8"

Trimmer pad 1/2" × 6-1/2" × 6-3/4"

1"-dia.

1/4"

60°

1"

2"

3/4" × 3" × 6-1/2"

Base 3/4" × 6-1/2" × 22"

WOODCRAFT MAGAZINE TIPS & TRICKS FOR WOODWORKING 141

Panel-raising guard

Success at raising panels on the router table means that the panel profile ends up neat, clean, and consistent, and that you don't lose any blood in the process. The two router table accessories that ensure this success are a featherboard and a bit guard. The featherboard holds the work firmly against the table throughout the cuts, ensuring a smooth profile with an edge that fits the frame grooves perfectly. The bit guard, of course, keeps fingers away from that vicious cutter.

Unfortunately, some guards can impede the use of featherboards and vice-versa. To allow the use of both, I cobbled up this simple L-shaped hardwood guard that clamps to the fence while wrapping around a 3/8"-thick shop-made featherboard. Size the 1/2"-thick vertical piece to suit your fence height, angling the business end to accommodate the slope of the featherboard. The 3/8"-thick horizontal piece extends out around the featherboard and over the bit. In use, set up your featherboard first, then clamp the guard to your fence so that it rides just slightly above the workpiece panel. Now rout your panel by taking a series of shallow, successively deeper cuts.

—*Paul Anthony, Riegelsville, PA*

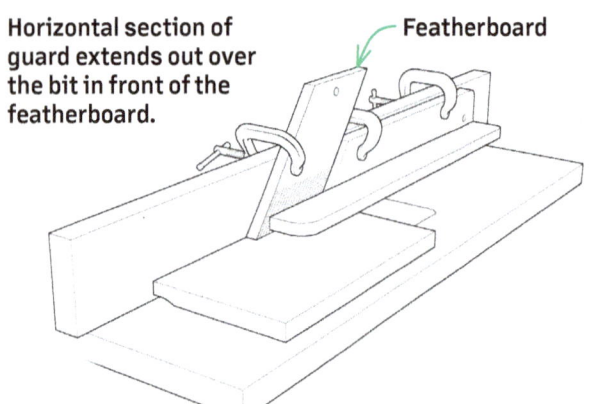

Horizontal section of guard extends out over the bit in front of the featherboard.

Featherboard

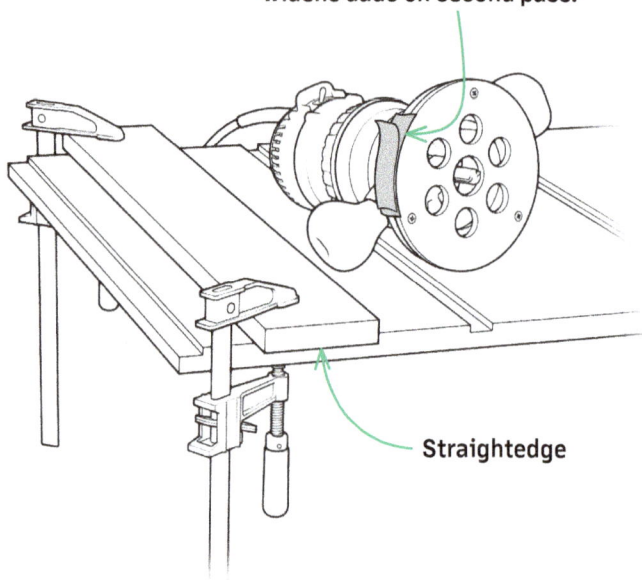

Layers of tape on edge of base widens dado on second pass.

Straightedge

Tape shim for perfect plywood dadoes

Routing dadoes for hardwood plywood can be problematic because the stuff is notoriously inconsistent in thickness, often coming in as much as 1/32" less than its nominal size. And that's not good because a gap of even a few thousandths of an inch can compromise joint strength. That's why router bit manufacturers offer "undersized" straight bits, such as a 2-3/32"-diameter bit for use with 3/4" plywood. These bits are great, but you often have to widen the cut a tad, again due to material inconsistency. So here's the tip: Rather than shifting your router straightedge, just apply a few layers of masking tape to the edge of your router base that rides the straightedge. It's fast, and a lot less risky than repositioning the cutting setup.

—*Stan Kowalski, Jersey City, NJ*

Routing through-mortises in thick stock

When faced with cutting a through-mortise in a 3"-thick slab, I opted to rout it using a combination of commonly available pattern and flush trim bits. First, I made a template from 1/2" plywood, cutting an opening in it the exact size of my desired mortise. After securing the template in place, I installed a 2"-long, 1/2"-diameter pattern-routing bit (with a top mounted bearing) in my handheld router. I routed out the waste, keeping close to the edge without hitting it. When the mortise was deep enough for the bearing to ride the template, I routed the full perimeter. After drilling out most of the remaining waste with a large spade bit, I switched over to a 1/2"-diameter flush-trim bit (with a bottom bearing). Entering from the opposite side of the slab, I trimmed away the remaining stock with the bearing riding against the previously routed surface. The result was a hole with straight sides completely through the workpiece.

—Stephen Gross, Santa Fe, NM

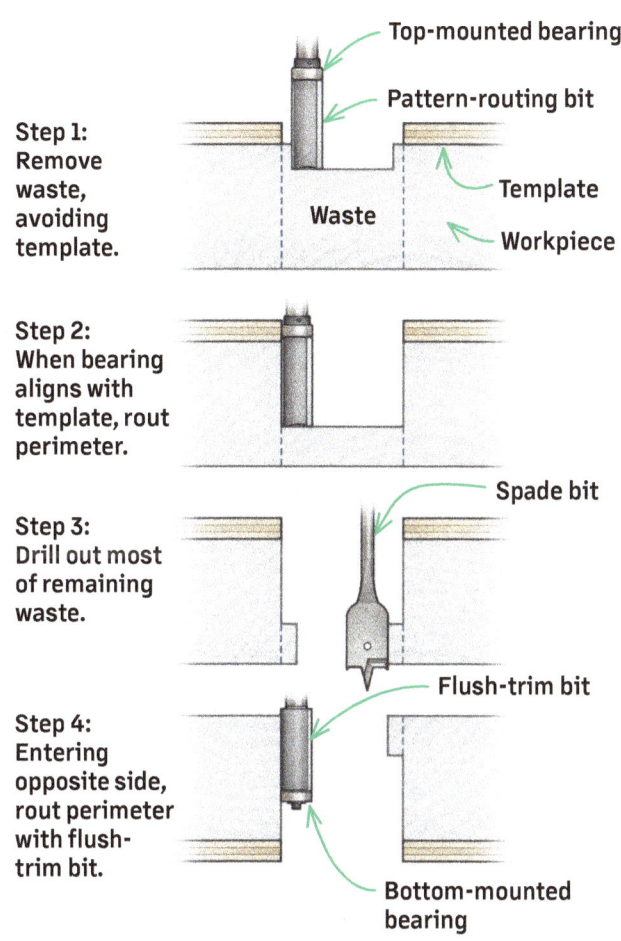

Step 1: Remove waste, avoiding template.

Step 2: When bearing aligns with template, rout perimeter.

Step 3: Drill out most of remaining waste.

Step 4: Entering opposite side, rout perimeter with flush-trim bit.

Stand-up rule jig

I find that the best tool for adjusting the bit height on a table router is a 6" steel rule with fractional increments on its end. The only problem is holding the rule on edge, since my hands are both occupied adjusting the router. To create a "third hand," I kerfed a block of wood to squeeze the blade and hold it on edge while I adjust the bit height to the end increments. (I made the cut with a hacksaw, but any saw whose kerf equals the rule's thickness will do.) Use the same trick to stand straightedges for adjusting jointer knives and aligning surfaces.

—Serge Duclos, Delson, Québec

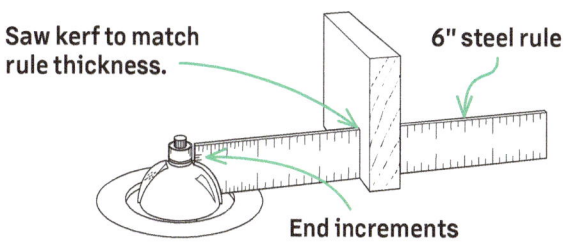

TOOLS > ROUTER

Keep hands safer with upgraded pushpad

To give my pushpads an "extra edge" in safety and control when profiling workpiece edges on my router table, I upgraded my store-bought pushpad as shown. To add a blade-safe ledge, drill a 5/16"-diameter hole through one corner, then use a 3/8-16 tap to cut threads to fit a nylon toilet seat bolt. (Aim for tight-fitting threads.) Screw the nylon bolt in or out to match the stock's thickness, or restore a nicked tip. For extra sideways support, such as for holding narrow stock against a router table fence, screw on a 3/4" thick ×1-1/4" wide piece of scrapwood along the edge of the pushpad. Stick a strip of 150-grit sandpaper to the inside edge of the wood to improve the pushpad's grip.

When using the jig at the table saw, you'll want to detach the wood edging. (Or you might consider making a second pushpad.)

—Roger McClure, Louisville, KY

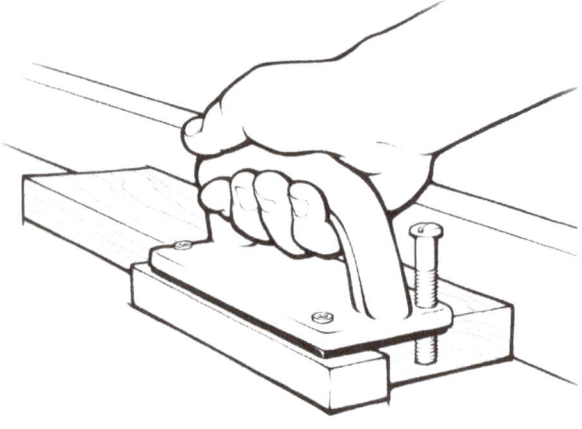

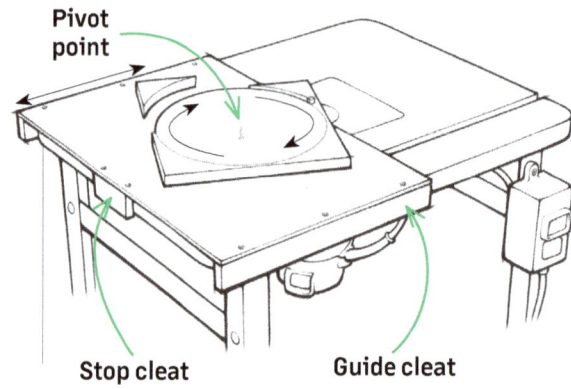

Rout circles with a slide-on top

Instead of cutting circles with my handheld router, I use my table-mounted router and the simple slide-on auxiliary top as shown. The sliding top not only enables me to make the cut in safe increments without stopping to raise the bit, but also allows adjustment of the circle's size without repositioning the pivot nail.

To make this jig, cut a piece of 1/4" hardboard slightly wider than your router tabletop and attach a pair of side cleats and stop cleat as shown. (Position the stop cleat so that the router bit grazes the inside edge.) Using the cut made by the bit, measure your desired radius, then drill a hole through the hardboard and insert a finish nail to serve as a pivot point. To rout a circle, place your workpiece on the pivot point and rotate it counterclockwise as you gradually slide it, and the table, into the bit. To rout a larger circle with the same pivot point, attach a clamp to the edge of your router table to stop the front edge of the sliding table.

—Charles Mak, Calgary, Alberta

Angled fence for routing discs

Here's a router table fence that I devised to rout the edges of circular discs with bearingless bits. Starting with a 3/4" × 12" × 21" piece of MDF, I used my framing square to lay out a right triangle with 12" legs. I drilled a 2"-diameter hole through the inside corner, and then removed the triangular cutout.

To set the V-shaped fence, place it on your router table so that the bit rests in the center hole, and clamp one end to your router table. Position the workpiece into the V, and then pivot the fence until the piece contacts the bit. Clamp the fence's other end. (For safe feeding when cutting a heavy profile, plan on taking a series of shallow cuts, readjusting the fence after each one.)

To rout, place the disc against the right-hand fence, and then roll it forward to make contact with the left-hand fence. With the disc touching both fences, spin it counter-clockwise until you have completed the cut. (For routing thick material, use a fence that's thick enough to provide bearing for the unrouted section.)

—Serge Duclos, Delson, Quebec

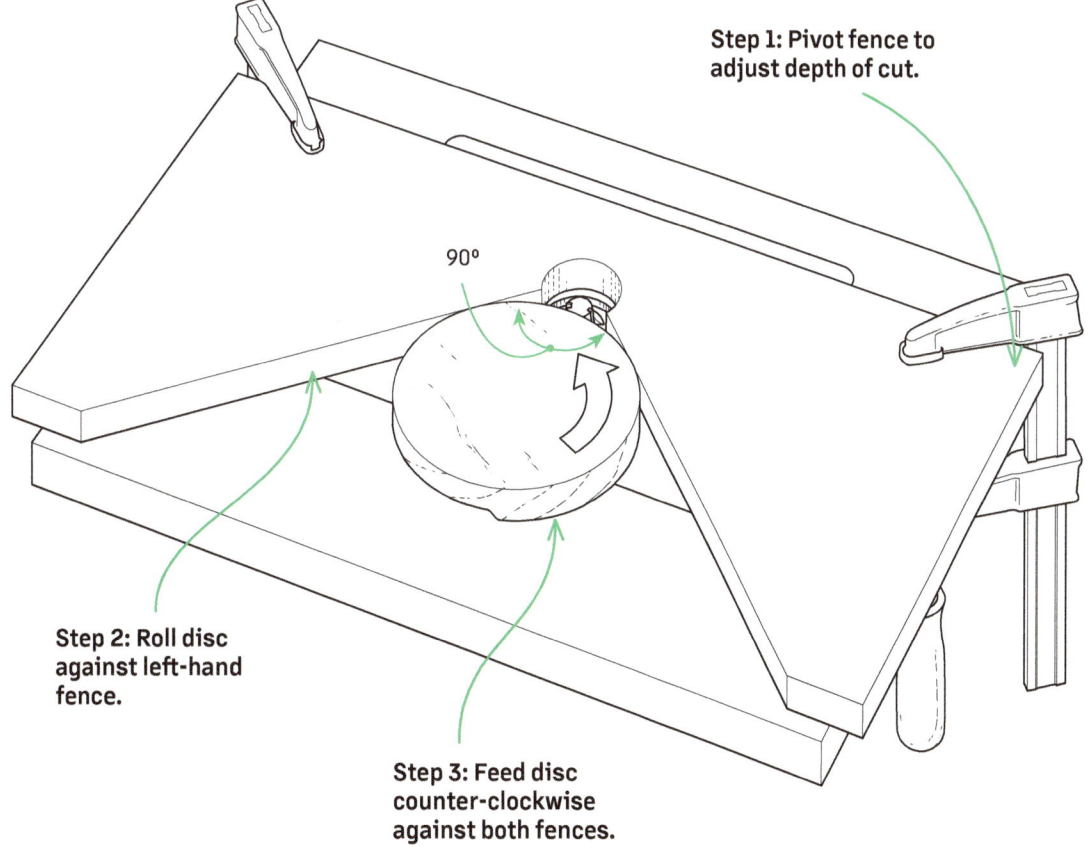

Step 1: Pivot fence to adjust depth of cut.

Step 2: Roll disc against left-hand fence.

Step 3: Feed disc counter-clockwise against both fences.

Rock-steady flush trim support

For years, I have been trying to balance my router on its edge to trim the hardwood edge banding attached to plywood. I've also tried using the router in a table, but found it difficult to hold the board vertical. To solve the problem, I simply attached a guide to the top of my fence.

Make the guide from any shop scrap, cut to a size that's easily mountable to the top of your router table's fence. Cut the guide on one side so it comes to a slightly rounded point. Attach it to the fence with screws, and adjust the fence so the pointed tip of the guide block aligns exactly with the bearing on a flush-trim bit mounted in your router. (Use a square to be certain the bearing and guide block are aligned vertically.)

Hold the workpiece to be trimmed against the cutter bearing and fence guide, and you'll get a perfect trim every time. For additional control and support, start the trim cut with the trailing edge of the workpiece against the infeed side of the router fence for three-point support, then as you pass the center, angle the workpiece so that the leading edge is against the outfeed side of the fence.

—*Vell H. Holcombe, Milton, PA*

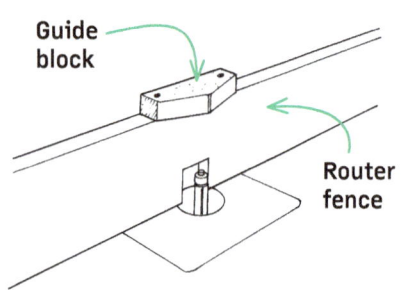
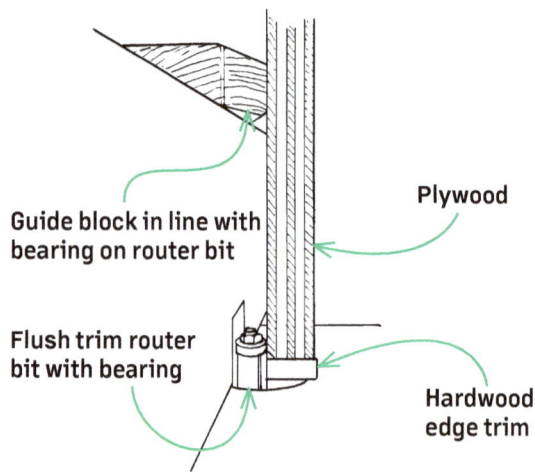

Router power lift

As I was cranking up my router for what seemed like the hundredth bit-change of the day, it dawned on me that the drive on the lift was the same hex drive as on my small cordless screwdriver. Now, I can power the lift up and down at the touch of a button. When I get close to the desired setting, I lock the screwdriver in manual mode to make the final adjustments.

—*Ron Moss, Statesboro, GA*

A helpful lift from I-beam risers

It often helps to raise a workpiece up off the bench, especially when you need clamp access underneath. Although you can sometimes just use thick boards as risers, I've found that I-beams work much better because you can clamp them to the benchtop, then secure the workpiece to the top beam flange. This works perfectly, for example, when you need to clamp routing guides to a panel for dadoing or cutting tenons for a breadboard end, as shown in the drawing. Even simple edge profiling is more easily done on a secured workpiece, and raising the work means you don't have to crouch at the bench. My risers span the width of my workbench to allow easy clamping anywhere along its length. Made of plywood, they raise a workpiece about 7" off the bench, which works fine for most operations. I screwed and glued the pieces together, counterboring the screws to prevent possible damage to workpieces.

—Paul Anthony, Riegelsville, PA

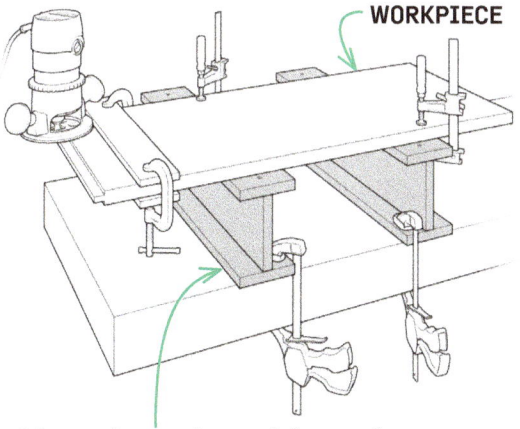

I-beam risers raise work for comfort and allow securing work to a bench with clamp access underneath.

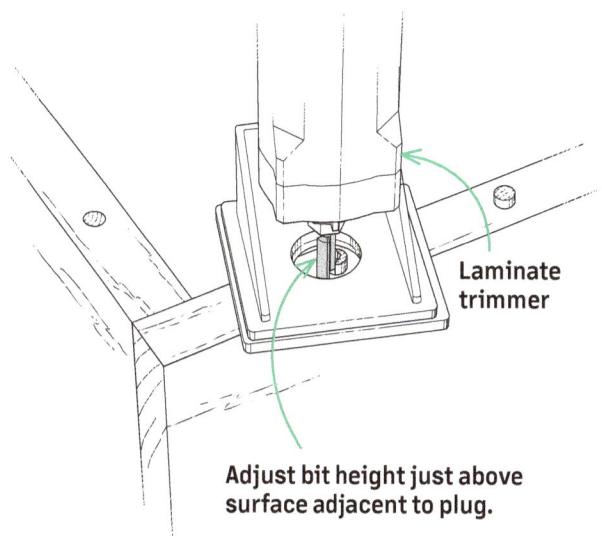

Adjust bit height just above surface adjacent to plug.

Flush-routing plugs

I've found that a router equipped with a straight or spiral flute bit does a much faster (and free of tear out) job of cutting plugs flush than does the old saw-and-chisel approach. I simply adjust the tip of the router bit shy of the workpiece surface by about the thickness of a sheet of loose-leaf paper, and then tilt the router to lower the spinning bit onto the end of the plug. The few thousandths of an inch of plug projection that remains is easily sanded or scraped away.

A laminate trimmer works best because of its maneuverability and small footprint. However, sometimes adjacent plugs prevent setting the subbase completely onto the work surface. In that case, you may have to trim a few plugs the old-fashioned way to create a landing pad for the base.

—George Aspinall, Tacoma, WA

TOOLS > ROUTER

Perfect router-cut dadoes

Hardwood plywood usually doesn't match its nominal thickness; it's typically undersized between 1/64" and 1/32". Therefore, when routing dadoes, a single pass with a single bit is unlikely to yield a perfect fit. (Even "undersized" panel bits sold for the purpose may not exactly suit the thickness of your particular stock.) To solve the problem, I've come up with a two-spacer trick to rout perfectly sized dadoes. All you need is a bit that's a smaller diameter than the desired dado width, a couple of scraps of wood, and a straightedge fence to guide your router.

First, make a spacer that's exactly the same thickness as your bit diameter. To set up the cut, sandwich the spacer between the fence and router base; align the bit with the dado layout line that is nearest the fence. Secure the fence and rout your first pass. Next, replace the spacer with a scrap strip of your plywood stock, standing it on edge. Make a second pass with the same bit to create a dado of perfect width.

—Ryan Reese, New York, NY

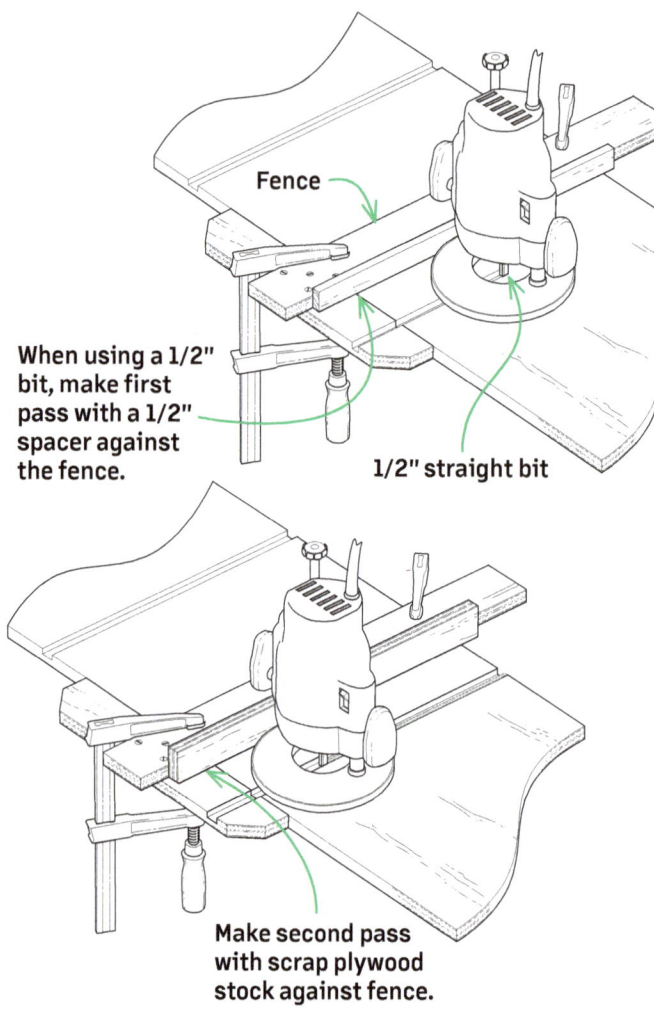

Fence

When using a 1/2" bit, make first pass with a 1/2" spacer against the fence.

1/2" straight bit

Make second pass with scrap plywood stock against fence.

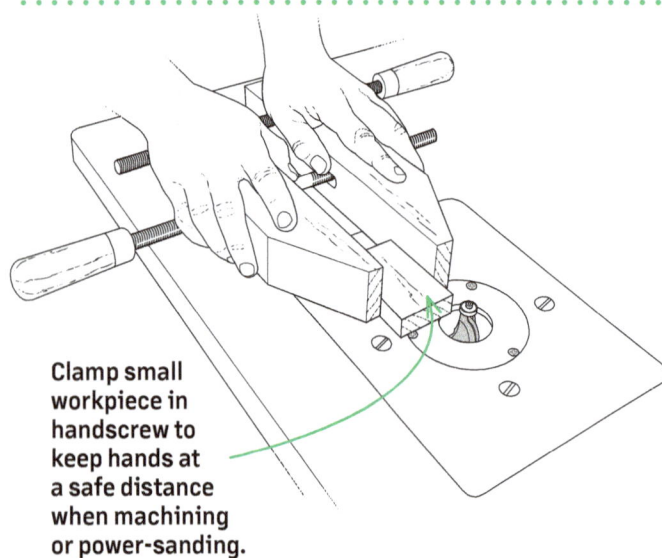

Clamp small workpiece in handscrew to keep hands at a safe distance when machining or power-sanding.

A handscrew helper

Wooden handscrews are great for a variety of clamping chores, but I also find myself reaching for them when I need to sand or machine small parts. Their long reach and solid grip allow you to safely perform otherwise dicey operations like routing or power-sanding the edges of small blocks. They'll keep your fingers out of harm's way, and the wooden jaws won't damage an expensive cutter in case of accidental contact.

—Jack Preston, Tucson, AZ

A quick corner rout

When making shelves and small table tops, I like to radius the corners for both aesthetics and safety. I find that the most efficient and consistent way to do it is using a template on a table router outfitted with a flush-trim bit. A pair of fences on the template allow for quick, accurate positioning of the workpiece. Make the template from a piece of 1/2" hardwood plywood, shaping one of the corners as desired with a jigsaw or bandsaw. If necessary, smooth and fair the profile by filing or power sanding. Attach two fences as shown, keeping them back from each end of the curve by a couple of inches so they don't impede bit travel.

To shape your workpiece, first trace its corners using the template, then saw to within 1/8" of the line. Install a flush-trim bit with a shank-mounted bearing into your table router, and adjust the projection of the bit so the bearing contacts the pattern. Holding the workpiece firmly against the template fences, trim the corner to shape, making sure to move the workpiece against the rotation of the bit.

—*Marvin Mertz, Baton Rouge, LA*

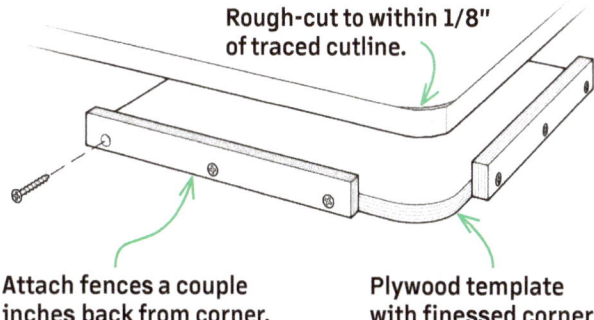

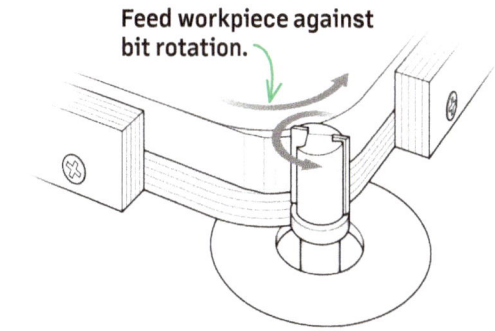

Small-parts finger saver

Routing small parts is not only hard to do safely, but it also produces a double dose of ruined or kicked-back parts. Attaching a dowel to the work keeps my fingers out of the equation and gives me a solid handle to control the cut. Depending on the size of the piece and depth of cut, you can use double-stick tape, but for the strongest bond, I recommend a thick bead of hot glue. Once routed, you can soften the glue bond with a few drops of mineral spirits.

—*Jim Young, Springfield, MO*

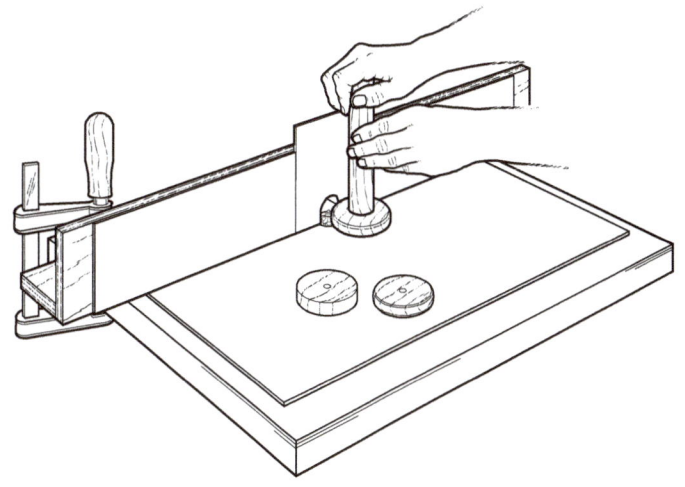

Keyhole slot routing jig

Routed keyhole slots provide a great way to hang everything from picture frames and plaques to small cabinets. Plunging the bit into the work, and then moving it forward about 3/8" creates a keyhole-shaped slot that accepts the head of a screw. Here's a simple jig to help with the job. It's nothing more than a small panel of 1/4"-thick plywood or hardboard with a frame of fences attached to guide the router. The panel "wings" allow clamping of the jig to a cabinet. For smaller workpieces, attach the panel with double-faced tape or hot-melt glue.

—Paul Anthony, Riegelsville, PA

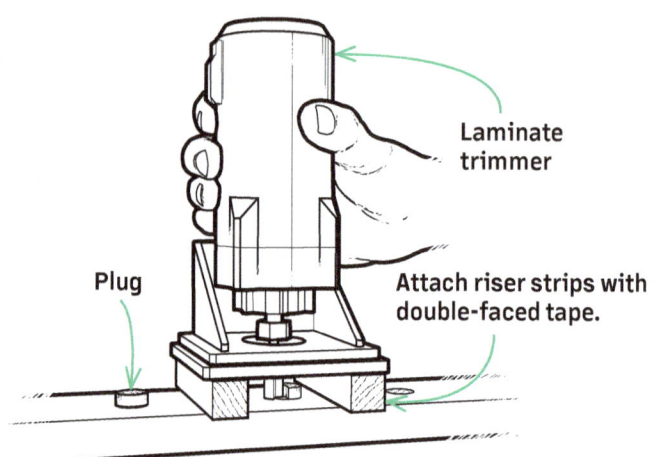

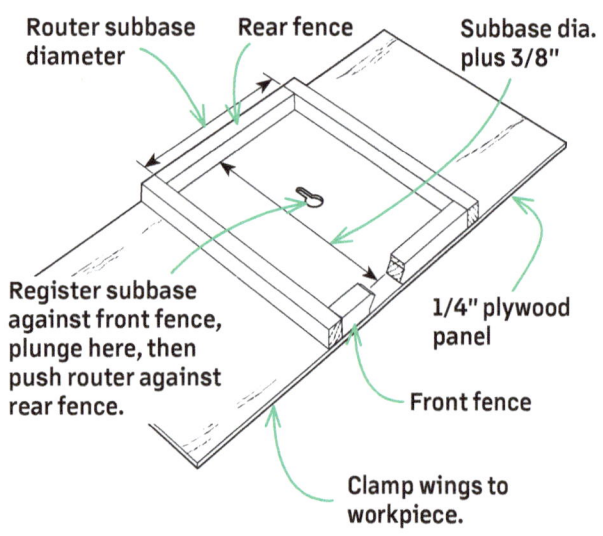

Flush-routing riser for plugs

When trimming wooden plugs with a chisel, it's easy to mar the adjacent surface or tear out the plug grain. When you have more than a few plugs to trim, using a router is a much cleaner, easier approach. To do the job, attach a couple of "riser strips" to the base of a laminate trimmer or other router using double-faced tape. The strips enable the router base to ride over the plugs while a straight bit adjusted a hair shy of the work surface trims the excess. Finish up the job with sandpaper.

—Paul Anthony, Riegelsville, PA

Block router table sag

Over the years, my old router table surface sagged until it was unusable. I recently upgraded the top and insert, and I wanted to make sure that my new investment stayed flat.

I figured that the constant weight of the router led to the dishing of my old table, so now I elevate the router on a piece of scrapwood when it's not in use. This takes the pressure off the table surface so that it's much less likely to sag. If your router table doesn't have a surface below it for the block, simply remove the router insert assembly and store it on a shelf.

—Richard Huck, Minneapolis, MN

TABLE SAW

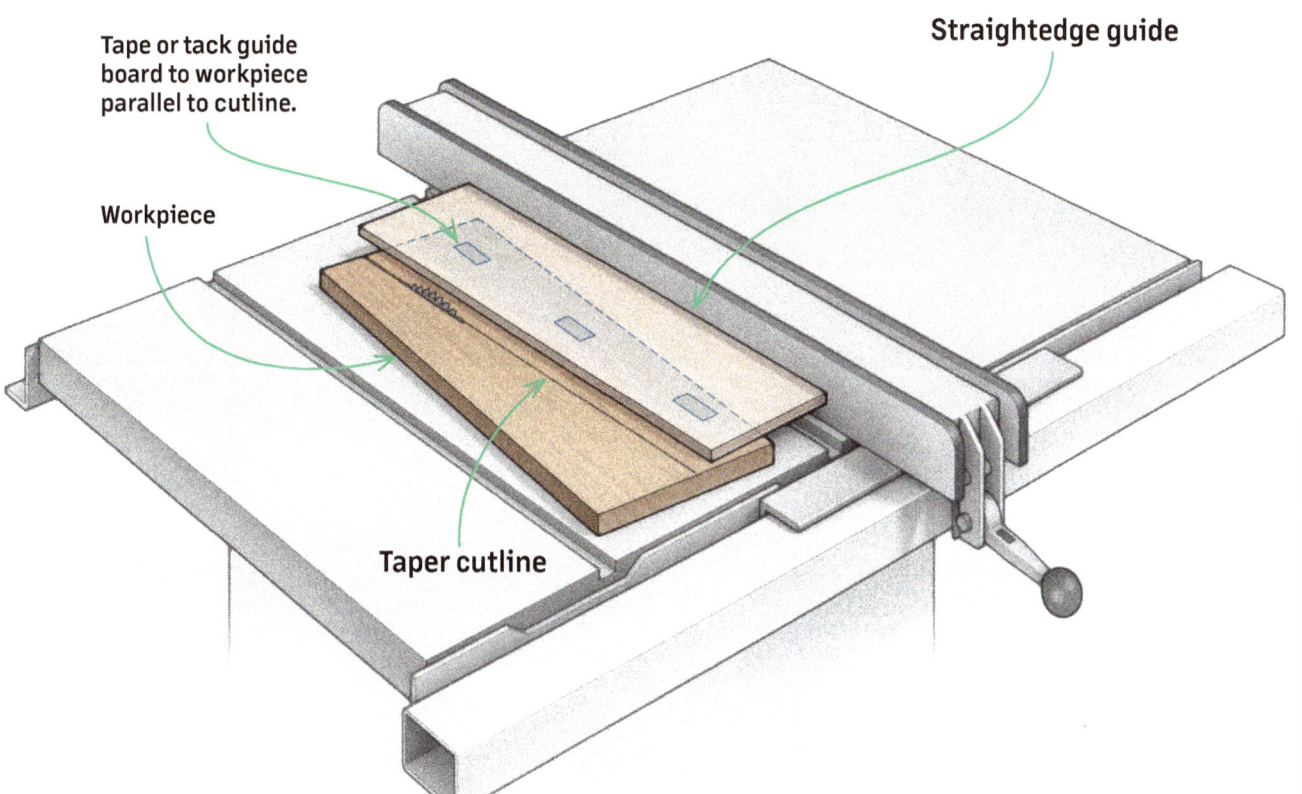

Tape or tack guide board to workpiece parallel to cutline.

Straightedge guide

Workpiece

Taper cutline

Tapering boards

I was working on a project that called for tapering long, wide boards, but my commercial tapering jig wasn't big enough for the job. To make the cuts, I used a strip of 1/4"-thick plywood to serve as a straightedge guide against the rip fence. After marking out the taper on the workpiece, I tacked the plywood to it, aligning the plywood's fence-bearing edge parallel to my cutline. At that point, it was a simple matter of ripping to the cutline in the usual fashion. To prevent marring, begin with a workpiece that's oversized in length and tack into the excess; you could also use double-faced tape.

—*Mark Clement, Phoenix, AZ*

Skinning a crosscut sled

I love my table saw crosscut sled because it allows me to crosscut large panels and other workpieces that would be too unwieldy to feed with my saw's miter gauge. Not only that, but the sled's base serves as a zero-clearance backup to minimize exit tear out. Unfortunately, I recently used the sled with a cheap blade that had enough wobble to widen the kerf in the base, compromising its zero-clearance support. The real fix would have been to cut out and replace the central section of the base, but I didn't have time for that yet. Instead, I discovered that you can use double-faced tape to attach a piece of 1/4"-thick hardboard or plywood to restore the zero-clearance support. For cutting accuracy, make sure to use enough tape to keep the thin panels from bowing. Keep in mind that the new "skin" doesn't necessarily have to completely cover the sled base; it just has to provide sufficient support for your workpiece.

—Steve Wentworth, Salt Lake City, UT

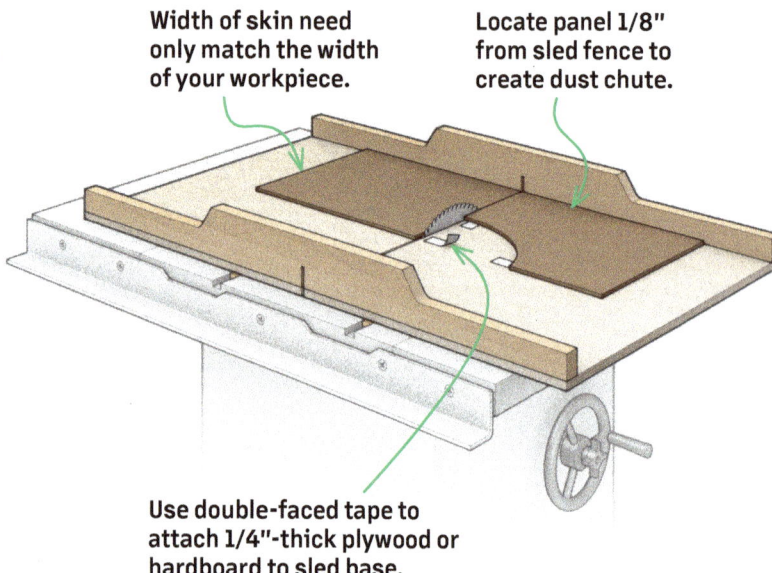

Width of skin need only match the width of your workpiece.

Locate panel 1/8" from sled fence to create dust chute.

Use double-faced tape to attach 1/4"-thick plywood or hardboard to sled base.

Outdoor safety strips prevent slips

I recently started a project that required mortise-and-tenon joints. I decided to make the tenons on the table saw using the miter gauge with an extension and a stopblock. To keep workpieces from slipping, I used PSA sanding discs on the miter gauge. However, no matter how well I cleaned and prepared the surface on the miter gauge and extension, the discs always popped loose.

Finally, I found a solution at the local hardware store: outdoor safety strips, the kind used on stairs and ladders to prevent slipping. The adhesive is much more robust than the PSA sanding discs, and their size worked perfectly on the miter gauge.

—Lewis Kauffman, Chambersburg, PA

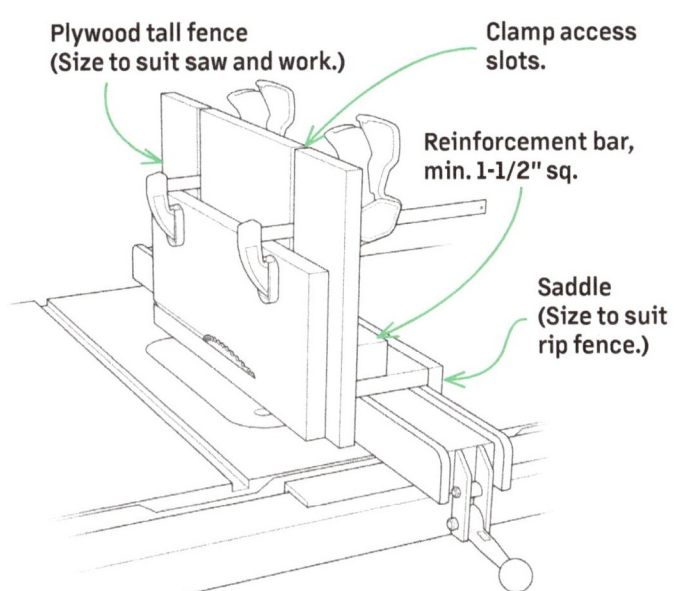

Plywood tall fence (Size to suit saw and work.)

Clamp access slots.

Reinforcement bar, min. 1-1/2" sq.

Saddle (Size to suit rip fence.)

Sliding tall fence

This sliding tall fence jig serves as a carrier for ripping knife-edge bevels on smaller boards, and also makes a great tall fence for vertically supporting work to saw beveled edges for door panels and traditional solid wood drawer bottoms. The fixture straddles the fence for stability and includes slots for clamp access. Size and slot the unit to suit your work, making the saddle section fit your fence snugly enough to slide easily but without slop.

—Russ Svendsen, Olean, NY

Table saw router fence

In space-starved shops, a table saw side-extension table can be pressed into service as a router table. One of the advantages is that your table saw rip fence can then double as a router table fence. To accommodate edge shaping and other operations that require setting the router bit back from the face of the fence, you can create a wood split-fence. It's an easy matter to attach a wooden fence like this to any one of the millions of Biesemeyer-style rip fences out there.

Using a piece of 8/4 stock a few inches shorter than the length of your rip fence, dress it straight and square to a thickness of 1-3/4" and just 1/2" or so wider than the height of your fence. Crosscut it into two, and rout a countersunk slot in each end to about 2" long. Butt the two pieces together end-to-end over your router opening, and attach them to your rip fence with 3/8-16 × 2-1/2" self-tapping screws, such as Tap-Flex.

Install each screw at the end of the slot furthest from the bit opening to allow maximum outward movement of the fence halves. The split fence will not impede normal table saw operations; you'll need to remove it only for those infrequent ripping maneuvers that require locating the fence to the left side of the blade.

—Paul Anthony, Riegelsville, PA

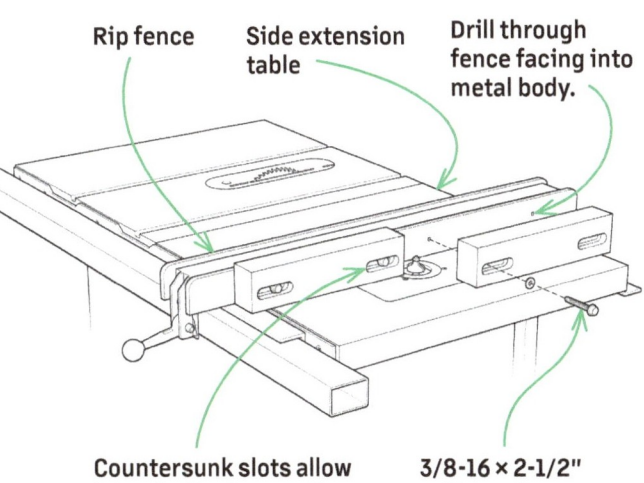

Rip fence

Side extension table

Drill through fence facing into metal body.

Countersunk slots allow lateral adjustment of router fence halves.

3/8-16 × 2-1/2" self-tapping screw

Small parts hold-down

Even with a crosscut sled, trimming small parts on my table saw requires placing my fingers uncomfortably close to the blade. For safety, I made this simple handheld hold-down, which consists of a riser block screwed to a beam. The beam provides downward pressure on a workpiece while keeping my hands out of harm's way. To maximize workpiece contact, the thickness of the riser should equal the workpiece thickness. To increase stability and grip, I glued thin rubber scraps to the undersides of the riser and beam end. The hold-down also works to secure small pieces at my power miter saw. It's helpful to have at the ready several of these hold-downs, with risers of different thickness.

—Bill Schneider, Athens, OH

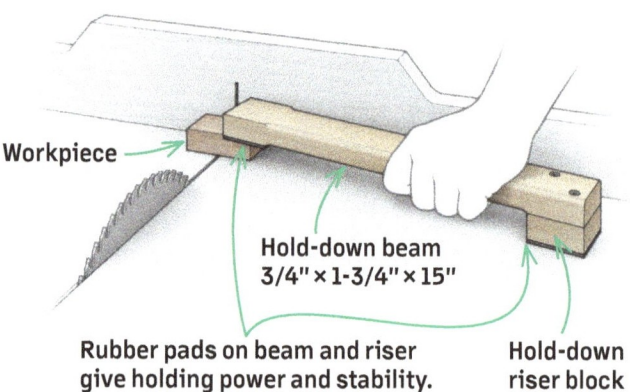

Ripping knife-edge bevels

Ripping a knife-edge bevel of less than 45° is challenging because you can't feed the board on-the-flat since the blade won't tilt that far. Instead, you have to feed it on its edge. Unfortunately, this can be awkward and, because the work exits the blade traveling on the knife edge, it's subject to damage. In these cases, I use a thick, squarely dressed carrier board to do the job safely and securely. Although you can clamp the workpiece to the carrier board, I prefer the less cumbersome approach of making the workpiece a bit oversized in length, then screwing it to the carrier board at both ends. Afterward, I cut away the screw holes.

—Paul Anthony, Riegelsville, PA

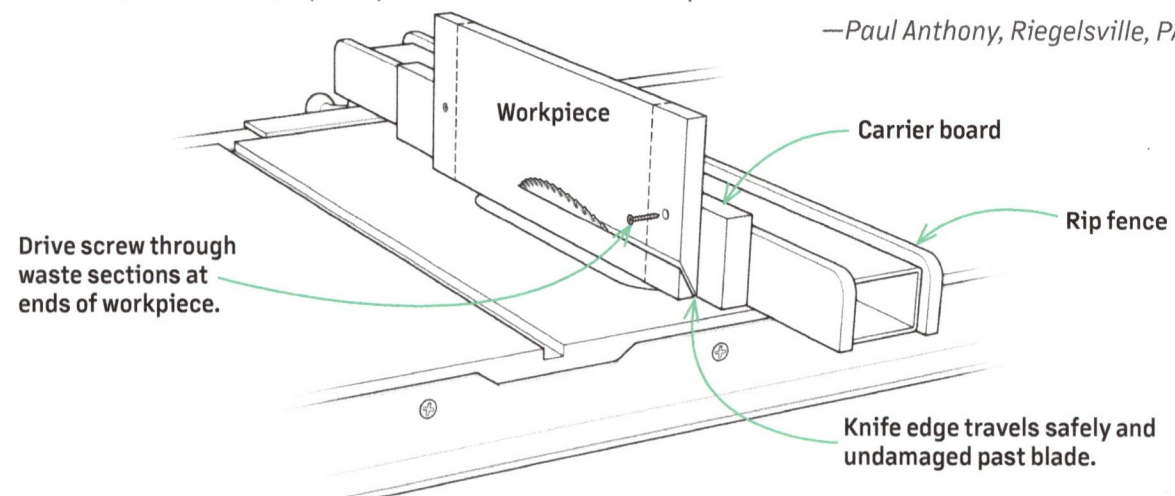

Wobble-widening a dado

I recently had to outfit a set of drawers with 1/8"-thick dividers. I needed the dadoes in the drawer sides to be snug, but not so tight that the dividers couldn't be removed easily by hand. A standard, 1/8"-wide saw kerf was a little tight. To get the saw to make a slightly wider cut, I made a "washer" from a 2" × 2" sticky note that matched the diameter of my table saw's arbor washer. I then cut this paper washer in half and stuck one half to the arbor flange and the other to the arbor washer. I then installed the blade as usual, taking care to align the two shims opposite each other. The shims turned my saw blade into a very subtle "wobble dado," which made a kerf about 5/32" wide—just what I needed for the dividers. With further experimentation, I found using a playing card as the washer yielded a kerf just under 3/16" wide.

—Ken Burton, New Tripoli, PA

Baby powder for surface slick

When pushing heavy sheet goods across your table saw, it helps to have a top that's super slick. Wax is good, but talc, a.k.a. baby powder, is even better. Sprinkle on a light dusting and brush off most of the excess. Unlike some other solutions, talc does not cause any finishing problems, and also seems to help protect the metal surface against rust.

—Mack Stolarski, Williamburg, VA

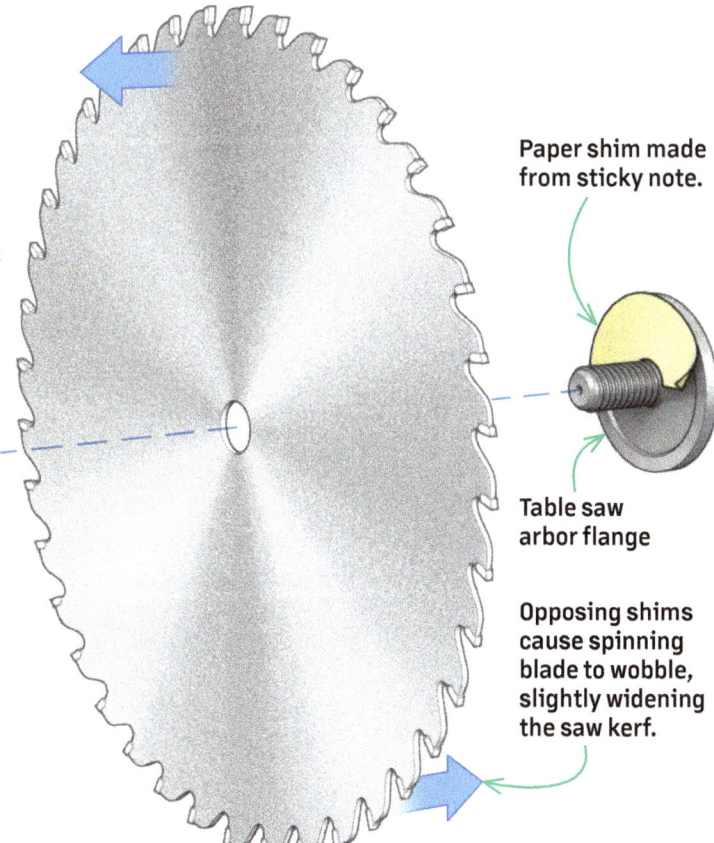

Arbor nut

Arbor washer

Locate paper shim on arbor washer to oppose shim on arbor flange.

Paper shim made from sticky note.

Table saw arbor flange

Opposing shims cause spinning blade to wobble, slightly widening the saw kerf.

Simple tapering

I was working on an outdoor seating project recently that called for tapering some 3/4"-thick boards. I own a tapering jig, but it wasn't big enough for the job. So, to make the cuts, I used a straight-edged board to serve as a guide against the rip fence. After marking out the taper on a workpiece, I used double-faced tape to attach the guide board, aligning its fence-bearing edge parallel to my cutline. (If marring the workpiece isn't an issue, you can use nails instead.) At that point, it was a simple matter of ripping to the cutline in the usual fashion.

—Mark Clement, Phoenix, AZ

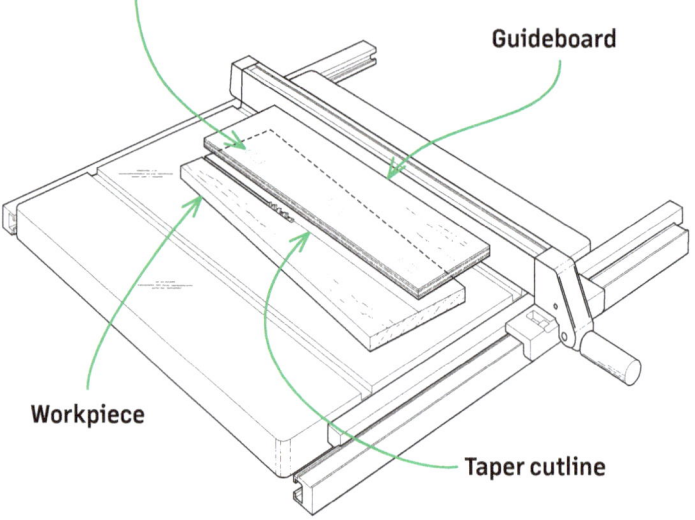

Tooth- and knuckle-saving blade changer

Wanting some insurance against any blade-meets-wrench or blade-meets-knuckle incidents when changing blades on my table saw, I came up with this shop-made solution. The jig is simply a narrow plywood box with a center cavity designed to shroud and snag the blade. The front nub helps lever the jig into the saw teeth, so that the blade doesn't spin when tightening or loosening the arbor nut.

To make the blade remover, use a spare blade as a guide to sketch out the basic dimensions of the inner and outer laminations onto some 1/4" plywood scrap, then glue together a three-ply sandwich, as shown. Adjust the size of the back nub as needed to fit your saw.

—Mark Koritz, St. Louis, MO

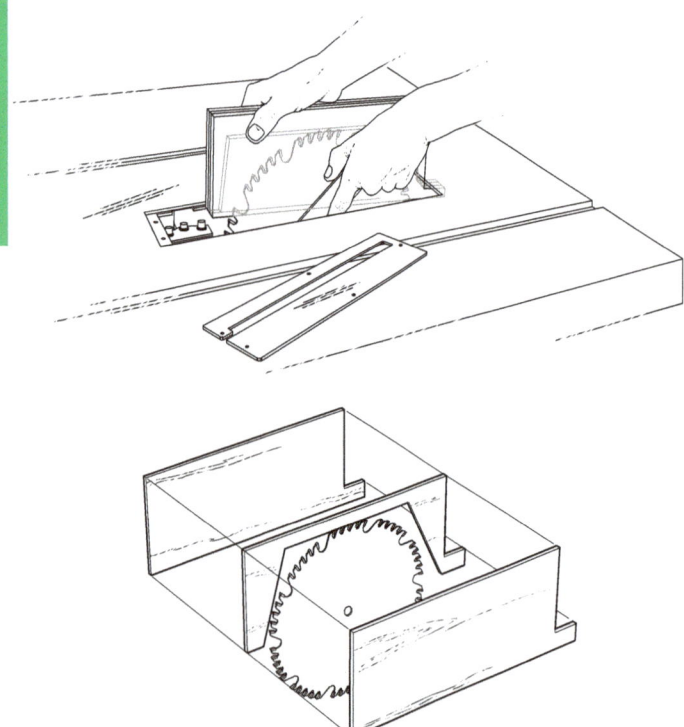

Zero-clearance throat plate

A zero-clearance throat plate on a table saw leads to cleaner cuts because the work is supported right up to the blade, minimizing exit tear out. It also prevents small offcuts from jamming between the blade and slot. Commercial blanks are available, but it's easy to make your own. You can use plywood or straight-grained hardwood, but I find that 1/2"-thick MDF faced on both sides with plastic laminate provides the best flatness and stability.

To make a throat plate, rip your stock to fit the opening exactly, trace the rounded ends from your stock throat plate, then bandsaw and disc-sand to the lines for a perfect fit in the opening. Also drill a finger access hole.

Next, level the plate to the saw table. If it's too thick, rout away the areas that contact the opening's support tabs. If it's too thin, shim with tape. Alternatively, tap the plate for Allen screws, which allow fine adjustability.

Cutting the blade slot in a plate blank can be tricky because a full-sized blade won't retract enough to allow the blank to seat fully. To do the job, fully retract the height-adjustment screws in your stock throat plate, and then place the blank atop it in the resulting shallow recess. Clamp a hold-down board across the blank, and raise the spinning blade partially through it. Finish the cut after placing the blank fully in its recess, again clamped down for safety.

—Paul Anthony, Riegelsville, PA

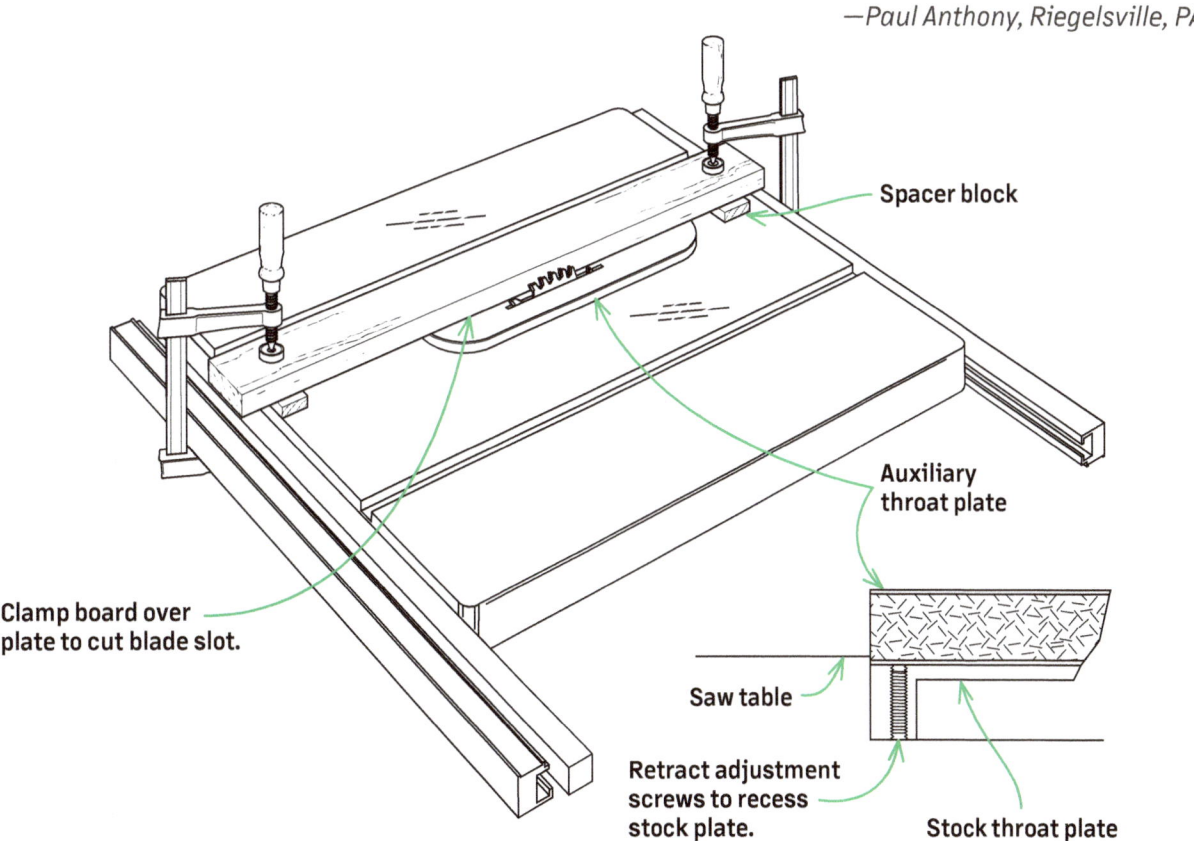

TOOLS > TABLE SAW

Computer-magnet featherboard holder

I found a simple solution to the problem of clamping a featherboard to my table saw in an unlikely place—inside a malfunctioning computer. When I disposed of the computer, I first removed the hard drive for security purposes. Inside the hard drive container, I found two extremely powerful magnets.

After making all the necessary cuts to the featherboard, I cut out the profile of the magnets using a 3/8" Forstner bit deep enough so the magnet was flush with the featherboard. The magnets hold the featherboard with more force and less clutter than a number of clamps.

—Jerald E. Larson, Irmo, SC

Ergonomic pushstick

As a custom furniture maker, I have been fine-tuning my pushstick design for decades, having found fault with many commercial versions. Made from maple or beech, my shoe-style pushstick features a gently curving rounded-over handle that fits comfortably in my palm. It also eliminates the kind of wrist strain that can lead to carpal tunnel syndrome when performing repetitive tasks at the table saw or jointer. Bandsawn kerfs in the heel serve to catch the edges of cutoffs, allowing me to safely push them out of the way.

Better still, the 14-1/2" length keeps my hand well out of harm's way without compromising control. To cover a variety of needs, I make my pushsticks in batches from 1/4"-, 1/2"-, 3/4"- and 1"-thick material.

—Tom Svec, Lock Haven, PA

Half-Sized Pattern
Enlarge 200%

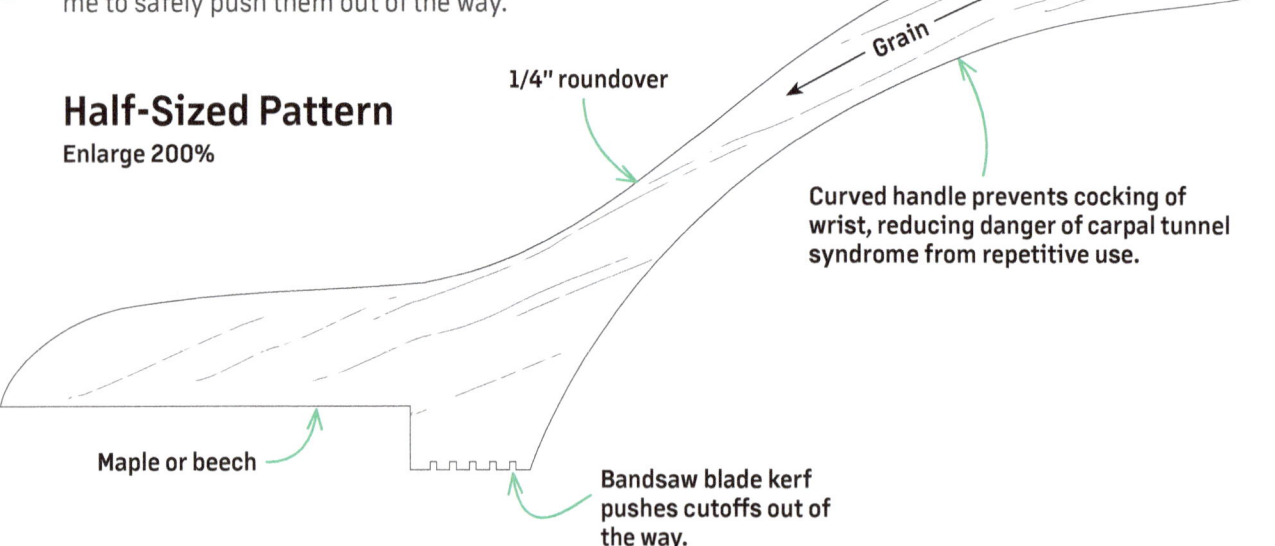

1/4" roundover

Grain

Curved handle prevents cocking of wrist, reducing danger of carpal tunnel syndrome from repetitive use.

Maple or beech

Bandsaw blade kerf pushes cutoffs out of the way.

Drive belt memory is a thing of the past

Ordinary motor drive belts develop a "memory" of their shape around pulleys whenever the machine isn't running. Starting up the motor moves these humps rapidly, creating noise and accuracy-robbing vibration in a table saw, bandsaw, drill press, and any other drive-belt tool.

I recently replaced the old-fashioned drive belt on my table saw with a link belt, and noticed an immediate reduction in both noise and vibration. And I'm sure it's not my imagination that my cuts seem smoother. The link construction made it easy for me to match the length of the new belt to the old one. When you have the old belt off, use a straightedge to check the alignment of the pulleys on the arbor and motor. Move one pulley or the other to ensure that they are parallel and in the same plane. Be sure to replace all belt guards after the installation.

—Audrey Beers, Parkville, MO

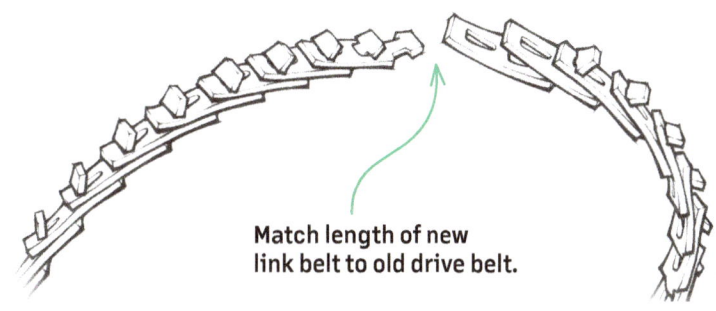

Match length of new link belt to old drive belt.

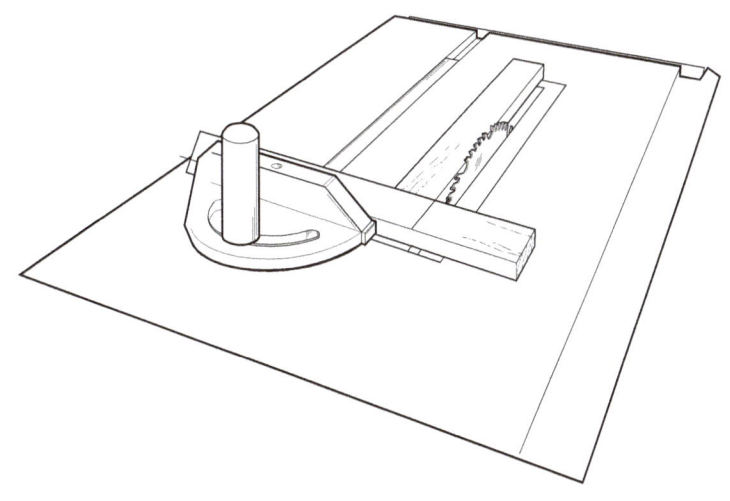

Precision alignment for crosscuts

I always get frustrated when I am trying to crosscut a board or plank on my table saw. In order to get a perfect cut, I have to mark it on the front and look over the board to see my mark. I came up with this idea, which I think is an easy solution. I take a piece of scrap board and lay it alongside my blade and line it up with the mark on the board I want to crosscut. I get a perfect cut every time. The scrap board and the crosscut board have to be the same thickness. I put a few pieces of various sizes of scrap board by my saw, and I became a happier hobbyist.

—Bob Pavek, Montgomery, MN

Ripping scrappy-edged stock

I typically mill my project stock from rough-sawn lumber slabs with "live" edges. To rip boards safely, I first have to establish one straight edge to feed against the rip fence. Although I've seen lots of jigs cobbled together with carrier boards and toggle clamps for this purpose, they strike me as over-engineered. Truth is, a simple 6"-wide straightedge panel of 1/4"-thick plywood or MDF does the job nicely. Here's my approach:

Begin by marking the desired cutline with a wide-lead carpenter's pencil or a chalk line. Next, roughly align your straightedge panel parallel to the cutline, allowing minimal overhang on the opposite edge to stabilize the setup. Using 1" nails, tack the straightedge to the board near the edges, which will be cut away later. Leave the nailheads proud for easy removal. (For scrappy-edged thin materials, use double-faced tape or hot-melt glue instead of nails.) Measure from the outside edge of the straightedge to the cutline, set your rip fence to that measurement, and make the cut with the straightedge bearing against the fence.

—Paul Anthony, Riegelsville, PA

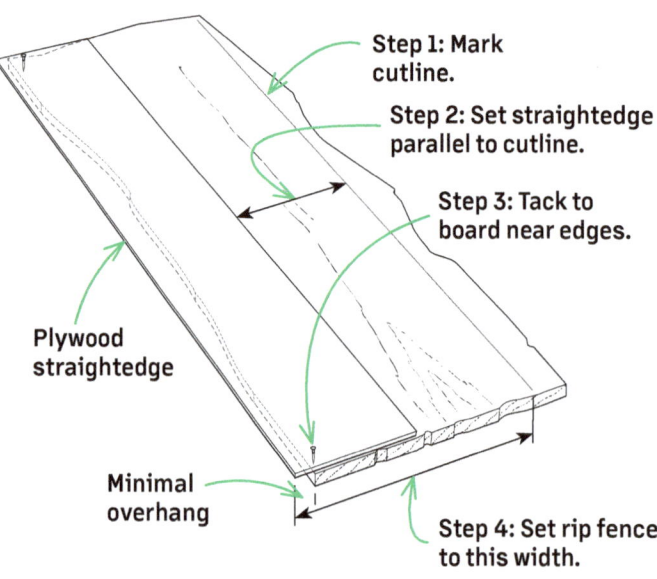

Reversible dual fence

Half-length table saw fences are common in Europe; they allow room for the movement of stressed lumber when ripping. I tried one and really liked it for ripping lumber, but didn't care for it when cutting sheet goods. I made a snug-fitting fence cover that I could reverse, thus presenting a choice of a half-length or a full-length sacrificial fence facing the blade. You'll need to adjust or modify the measuring pointer on the fence rail to compensate for the thickness of the new fence cover.

—Dick Ayers, Barron, WI

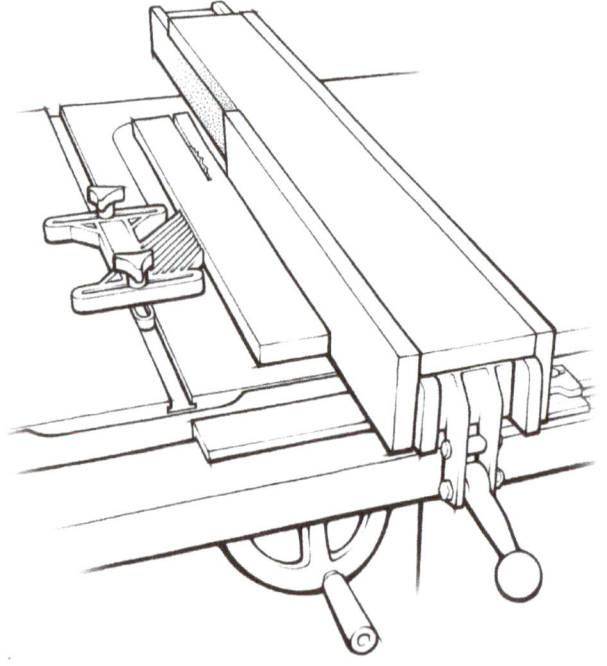

Flush-trimming at the table saw

I make a lot of utilitarian boxes by simply gluing the bottom panels to the undersides of the box walls. For efficiency and accuracy, I make the panels slightly oversized, then trim their edges flush to the box walls. I find that a table saw fence jig works great for the job. It's basically a template-sawing setup that consists of a guide board that's glued and screwed off-center to a mounting board that's clamped to my rip fence.

To use the jig, clamp it to your table saw fence so that the guide board sits about 1/4" above the material to be trimmed. (The offset accommodates materials of different thicknesses by inverting the jig.) Raise your blade just shy of the guide board, and set your rip fence to locate the edge of the guide board just a hair past the outermost edges of the blade teeth. To make the flush-cut, feed each box wall in turn against the guide, beginning by crosscutting the ends to eliminate tear out. Alternatively, if you want an offset cut, simply locate the rip fence to suit.

—Bill Sands, Lubeck, WV

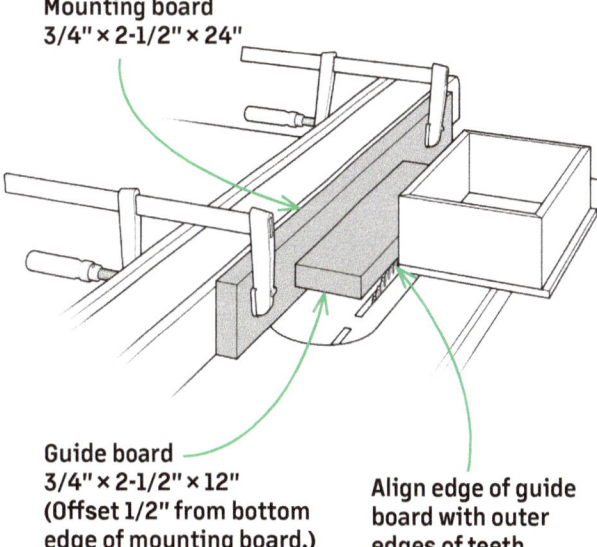

Mounting board 3/4" × 2-1/2" × 24"

Guide board 3/4" × 2-1/2" × 12" (Offset 1/2" from bottom edge of mounting board.)

Align edge of guide board with outer edges of teeth.

Fine-tuning sled runners

When making a table saw sled, there's often a bit of final fussing with the wooden runners to ensure that the sled slides easily but without side-to-side play. This usually involves selectively sanding, scraping, or planing away any deviant sections on the runners. I've found that the best way to target the problem areas is to first scrub a wide-lead carpenter's pencil across the shoulders of the saw table slots to load them with graphite; then, push the sled back and forth. This transfers the graphite to the errant spots for easy identification.

—Mark Bannon, Denver, CO

Cheap rust inhibitor

Having run out of my favorite rust inhibitor, I needed a quick replacement to keep my cast-iron table saw protected. The solution was as close as my second hobby across the garage. The chain wax that I use for my dirt bike was just the fix. It not only works as well or better but it is half the cost for twice as much. It is now the only product I buy.

—Jay Williams, Shirleysburg, PA

TOOLS > TABLE SAW

Magnetic crosscut standoff

When crosscutting at the table saw, never use the rip fence as a stop. That's because the freed offcut, being trapped between the blade and the fence, wants to kick back. One traditional approach is to clamp a thick stopblock/standoff to the rip fence forward of the blade, which both registers the cut and creates a safe "fall-off" space for the offcut between the blade and fence. To make things even easier, I created a magnetic block for the job by installing a switchable magnet, such as a MagJig 150, in a piece of 3/4" × 2-1/2" × 3" wood. I use my rip fence scale to set up the cut, adding 2-1/2" to my desired crosscut length. Then, I simply place the magnetic block against the fence, and I'm ready to cut.

—Tom Roessler, Appleton, WI

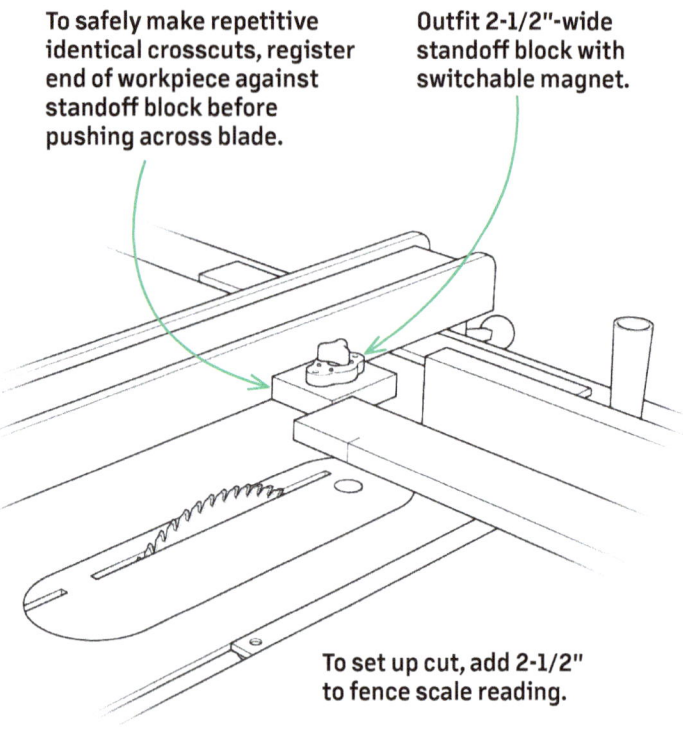

To safely make repetitive identical crosscuts, register end of workpiece against standoff block before pushing across blade.

Outfit 2-1/2"-wide standoff block with switchable magnet.

To set up cut, add 2-1/2" to fence scale reading.

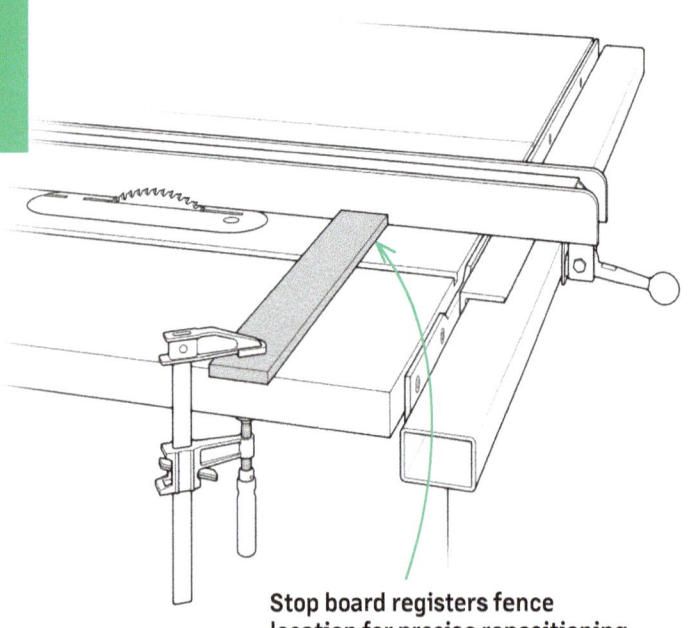

Stop board registers fence location for precise repositioning.

Quick rip fence reset

There are times when your table saw rip fence is precisely positioned for a job, but sitting atop your throat plate when you need to change blades or adjust the width of a dado head. To save yourself the hassle of fussing a displaced fence back into position afterward, simply butt the end of a board against it and then clamp the board to your saw table before moving the fence. When done with the blade change, slide the fence against the board, lock it down, and remove the board; you are exactly back in action.

—Quinn Jackman, St. Charles, MO

Fence-free tapering

Making a shelf for a wedge-shaped cabinet I built a while ago required sawing a fairly extreme taper on a 2×4' sheet of 3/4"-thick plywood. I wanted to use the table saw because it provided a much cleaner cut than my portable circular saw, but the piece was too large, and the angle too severe to use a typical tapering jig. After a bit of thought, I realized that the solution was to guide it with a runner that slid in my saw table groove.

I began by laying out a cutline on what would be the underside of the finished piece. Then I cut a straight-grained, table-slot-sized strip of wood to the approximate length of my cutline. I measured the distance from the saw blade to a table groove, then transferred that measurement from my cutline onto the "keeper" section of the workpiece. After using a straightedge to draw the full-length offset, I screwed the runner to the workpiece adjacent to that straight line. All that was left was to insert the runner in the table groove and make the cut.

—Russ Svendsen, Olean, NY

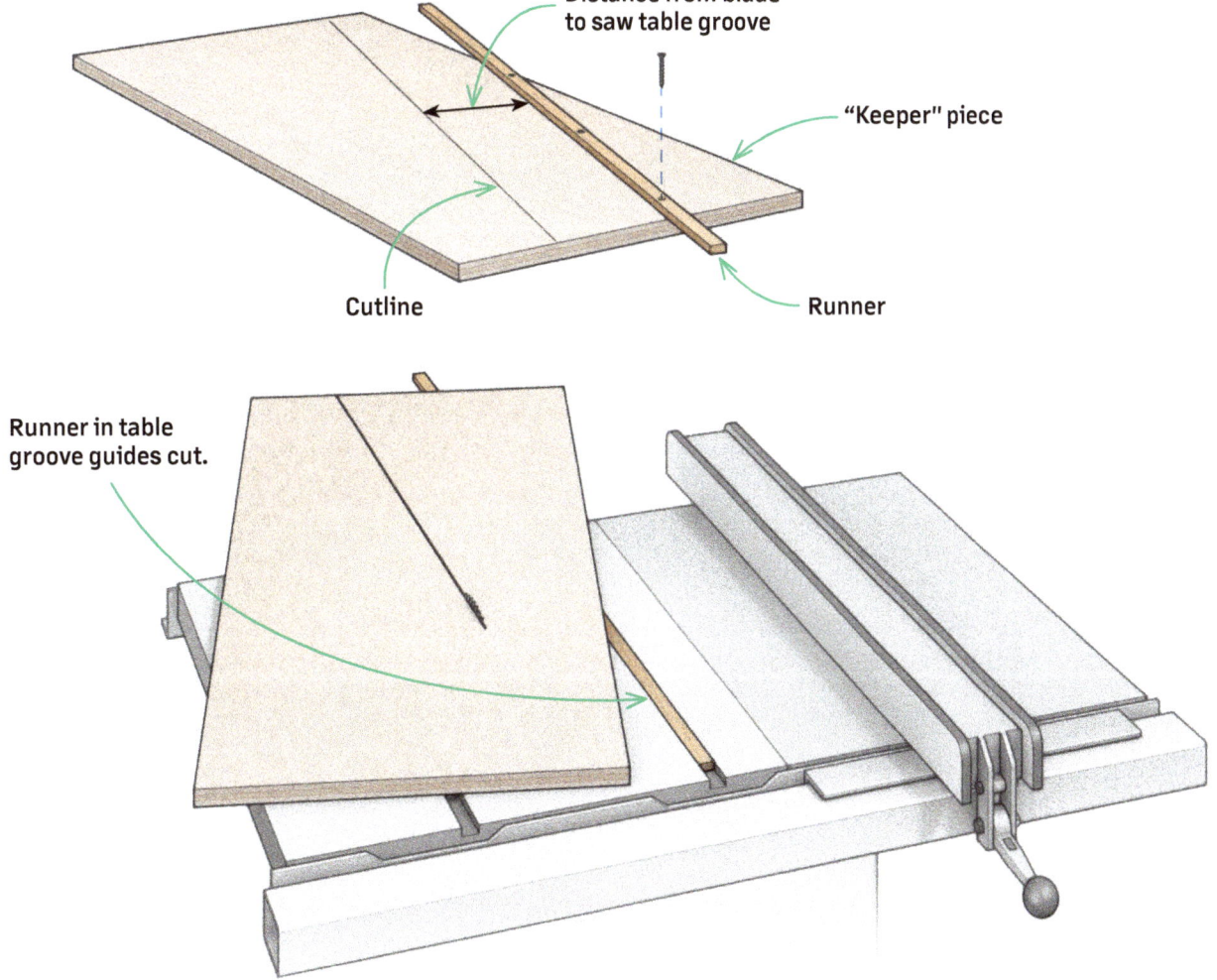

Self-gripping springboard

This magnet-assisted spring-loaded jig holds sawing stock in place, but is a lot easier to use. Instead of fussing with clamps, all I need to do is flick a switch. Because it's conveniently sized and comes with its own built-in clamping mechanism, I find myself using it more often, resulting in cleaner cuts and less risk of kickback.

As shown in the drawing, the jig is a simple, two-piece project sized to fit a pair of 20mm switchable magnets, such as MagJigs. I cut the parts as shown, drilled the spring holes, then hinged the two pieces together using a strip of plastic cut from a milk jug and a few short screws.

To use this jig, simply position it about 1" in front of the blade, press the jig so that the curved nose is tensioned against the edge of the board, then switch on the magnets. As the board passes the jig, the curved trailing end gradually reduces pressure so that the jig doesn't snap back or spin the board at the end of the cut.

—*Tom Roessler, Appleton, WI*

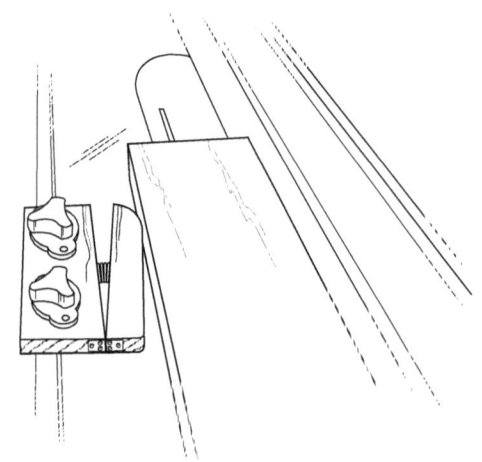

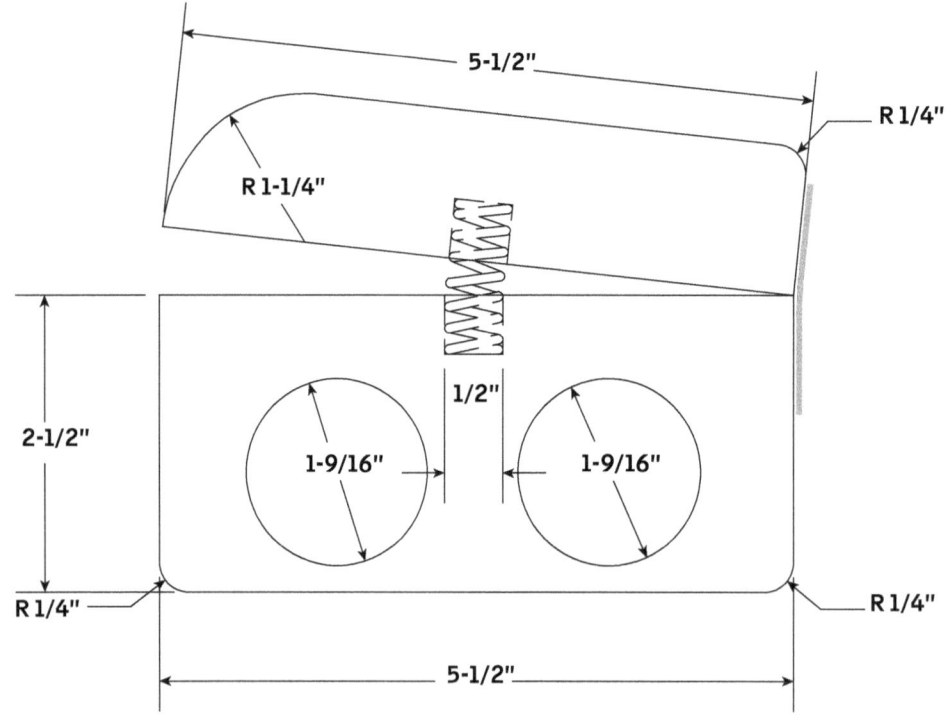

Let a kerf mark the cut

The problem with most etched-line saw-blade indicators is that it's too easy to make an incorrect reading if you're not looking through the acrylic at just the right angle. And for those times when you're cutting a dado or groove, the single line doesn't indicate the exact location or full width of the blade. Kerfing the gauge as shown (I replaced mine with a scrap of clear acrylic) solves both problems in one quick cut.

To make the gauge, affix the acrylic to the end of a scrap 2×4 with a few dabs of hot glue; then, notch it with your table saw for an exact blade-width kerf. Next, set the indicator by positioning the rip fence against the right side of the blade, and adjust the left-hand edge of the kerfed acrylic to your zero mark.

—Terry Dillon, Mineral Point, WI

Rapid repeatability

I recently had to make several curved glue-ups from 1/8" slats. I could have used my bandsaw to resaw the stock, but because the slats were cut from 2×4s, I figured my table saw would be faster and would make a smoother cut. However, moving the rip fence exactly the right distance after each rip operation would not only be very time consuming, but difficult to measure exactly right each time it was moved. Instead, I created this setup that required the exact measurement to be made only once.

Set up the rip fence so that the resulting slat is the exact size you want. Before cutting, clamp a stop block to the saw table at the left edge of the workpiece. After each rip operation, simply place the workpiece against the stop block and slide the rip fence left to meet the stock and lock it down. The stop block, which is offset from the saw kerf by the distance of the first slat, will automatically set the workpiece—and the rip fence—at the exact spot each time.

—Lewis Kauffman, Chambersburg, PA

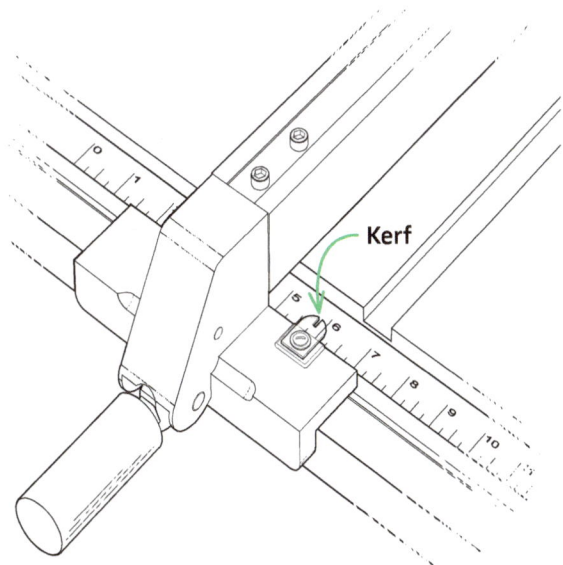

Kerf

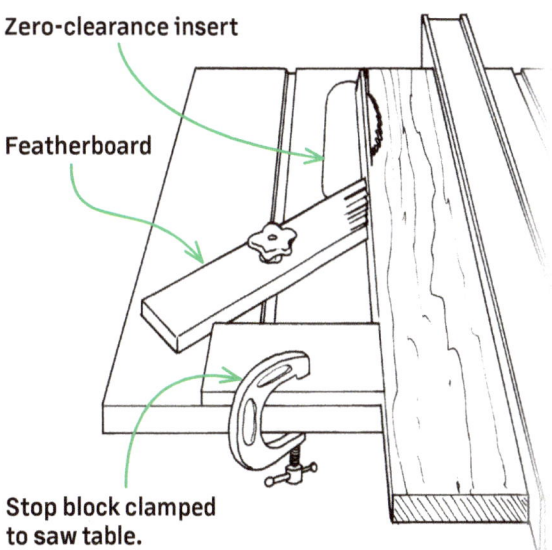

Zero-clearance insert

Featherboard

Stop block clamped to saw table.

TOOLS > TABLE SAW

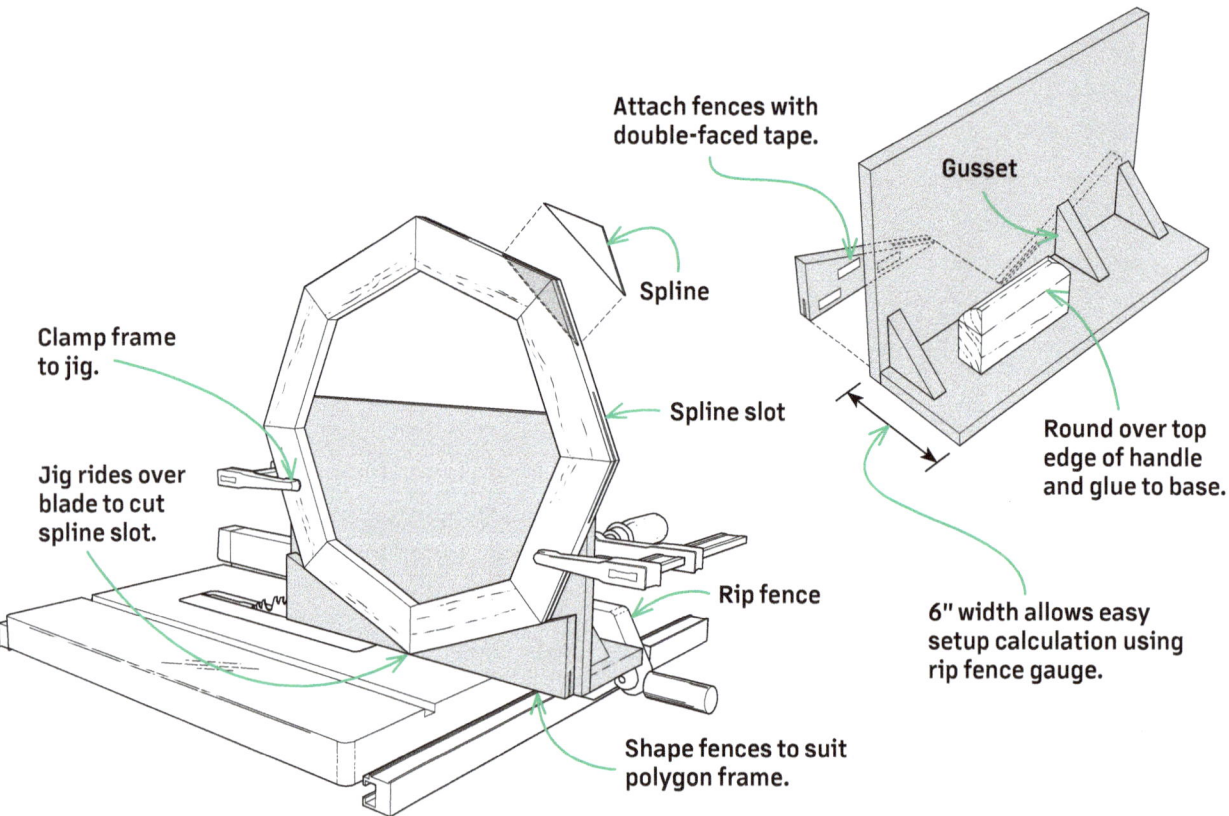

Splining polygons

Sometimes I make six- or eight-sided frames, reinforcing the otherwise weak joints with splines. As when splining square frames, these polygons are first glued together, and then the frame is held vertically in a jig and fed across the table saw to cut the spline slots.

The trick is in the jig. Many woodworkers have a dedicated jig for spline-slotting square frames. It's typically constructed somewhat like a tenoning jig, except it has two fences—perpendicular to each other and at 45° to the saw table. These are usually screwed to the jig face. I attach my fences with double-faced tape rather than screws. This gives me the flexibility to attach or rearrange any type or number of fences to suit a frame of any shape. (I can also use the jig for tenoning by attaching a single vertical fence.)

The jig itself is nothing fancy—just a couple of 3/4"-thick MDF or hardwood plywood panels attached and gusseted at a perfect 90° angle with a handle on the base for keeping the jig against the rip fence when in use. For safety, always clamp the workpiece to the body of the jig when sawing.

—Bill Sands, Lubeck, WV

Handy miter fixture

Making perfect miters can be a challenge, but with this fixture, you only have to measure a miter angle once.

Start with a piece of 1/2" or 3/4" plywood measuring 12" × 22". Cut a hardwood guide bar sized to your miter slot that will mount to the underside of the plywood so the plywood extends 1/4" past the cutline of the table saw. Double-check the guide bar for straightness (so it doesn't bind in the miter slot), and attach it to the plywood with glue and flat-head screws.

Place the fixture with the guide bar in the miter slot and cut off the excess along the cutline of the table saw—the edge is now perfectly parallel to the guide bar.

Make two hardwood fences measuring 1" × 1-1/2" × 14". Glue and screw one fence to the top of the fixture at 45° to the cutline edge; measure perfectly, then measure again to ensure the angle is exact. Using an accurate framing square, attach the second fence at exactly 90° to the first fence.

Glue 80-grit sandpaper to the outside fence faces to keep workpieces from slipping when you make your 45° cuts.

—Arthur Chism, Hot Springs Village, AR

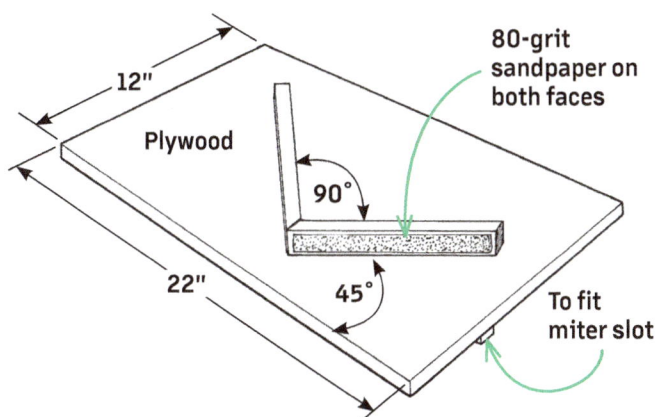

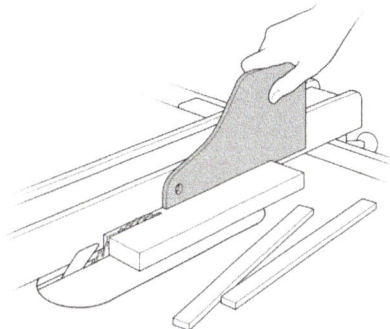

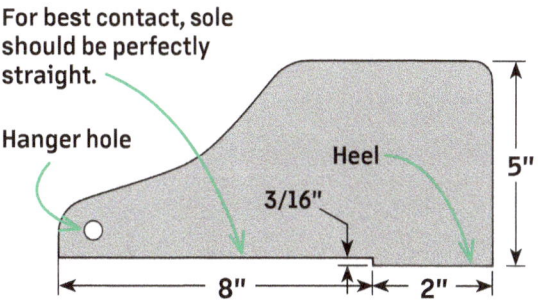

Shoe-style pushsticks

A shoe-style pushstick offers the best control over your workpiece. The long sole allows good downward pressure while the heel hooks over the end, offering positive forward feed force. The straight sole also provides enough bearing to help keep the workpiece against the fence to prevent kickback. Commercial models are available, but you can make your own from 1/4"- and 1/2"-thick plywood. Because they're cheap and easy to make, you can consider them sacrificial, meaning that they're perfect for ripping thin strips that require cutting into the pushstick as part of the process. You can make a pushstick any size you like, but it should be tall enough for your hand to pass over a tall splitter during narrow rips. The heel should be deep enough to positively grab the workpiece without slipping, but not so deep as to prevent solid sole contact on thin workpieces.

—Paul Anthony, Riegelsville, PA

TOOLS > TABLE SAW

Miter gauge quick-slip

Rather than trying to insert the washer end of a miter gauge bar in from the front of the table saw's T-slot, drop the bar in the slot with the washer cantilevered at the rear, and pull the miter gauge toward you.

—Paul Anthony, Riegelsville, PA

Dado blade tray

I find that stacking dado blades and chippers on a spindle often makes it a pain to get to a specific chipper when you need it. To make all my dado components much more accessible, I made a tray to accommodate them, placing it atop a cabinet under my saw's side extension table. To make the tray, I traced out the shape of each blade and chipper onto a piece of 3/8"-thick MDF, incorporating adjacent cutouts for finger access. After cutting out the shapes with a jigsaw, I glued the cutout panel onto another sheet of MDF, creating a custom-fitted tray that organizes and protects my now very accessible cutters.

—Rob Spiece, Berea, KY

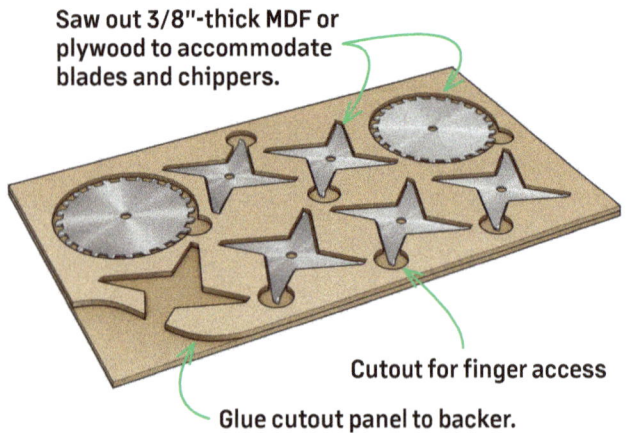

Saw out 3/8"-thick MDF or plywood to accommodate blades and chippers.

Cutout for finger access

Glue cutout panel to backer.

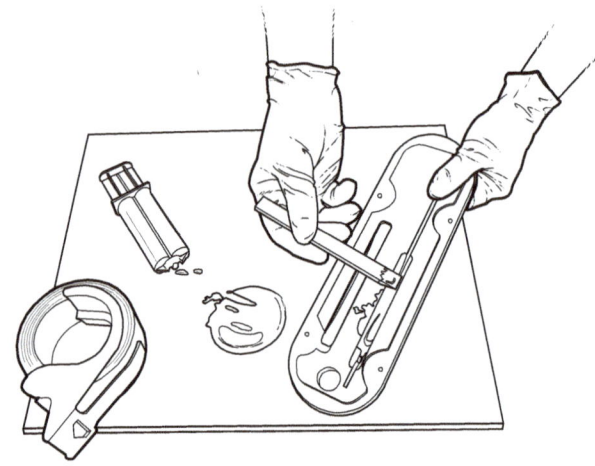

Re-zeroed table saw insert

Zero-clearance inserts prevent splintering and chip-out only as long as they remain zero-clearance. After a few years of use and several different blades, the slot on my insert had become too wide to do the job right. Rather than make or buy a fresh insert, I found a way to get a few more clean cuts from my old one.

To give your insert new life, affix a strip of clear packing tape over the slot from the top of the insert. Now flip it over and drip epoxy into the slot. (To save epoxy, use only as much as is needed to patch the slot top face.) Once cured, sand flush, reinsert the insert in your saw, and raise the blade to cut a fresh slot.

—Jay Trinidad, Bainbridge Island, WA

Not quite 90°

After making a table saw cut that's just slightly off 90°, immediately reset the blade square again or else place a reminder of some sort next to it. It's too easy to overlook a slightly tilted blade when you return to make a 90° next time. Oops!

—Paul Anthony, Riegelsville, PA

TABLE SAW < TOOLS

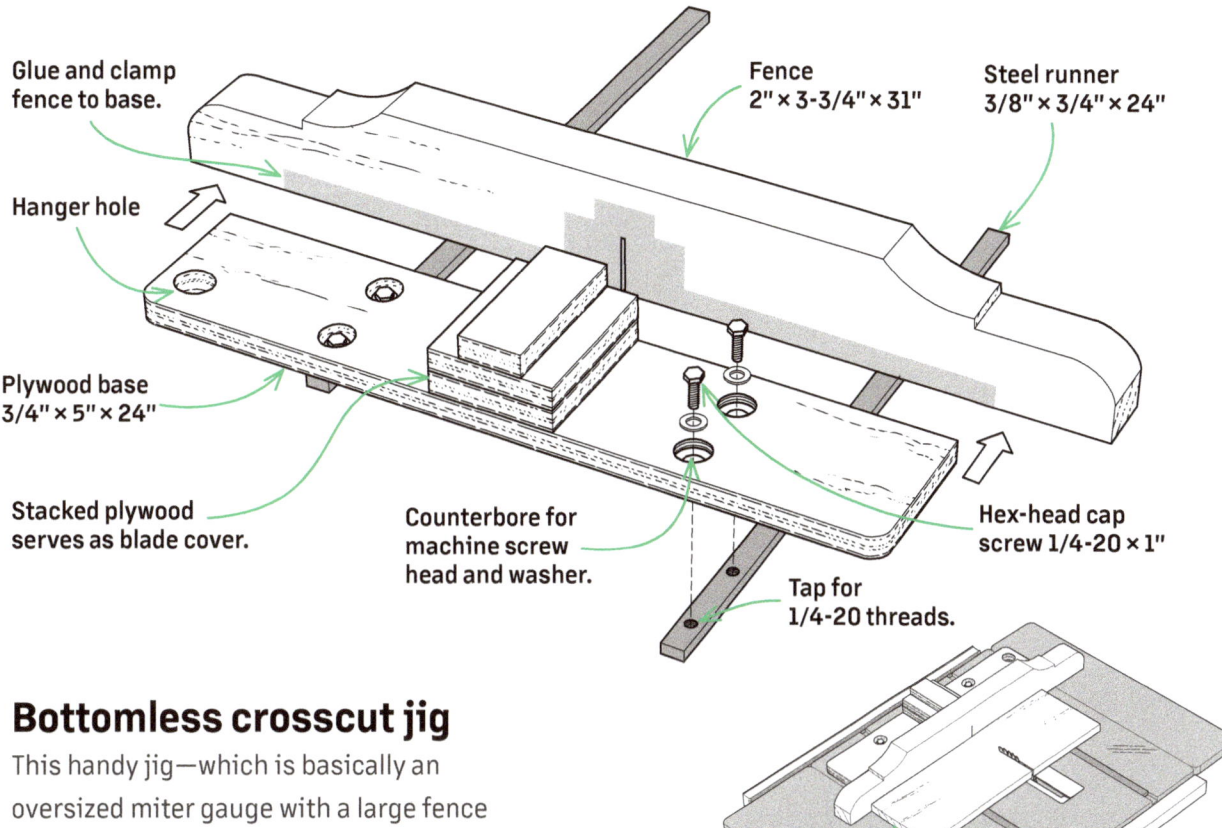

- Glue and clamp fence to base.
- Hanger hole
- Plywood base 3/4" × 5" × 24"
- Stacked plywood serves as blade cover.
- Fence 2" × 3-3/4" × 31"
- Steel runner 3/8" × 3/4" × 24"
- Counterbore for machine screw head and washer.
- Tap for 1/4-20 threads.
- Hex-head cap screw 1/4-20 × 1"
- Workpiece

Bottomless crosscut jig

This handy jig—which is basically an oversized miter gauge with a large fence and double runners for better workpiece bearing and stability—lets you crosscut large workpieces with accuracy and ease. Its advantage over a traditional crosscut sled is the ability to make a full-depth cut, as there's no bottom sled panel raising the workpiece. The plywood base keeps the fence dead-straight and serves as a solid connection for the runners while allowing adjustment if necessary to square up the fence. The tapered ends of the fence allow better hand access for holding down narrow work.

Use quartersawn hard maple or other straight-grained hardwood for the fence, and 3/4"-thick hardwood plywood for the base, stacking pieces at the center to serve as a blade cover. Drill the attachment holes through the steel bar stock with a #7 bit before cutting the threads with a 1/4-20 tap.

Trim the leading edge of the base flush and square, and then glue the fence to it.

With the runners in their slots, measure the precise distances between the hole center points, and transfer those locations onto the base. Drill 5/16"-diameter holes at those points, also counterboring to recess for 1/4-20 × 1" hex-head cap screws and washers. Loosely attach the runners with the cap screws and washers, square the fence to the fully raised blade, and then tighten the screws. Make a test cut, and readjust if necessary. When correct, you'll get perfectly square crosscuts every time.

—Andy Rae, Asheville, NC

TOOLS > TABLE SAW

Fence auxiliary facing

Sometimes I need to attach an auxiliary wooden fence, or facing, to prevent damage to the aluminum fence when performing operations like sawing rabbets with a dado head. The typical approach is to drill holes through it for securing a facing with screws. This setup is quicker to attach.

I made the 3/4"-thick MDF facing wider than the height of the fence and screwed on a spacer for mounting three toggle clamps. Now it's a matter of simply clamping the facing in place instead of messing with attachment screws.

—*Dick Reese, Centerville, OH*

When to sharpen saw blades?

It can be hard to know when to sharpen a table saw blade. If you wait until teeth tips start rounding over and your work starts burning, you've waited too long. Your best reference is to compare a current cut against test cuts made when a blade is brand new or freshly sharpened. Whenever I get a new blade, I take a series of rips and crosscuts in both hard and soft wood, marking the pieces with the date and blade identification. I then stash them in a cabinet with extra test-cut stock. When a blade starts cutting questionably, I clean it with concentrated citrus cleaner, then take a few cuts in my stashed test stock. Comparing these current cuts with my initial test cuts under a strong raking light shows how much the blade has dulled. Just as importantly, comparing the results of a freshly sharpened blade against your original test cuts indicates the quality of your sharpening service.

—*Paul Anthony, Riegelsville, PA*

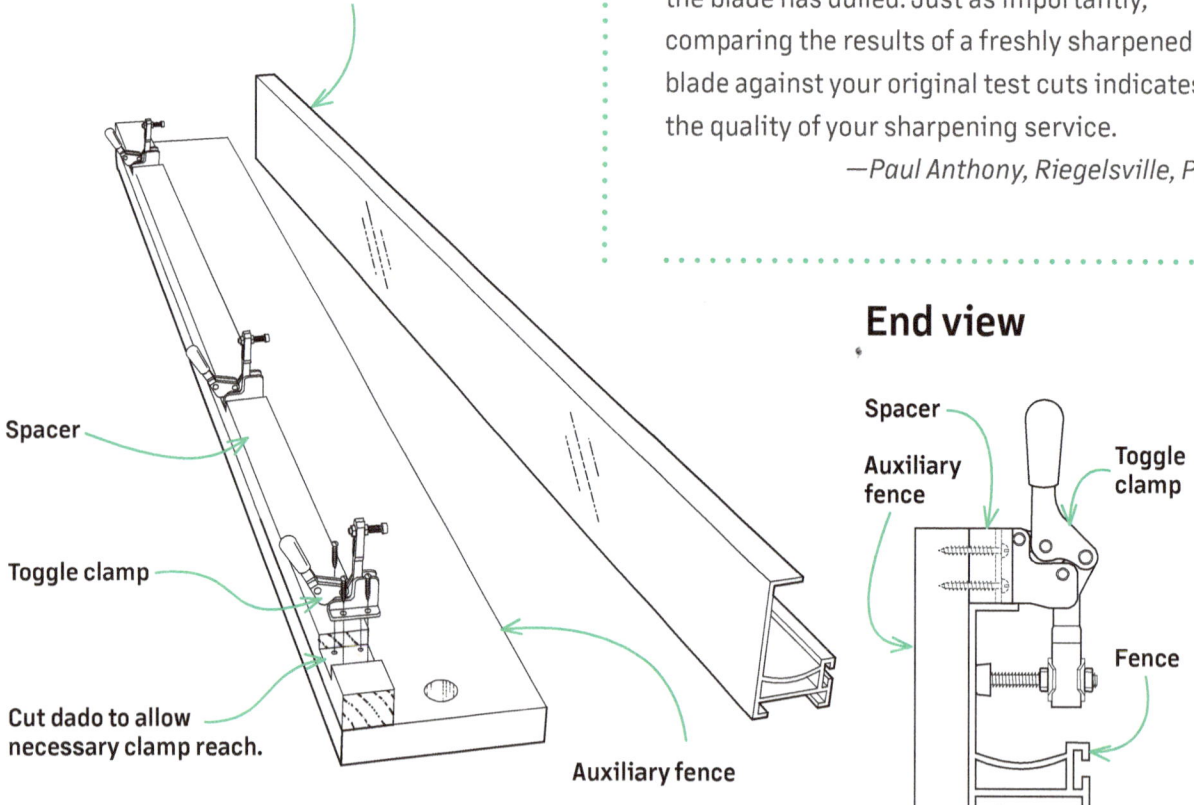

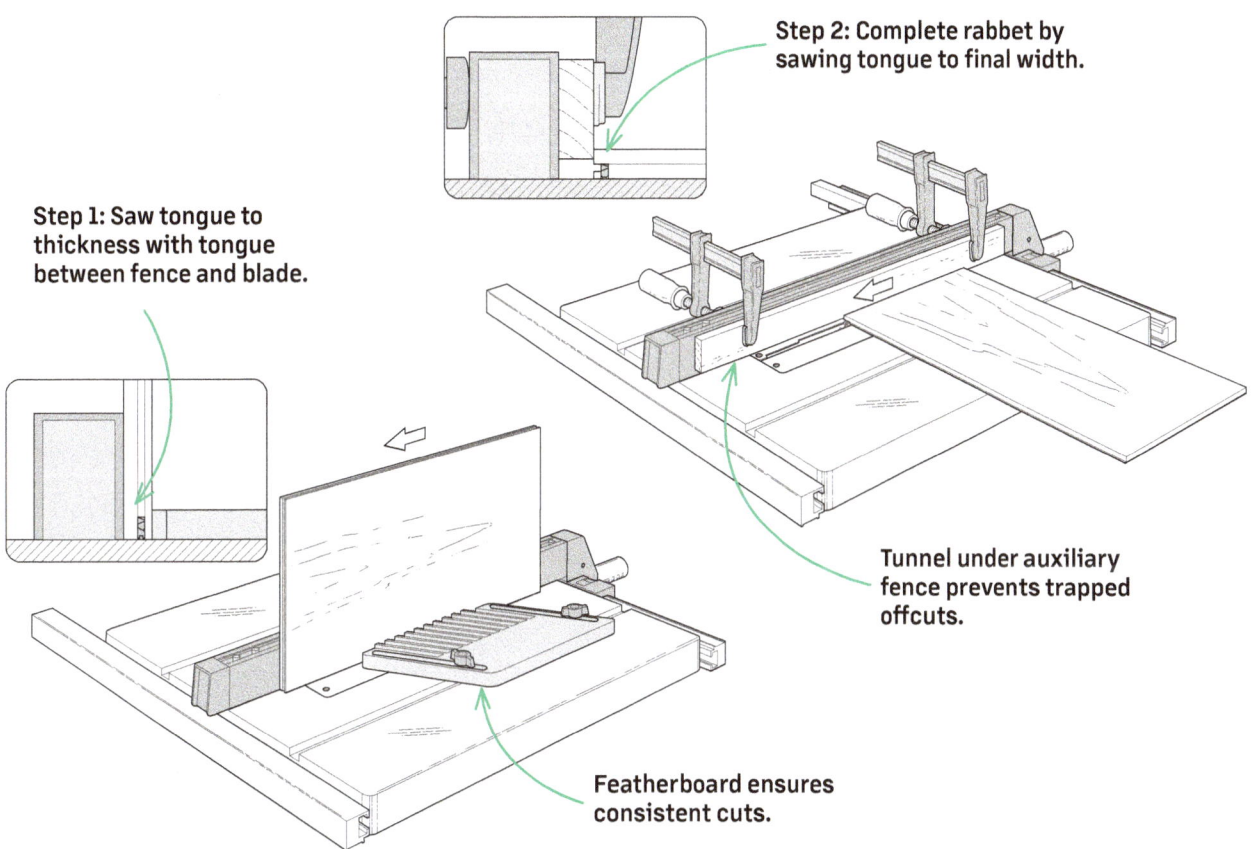

Step 2: Complete rabbet by sawing tongue to final width.

Step 1: Saw tongue to thickness with tongue between fence and blade.

Tunnel under auxiliary fence prevents trapped offcuts.

Featherboard ensures consistent cuts.

Perfect tongue-and-groove fit

Project plans often call for rabbeting the edges of a panel in order to create a tongue that slips into a drawer or rail groove. This is often done with a router bit or table saw dado head, with the work fed flat on the table. Unfortunately, done this way, any inaccuracy in the thickness of the stock is transferred to the thickness of the tongue, creating an ill fit in the groove.

One way to ensure a perfect tongue-and-groove fit is to create the rabbet by making two intersecting cuts on the table saw, feeding the edge to be rabbeted against the fence. Set up the first cut to rip the tongue to thickness, feeding the panel on edge with the tongue face against the fence. Use a featherboard to ensure consistency of cut. Now set up to make the intersecting cut against a thick auxiliary fence, raising it enough to create a tunnel for the freed offcut to fall away without being pinched between the blade and fence, eliminating violent ejection of the piece.

—*Harvey Mickelson, Reno, NV*

TOOLS > TABLE SAW

Wedge-cutting revisited

My wedge-cutting method can be done on either the bandsaw or table saw and doesn't require making a jig.

Begin by thicknessing a board to the desired width of your wedges, and then crosscut away a piece that equals the desired wedge length. Outfit your miter gauge with an auxiliary fence, and set the gauge to half the desired wedge angle. (It's best to set it to create an obtuse angle between the fence and blade.) Also outfit your saw's throat opening with a zero-clearance insert. Trim the end of your blank, flip it 180º, shift it the desired amount, and make another cut to complete the wedge. To make multiple identically sized wedges, set up a stopblock, as shown. (I use the back edge of my featherboard.) To prevent binding, place the stopblock forward of the blade a distance equal to or greater than the length of your wedges.

—Philip Houck, Boston, MA

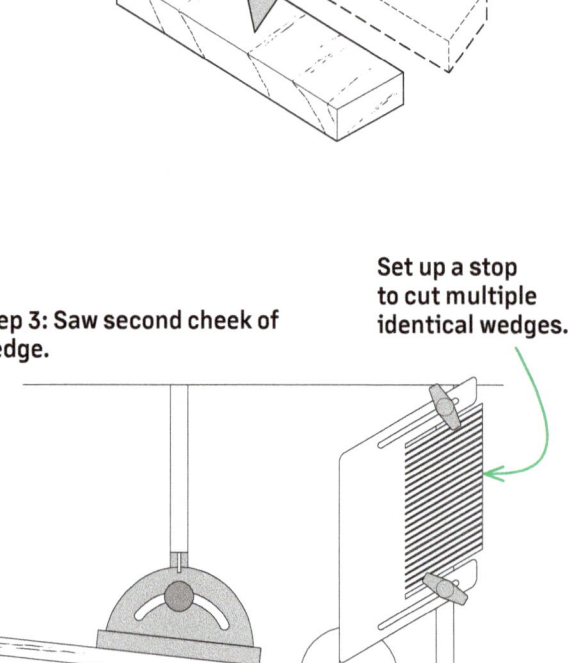

Step 2: Flip blank.

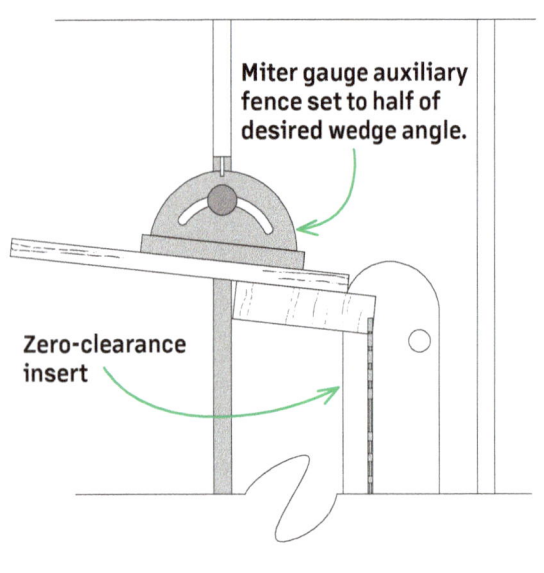

Step 1: Trim end of wedge blank.

Miter gauge auxiliary fence set to half of desired wedge angle.

Zero-clearance insert

Step 3: Saw second cheek of wedge.

Set up a stop to cut multiple identical wedges.

Ripping thin strips

Ripping multiple thin strips on the table saw in traditional ripping fashion can be dicey. The blade is so close to the fence that it tends to chew up your pushstick, which is also usually too thick to bypass a splitter. This is when it's better to rip from the outer edge of the board. But the trick is being able to quickly and accurately reset the fence for subsequent identical cuts. Here's how it works:

Adjust the rip fence so that the blade will slice your desired width of cut from the edge of the board that's opposite the fence. With the board at the ready for cutting, set up a stop of some sort against the edge that's being trimmed. Make the cut, and then set up for the next cut by resetting the fence with the board pinched between it and the stop. For a stop, I use a simple jig like the one shown. It's just a small piece of wood glued or screwed to a runner that rides in the table slot. The screw allows fine adjustment for the cut. Instead, you could use a stout featherboard or a stick clamped to your miter gauge.

—Harold Coverson, Salt Lake City, UT

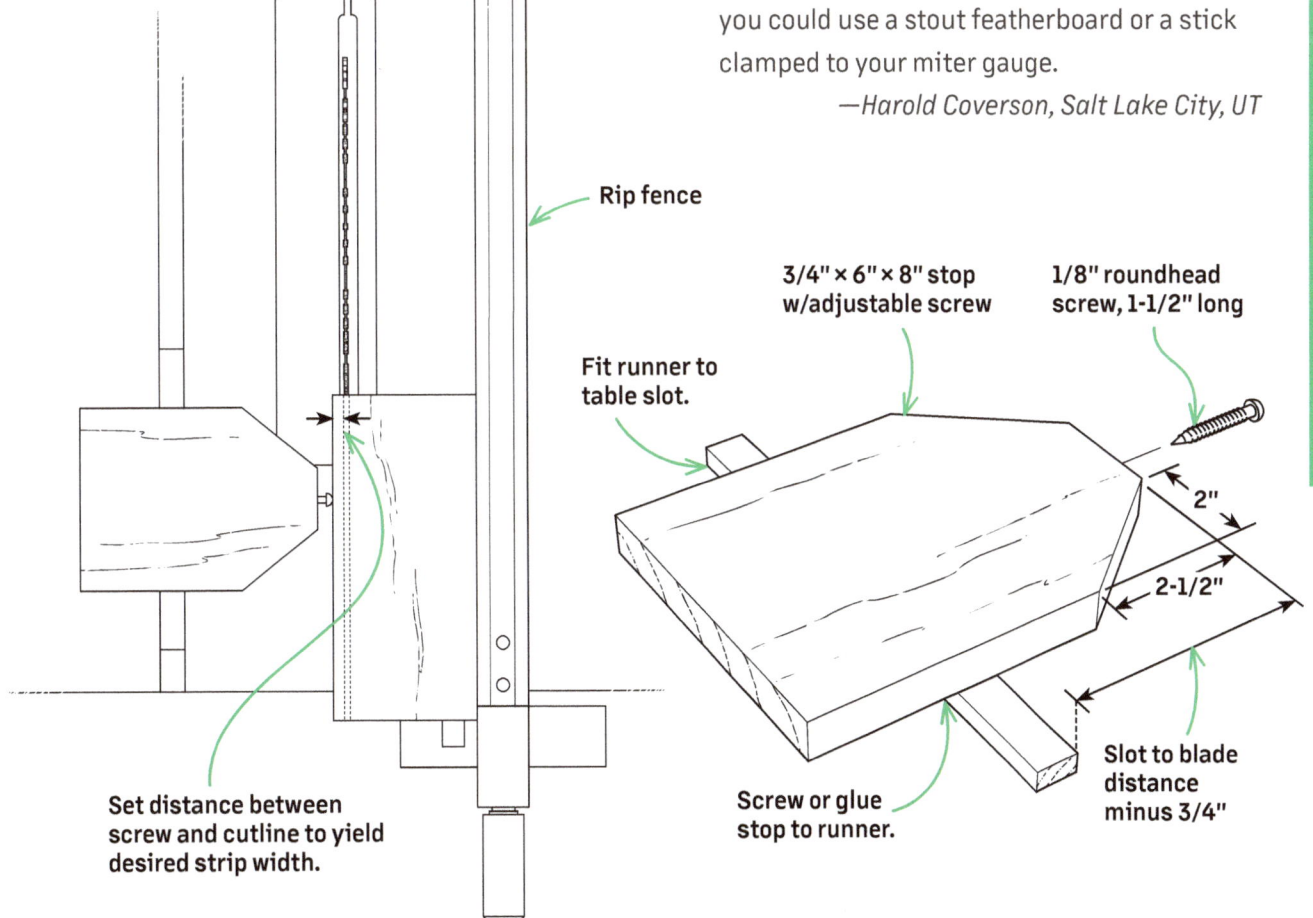

TOOLS > TABLE SAW

Zero-clearance laminate panel

When ripping narrow pieces from wide stock, I was having trouble because the opening on my table saw's stock throat plate was too wide to offer good support for the resulting strips. I hadn't yet made a zero-clearance replacement throat plate, and needed a quick fix. I ripped a piece of plastic laminate about a foot wide and crosscut it to match the front-to-back depth of my table saw. I used double-faced tape to affix the laminate to my table saw top, with its edge butted against my pre-set fence. I clamped a board to the fence to hold the laminate down as I raised the saw blade through it. After removing the hold-down, I was ready to go, with the laminate serving as a zero-clearance panel.

—Bill Wells, Olympia, WA

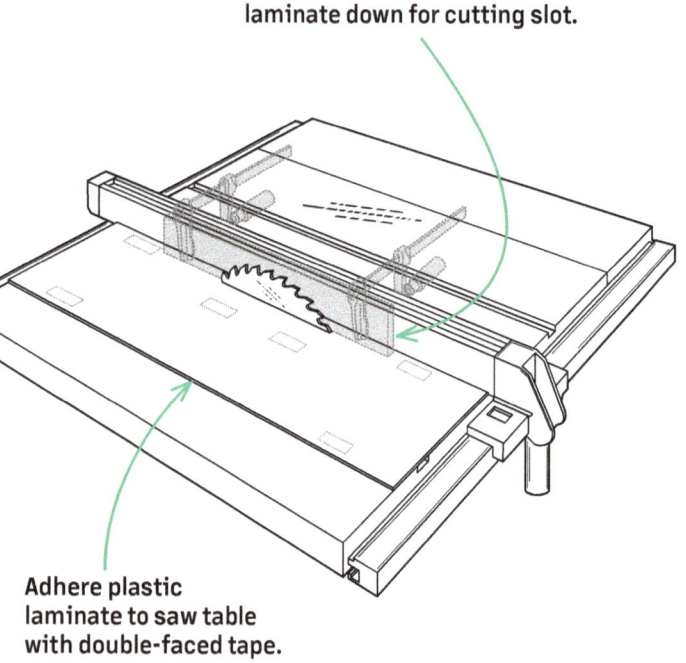

Temporary board holds laminate down for cutting slot.

Adhere plastic laminate to saw table with double-faced tape.

Butcher block facing

Stock fence

Butcher block fence

The MDF face of my fence wasn't perfectly straight, so I added a strip of 1-1/4"-thick maple butcher block. Attaching the strip to the fence will vary from saw to saw, but in my case I popped the MDF face off the fence and screwed the MDF to the maple. Easy peasy.

Besides providing a straighter bearing surface, the maple face is taller than the original. I find the extra surface area helpful when ripping stock on edge, or when I want to clamp on featherboards or stops. Should it get damaged, the hardwood facing can be restored with a jointer and planer.

—Tommy MacDonald, Boston, MA

TABLE SAW < TOOLS

Rip-fence repeater

In a perfect world, you'd make all the cuts for same-width project parts at the same time. There are instances, however, when you need to set the rip fence for other cuts, and then must return to the original table saw setup. That's when you need this jig. Its adjustable arms allow you to quickly reset your rip fence for two repeatable settings without fussy measuring or test cutting. I mostly use the jig with my table saw, but it works just as well with a router table equipped with a miter gauge slot. Build it as shown, making sure that the miter slot strip fits your saw.

To use the jig, set your rip fence, then position the jig into the miter slot, loosen the wing nut, and slide one of the wood arms so that its end touches the fence. To use the second arm, rotate the jig end for end. For greater versatility, consider making one arm 12" long; the other, 18" long.

—Tim Rusch, Tampa, FL

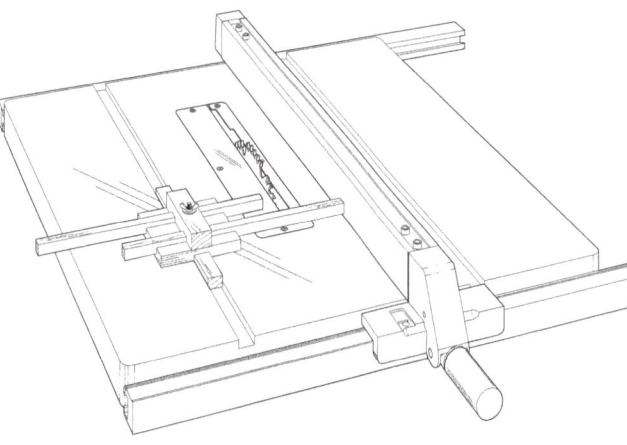

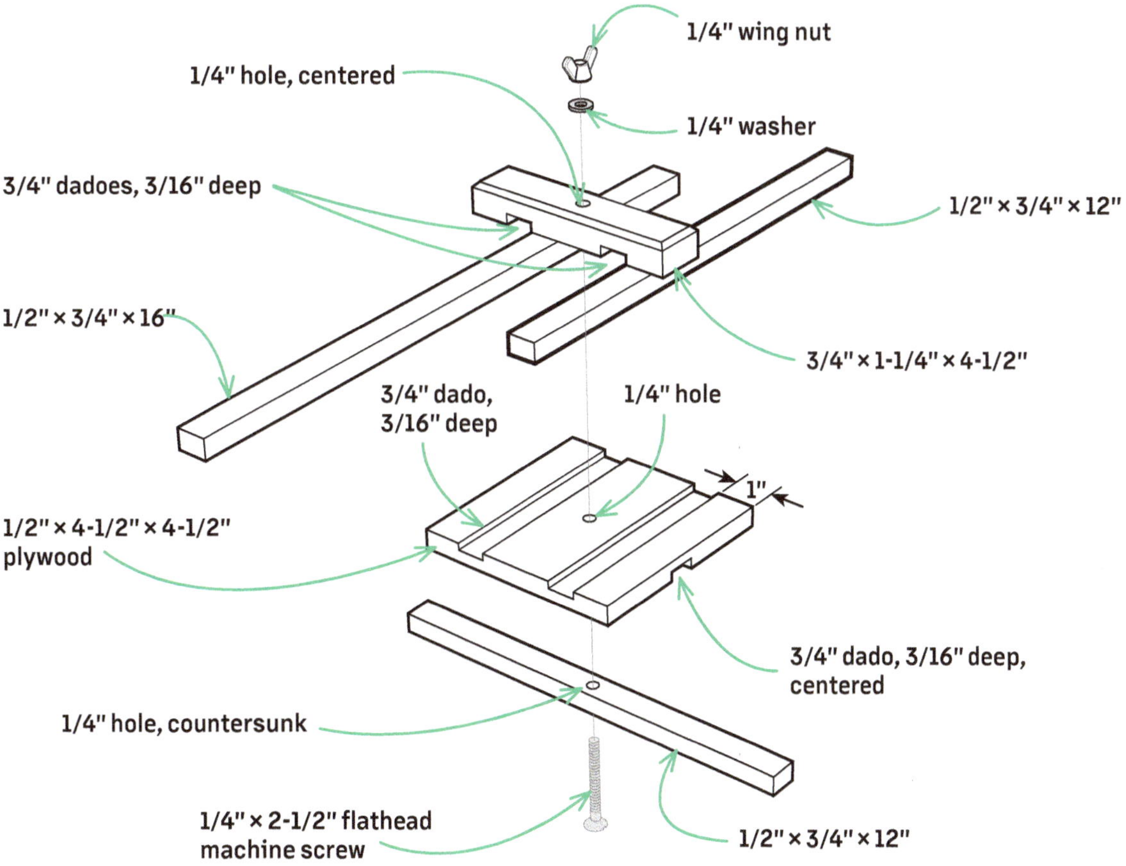

- 1/4" wing nut
- 1/4" hole, centered
- 1/4" washer
- 3/4" dadoes, 3/16" deep
- 1/2" × 3/4" × 12"
- 1/2" × 3/4" × 16"
- 3/4" × 1-1/4" × 4-1/2"
- 3/4" dado, 3/16" deep
- 1/4" hole
- 1"
- 1/2" × 4-1/2" × 4-1/2" plywood
- 3/4" dado, 3/16" deep, centered
- 1/4" hole, countersunk
- 1/4" × 2-1/2" flathead machine screw
- 1/2" × 3/4" × 12"

WOODCRAFT MAGAZINE TIPS & TRICKS FOR WOODWORKING

Featherboard riser

A featherboard is great for controlling feed at the table saw, bandsaw, or router table, preventing kickback and keeping a workpiece firmly pressed against a fence for both safety and accuracy of cut. But there are times when a featherboard is best raised up off the table. For example, when rabbeting at the table saw, a table-mounted featherboard will press against the freed offcut, causing it to eject violently. Raising the featherboard prevents this. A raised featherboard also keeps tall panels and other workpieces perfectly vertical, which helps when resawing against a tall fence, among other operations.

This simple riser jig works with commercial featherboards, most of which include hardware that locks the unit in your machine table slots. Make the jig base from 3/4"-thick plywood, about 3" wide and a few inches longer than your featherboard width. Glue on a hardwood mounting bar, the width of which raises your featherboard to the desired height. Install the featherboard locking hardware in the jig base, and then mount the featherboard to the mounting bar with hanger bolts from the hardware store and female jig knobs.

—Dan Martin, Galena, OH

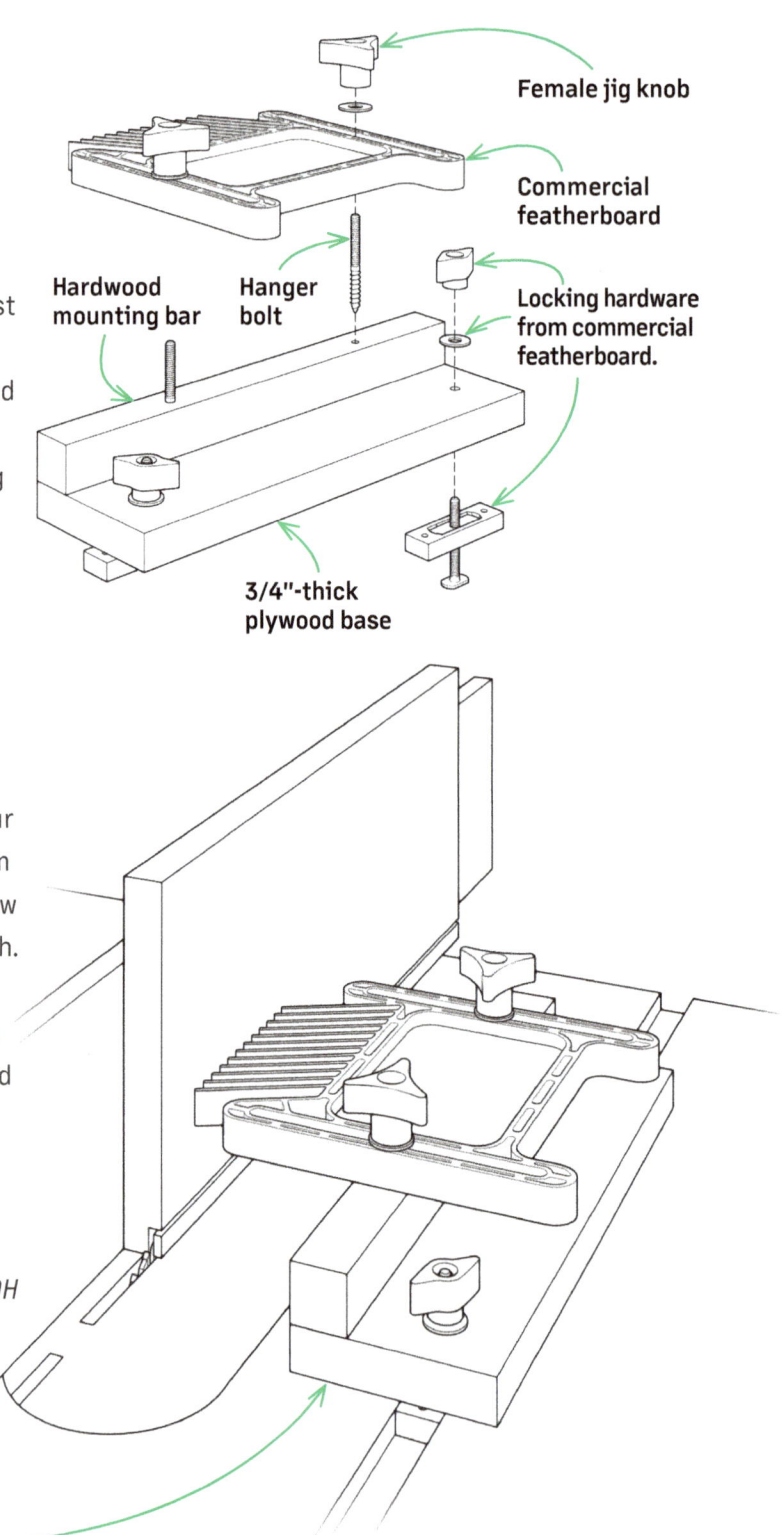

Riser jig raises featherboard off the saw table when appropriate for operation.

Double-slot zero-clearance hold-down

For my table saw, I like to use a two-slot zero-clearance insert (ZCI) that will accommodate both a standard blade and a thin-kerf blade. As with any ZCI, it's best to secure the rear end of the insert to prevent it from lifting. With a single-slot insert, a flat washer screwed to the underside at the rear will do the job. However, that won't work when you rotate a ZCI like this to use the opposite slot.

To solve the problem, I screwed a figure eight tabletop fastener to each end of the insert. Now, depending on which blade I'm using, I rotate the rear fastener outward to catch the underside of the saw table and rotate the front fastener inward, out of the way of the slots.

—Father Chrysanthos Agiogregorites, Etna, CA

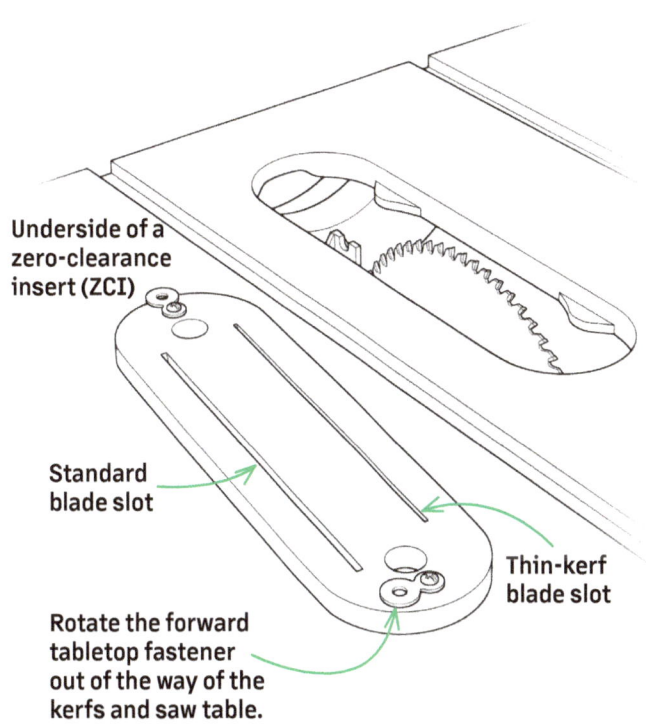

Underside of a zero-clearance insert (ZCI)

Standard blade slot

Thin-kerf blade slot

Rotate the forward tabletop fastener out of the way of the kerfs and saw table.

Multipurpose crosscut sled

If you have a crosscut sled for your table saw, you actually have much more than just a crosscut sled. What you have is a sliding base to which you can attach all sorts of custom fences and hold-downs to accommodate specialty cuts. For example, say you need to saw multiple plywood gussets for a project. Simply tack or screw two fences to your sled base, as shown, to quickly and accurately make the cuts. You can even outfit the sled with fences and hold-downs to safely cut tapers on small workpieces. Using a sled like this can be a great labor-saving alternative to making dedicated jigs that will see service only once or twice.

—Paul Anthony, Riegelsville, PA

Workpiece

Attach appropriate fences to sled base to support odd-shaped workpieces.

TOOLS > TABLE SAW

Laminate-sawing auxiliary fence

When feeding plastic laminate on the table saw, the material tends to pinch in the gap under the rip fence. It also wants to ride on top of the spinning blade if the sheet isn't held down. Furthermore, the heel of a pushstick too often slips upward off the thin stock. This simple jig neatly solves all three problems. Make the parts from plywood or MDF, gluing the riser strip to the bottom edge of the auxiliary fence. This configuration prevents the material from slipping under the rip fence, and lifts it enough for a pushstick heel to easily catch. The hold-down, of course, prevents lifting.

I use double-faced tape to attach the hold-down board in case I need to raise it more than 1/8" to accommodate acrylic or other slightly thicker material. The hold-down is a few inches shorter than the auxiliary fence to allow inspection of workpiece/fence contact at both ends of the fence. For most cuts, you can simply clamp the jig to your rip fence. However, clamps can impede pushstick travel on very narrow cuts, in which case I attach the jig to my rip fence with double-faced tape, applying clamp pressure to the taped areas for a few moments to ensure a good bond.

—*Paul Anthony, Riegelsville, PA*

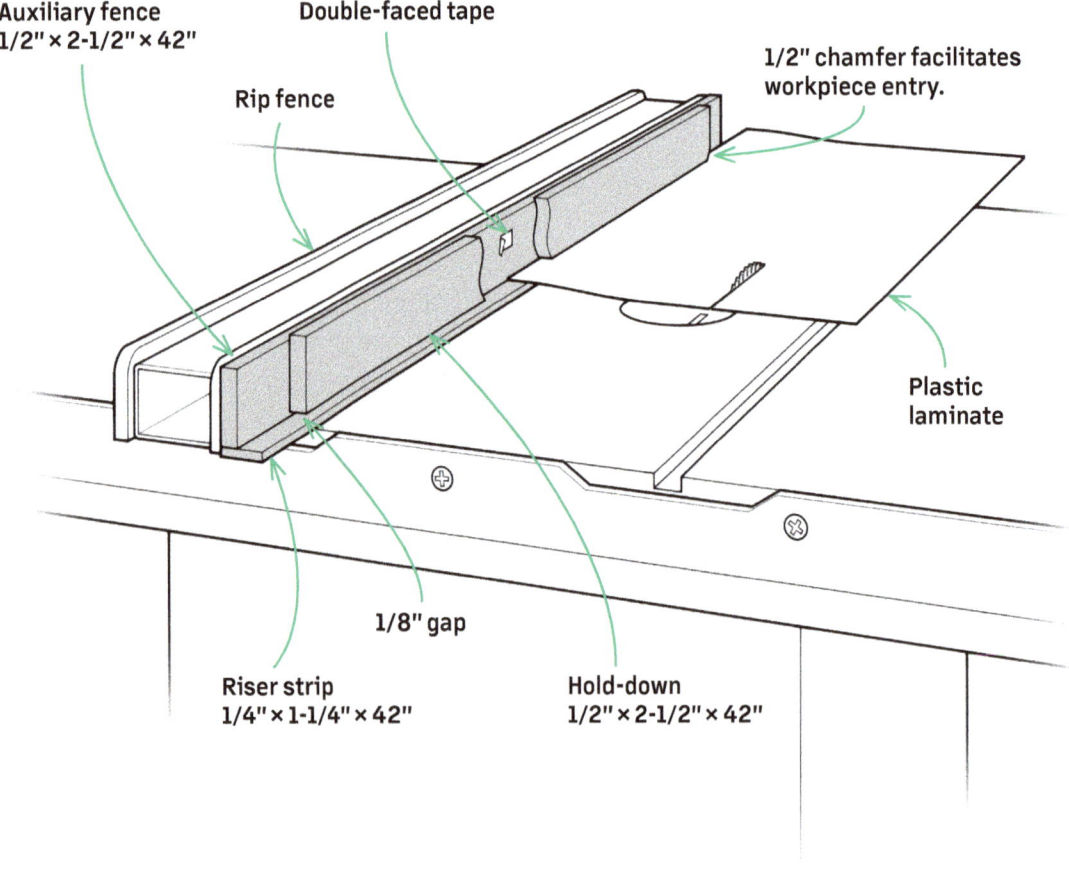

Thin-plate zero-clearance insert

My hybrid table saw has a 1/8"-thick metal throat plate that sits in an opening with very shallow ledges. This shallow recess complicates making a zero-clearance insert for the opening. My solution is to modify the stock throat plate.

Make a sub-plate by cutting a piece of 3/8"-thick plywood to fit between the leveling screw tabs in your table opening. Wax the underside of the stock plate and the inside edges of its slot (to resist glue when attaching the filler strip later), and then screw the plate to the plywood with flat-head screws driven through six countersunk holes you drilled through the plate. Next, thickness a hardwood blank to match the width of the slot, and then rip a strip from the blank that's just a hair wider than the thickness of the plate. Crosscut this slot-filler strip to the slot length, and then glue and clamp it to the underlying plywood, topping the strip with waxed paper and a caul. After the glue dries, sand the strip flush to the plate. (To avoid scratching your plate, mask off the surrounding area with tape.) Alternatively, unscrew the stock plate and handplane the strip, testing the fit as you work. Finally, clamp down the finished insert and raise the spinning blade through it.

—David Schermock, Humble, TX

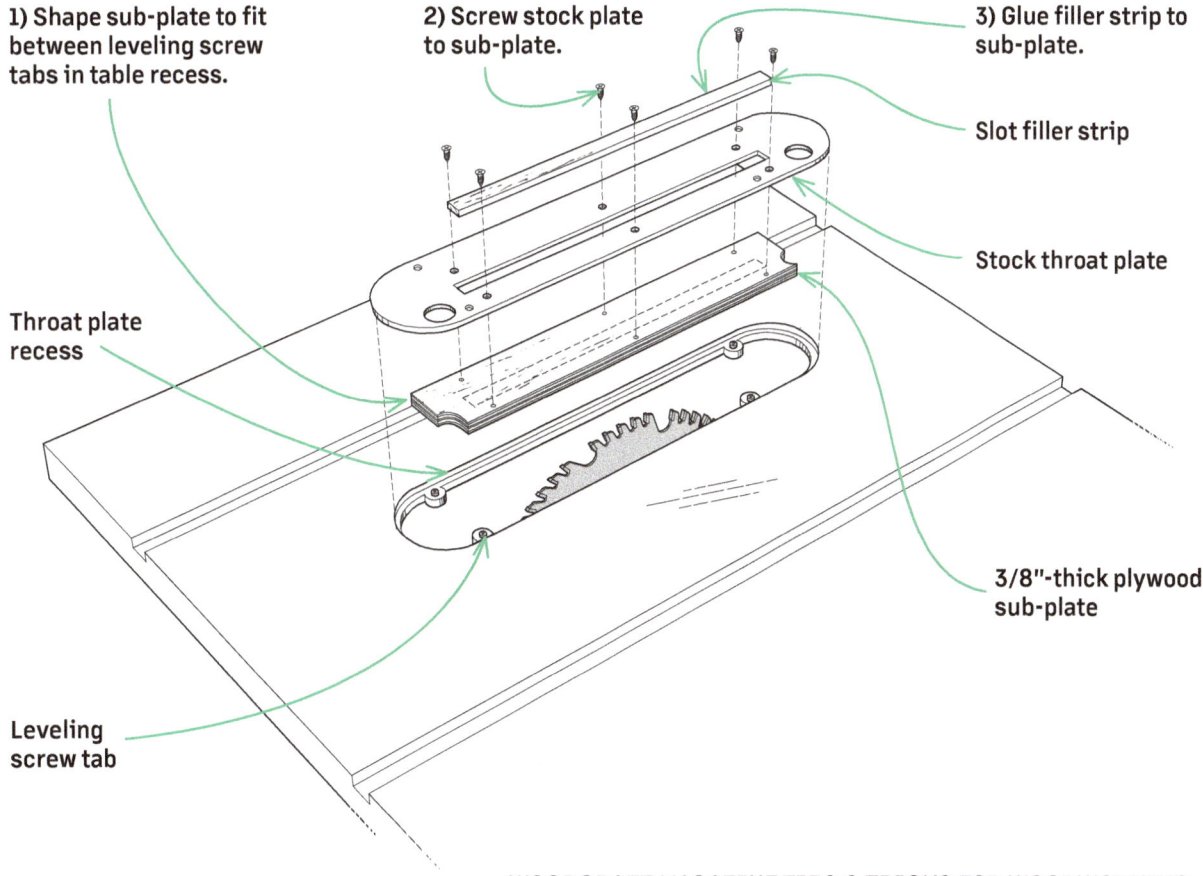

1) Shape sub-plate to fit between leveling screw tabs in table recess.

2) Screw stock plate to sub-plate.

3) Glue filler strip to sub-plate.

Slot filler strip

Stock throat plate

Throat plate recess

3/8"-thick plywood sub-plate

Leveling screw tab

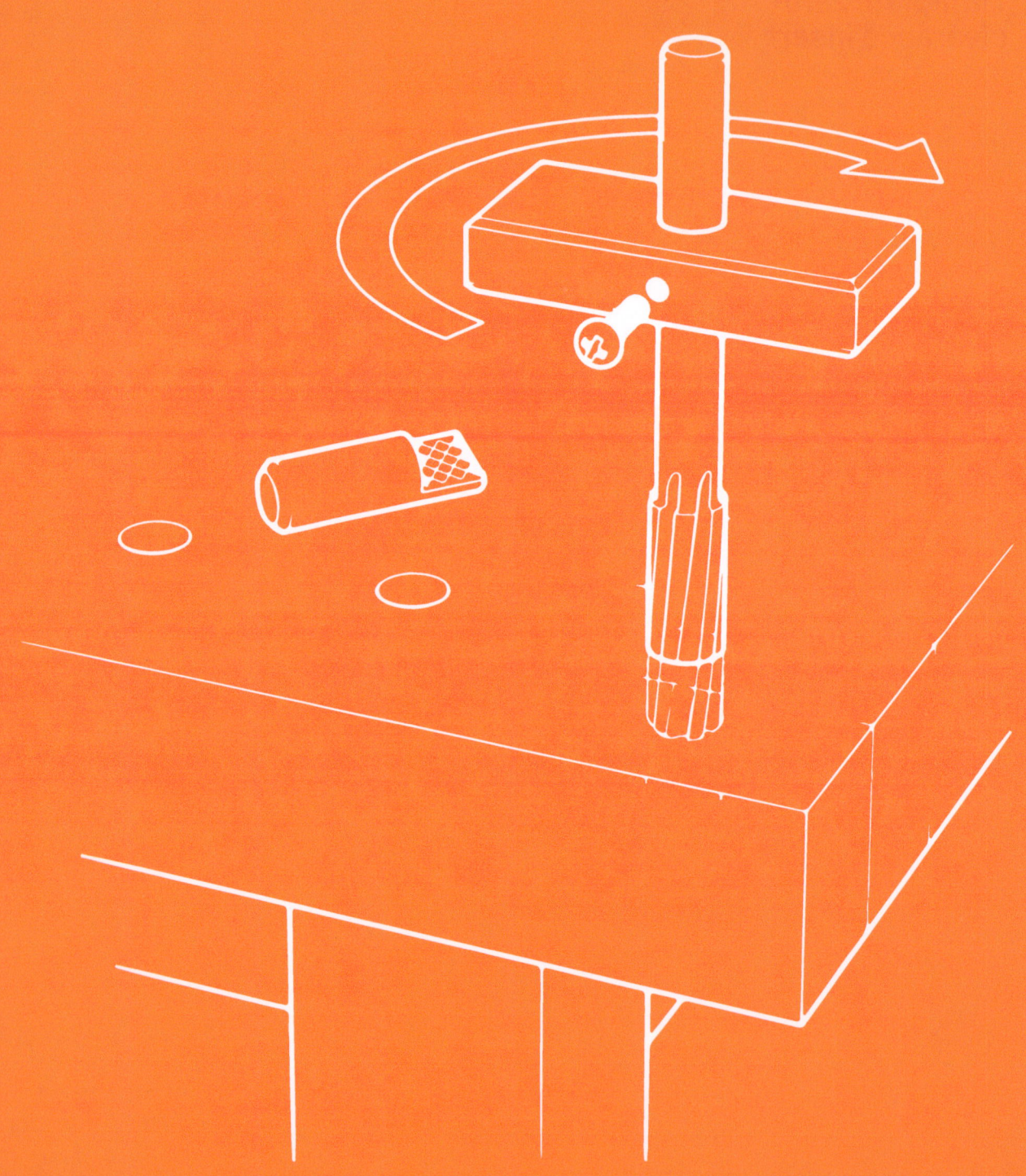

WORKSHOP

CLAMPING & WORK-HOLDING............ **182**

CLEANUP **206**

DUST COLLECTION **210**

ORGANIZATION & STORAGE **214**

SHOP **228**

WORKSHOP > CLAMPING & WORK-HOLDING

CLAMPING & WORK-HOLDING

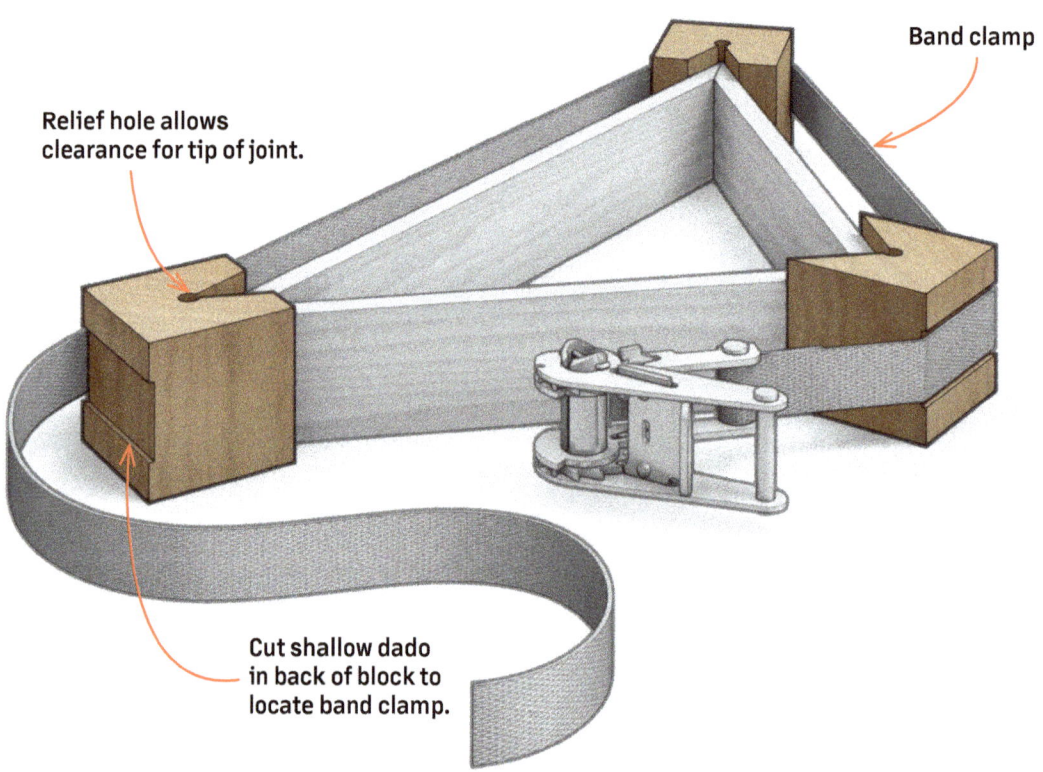

Corner clamping cauls

I'm an old Marine and—more often than I like—I make flag display boxes for the families of fallen comrades. The triangular boxes are finicky to clamp up, so I devised a brilliant (for me) but simple solution. Beginning with three 3" long pieces of scrap 4×4, I bandsawed a 90° notch into one and a 45° notch into each of the others. Then I drilled a small relief hole at the apex of the notches and cut a shallow dado on the back to locate a clamp strap. Voila! The cauls pull the box walls together tightly, spreading clamping pressure across the joint, which also eliminates the need for multiple band clamps.

—J. M. "Mike" Jeffries, Millbrook, AL

Bar clamp hold-down

During a recent project, I realized that I needed a bench hold-down. I've seen commercially available toggle-style hold-downs that fit in 3/4"-diameter bench dog holes like mine but wanted the kind of extra strength that a screw clamp can apply. I couldn't find what I wanted, so I created one by modifying a clamp I already had. I began by sawing the head off of a 12"-long F-style clamp that has a 3/4"-wide bar. Then, using an angle grinder outfitted with a 1/16" disc, I ground a dozen or so pairs of opposing notches about 1/8" apart at the end of the bar, angling them at about 60°. Finally, I filed the sharp edges of the notched section for safety and for an easier fit in my dog holes. The modified clamp works great! It's remarkable how often I find myself using it.

—Don Stump, Grand Rapids, MI

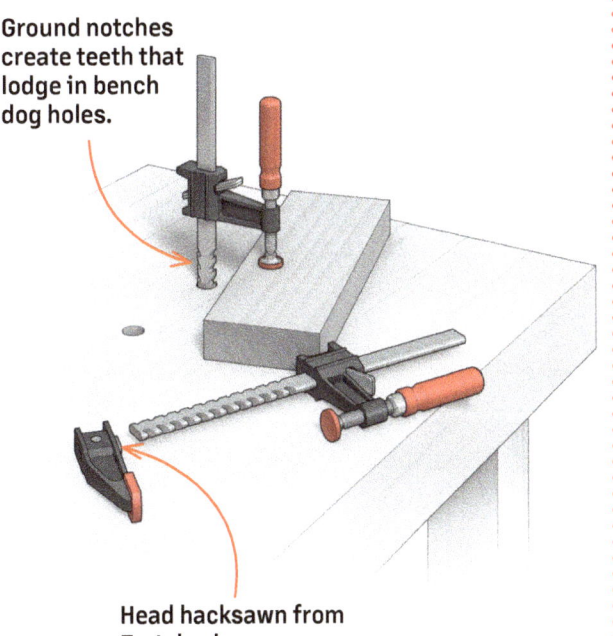

Ground notches create teeth that lodge in bench dog holes.

Head hacksawn from F-style clamp.

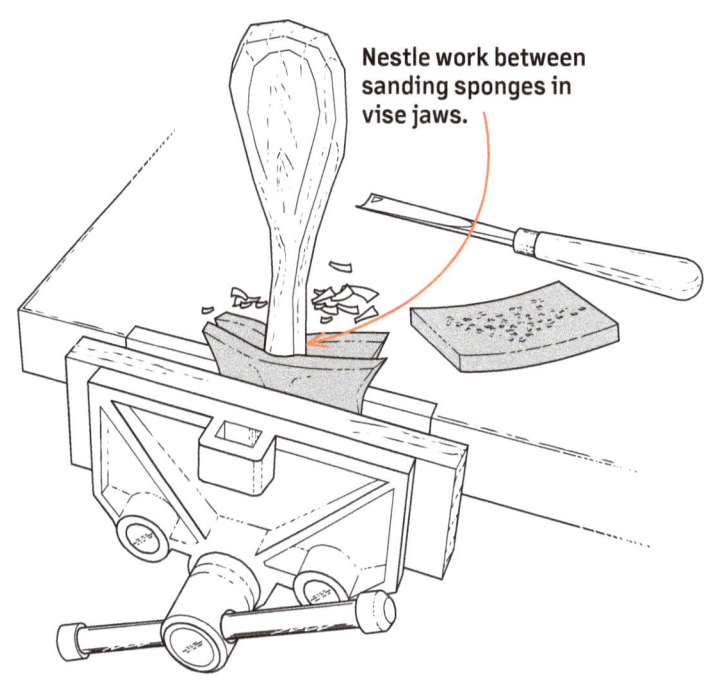

Nestle work between sanding sponges in vise jaws.

Vise-assistance from sanding sponges

When I started making wooden spoons using gouges, spokeshaves, and a drawknife, the biggest problem was clamping the curved spoon blanks in my vise for shaping. As I was smoothing a completed spoon one day, I realized that the sanding sponge I was using might do double-duty to help hold the workpiece in the vise. Sure enough, I found that sandwiching the spoon blank between two sponges (grit against the wood) considerably increased the grip of the vise on the work. Sponges with grit on both faces work even better. Obviously, this technique can help when clamping any number of odd shapes in a vise.

—Alejandro Balbis, Longueuil, Quebec

WORKSHOP > CLAMPING & WORK-HOLDING

Taping your cauls

Effective glue-ups often require using clamping cauls to pull joints home, especially when assembling casework. But holding long cauls in place while trying to clamp them down can be octopus work, especially on vertical surfaces. Since I don't have extra arms, I use double-faced tape to do the job. It works great, but do yourself a favor and apply wide cellophane (packing) tape to your workpiece first, especially if it's plywood. Otherwise, you may tear off the top veneer when removing the cauls.
—Chad McClung, Vienna, WV

Underlying cellophane tape allows easy, clean removal of caul after assembly.

Caul spreads clamping pressure across joint.

Double-faced tape holds caul in place on vertical surfaces for clamping.

Miter clamping cauls

Need to glue up a mitered frame but don't have a strap clamp? Raid your scrap bin to make some miter clamping cauls. To make each caul, glue a triangular clamping block to the end of an "anchor" board that's about as wide as your frame pieces. When gluing a frame corner, locate a pair of cauls so that the outermost faces of the triangular blocks will direct clamping pressure across the joint faces as shown. (This will vary depending on the size of the blocks and thickness of your frame.) Secure the anchor boards to the frame, and then clamp across the blocks to produce full force on the joint faces.
—Leonie Ward, Jackson, MS

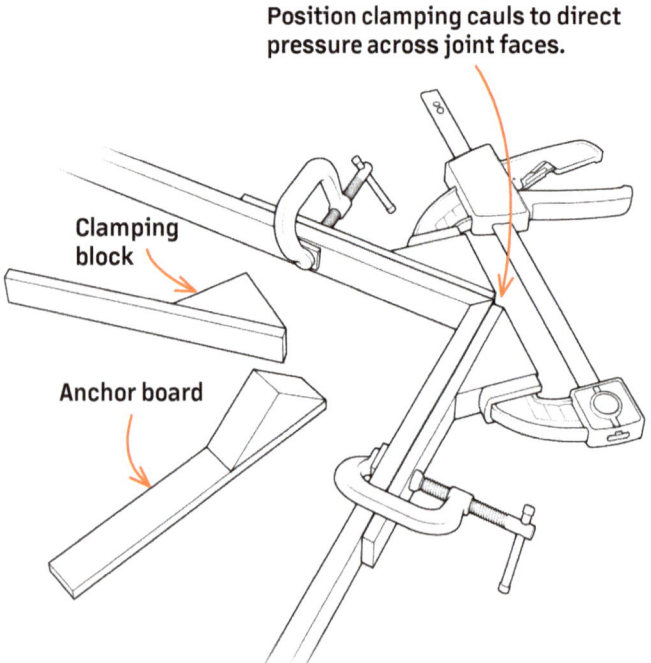

Position clamping cauls to direct pressure across joint faces.

Clamping block

Anchor board

A tall-vise handscrew

There were times when I used to wish my vise jaws could project above the bench top, which would be helpful when securing workpieces for biscuiting and other operations. I got my wish recently when I realized that all I have to do is clamp a large wooden handscrew into the vise as shown. It sure makes a lot of jobs quicker and easier now.

—William Purcell, Laurinburg, NC

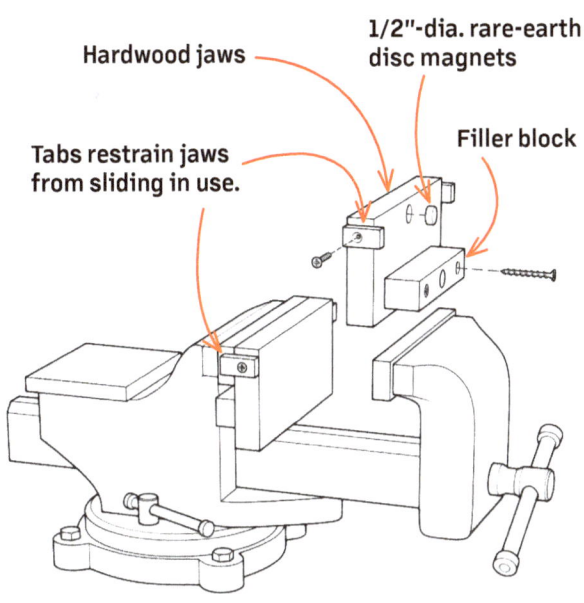

Vise conversion

Not having a proper woodworking vise, I've been forced to use my metalworking vise. However, its narrow, relatively small jaws are hardly ideal for woodshop chores. To solve the problem, I cobbled up these wooden inserts, which mimic the wide, flat jaws on woodworking vises. As shown, the magnetically attached 3/4"-thick hardwood jaws extend from the top edges of the metal jaws fully down the opening. Wooden tabs screwed to the ends of the jaws prevent them from sliding in use, and the filler blocks direct clamping pressure fully across the faces of the jaws when closed. The inserts don't take long to make, and work great. Just make sure to inset the magnets absolutely flush to the surface of the wood.

—Wayne Johnson, Grand Ledge, MI

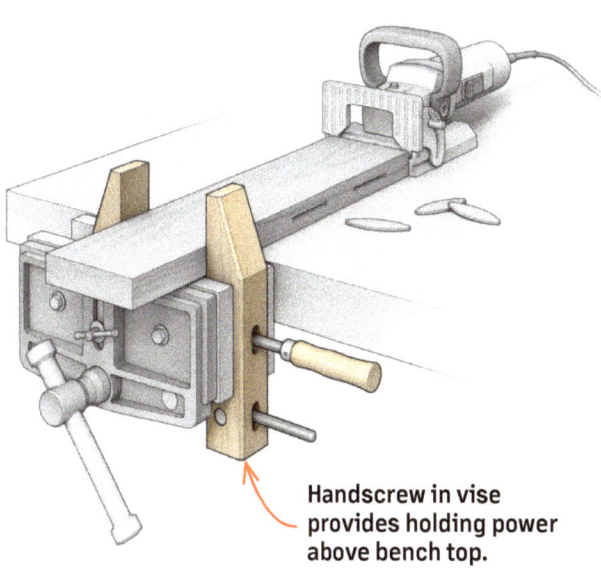

Handscrew in vise provides holding power above bench top.

See-through clamping pads

Acrylic that's at least 1/4" thick makes for great clamping pads. The material is flat, non-stick, and transparent, making it particularly useful for viewing patchwork. Sheet cutoffs are often available from glass shops at reasonable prices.

—Craig W. Bentzley, Chalfont, PA

Blade-friendly bench dogs

In our shop, bench dogs disappear almost as quickly as donuts. Our solution was to make a large batch of inexpensive dogs using dowels tipped with vinyl tubing cut with a utility knife (or a table saw or bandsaw after fitted onto the dowel). The soft vinyl-capped dowels will not damage plane blades, scrapers, or sandpaper and are more grippy than metal or wooden dogs. If a dog is slightly taller than the stock, simply touch the end against a belt sander or give it a few swats with a block plane. When working with super-thin stock on your benchtop, trim a narrower ring from the tubing and replace your standard-sized tip.

Find the dowels that fit your dog holes before you buy the vinyl. A foot of tubing (purchased at home centers) will make 6-8 dogs and provide extra material for replacement tips.

—Joe Hurst-Wajszczuk, Birmingham, AL

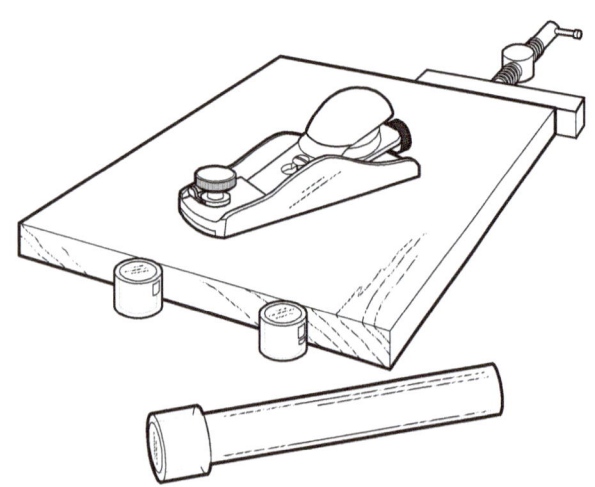

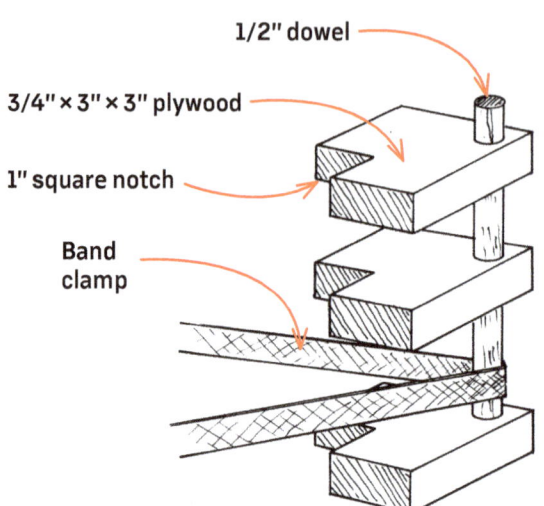

Corner clamping aid

When gluing up boxes using band clamps, I like to add blocks that help align the sides and spread the clamping force at each corner. Lacking enough hands to hold all the blocks in place, while at the same time tightening the band clamp, drove me to devise this simple solution. Using some scrap 3/4" plywood and 1/2" hardwood dowels, I made a set of four self-standing, adjustable corner blocks.

Start by cutting four 10" lengths of dowel. Cut the plywood into a dozen 3" squares, then cut a 1" square notch out of each corner. Drill a 1/2" hole in the opposite corner from the notch. It's helpful to stack and clamp each set of three blocks when cutting the notch and drilling the hole, to ensure that each corner block is perfectly aligned.

Glue a dowel into the bottom square of each set, leaving the other two squares unglued and free to slide up and down the dowel as needed.

Because the base square is glued into place, the corner block set will stand in place, allowing me to concentrate on positioning and tightening the band clamps.

—R.B. Himes, Vienna, OH

Cocking clamps for square assemblies

The best way to ensure a square glue-up of just about any kind of box is to cut your joints accurately, work on a dead-flat surface, and carefully center the clamping pressure across the joint. However, it's not unusual to find that you're still a bit out of square. It's time to get cocky with your clamps: simply shift them slightly in the direction of bringing the clamp bars parallel to the assembly's longer diagonal. Recheck for square by comparing your diagonals again, and make any adjustments until the diagonals match.

—Jean Devine, Santa Rosa, CA

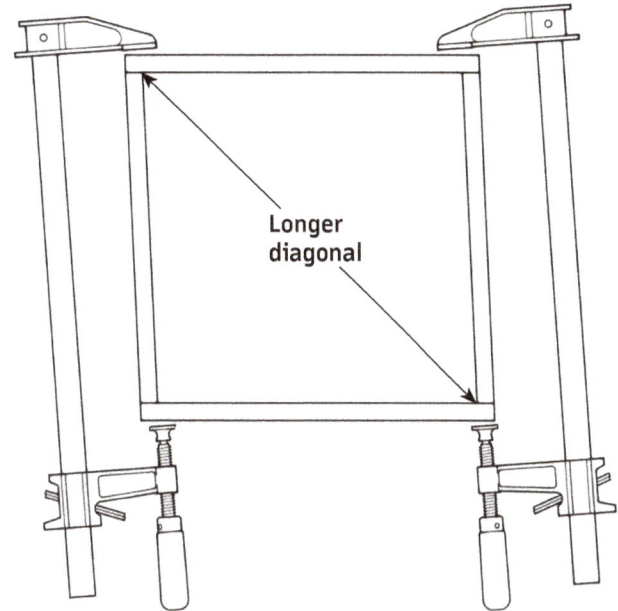

To bring assembly into square, cock clamps slightly, as though bringing their bars into parallel with the assembly's longer diagonal.

Spin-free pipe clamp pads

Frustrated by rubber pads that don't stay securely on my pipe clamp jaws, I made these 3/4"-thick wooden pads that attach using rare-earth magnets. My first attempts were square pads, which worked okay, but tended to rotate and shift in use. I fixed that by attaching plywood strips that hug the sides of the clamp jaw as shown. For the most secure attachment, make sure the face of the embedded magnet is very flush to the surface of the block. I used steel mounting cups designed to attach the magnets, but you could just epoxy them into their recesses instead.

—Richard Melpignano, Bellingham, MA

WORKSHOP > CLAMPING & WORK-HOLDING

Vise-assist from a bench dog

Clamping a long board in a face vise for edge-planing or other operations can be difficult because one end of the board is unsupported. Some woodworkers use a freestanding or bench-mounted jack to support the extended end, but there's an easier way if your bench includes dog holes.

I simply raise a bench dog near the unsupported end of the board and then clamp against the board and the dog as shown, using a thick spacer block between them to prevent board twist. If your inner vise jaw is flush to the edge of the bench, the spacer need only extend between the board and the dog. If your inner vise jaw stands off from the bench edge, make an L-shaped spacer that also fills the offset. To prevent the extended end of the board from slipping, it can help to glue sandpaper to the contact face of the spacer.

—Alejandro Balbis, Longueuil, Québec

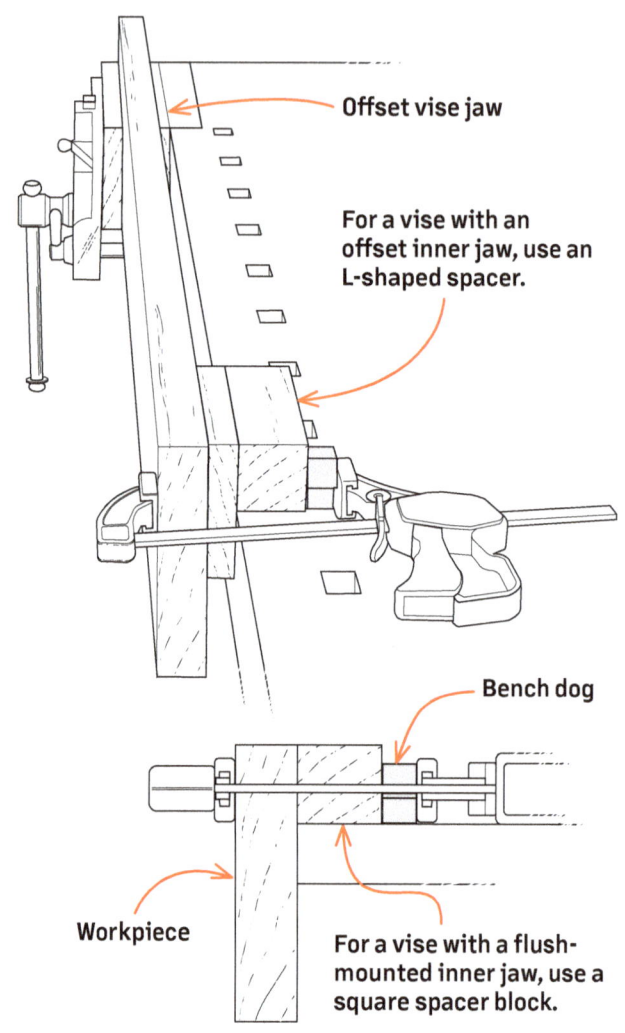

Offset vise jaw

For a vise with an offset inner jaw, use an L-shaped spacer.

Bench dog

Workpiece

For a vise with a flush-mounted inner jaw, use a square spacer block.

Bench dog bumper

Brass isn't as hard as steel, but it is still hard enough to dent wood. To protect finished edges from bench dog damage, I affixed strips of leather with contact adhesive to the checkered face. This "muzzle" provides a non-marring, non-slip face, much like commercial slip-on collars, but mine won't slip off and run away, even when the dog is set flush with the benchtop.

—Tommy MacDonald, Boston, MA

Handscrew vise

I work for a custom stair builder and often find myself working on small or odd shaped pieces such as handrail fittings. Unfortunately, I have a hard time holding them for sanding or shaping, and the boss won't spring for a bench vise. To make do, I've found that I can substitute a large handscrew for the job. I clamp my workpiece in it, and then secure the handscrew to the bench with a couple of F-style clamps. The setup actually works pretty well. Even clamped down, the handscrew can still be adjusted enough to allow repositioning of the workpiece without a lot of hassle.

—Jonathan Wisher, Matthews, NC

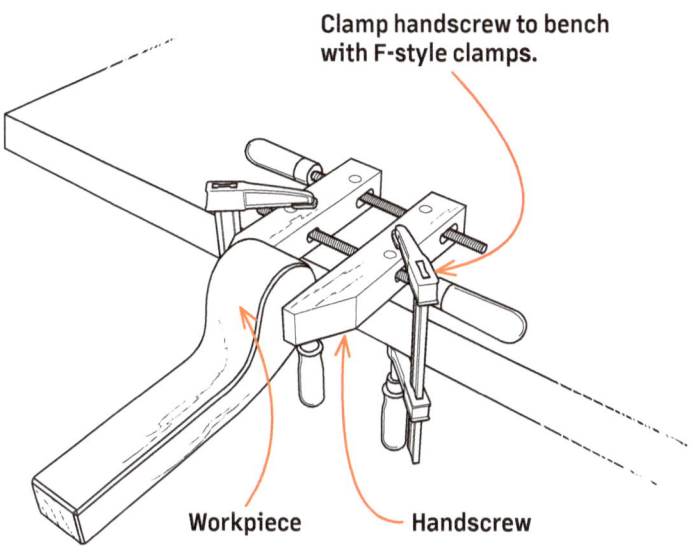

Clamp handscrew to bench with F-style clamps.

Workpiece   Handscrew

Daisy-chaining pipe clamps

Although I have plenty of pipe clamps in various lengths, there have been times when I needed more reach. Yes, I know that you can attach pipe couplers to the tail end of a pipe to extend it, but that's too much hassle. There's a much quicker and easier way.

I just select two clamps of appropriate length and rotate their jaws to interlock as shown. While this isn't necessarily the best approach for edge-gluing panels, it works great for assembling very wide cabinets, attaching edging from a distance, and other long-reach clamping chores.

—Mark Clement, Biloxi, MS

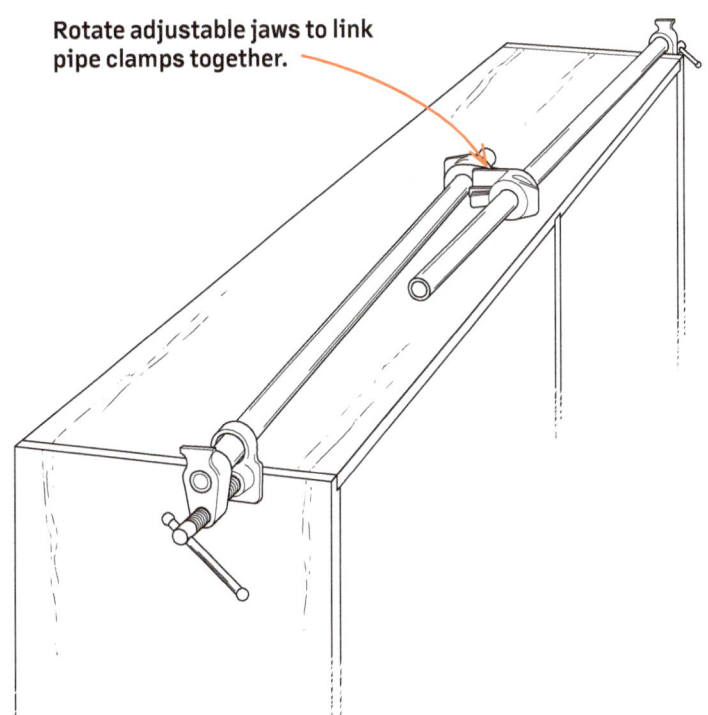

Rotate adjustable jaws to link pipe clamps together.

WORKSHOP > CLAMPING & WORK-HOLDING

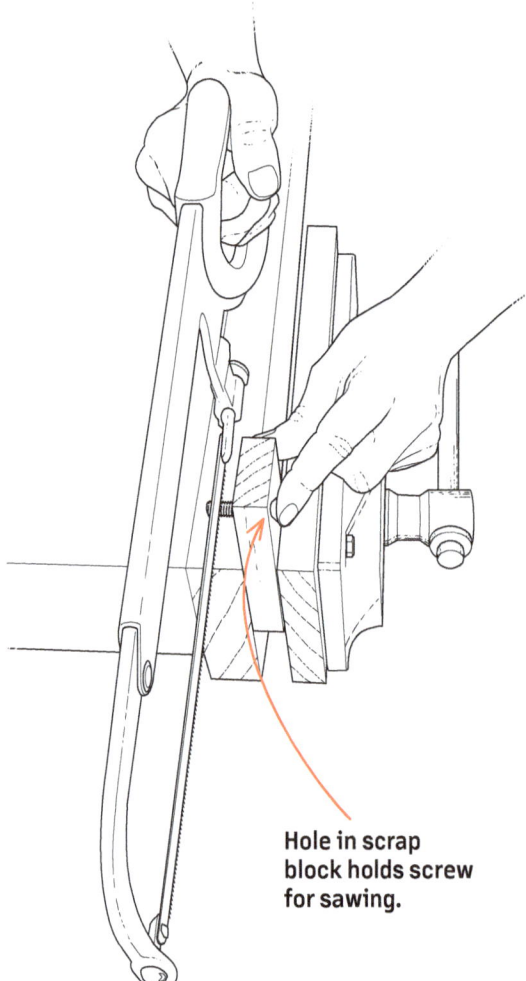

Hole in scrap block holds screw for sawing.

Shortening screws

It's not uncommon to have to shorten a machine screw, bolt, or other threaded fastener. Unfortunately, it can be difficult to secure the fastener in a vise in order to hacksaw it to length. My solution is to drill a hole in a scrap board using a bit whose diameter exactly matches the outside diameter of the fastener threads. I clamp this "holder board" in my vise, slip the fastener through it, and hold its head while sawing the shank to desired length.

—Alejandro Balbis, Longueuil, Quebec

Clamp-on saw guide

I discovered that I needed to trim several 4×4 posts on an outdoor project. I was unwilling to attempt the cut with a portable circular saw, so I devised this self-clamping jig to guide a handsaw for the job. The jig consists of two 3/4"-thick wooden bars connected by a pair of carriage bolts and lock knobs. I sized the bars a few inches longer than the width of the pieces to be cut, and ensured alignment of the bolt holes by stack-drilling them on the drill press. A ledger strip on the top of each bar provides a wider bearing surface for the handsaw. I used polyethylene for the strips for durability and minimal friction, but dense hardwood would work. The jig is so accurate and easy to set up that I now use it on other parts that are too big or awkward to cut on a stationary machine.

—David Miller, Clemmons, NC

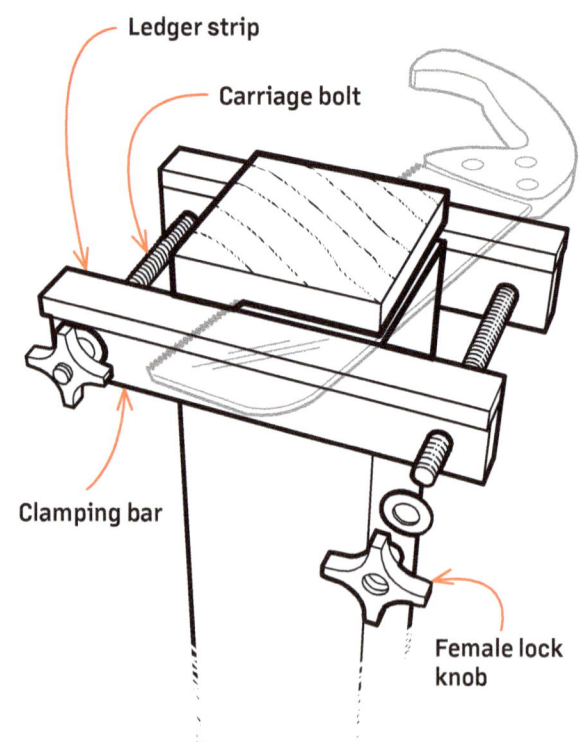

Well-behaved bench dogs

Conventional bench dogs are usually outfitted with sprung metal or wood strips to hold them in place at your desired working height. They work well enough at an inch or so above the benchtop, but lack bite when standing tall to hold higher work. This dog relies on 1/4-20 × 1/2" nylon-tipped set screws to keep it precisely where you want it, even when projecting 4" above the work surface. To make a good dog like this, saw your stock from a dense hardwood like maple, sizing its body to suit your benchtop's dog holes. Then drill a series of 3/16"-diameter holes through the back of the dog (there's no need to tap them). Drive the screws through until their nylon tips protrude from the opposite face and bear lightly against the inside of the dog hole. It will then sit where you want it to without further commands to "stay!"

—*Andy Rae, Asheville, NC*

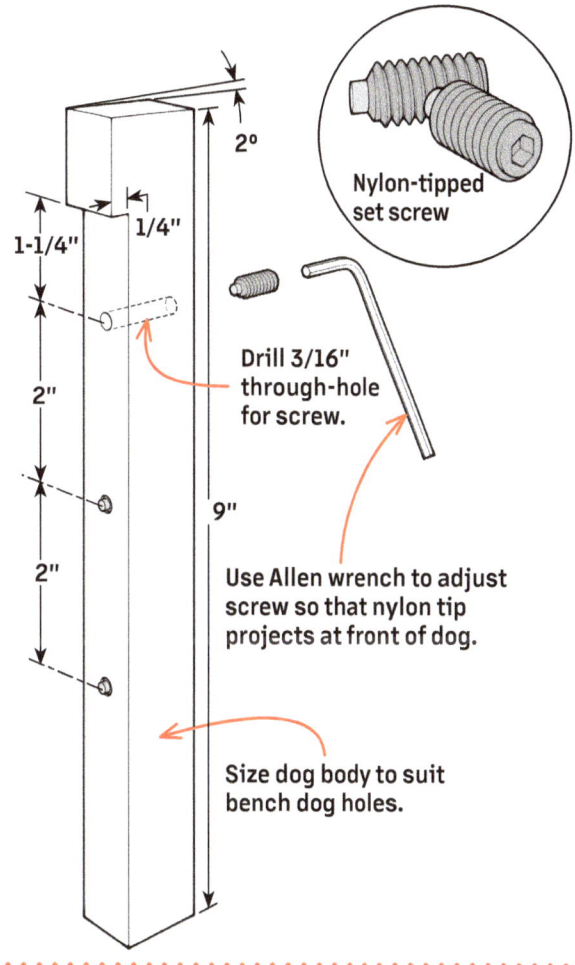

Drawer planing platform

When planing drawers to fit their openings, it's important that the surface being planed remains flat during the process. If a drawer side flexes under the pressure of the tool, you won't be able to plane it evenly. My solution is to use a 3/4"-thick MDF planing platform that I slot to accommodate drawers of different sizes. I cantilever the slotted section off the edge of the bench as shown, and clamp the platform in place. Fine sandpaper adhered to the section under the clamps helps keep the panel from shifting in use.

—*Mark Schuman, St. Paul, MN*

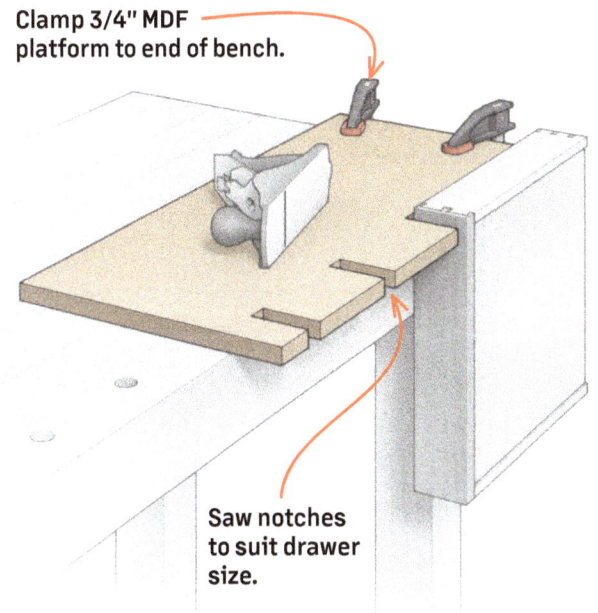

WORKSHOP > CLAMPING & WORK-HOLDING

Bench slave

I have a couple of these "slaves" mounted under my workbench top to allow for easy clamp-free support of long stock for edge-planing. Each unit is basically a bracket that houses a stick that can be extended for board support when necessary, and retracted when not in use. These slaves are simple to build, as shown. Just make sure to use a strong hardwood, such as maple or birch, for the bracket, and an even stronger wood, such as rosewood or osage orange, for the stick. After shaping the center block and gluing it between the outer blocks, drill and counterbore clearance holes in the outer blocks and screw the bracket to the underside of your bench. Make sure that the retracted stick is inset about 1/2" from the edge of the bench. Consider mounting one slave in the middle of your bench, and one at the far end opposite the vise to accommodate boards of various lengths.

—Andy Rae, Asheville, NC

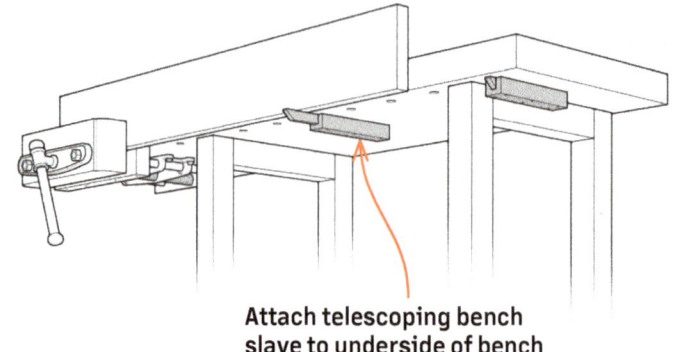

Attach telescoping bench slave to underside of bench to support boards.

Cut a 1" × 9-1/2" rabbet in center block.

Center block 5/8" × 1-1/2" × 10"

Support stick 5/8" × 1" × 10-1/2"

Glue and clamp 3 blocks together.

Outside block 5/8" × 1-1/2" × 10"

Avoid pipe clamp stains

Wet glue squeeze-out contacting black iron pipe clamps can stain workpieces. To prevent it, cut a roll of wax paper into 2" lengths and place the strips of paper between the pipes and the work. Tape will hold the strips to the pipes resting on the bench.

—Larissa Huff, Schwenksville, PA

Self-positioning assembly braces

Squaring braces can be very helpful for assembling cases and drawers. Expensive commercial versions are available, but simple plywood triangles with notches or holes serving for clamp purchase work pretty well. However, I decided to upgrade to the shop-made fenced versions shown for a recent large cabinet project. Unlike standard flat triangles, these braces can rest atop case or drawer side edges, holding the parts together while you set the clamps.

I recommend making large and small braces to accommodate different size cases. The dimensions aren't critical, but the outermost corner must be an accurate right angle. Locate the fences about 1" out from the inside corner so that they don't get in the way when positioning a divider or shelf in the middle of a case. These braces are designed for 3/4"-thick adjoining pieces. For thicker wood, or for assembling face frames or other projects, they can be clamped to the inside corners, like simpler fence-less braces.

—Joe Hurst-Wajszczuk, Birmingham, AL

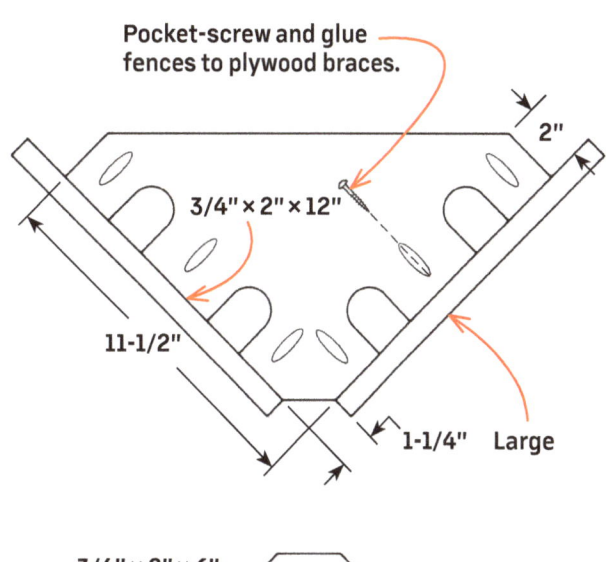

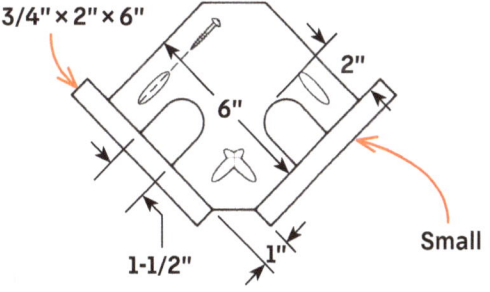

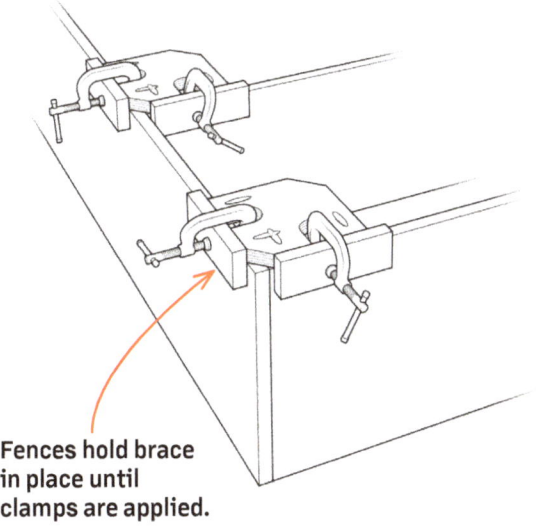

Fences hold brace in place until clamps are applied.

Ratchets for frames

There are lots of jigs for gluing up frames, both homemade and manufactured. I find that straps with a tightening ratchet work perfectly without a jig. For wide material, the joints line up automatically at a right angle as long as care is taken cutting the miters. For narrower material it is necessary to use a square inside the corners to make sure the frame is correct. A piece of wax paper inside the strap over the corner prevents squeeze-out from getting on the strap. Ratcheted straps from an automotive store work fine and are much less expensive than those found at wood stores.

—Don Ernst, Olympia, WA

Clamping with foam

I do restoration work that often requires gluing on odd-shaped pieces such as moldings and carvings. I discovered that scraps of polystyrene foam serve as great clamping cauls for pieces that lack flat clamping surfaces. Just cover the part to be clamped with waxed paper or cellophane, and then lay a piece of foam about 1" thick over it, topped with a wooden caul for support. Under clamp pressure, the foam will compress over the part, providing fairly consistent pressure overall. This technique works not only for moldings and carvings, but also for inlay repairs where the patch might initially be a bit thicker than the underlying area.
—Brian Hillman, Stockbridge, GA

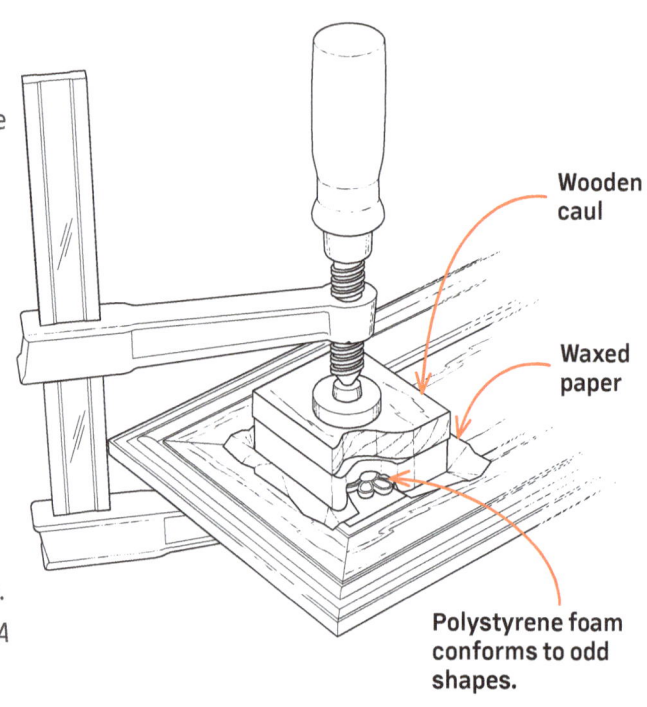

Wooden caul

Waxed paper

Polystyrene foam conforms to odd shapes.

Inner tube clamps

Woodworking often requires glue-ups that traditional clamps can't handle, so sometimes you need to think outside your wheelhouse. Inner tubes can apply pressure where ordinary clamps can't, making them invaluable for nonlinear assemblies, such as curved or twisted work. To turn a trashed tube into a valuable clamp, cut off the valve stem and slice the tube into 3/4"- to 1-1/4"-wide strips to suit your needs. Wrap a strip around the assembly as necessary, tucking each end under a previous wrap to secure it. If you don't have any old tubes hanging in your garage, check out your local bike or motorcycle shops. Regular tubes are thin and stretchy, while heavy-duty tubes are made from thicker material, which stretches less but is more durable.

—Andy Rae, Asheville, NC

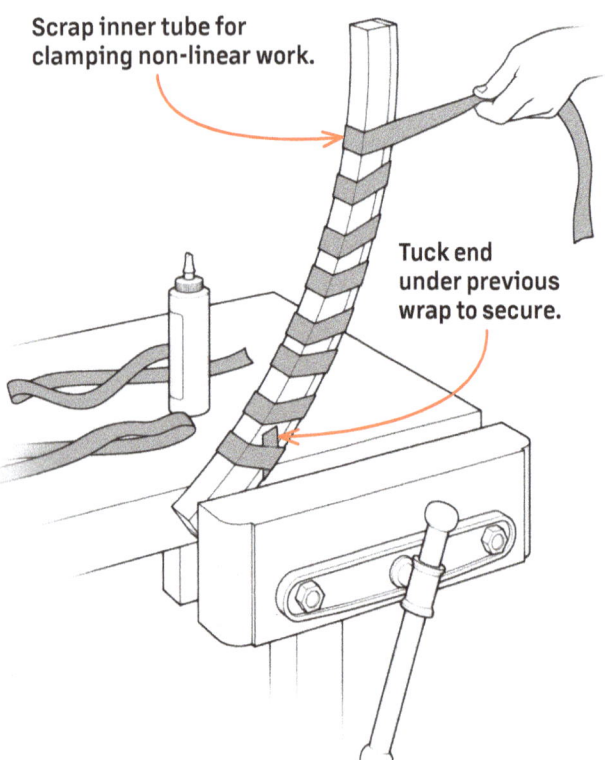

Scrap inner tube for clamping non-linear work.

Tuck end under previous wrap to secure.

Versatile vise jaws

In my work, I often need to secure oddly shaped pieces in my bench vise. To do the job, I devised a pair of auxiliary cauls that attach via rods to thick wooden pads on my vise jaws. One of the auxiliary jaws is fixed, while the other one can swivel to accommodate pieces with non-parallel sides.

I began by making a 1"-thick hardwood facing block for each jaw, boring three equidistant 1/2"-diameter holes through the edge of each block to accept the rods. (Through-holes prevent clogging from detritus.) I screwed the blocks to the jaws, aligning their top edges with my workbench surface. Next, I used dowel centers to transfer the hole locations to the underside of each caul. The swiveling caul needs only one hole in the center, while its mate is drilled to match only the two outer holes, all three of which I then drilled 3/4" deep using the drill press. To finish up, I glued 2-1/2"-long, 1/2"-diameter steel rods into the cauls, and faced the caul's bearing surfaces with cork to aid gripping. When I need to hold curves and odd-shaped pieces, I attach a suitably shaped block to one or both of the cauls with double-faced tape.

—Bill Mitchell, Hellertown, PA

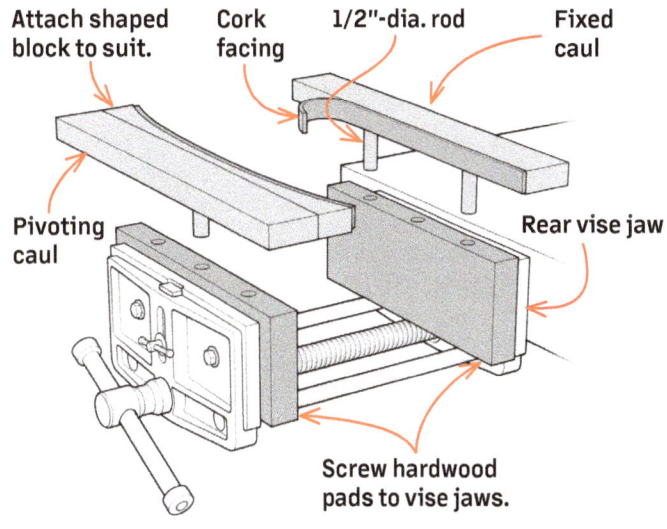

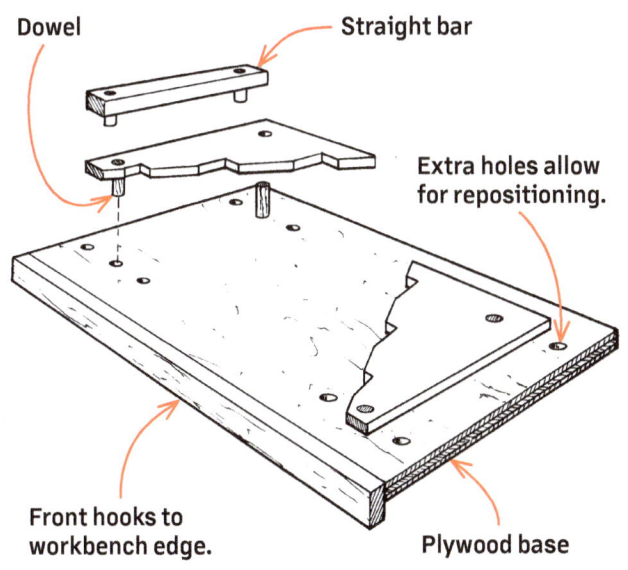

Versatile bench hook

Whether I'm using it for planing, sanding, or carving, I find this bench hook very versatile. It's great for holding all kinds of differently shaped items, especially odd or round shapes. By using a wide base and adding some extra holes, I gained the ability to easily adjust the width of the jaws. I also made up a straight bar that can replace the angled jaws when that suits my purposes better.

—R. B. Himes, Vienna, OH

WORKSHOP > CLAMPING & WORK-HOLDING

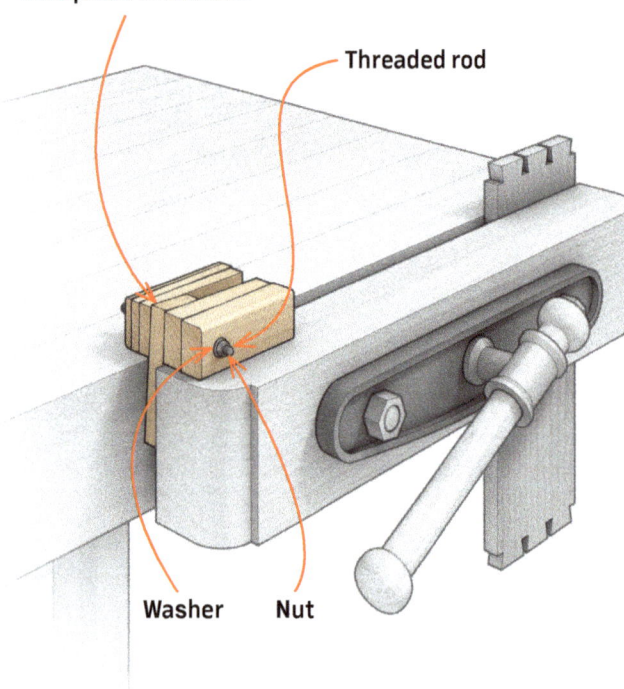

Use spacer that matches workpiece thickness.
Threaded rod
Washer
Nut

Anti-rack vise jig

Clamping a workpiece at one end of a wooden bench vise often racks the jaw, compromising its grip. The common prevention for this is to clamp a scrap of equal thickness at the opposite end. But it's a nuisance searching for the right size scrap and unwieldy trying to hold both pieces in place while tightening the vise. This multi-fingered jig—consisting of various spacers mounted on a threaded rod—provides a great solution. Simply place it atop the bench with the appropriate-sized finger dangling between the vise jaws. To make the jig, drill a 1/4"-diameter cross-hole in one end of a 4" long 2×4. Rip the piece to yield a series of incrementally sized strips. Mount the strips on threaded rod between washers and nuts.

—John Esposito, Foster, RI

Handscrew saw guide

I was trying to cut tenon shoulders on the end of an odd-shaped workpiece, and I was having a hard time keeping my handsaw on target. Then it occurred to me that I could use a wooden handscrew as a saw guide, clamping the jaws of the tool adjacent to my cutline opposite the waste side. To prevent scarring the jaws with the saw teeth, I used a flush-cutting saw, which worked great. As a bonus, the jaws also served as a chisel guide for cleaning up any sections afterward where necessary.

—Dean Laughren, Winnipeg, Manitoba

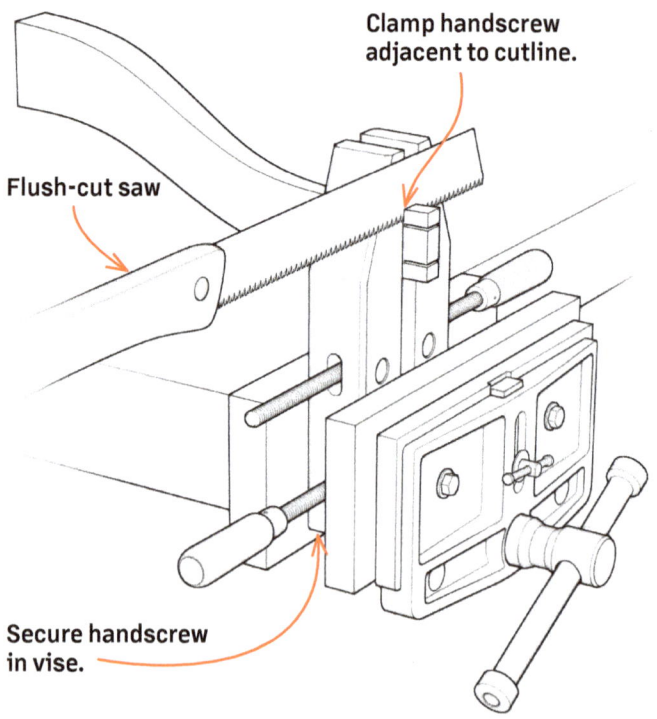

Clamp handscrew adjacent to cutline.
Flush-cut saw
Secure handscrew in vise.

Stop feeling the pinch

It happened again. I was adjusting my metal bench vise to put the squeeze on a workpiece when the handle bar suddenly slid full force through its hole, slamming my fingertip between the ball-end of the bar and the head of the vise screw. (A bunch of you out there know exactly what I'm talking about.) I finally decided I had had quite enough of that smooth move and rifled through my collection of rubber washers and O-rings looking for a fix. I found a couple of thick rubber washers that fit nicely onto the ends of the handle just below each ball. No more blood blisters.

—Willard Knight, Bellingham, WA

Fit rubber washers on ends of bar below ball.

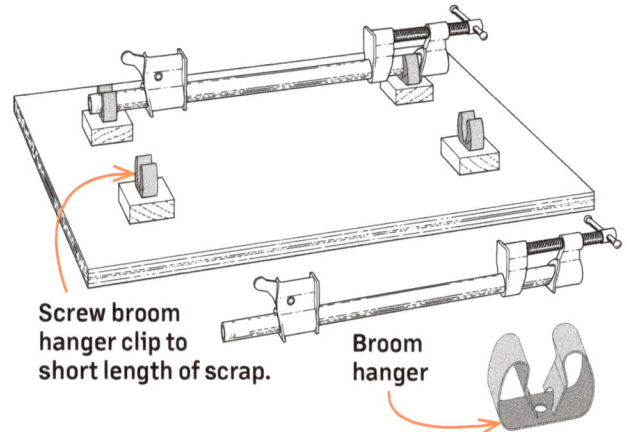

Screw broom hanger clip to short length of scrap.

Broom hanger

Pipe clamp stands

For some time, I struggled when gluing up projects with my vintage 3/4" pipe clamps. Their narrow footing often caused them to tip when loading boards onto them. During a glue-up one day, I realized that the answer was right in front of me on the wall, holding my shop brooms. These metal spring clips—designed for storing housekeeping equipment—can be screwed to stands made of shop scrap. As an added benefit, the setup raises the clamps enough to facilitate easier turning of the clamp handles.

—Robert Smith, Churchville, NY

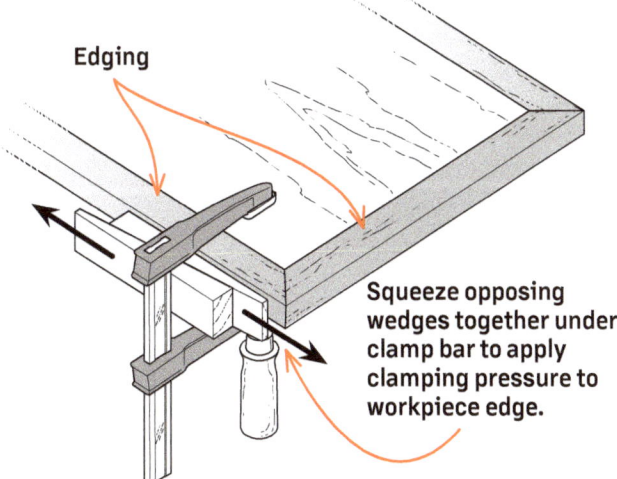

Edging

Squeeze opposing wedges together under clamp bar to apply clamping pressure to workpiece edge.

Improvised edge clamp

I needed to glue a piece of edging to a panel where it would have been awkward to span the panel's surface with long bar or pipe clamps. Then I remembered a trick a friend showed me a long time ago. I secured a couple F-style clamps to the panel as shown, and slipped opposing wedges between the clamp bar and the edging to apply clamping pressure.

—Alan Wahlburg, Knoxville, TN

WORKSHOP > CLAMPING & WORK-HOLDING

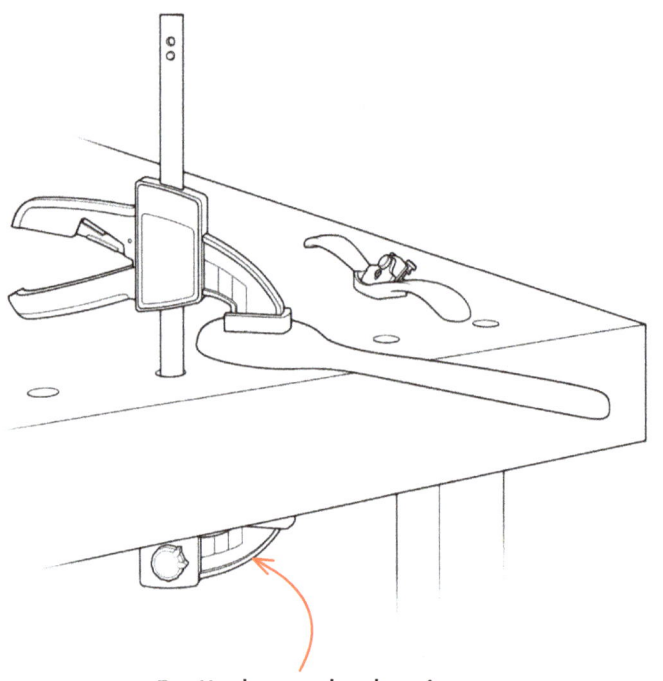

Reattach spreader clamp's removable jaw after inserting clamp bar through bench dog hole.

One-handed hold-down

I carve a lot of spoons. Most of the post-bandsaw shaping takes place with the work secured in my bench vise. However, sometimes I need more positioning flexibility. It turns out that a spreader bar clamp is just the thing. You can remove its reversible jaw in order to slip the bar through a standard 3/4"-diameter dog hole. Replacing the jaw in its normal orientation—but below the benchtop—then creates a very effective bench hold-down. It can be operated with one hand so I can quickly and easily reposition a workpiece as needed to finish shaping and smoothing it.

—Bob Poling, Parkersburg, WV

Square deal

Indestructible and inexpensive, my aluminum square has earned its keep by doing basic layout work and guiding the edge of my circular saw when making square cuts in framing lumber. But I recently discovered a new use that has been keeping this tool a lot busier. Thanks to the open interior and the flange along one edge, it's easy to use the square as a clamp when I need a right-angled assembly. Plastic versions of this square don't have the same open configuration, so look for an aluminum model if you want this added functionality.

—Tim Snyder, Sandy Hook, CT

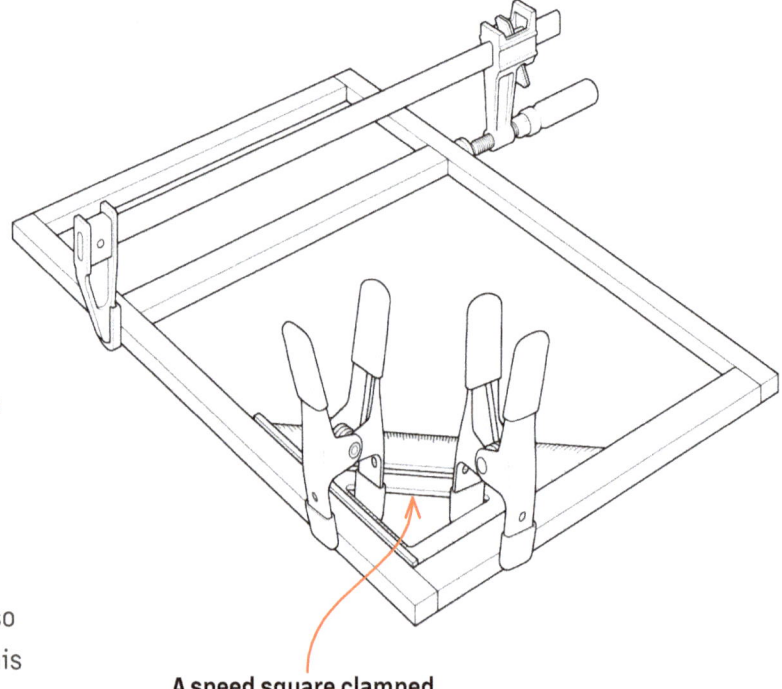

A speed square clamped to an assembly will keep it square during glue-up.

Better clamp purchase on machine tables

I frequently find myself clamping fences and other fixtures to my table saw, bandsaw, and other machine tables. Unfortunately, the cast iron webbing on the underside of the tables can make finding solid footing for clamps tricky. To remedy this, I fit and epoxied filler blocks of 3/4" plywood between the webbing ribs to create flat surfaces that are much more clamp-friendly.

—Rick Lombardi, Dublin, OH

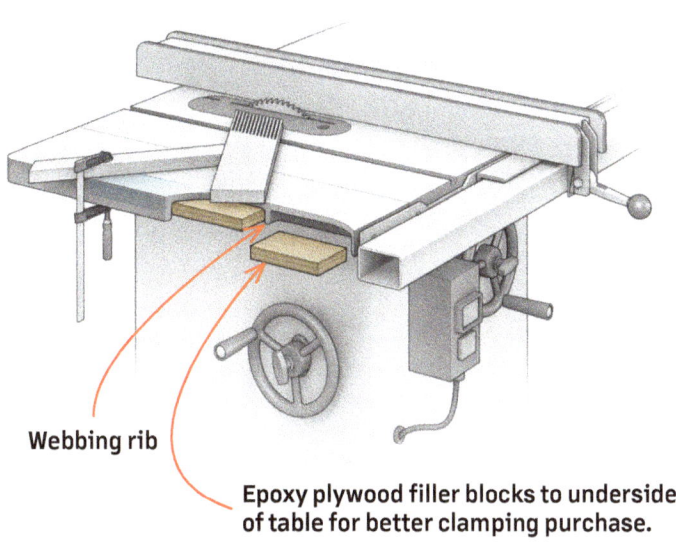

Webbing rib

Epoxy plywood filler blocks to underside of table for better clamping purchase.

A simple spreader

Like many furniture makers, I do my fair share of repair work, often involving disassembly of chairs and other pieces. I have a reversible-jaw pipe clamp that can be used as a spreader clamp, but the jaws aren't very long. Plus, I often need more than one spreader in play, so I devised this wooden spreader jig, based on something similar I saw once. The jig is simply a long hardwood bar with a fixed crossbar at one end and a pivoting bar at the other, with a bar clamp wired to the fixed and pivoting bars as shown. Tightening the clamp creates a strong, controlled spreading action on the opposite side of the spreader. Size the jig to suit the job, and drill extra holes in the long bar when necessary.

—Martin Grasse, Denver, CO

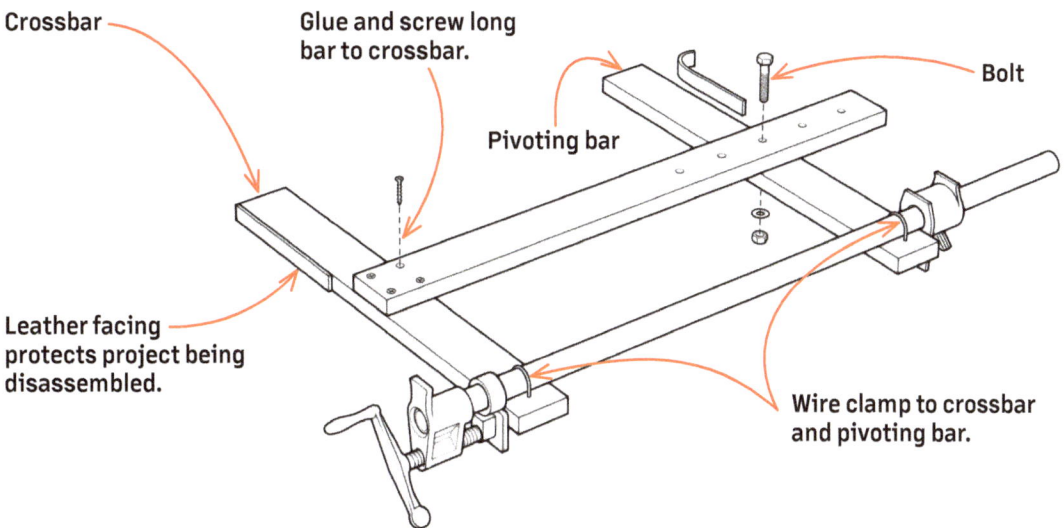

Crossbar

Glue and screw long bar to crossbar.

Pivoting bar

Bolt

Leather facing protects project being disassembled.

Wire clamp to crossbar and pivoting bar.

WORKSHOP > CLAMPING & WORK-HOLDING

Affordable carving vise

For shaping cabriole legs, I needed a way to secure the leg at different angles so that I could carve the ball and claw foot. Wanting a less-expensive alternative to a patternmaker's vise, I made a minor upgrade to a T-bar sash clamp with flanged ends. After bolting it to a wooden arm (I used a 2×4, as shown), I then gripped the clamp-turned-vise in my basic bench vise.

—Tommy MacDonald, Boston, MA

Handscrew vise helper

Sometimes you need to clamp a long board on edge on your benchtop. There are several ways to do this, but one of the easiest is to lock the board in a handscrew clamp held in a bench vise as shown. The most secure approach is to clamp the handscrew to the board before locking it in the vise.

—Frank Burnside, Miami, FL

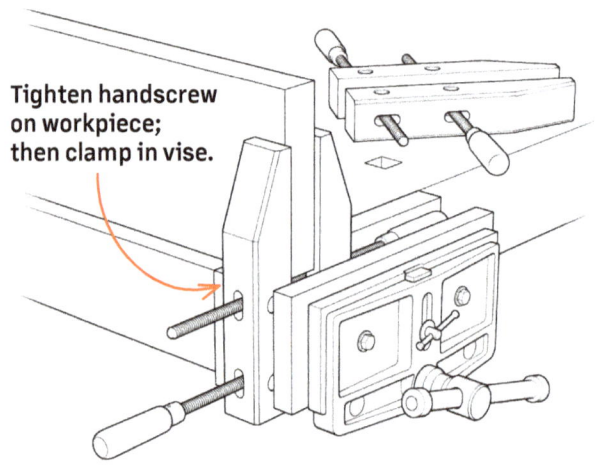

Tighten handscrew on workpiece; then clamp in vise.

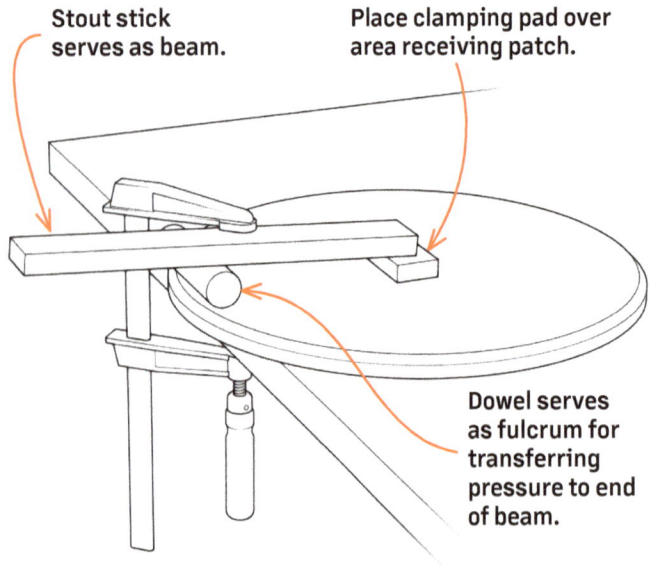

Stout stick serves as beam.

Place clamping pad over area receiving patch.

Dowel serves as fulcrum for transferring pressure to end of beam.

Cantilevered clamping

The next time you need to clamp an area that's out of the reach of your clamp jaws, such as gluing a patch in a tabletop, try this: Place a dowel or triangular strip of wood near the edge of the workpiece to serve as a fulcrum, and place a protective clamping pad over the area to be clamped. Straddle the two with a stout beam, and then put clamp pressure on the stick on the inward side of the fulcrum as shown.

—Natalie Simmons, San Diego, CA

Angle clamping jig

As I was making a corner cabinet out of birch plywood with cherry facings and five-sided shelves, I encountered a problem. My design called for gluing cherry facing strips to the front edges, which I would then shape. However, the long front edge of the shelf had no opposing parallel edge to use for clamping. I developed this jig so I could clamp the facings to the front edge of the plywood.

I made the three-part jig from scrap plywood. The tongue is about 7" long and 1-1/2" to 1-3/4" wide and should be made from the same thickness of plywood as the workpiece to which you will be clamping the facing. Cut the tongue to give a 45° end. The final length should be about twice as long as that of the cheeks, so that a bar clamp and a C-clamp do not interfere with each other. Make the two cheek pieces from scrap the same width as the tongue and about twice as long as the width (3 to 3-1/2"). Screw or glue the cheeks to the tongue with a mitered edge facing away (sort of like a miter saw gone awry) to form a cradle.

To use the jigs, slide one onto the workpiece and move it up or down the long edge until the mitered edge is directly opposite the desired clamp point. Use a C-clamp to clamp the cradle tightly to the workpiece. A long bar clamp will then span the two parallel clamping surfaces. I used one of the jigs near the back corner and positioned two down the length, giving three points for clamping.

—*Willard Anderson, Chapel Hill, NC*

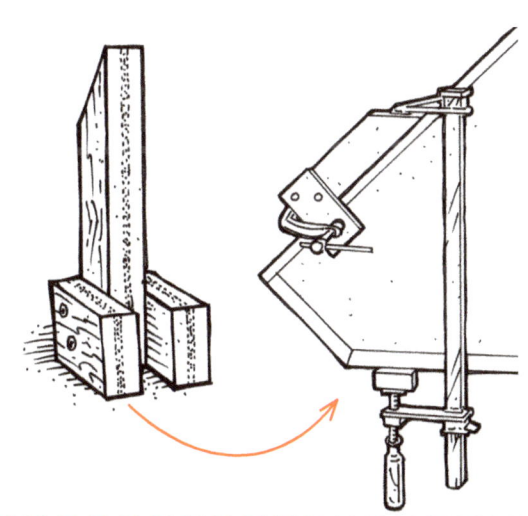

Support while planing

Unless your bench has a board jack, planing long boards requires some kind of makeshift support. Using a piece of scrap I had on hand and a little time, I created a neat alternative. The contraption is simply a tray arrangement with arms. These arms have pegs (round or square, depending on your bench) that slip into the dog holes along the front. I made my tray with a front lip, enabling me to shim boards for a tighter fit, but the lip may be omitted if you prefer.

—*R.B. Himes, Vienna, OH*

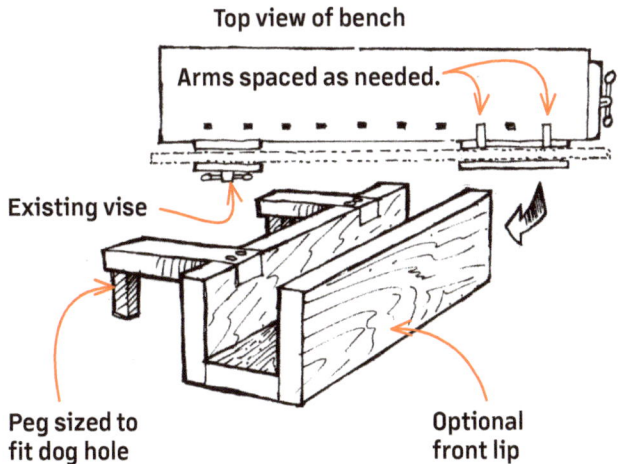

WORKSHOP > CLAMPING & WORK-HOLDING

On-top stop

Not all workbenches are cut out for dog holes. If your workbench is less than 1-1/2" thick, it may not have enough meat to adequately support a bench dog. When faced with this problem, I glued and screwed two stops to opposite faces and ends of a piece of MDF to make a stop that would work on any work surface. The 1/4"-thick strip at the back edge doesn't interfere with most planing chores, but it won't damage my blade if it does.

Even though I now have a better bench, I still use my benchtop stop. The long strip at one end provides a wider bearing surface than dog heads. This enables me to arrange stock pieces side by side and smooth them at the same time. And, compared to a bench dog, it's easier to find when I'm ankle deep in shavings.

—Tommy MacDonald, Boston, MA

1/4"-thick stop

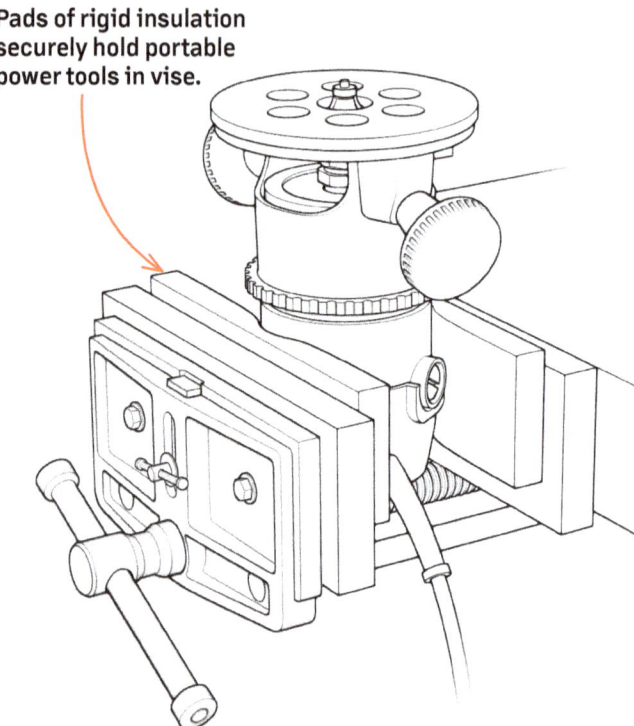

Pads of rigid insulation securely hold portable power tools in vise.

Vise pads for power-tool mounting

It can be difficult to rout or sand small workpieces with portable power tools. In those cases, it's best to take the work to the tool instead of the other way around. But what do you do if you don't have a router table or stationary sander? Well, you could construct a custom platform of some sort for your router or sander, but there's an easier approach. I just cut some appropriately sized pads from 3/4"-thick rigid insulation and squeeze the tool in my vise between the pads. The soft but firm material conforms to the tool, holding it very securely without damaging it. If necessary, knife out any sections on the pads to accommodate large protrusions, and make sure not to block any tool vents.

—Roger Townshend, New Britain, CT

String-and-sticks clamping

While serving in the US Navy during the Vietnam War, I picked up this tip working in the carpenter shop on an aircraft carrier. It allows you to clamp up a frame with nothing more than string and sticks. Begin by placing the unglued finished frame parts together. Next, wrap stout string at least four times around the perimeter of the frame. Add a foot or so to that, and cut the string to length. Now crosscut eight 1/4" × 1" sticks of wood to about 3/4" longer than the thickness of the frame stock.

Glue the frame joints, and place the parts together on a flat surface. Wrap the string as tightly as you can around the frame, and then tie it off with a square knot at one of the corners. Using a putty knife, pry the string away from the frame, and insert two sticks near the center of each frame side. Then spread the sticks apart as far as they will go while keeping the frame flat. This will effectively tighten the string to apply clamping pressure at the corners.

—Earle Darrow, Thousand Oaks, CA

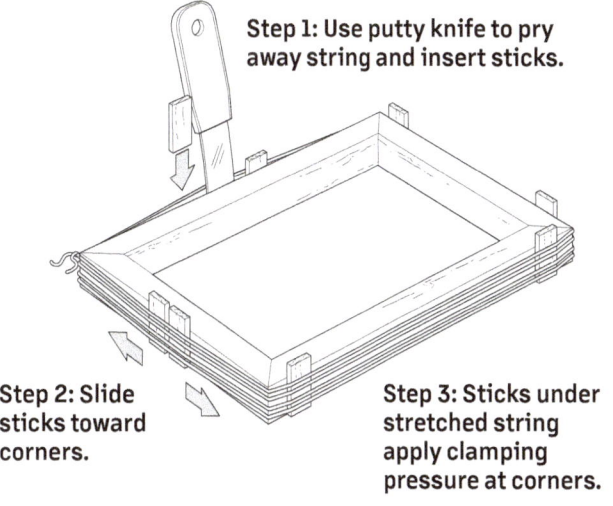

Step 1: Use putty knife to pry away string and insert sticks.

Step 2: Slide sticks toward corners.

Step 3: Sticks under stretched string apply clamping pressure at corners.

Tap-'n-lock vise

To secure a board to your workbench without a standard vise, all you need is a pair of round dogs (in matching dog holes, of course) and a wooden wedge. Place your board between the two dogs, insert the wedge, and give the end a light tap. As it's driven in, the wedge will rotate the adjacent dog to redirect pressure against the end of your stock and lock the board to your bench.

You can easily make wedges of different widths and thicknesses as needed to suit different lengths and thicknesses of stock. The taper angle isn't critical, but I find that a shallow angle works best.

—Alejandro Balbis, Longueuil, Quebec

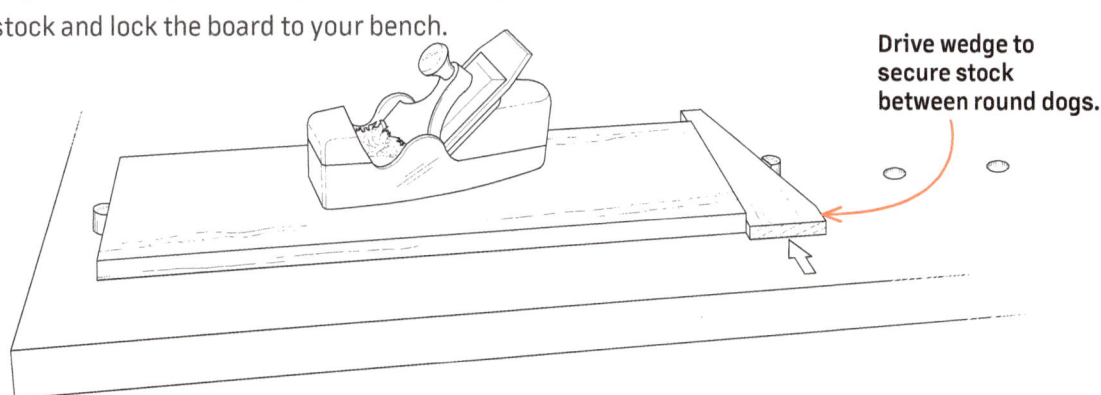

Drive wedge to secure stock between round dogs.

WORKSHOP > CLAMPING & WORK-HOLDING

Dual-purpose bench stops

Over the years, I've seen a variety of bench-mounted stops, some designed for planing and some for sawing. One of my favorite designs is this dual-purpose stop that mounts out of the way on the end of a bench to serve for small planing and sawing tasks. To use as a planing stop, rotate either stop so that it projects above the benchtop. To use as saw stops, place the overhanging workpiece against the appropriate stop—one suiting push saws, and the other pull saws. For strength, make the stops from a dense wood, like hard maple or rosewood, and take your time locating and installing the parts so that they rotate correctly into position. For proper tension, place a drop of thread-locking adhesive on the screw that holds each stop, then tighten the screw until the stop rotates easily but without play.

—Andy Rae, Asheville, NC

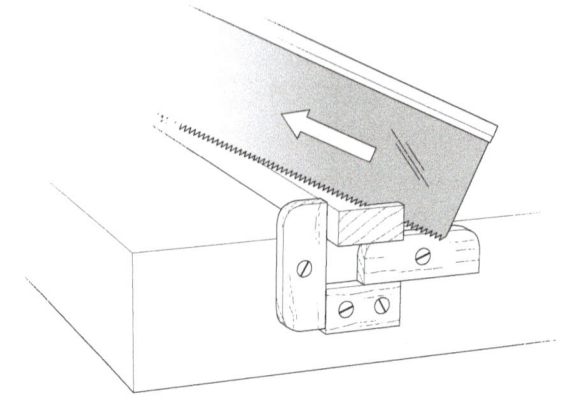

Use 3/8" × 1" dense hardwood for the three parts.

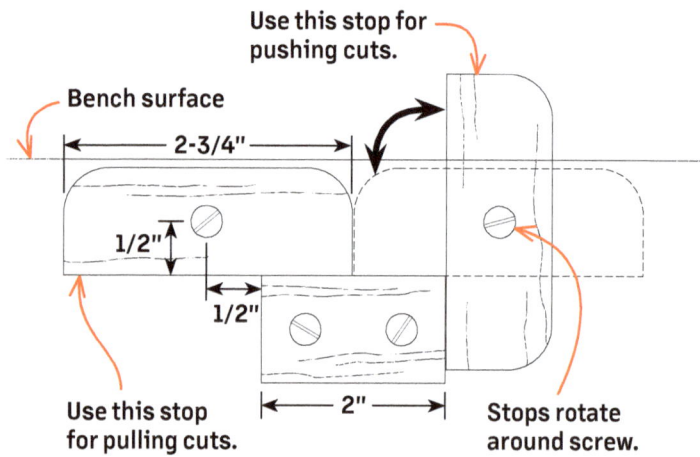

Quick-fix edge clamps

If you find yourself gluing up edge trim and running short of edge clamps, here's a fast alternative. With the trim in place, firmly attach C-clamps to the workpiece edge so there's a small gap between the trim and the inside surface of the clamps. (Use pieces of scrap to protect the surface of the workpiece.) Then, just slip wooden shims in the gaps between the clamps and edge trim and tap them into place until snug.

—Jim Chappel, Wausau, WI

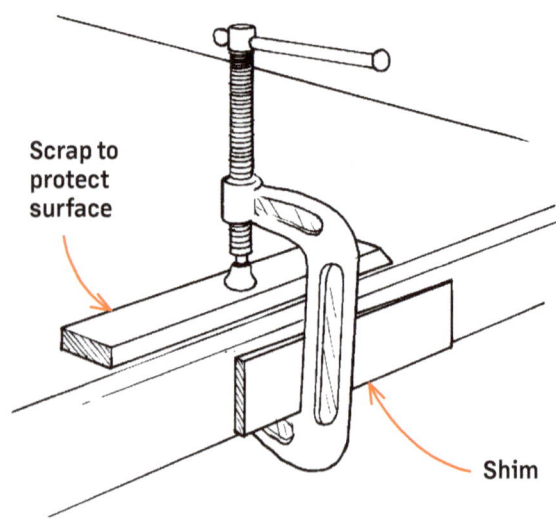

Leather-clad clamps

As much as I love my parallel jaw clamps, I don't have a lot of them, and often have to bring pipe clamps into play on a project as well. Pipe clamps work fine for many jobs, but their unevenly cast jaws have the unfortunate tendency to mar workpieces. I've found that the solution is to attach thick leather pads to the jaw faces using contact cement. In addition to preventing dents, the leather helps keep the jaws from sliding around while positioning the clamps for case glue-ups and other operations.

—Shelly DuBois, New Orleans, LA

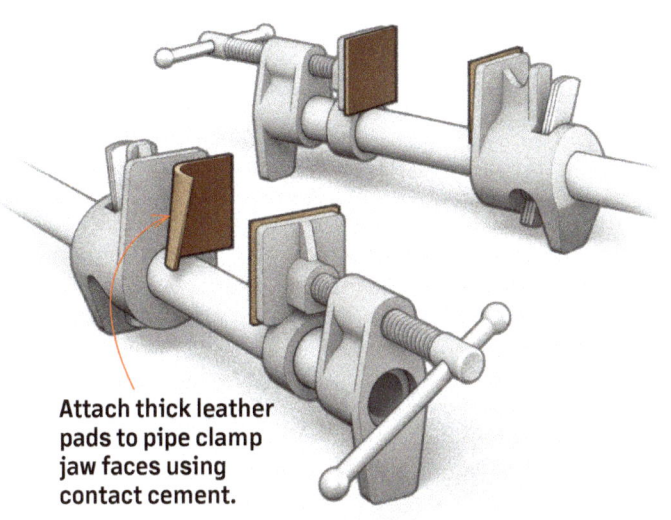

Attach thick leather pads to pipe clamp jaw faces using contact cement.

Telescoping hold-down

Hold-down clamps are an effective way to secure work in process. Unfortunately, most commercial hold-downs are restricted to a fairly limited reach. If the sizes of the workpieces vary, you need to remove and reposition a clamp in another jig mounting hole. Not wanting to turn my templates into Swiss cheese or waste time rearranging clamps, I make my own wooden versions. These include long slots that allow easy extension or retraction to increase or reduce reach. They cost a fraction of the price of commercial versions, and are quick and easy to produce. I have made enough that I can dedicate a batch to any particular jig, which is less time-consuming than switching them out from one setup to another.

—Scott Grove, Canandaigua, NY

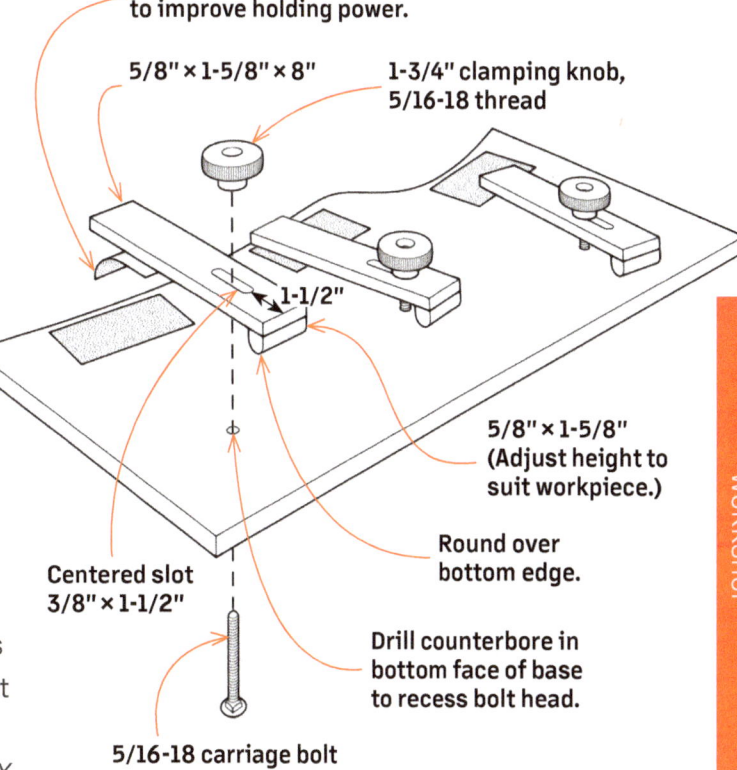

Affix sandpaper to bottom to improve holding power.

5/8" × 1-5/8" × 8"

1-3/4" clamping knob, 5/16-18 thread

1-1/2"

5/8" × 1-5/8" (Adjust height to suit workpiece.)

Round over bottom edge.

Centered slot 3/8" × 1-1/2"

Drill counterbore in bottom face of base to recess bolt head.

5/16-18 carriage bolt

CLEANUP

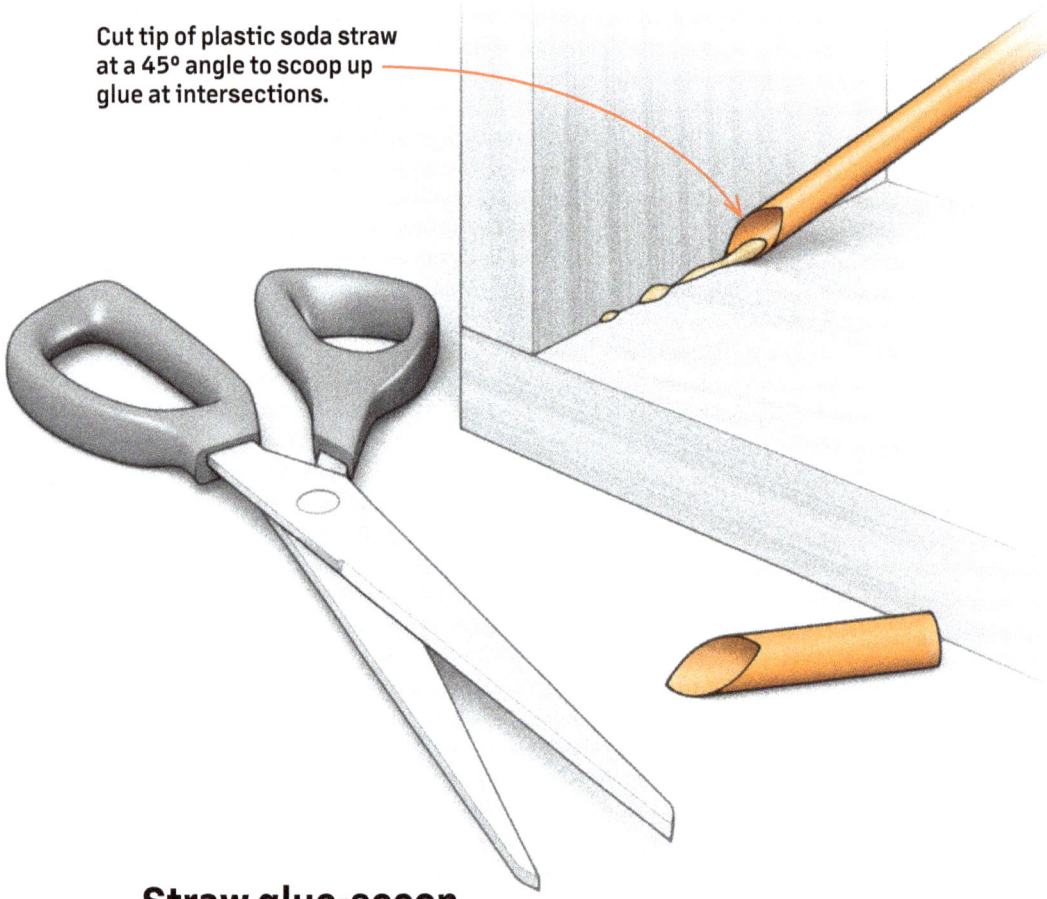

Cut tip of plastic soda straw at a 45° angle to scoop up glue at intersections.

Straw glue-scoop

Glue squeeze-out at panel intersections can be difficult to clean up. If you wipe it up with a wet rag, you risk dragging diluted glue into the wood grain, where it will resist finish. Scraping it up with a putty knife or other tool can be a similarly messy proposition. Try this instead: Nip the end off of a plastic soda straw at a 45° angle and use it to scoop up the wet glue. The sharp tip targets the corner, while the edges hug the walls, neatly forcing the glue up into the tube. Once you've gotten rid of the majority of the squeeze-out this way, a follow-up swipe with a clean, wet rag takes care of any residual glue.

—Kat Nash, Richmond, VA

It's in the bag

Using a magnet is a fast way to pick up dropped nails or screws, but picking all the nails off the magnet can be a chore, especially for those super-strong rare earth magnets. To make it a lot easier, turn a small snack-sized resealable bag inside-out over the end of your magnet before picking up the nails. Once the nails are all picked up and stuck to the magnet, just turn the bag right-side-out and pull it off the magnet.

—*Jim Brook, Denver, CO*

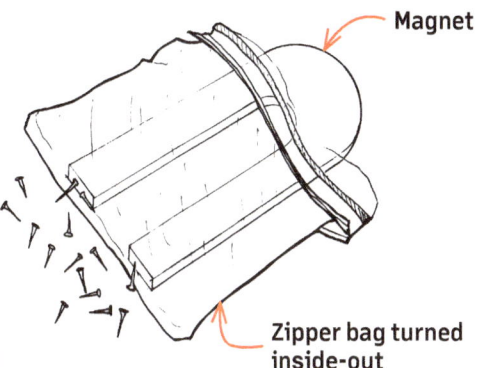

Glue cleanup detailing

It can be difficult to clean up glue in tight recessed spots like in beads and other small profiles, but here's a good approach. Begin by using a damp, short-bristled brush, pushing it forward to scoop up the majority of the glue. Keep the brush clean by washing it in clean water as you work. When most of the glue is gone, follow up by scrubbing the area with a wet tuft-head toothbrush, whose small cylindrical head easily gets into tight spaces. Again, keep it clean as you work to avoid rubbing diluted glue into the pores, but don't keep it sopping, as you want to prevent dripping water into the joint.

—*Frank Ellis, St. Louis, MO*

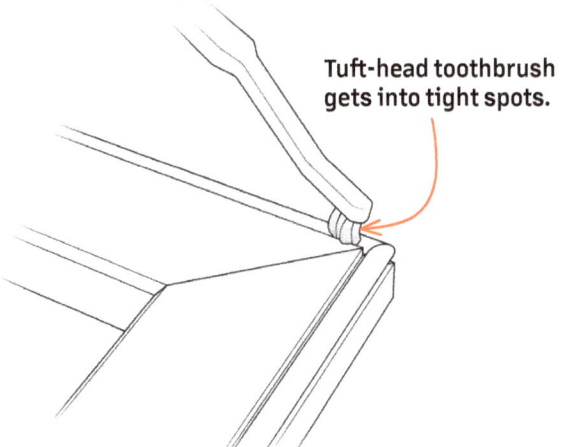

Tuft-head toothbrush gets into tight spots.

Glass as a scraper

Glass can be used as a wood scraper with the same results as a metal scraper. You can find 1/8" window glass scrap pieces at your hardware store for little to nothing. A plus in using glass is it can be cut straight or in any curve you need for the job.

To be safe, use a wood jig or gloves. I've also found glass to be efficient for removing old paint from wood.

—*Walter E. Erck, Mt. Prospect, IL*

Cleaner eraser

When erasing pencil layout lines, use a white polymer eraser (available at office supply stores). It won't smear like a typical rubber eraser.

—*Ken Burton, New Tripoli, PA*

Remove tape residue

An easy way to remove sticky tape residue from almost anything is by applying aerosol shaving cream to the residue and wiping it off. Works like a charm!

—*Jude Gagner, Bangor, ME*

WORKSHOP > CLEANUP

Easy pattern removal

It can be a hassle to remove glued-on pattern material from pieces after they've been sawn up. I find that a much easier approach is to completely mask a workpiece with wide painter's tape before applying the pattern with spray adhesive. It sure makes removal much easier.

—Dan Martin, Galena, OH

Turn up the heat on stubborn labels

Nearly everything you buy at a home center—including lumber, shelf boards, tools, and much more—will have at least one label on it. Some labels remove cleanly but others will shred into bits. And you'll find yourself doing a slow burn as you tediously scrape at the pieces.

Instead of raising your own temperature, turn up the heat on stubborn labels with a hair dryer or heat gun. The blast of heat will often make the label quickly surrender. If the hot air treatment fails, you can always resort to naphtha or mineral spirits on a cloth to dissolve the adhesive.

—Phillip Tucker, Tulsa, OK

Banish pitch with sunscreen

We all know that we should wear sunscreen, but now we have one more reason. After playing in the shop with some lumber and getting pitch on my hands, I applied some sunscreen and sure enough, all the pitch came right off! I tried it on a blade, and I now have a cheap new way to clean my blades and hands.

—Brian Wachs, Redmond, OR

Tight spot cleaning brush

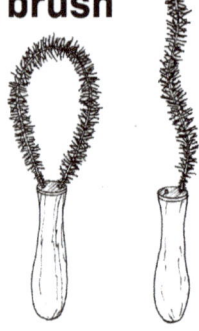

To get into hard-to-clean shop areas—such as inside your table saw cabinet, around bandsaw wheels, or anywhere else fine dust gets packed—modify an inexpensive loop-shaped vegetable brush.

Simply clip one end of the loop where it attaches to the handle and remove the extra wire. You're now free to bend the brush into any shape needed. In addition to its flexibility, the beauty of this little tool is that the really stiff bristles will loosen even caked-on stuff.

By the way, an unmodified vegetable brush used with cleaner is also a great tool to scrub the accumulated gunk off saw blades and drill bits.

—R.B. Himes, Vienna, OH

Mini-scraper

Use a burnisher to turn the edge on a common single-edged razor blade to create a small scraper for leveling dried finish drips and getting into tight spots.

—Craig W. Bentzley, Chalfont, PA

Plane iron chisel

I had built a small box, and needed to pare away some dried glue squeeze-out from the inside corners. Too bad all of my chisels were too long to fit inside the box. Standing there wishing for a short chisel, I suddenly realized I could just steal the blade from my block plane, which proved to do the job just fine.

—Anthony Warren, Las Vegas, NV

Cheap chisel champ

One of my favorite tools is one that protects several of my other tools. It's a very cheap chisel. You know the kind: They're often found dumped in a cardboard bin by the checkout counter at the hardware store. Buy one and hang it so that it's closer and easier to reach than your good tools. Then when you need to scrape glue off the floor, paint off tile, open a can of wood putty, or any of the scores of other tasks for which you really don't want to use a good tool, you'll have a quick and easy answer right at hand. And, if you do end up damaging it beyond repair, it's no big no loss—just throw it away and replace it. Your good tools will thank you for it.

—C. Alec MacLean, Fremont, CA

Spill absorber

Accidentally spill something? Open up that dust collector and throw some sawdust on it! After about 15 minutes, the sawdust will absorb most of the spill.

—Rob Spiece, Berea, KY

Wipe away pencil lines

Pencil lines are easy to sand or plane away, but there are times when you might miss a mark halfway into the assembly or finishing process. Instead of reaching for an eraser, try denatured alcohol. Unlike erasing, an alcohol wipe-down won't leave crumbs or any rubbery residue, or even raise the grain.

—Dan Nonte, Midlothian, VA

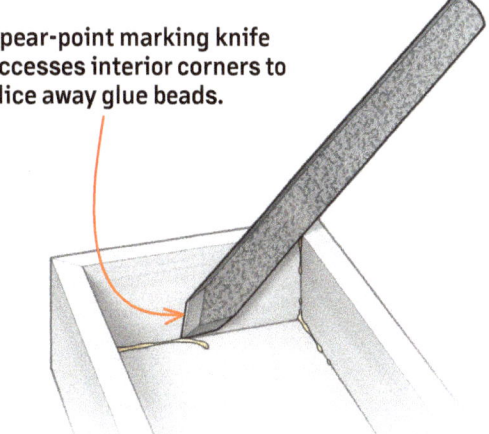

Spear-point marking knife accesses interior corners to slice away glue beads.

Marking knife glue cleanup

My Japanese "spear-point" marking knife is great for accurately marking out joinery. Because it has a flat face and no handle, it can register flush against a dovetail cheek, for example, to precisely lay out the mating socket, even between closely spaced tails. And the spear point allows both right- and left-hand use. Recently, I discovered another great use for the tool: glue cleanup inside the corners of boxes and other small cavities. The flat face and spear point allows the knife to cleanly slice away partially hardened beads of glue squeeze-out in corners where a chisel often won't reach.

—Dave Freedman, Highland Park, IL

Second life for old toothbrushes

Save those old toothbrushes for cleaning up excess glue. They reach into small reveals and other tight spaces where squeeze-out can be hard to access. Old toothbrushes are also great for brushing sawblade teeth after applying a cleaning solution.

—Rob Spiece, Berea, KY

WORKSHOP > DUST COLLECTION

DUST COLLECTION

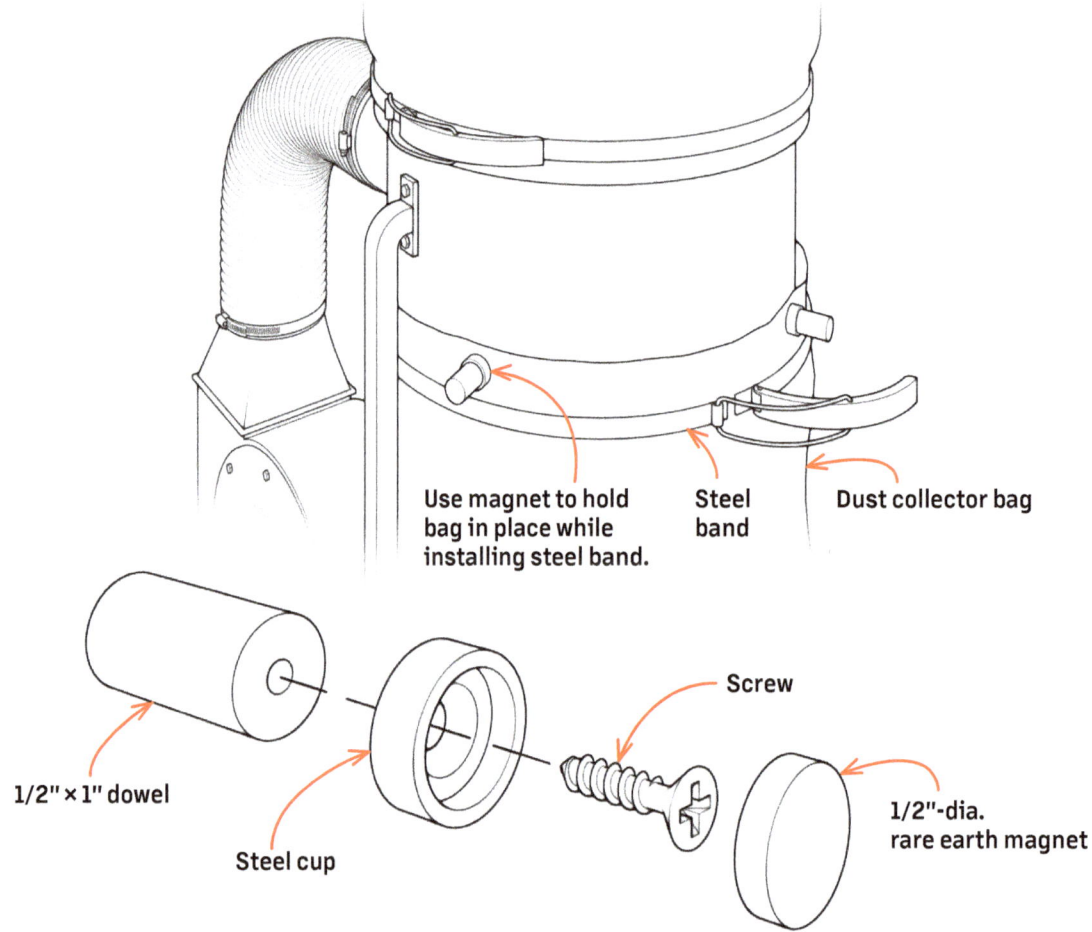

Mags to hold bags

Changing the bag on my dust collector always made me wish I had four hands—two to hold the bag in place, and two to replace the metal holding strap. Since I'm unlikely to grow an extra set of mitts, I decided to put a couple of 1/2"-diameter rare-earth magnets into play for the job. I screwed commercially available steel cups to the ends of short dowels to hold the magnets in place. They temporarily hang the bag in place while I apply the strap. Works great!

—Ed Williams, Makawao, HI

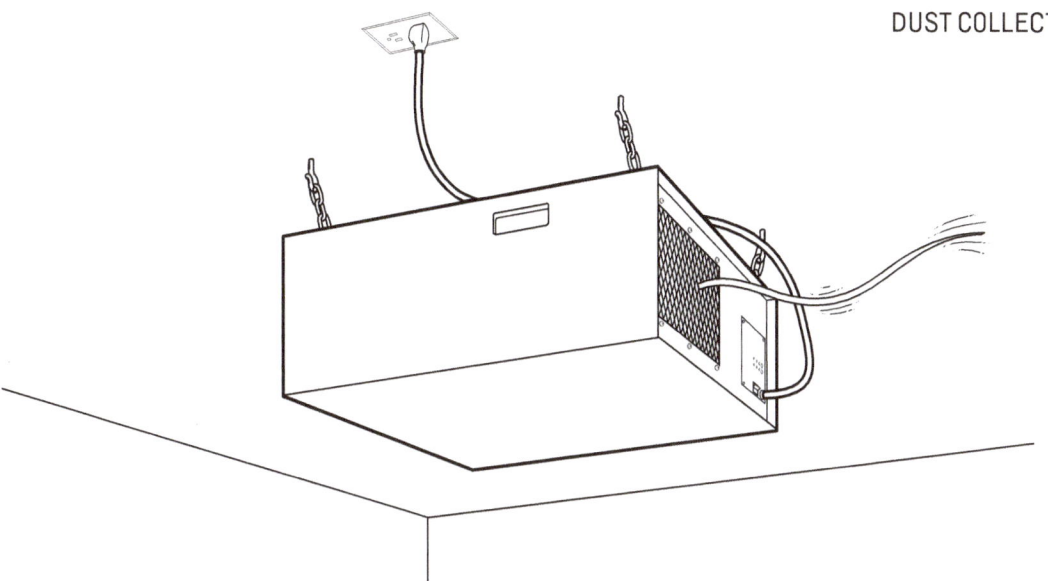

Dust filter detector

Taking a cue from the fan display at my hardware store, I attached a 24"-long ribbon strip to the exhaust grill of my ceiling-mounted dust filter. The ribbon provides an at-a-glance indication that the machine is running (this can be tough to tell when using other machines). The ribbon also serves as a handy airflow gauge. When the strip starts to sag, I know it's time to pull out the ladder and install a fresh filter.

—Steve Bruns, Lafayette, CO

Coffee can connector

Have you ever accidentally ripped a dust-collector hose and found yourself wishing you had a connector to fix it? Or have you ever wanted to connect a couple of shorter dust-collector hoses to give you extra reach, but didn't have the connector to do the job? Well, maybe you did after all. It's a good bet you have a 1-lb. coffee can sitting around your shop full of nails or other hardware. Just cut off the bottom of the can and—voila!—instant 4"-diameter dust-collector connector.

—Thomas Lagreca, Lockport, NY

Dust collector gate hack

Instead of using the thumbscrews on metal dust collector gates, place a few rare-earth magnets on the metal gate housing to hold the gate in place. It makes for much quicker operation.

—Paul Anthony, Riegelsville, PA

WORKSHOP > DUST COLLECTION

DIY dust filter

I found an inexpensive way to reduce the dust in my shop using a box fan outfitted with a furnace filter. Affixing the filter to the intake side of the fan using duct tape creates a sort of cheap ambient air cleaner that I can place at my sanding station, table saw, or wherever. It's best to place the unit in an open window, but at least avoid aiming it toward walls, which stirs up latent dust. No, it's not as effective as a commercial unit, and I still wear a dust mask since the filter only captures large particles. However, it sure does prevent working in a cloud of dust, and I can afford to put a few of them in convenient locations around the shop.

—Jesse Hodgman, Los Angeles, CA

Affix furnace filter to intake side of box fan.

Duct tape

Bicycle tube dust solution

How many of us have several tools in our collections with fractionally different exhaust diameters? I know I do.

One evening, while preparing to connect my shop vacuum to my bench-top sander with duct tape, my eye happened to catch an old bicycle tube hanging in the shop. I felt like Columbus discovering America. I cut a 3" piece of the old tube and slipped it over the exhaust port of the sander and the 1" connector on the vacuum hose for a perfect airtight connection. With the variety of bicycle inner tubes that are available, this would probably work with an infinite number of tools.

—Tom Warren, Oakland, NJ

Dust collector muffler

When I set up my cyclone dust collector, I had no idea how loud it would be. I decided to make my own muffler, using a pair of five-gallon buckets and some scraps I had in my shop. The collector's performance didn't change, but the muffler cut down the noise level so that I could find and fix the leaks in my ductwork by listening for the hisses of air at the fittings.

To make the muffler, I used a jigsaw to remove the bottoms from both buckets and then attached them, bottom to bottom, with foil tape. Next, I sliced an old foam camping mattress into 5"-wide strips on my bandsaw and glued the strips to the inside of the buckets with spray adhesive, leaving an 8"-diameter hole in the middle for air movement. To mount the muffler to a plywood base, I drove 3/4" screws through a plastic flange and then sealed the joint with caulk.

—*Rob Mousel, Hanover, MN*

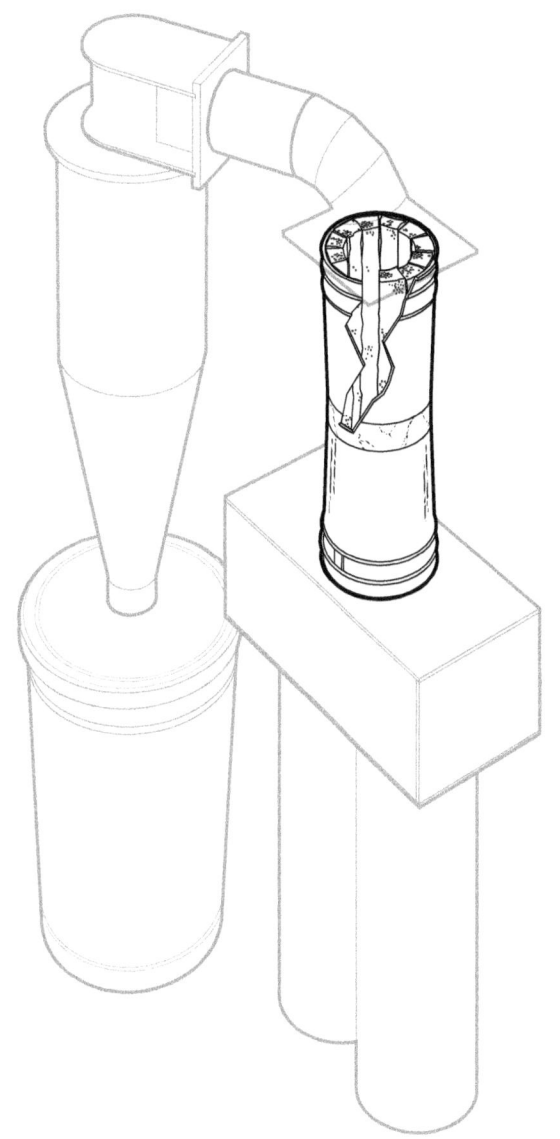

Hooks tame wild hoses

Hoses for a dust collector or shop vacuum can be unruly beasts, defying your best efforts to tame them. You lean them against a wall, but they quickly slither away, ending up underfoot. It's more than an annoyance—it's a real safety hazard.

Conquer the problem by draping each hose over a storage hook mounted high on the wall or screwed into a ceiling joist. You'll find hooks in several sizes at your home center. A bike hook will handle vacuum hoses, and a jumbo ladder hook is big enough to handle several hoses. Hooks with a foam surface help prevent the hose from sliding.

—*Glenn Varney, St. Louis, MO*

WORKSHOP > ORGANIZATION & STORAGE

ORGANIZATION & STORAGE

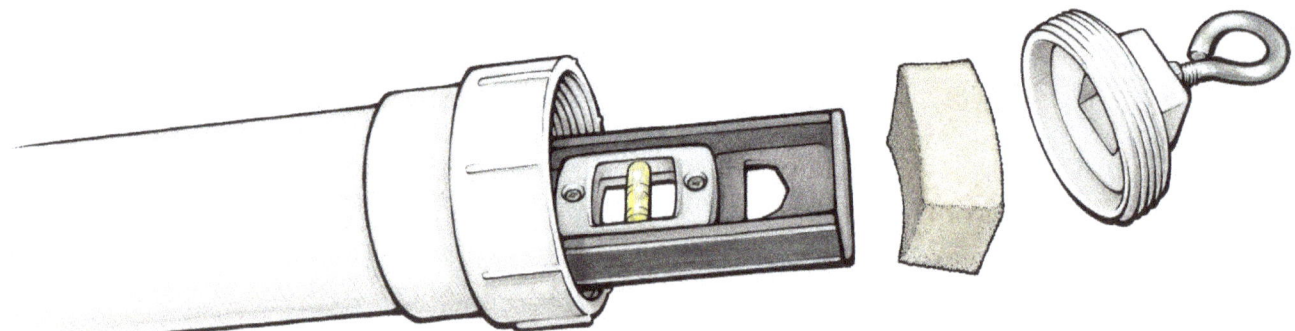

Making a strong case for the level

Installing cabinets requires a quality level, but the tool can lose its accuracy when dropped or banged around on its way to the job site. You can find a case manufactured for a 4' level, but there's nothing for a 2-footer. And finding a case for a pricey 6' level? Forget about it!

Fortunately, you can make a strong case for your level quickly and inexpensively from common PVC plumbing pipe and fittings. You'll find heavy-duty schedule 40 pipe and components at your local hardware store or home center. Solvent-weld a cap to one end of a 3"-diameter pipe, and push a block of foam to the bottom to cushion the tool. Cut the pipe to length (it's easy with your miter saw) and solvent-weld a female adapter in place. A screw cap completes the case. For quick and easy storage, drill through the cap to add an eye bolt with a couple of washers and nuts. A foam block at the top of the case completes the cushioning. Don't screw the cap on tightly until the solvent odor completely dissipates.

Another tip: If you don't like the printing on your pipe, remove it with a rag dampened with lacquer thinner.

—John Appleton, Spokane, WA

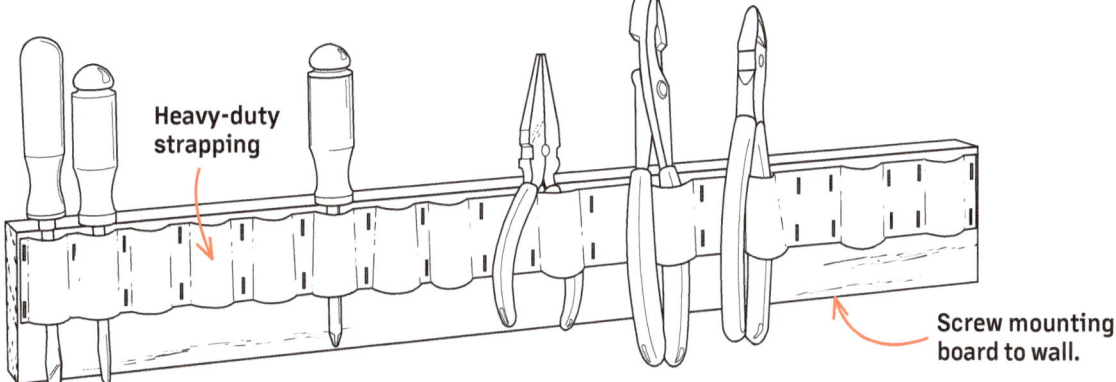

Strapping tool holders

My son, who is in the heavy equipment business, happened to have a few scraps of heavy-duty tie-down strapping lying around. I grabbed them, thinking they might come in handy for something, and they did. I found that they work great as tool holders for everything from screwdrivers and awls to pliers and wire cutters. I simply stapled the strapping to a board on the wall, bunching it up to create appropriately sized "pockets" to accommodate my tools.

—Oneil Long, Mound City, MO

Erasable notes

I am constantly making notes of measurements, shopping lists, and cutting dimensions in my shop. When I built my shop cabinets, I made the door panels out of white-coated 1/8"-thick fiberboard. I use dry-erase markers to make notes to myself for measurements, such as the spacing of drawers for a cabinet I recently built. When I no longer need the information, I simply erase, and I am ready for my next project or list.

—Roger Gall, New Cumberland, WV

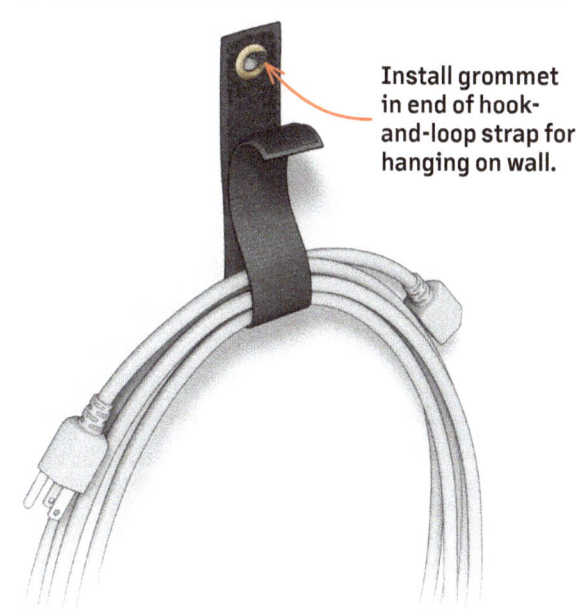

Hook-and-loop cord management

After a couple of shoulder surgeries, I found myself with several hook-and-loop straps that had been used to attach various therapeutic supports. I wanted to use them in some way, and realized that they would make great hangers for cords and other such items. All I had to do was attach a grommet to the end of a strap using a grommet installation kit. A strapped cord can then be neatly carried and hung anywhere you install a screw.

—Deanna Manke, Island Lake, IL

Quick-release magnetic pickup

It seems I'm always gathering up small screws and other hardware from the bench during hinge installation and other operations. I got tired of having to pick them up by hand, so I came up with this little solution. It's just a magnet attached to the end of a dowel that slides inside a 35-mm film canister. To "activate" the unit, slide the magnet to the bottom of the canister and pick up your hardware. To release the hardware, retract the magnet. Simple. It's also a great way to separate steel screws from brass and aluminum versions.

To make the pickup, attach a 1"-diameter rare-earth magnet to the end of a 1/2"-diameter dowel about 3" long. I screwed on a 1" steel cup designed for attaching magnets, but you could use epoxy instead. Drill a hole in the canister cap to accept the dowel, put the parts together, and it's ready to go.

—Lee Dabkey, LaGrange Park, IL

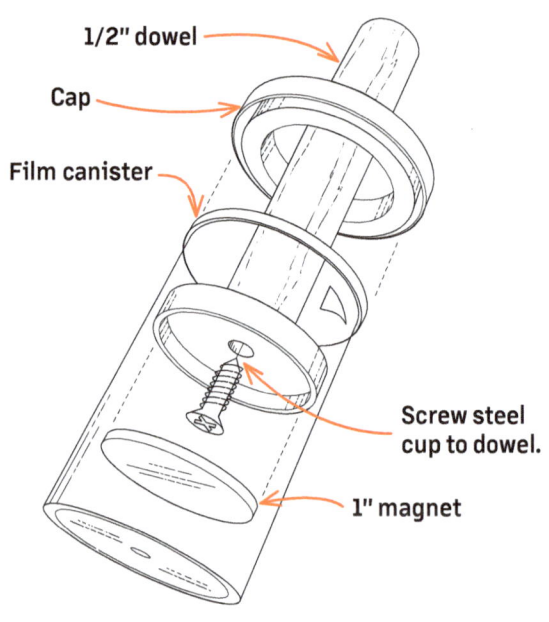

Quick I.D. for parts bins

How many times have you gone through every drawer in one of your parts bins looking for a single item?

For a fast, positive I.D. of a drawer's contents, take one of each like part from each drawer and use a dab of hot-melt glue to attach the part to the front. Now, one quick glance at the front of the drawer will instantly reveal what parts are inside.

If you ever decide to change the contents of a drawer, the hot-glued part pops right off the front of the smooth plastic drawer front with just a bit of prying with a screwdriver or chisel.

—Stan Zolenski, Plymouth, MA

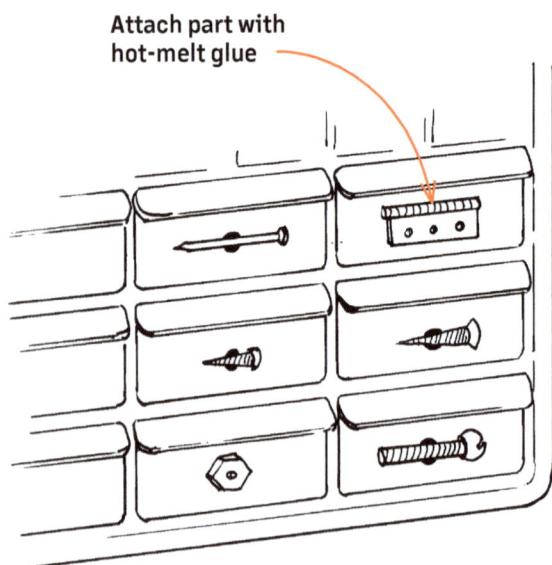

Economical lumber stickers

Use of wooden stickers to stack lumber for drying will sometimes result in mold or bugs between the sticker and the lumber. Store-bought stickers work well, but are expensive.

An alternate solution is to use 3/4" schedule 40 electrical conduit from the local home supply store. It can easily be cut into required lengths. Its advantages are: small contact area with the stacked lumber; very rigid; bugs and mold don't find it tasty; and sliding boards onto the conduit is very easy because it tends to act as a roller.

However, if the wood is going to be stacked on anything but level ground or the whole stack is going to be moved with a forklift, the roundness of the conduit will result in a pile of lumber that rolls onto the ground (and usually into the only mud puddle within 100 yards).

To solve this problem, purchase 1-1/2" conduit and cut it down the middle, making two stickers shaped like half circles. Make a jig using a scrap piece of 10"-long 4×4. Bore a 1-1/2" hole through the center of the 4×4; unless you have a long bit, you'll probably have to drill from each end. Raise the blade on your table saw to about 3" and cut a slot down the middle, bisecting the center of the bored hole. Next, attach the jig to the fence of the saw over the blade (make sure you cover the exposed blade completely). To use the jig, simply turn on the saw and feed the conduit through the hole bored in the jig. This will give you two stickers for the price of one.

—John P. Rose, Litchfield, OH

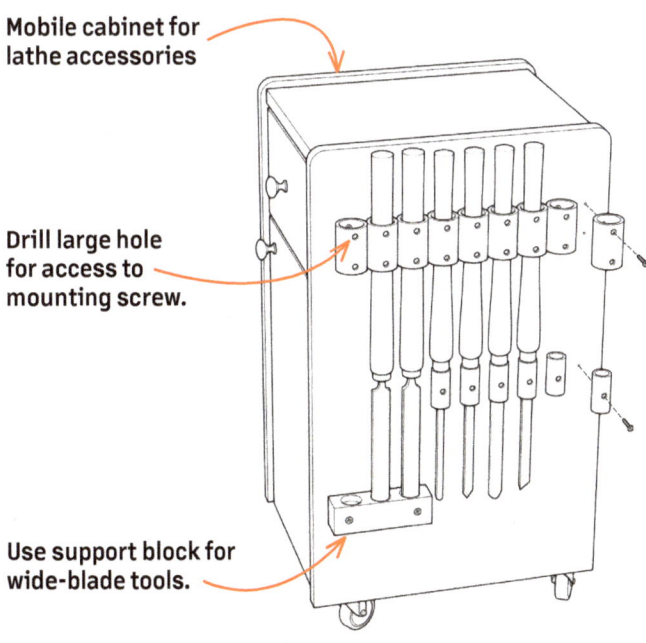

Mobile cabinet for lathe accessories

Drill large hole for access to mounting screw.

Use support block for wide-blade tools.

PVC lathe rack

For safety, I mount my tools cutting-edge down within short lengths of PVC pipe. The diameter of the lower length of pipe, which supports the tool, is slightly less than the diameter of the tool's ferrule. The tool handle sits inside a larger diameter pipe. In those cases where the blade is as wide as the ferrule, the cutting edge rests on a wooden block. I mounted this "rack" on the side of a mobile cabinet that includes a drawer and plenty of storage for drill bits, calipers, and other turning accessories. The unit has served me well for years.

—David Taft, Harpswell, ME

WORKSHOP > ORGANIZATION & STORAGE

Twin-handled tool rack

I use a lot of pliers, nippers, wire cutters, and other "twin-handled" tools at my bench. To keep them sorted out and at-the-ready, I took a tip from my electrician dad and created a rack for them on my bench wall using conduit clips. These inexpensive, commonly available saddle-shaped metal clamps, or "straps," are typically used to surface-mount electrical conduit. Available in various sizes, they're perfect for holding one handle of a tool solidly to a wall, leaving the opposite handle extended for easy grabbing. Installing them side-by-side, sharing a mounting screw, consolidates the tools into a small area. And unlike some pegboard hooks made for the purpose, the straps won't accidentally pull away from the wall.

—Bil Mitchell, Riegelsville, PA

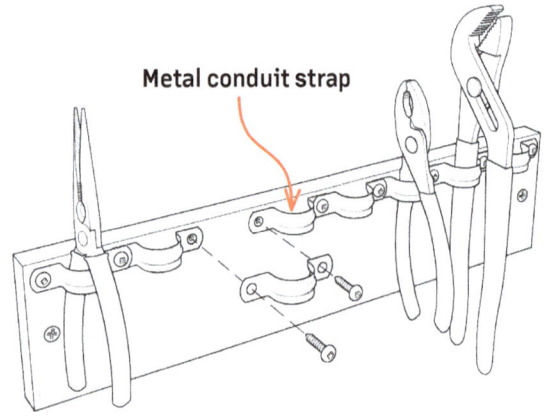

Metal conduit strap

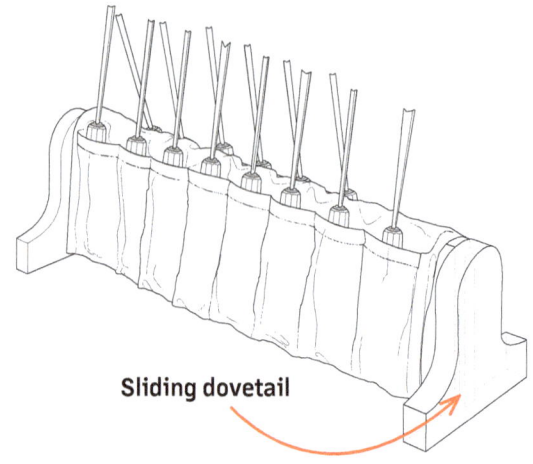

Sliding dovetail

Benchtop horse puts tools in easy reach

I like the convenience of storing my carving tools in a canvas roll, but pulling them out when I need them can be a pain (sometimes, quite literally). At a carving class I attended, I noted that the instructor draped his roll over a mini-sawhorse. Compared to a flat-laid roll, his setup required less bench space and put all the tools within easy reach.

My version takes the original design up a notch. After sizing the beam to match my roll, I routed a dovetailed groove into each leg and routed the dovetailed ends of the beam to fit. The knock-down joinery eliminates any need for additional parts or fasteners that could get lost in transit.

—Craig W. Bentzley, Chalfont, PA

Stretch wrap packing

Use a small roll of stretch wrap (available at office supply stores) for bundling organized lumber and project parts.

—Paul Anthony, Riegelsville, PA

218 WOODCRAFT MAGAZINE TIPS & TRICKS FOR WOODWORKING

ORGANIZATION & STORAGE < WORKSHOP

Lathe chisel rack

Lathe work typically involves using a fair number of tools in a session, which means they need to be organized and easily accessible. This rack provides those services while also protecting the tools from damaging each other by separating them with commonly available Shaker pegs. One of the beauties of this design is that the rack can stand alone, or it can be screwed to a wall or cabinet top—whatever serves best. As shown in the drawing, it's easy to build in any size to suit your collection, or perhaps just your most commonly used tools.

—Andy Rae, Asheville, NC

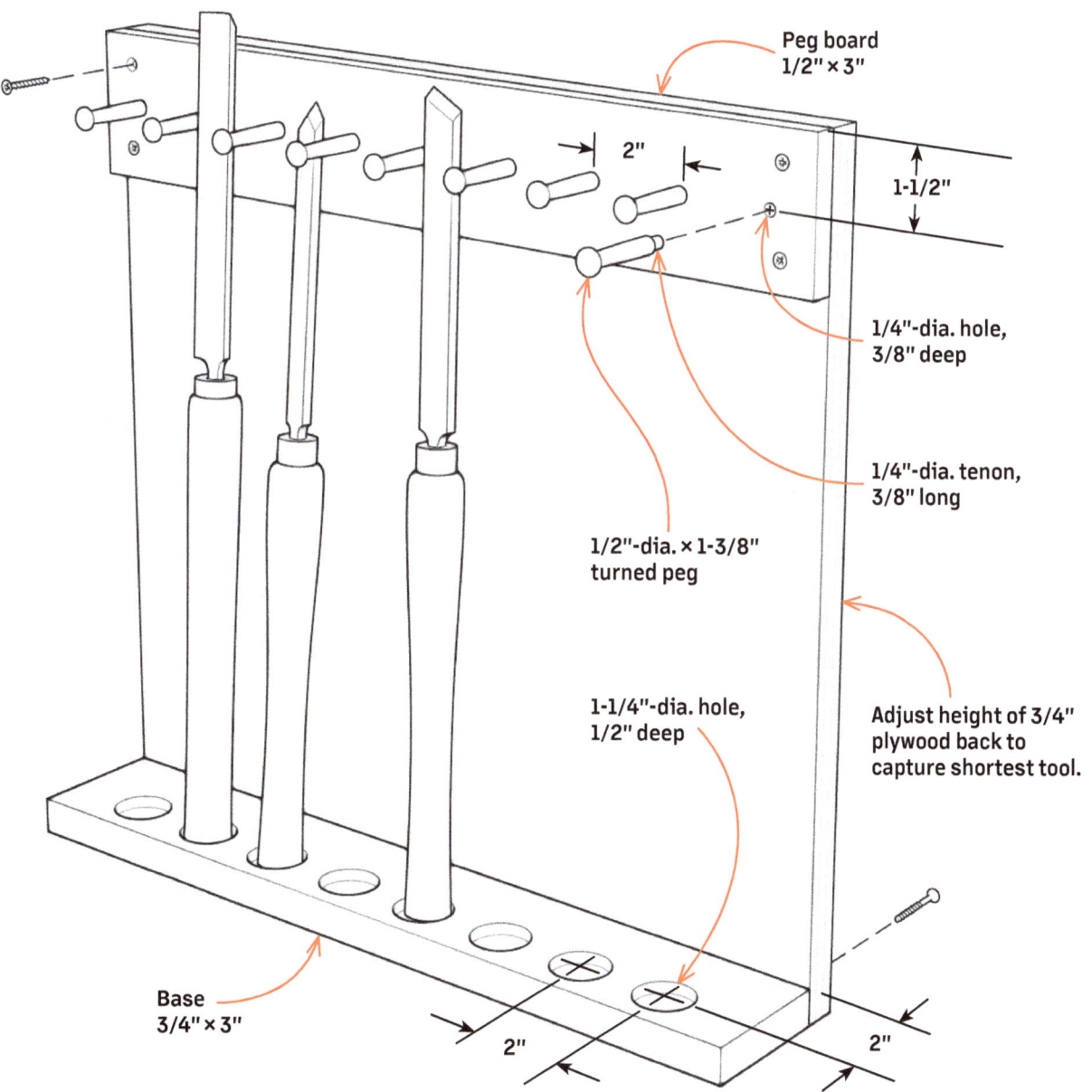

WOODCRAFT MAGAZINE TIPS & TRICKS FOR WOODWORKING   219

WORKSHOP > ORGANIZATION & STORAGE

Triangle marking system

I was in my shop trying to organize a jumble of cabinet parts when a friend dropped by and showed me an old layout trick that has since saved me lots of time and confusion. After parts are cut to size, and before you lay out any joints, select the show face of each piece, orient it for best grain composition, and then organize the pieces on your bench in their desired relation to each other. Now, it's a simple matter of pressing the pieces together and striking a few lines across their faces to create a triangle as shown in the drawings. A glance at the markings immediately identifies the show face, the top, the bottom, and the left- and right-hand sides of each piece. To identify multiples, strike additional lines that extend across the mating pieces.

—*Gary Goldthwaite, Indianapolis, IN*

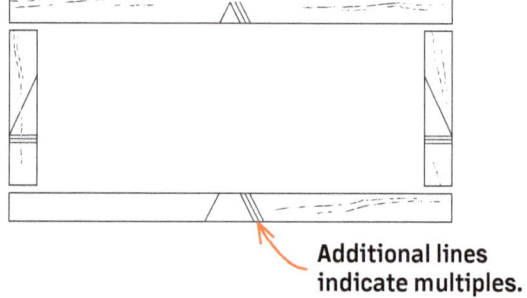

Additional lines indicate multiples.

Hang it all

Between protecting my workbench from glue spills and putting pieces between clamps and wood, I use a fair amount of waxed paper in the shop. To keep it handy, I cut a heavy plastic clothes hanger and slipped on a roll of waxed paper. It now hangs on the tool board above my workbench, where I can tear off just as much as I need.

—*R.B. Himes, Vienna, OH*

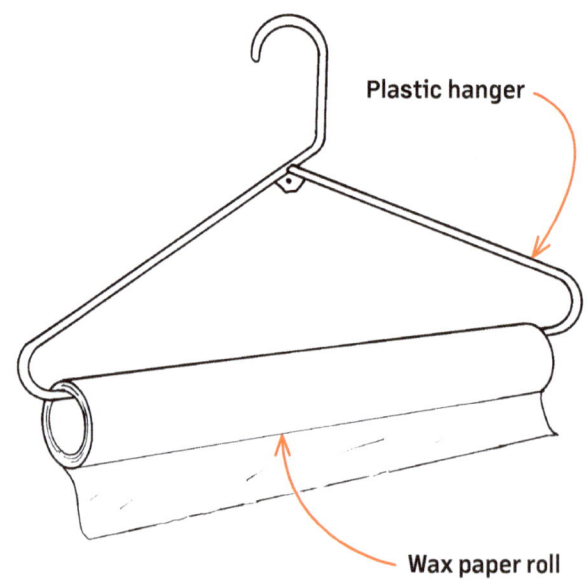

Detachable tool tray

Many workbenches have holes on their sides or ends, either for use with side-mounted hold-downs, or as installation holes for future vises. I built this small tool tray to keep tools and materials clear of my benchtop. By mounting dowels in the back to match the holes in my bench, the tray can be pressed into service when needed or pulled out when it's in the way. Snug-fitting dowels, coupled with the weight of the contents within, keep the tray firmly in place.

Design the tray to fit your bench. To maximize your benchtop surface, set the tray slightly below it. I made mine deep enough to store handplanes so that the handles don't protrude above the benchtop edge.

—*Mark Theil, Coral Springs, FL*

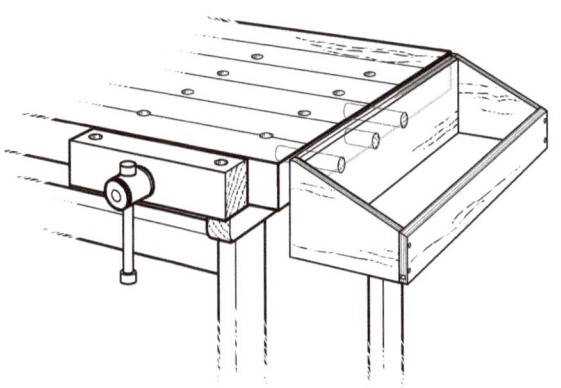

Steel wool dispenser

I use a lot of steel wool for rubbing out finishes. Like many woodworkers, I buy the stuff in rolls. Rather than stashing it in a cabinet, I hang it from the ceiling joists on a simple shop-made bracket screwed together from wood scraps and a section of old broom handle. It's the easiest thing in the world to simply pull down the amount that I need and trim it off with scissors.

—*Howard Hirsch, Malvern, PA*

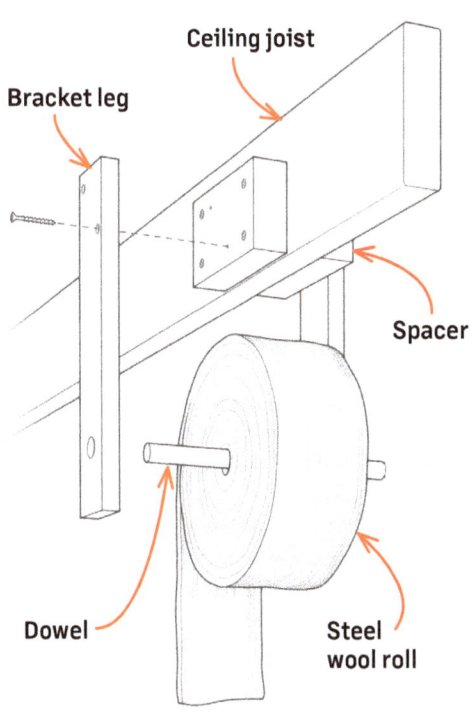

White board in the wood shop

Many contractors rely heavily on dry-marker white boards for scheduling, sketching, notes, and reminders, to name just a few uses. I find that they are just as useful in the shop. In addition to boards, the material is available in thin sheets with self-adhesive or magnetic backing. Suitably sized and strategically placed pieces of the material can be adhered to various machines to make notes regarding cutter details and settings, as well as machine maintenance records.

—*Larry Koch, North Adams, MA*

WORKSHOP > ORGANIZATION & STORAGE

Keep manuals handy

Even if you're the type of woodworker who brags about never reading tool manuals, you'll need to refer to one someday. But where do you keep the manuals so that finding one doesn't involve days of tedious searching?

Go to an office supply store, buy a three-ring binder, clear plastic page inserts, and a set of dividers. Use the dividers to keep the instructions for your accessories grouped with the appropriate tool. For example, one section will include your table saw, its stand, rip fence, and so on.

To keep track of information that can be useful for warranty purposes, staple the original purchase receipt to the manual.

—Deborah Lawrence, Madison, WI

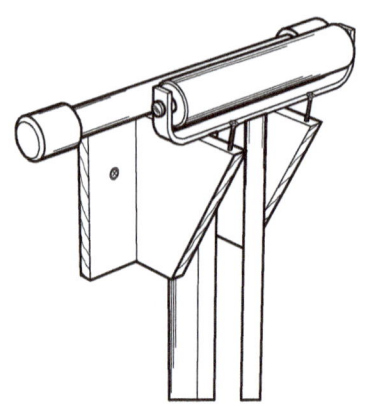

Roller stand wall rack

Folding roller stands see plenty of use at the table saw, drill press, thickness planer, etc., but they can be a nuisance when they're not needed. To keep my roller out of traffic, I cobbled together a simple rack using nails, glue, and a few scraps of pine. The nails on the top of the braces keep the roller from flipping open or falling off.

—Mark Koritz, St. Louis, MO

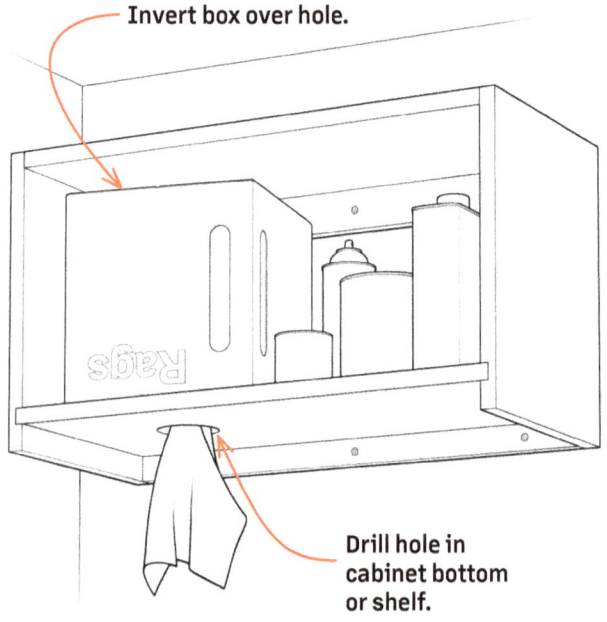

Invert box over hole.

Drill hole in cabinet bottom or shelf.

Paper rags at the ready

For cleanup around the shop, I use paper rags like those sold in boxes at home supply stores. They're convenient to use, but tearing off a perforated section can be a two-handed hassle, with one hand (often already fouled with finish) to hold the box, and the other to rip away the necessary rags. The easy fix is to store the box upside down in a cabinet whose bottom has been drilled to create a dispensary hole for the rags. A quick, one-handed sideways pull is all it takes to free up whatever length you want. If you don't have a suitable cabinet, you can create a simple shelf for the job, mounting it to a wall or perhaps between overhead joists.

—Carl Rettiger, Billings, MT

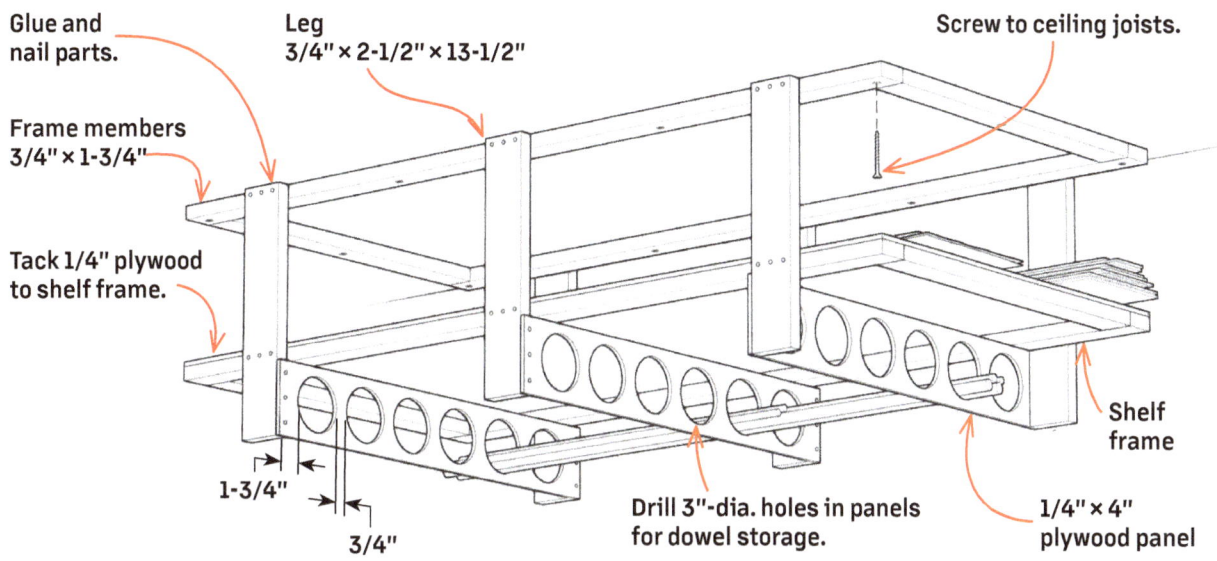

Ceiling-hung veneer and dowel rack

Pressed for storage space in a cramped shop? Look overhead. A ceiling-hung rack is the perfect place for somewhat large, but lightweight, shop materials and supplies. I made this rack to safely store veneers flat without taking up valuable floor space. By simply incorporating a few small panels with circular cutouts, I was able to add dowel storage that's still within my reach without a ladder. Construction simply involves making two frames: one for ceiling attachment and one to serve as a shelf. Use any frame joinery you like. The overall dimensions of my unit are 24-1/2" × 48" × 13-1/2", but size yours to suit your supplies and ceiling joist spacing.

—Paul Anthony, Riegelsville, PA

Keep dust brushes nearby

Frustrated at never having my dust brushes where I needed them, I drilled 1/4"-diameter holes and glued in 10mm-diameter rare-earth magnets into the bristle ends of my brushes. Now my brushes stay out of the way on the sides of the machines, but are nearby when it's time to clean up.

—Bill Sands, Lubeck, WV

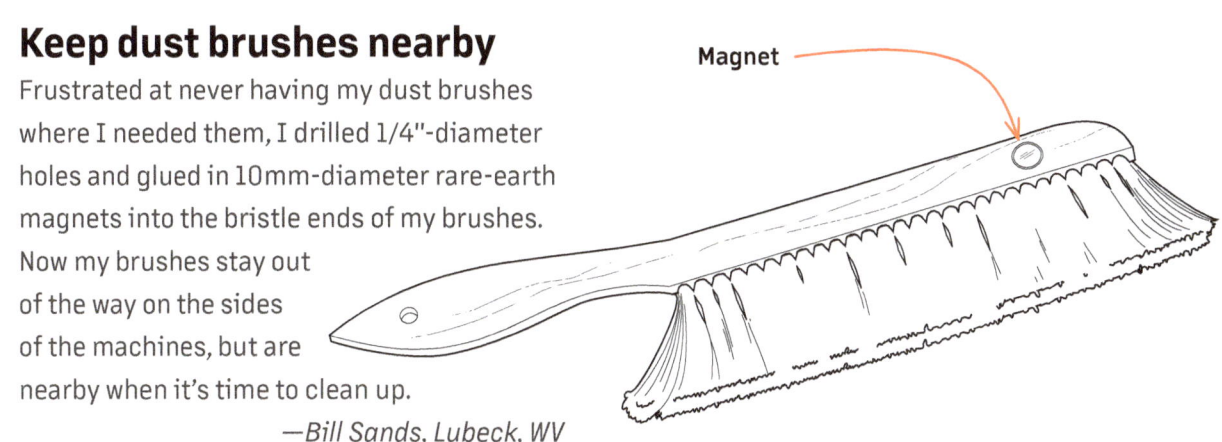

WORKSHOP > ORGANIZATION & STORAGE

Rack-in-waiting

Extra cabinet bases are perfect for storing short pieces of lumber and also serve as racks for longer boards. If you ever need storage relief, the boxes can be quickly put into play by adding doors and drawers.

—Tommy MacDonald, Boston, MA

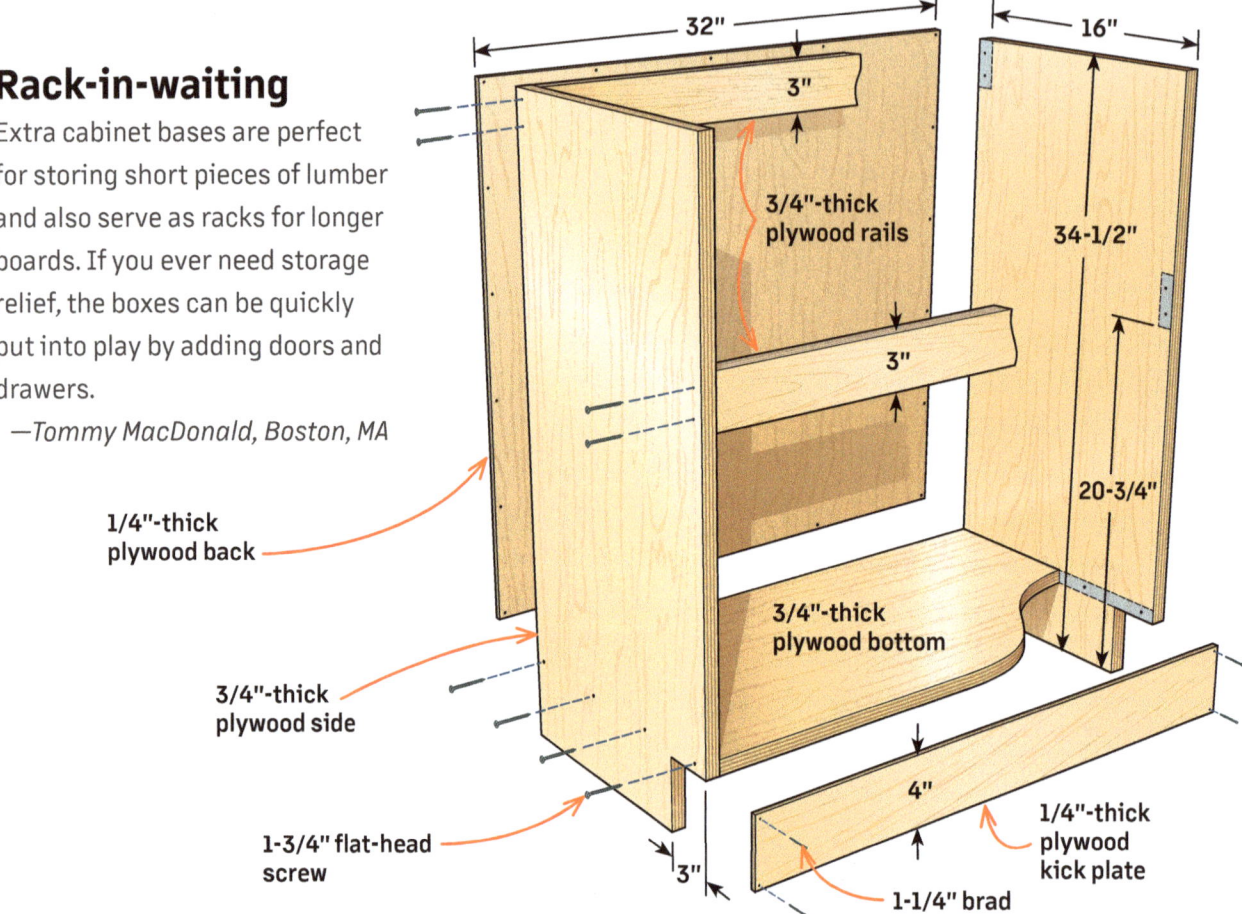

Jig pictures worth 1,000 words

Have you ever pulled out a jig that you haven't used in a while and realized that you don't entirely remember how to set it up or use it? Me, too. To prevent that, I've added a new tool to my shop—an inexpensive digital camera. After setting up a jig and any attendant tools, I take a few relevant snapshots, print them out, and tape them to the jig or stash the images in a "jig setup" folder for future reference. This approach works well as long as I can remember where I keep the camera.

—Robert Lopez, Los Angeles, CA

Protecting tool rolls

The sharp edges of my turning tools kept cutting the interior of their canvas carrying pouch. As a remedy, I cut the fingers off a pair of inexpensive leather work gloves, yielding ten protectors to fit over the business end of the cutters.

—Linda Halligan, Livonia, NY

ORGANIZATION & STORAGE < WORKSHOP

Nonslip chisel guard

My good bench chisels enjoy a safe home near my workbench, but my jobbers aren't so lucky, as they're typically banging around unfettered in my toolbox. Looking for a way to protect freshly honed edges from accidental abuse, I experimented with a few scraps of thick-walled vinyl tubing left over from a plumbing project. I found that the tubing offers good protection and even allows me to carry chisels safely in my shop apron. To outfit a chisel, simply pinch a short section of tubing to widen its opening, then slide it over the chisel tip. The vinyl springs back and clamps tightly onto the blade.

Matching tubing and chisel sizes involves some trial and error. For a nonslip fit, select a tube with an interior diameter (I.D.) that's slightly less than the width of the blade. Smaller-diameter tubes compress to only about 1/8" wider than their interior diameter, while larger tubes flex enough to fit blades 1/4" to 1/2" larger than the I.D.

—*Joe Hurst-Wajszczuk, Birmingham, AL*

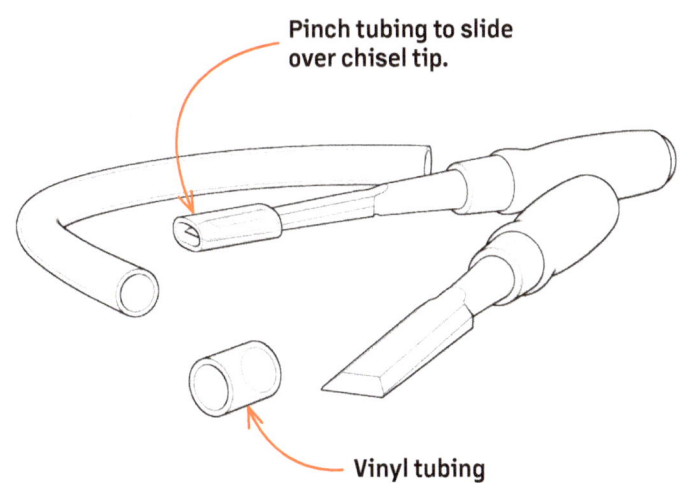

Pinch tubing to slide over chisel tip.

Vinyl tubing

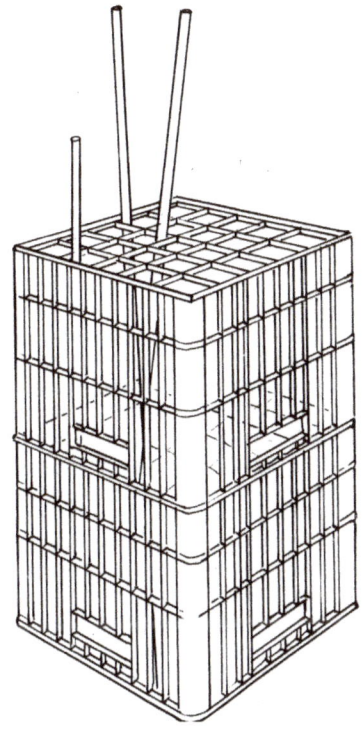

Stackable storage

I use a couple of milk-crate-style storage containers to keep a large assortment of moldings and dowels organized. The crates usually measure about 12" on all sides, and have a grid on the bottom. Start by screwing two of them together, one on top of the other. Turn them upside down and attach them to a piece of plywood sized to fit the opening (which is now on the bottom). The resulting storage unit is light and inexpensive, and the two grids keep thin stock organized.

You could keep the crates in the intended open-end-up position, still use the grid for long, thin stock, but also utilize the open part for storage of short pieces. You can add wheels for portability. You can even use it to store long-handled tools for the shop and garden with sufficient weighting on the bottom.

— *Kevin Hemmingsen, Wabasha, MN*

WOODCRAFT MAGAZINE TIPS & TRICKS FOR WOODWORKING

WORKSHOP > ORGANIZATION & STORAGE

Shop hangers from PVC pipe

Visitors to my shop often comment on my unusual system of hooks and hangers made from plastic pipe. The idea came about when I was given some short lengths of wide-diameter PVC pipe by a local plumber. I realized I could crosscut them into rings that I could screw to the ceiling joists for hanging dowels, pipes, and strip stock up out of the way. I took it a step further by bisecting some of the rings to create J hangers for extension cords, ropes, and even rolled drawings. I used a reciprocating saw to do the cutting, but a hacksaw or handsaw will work.

—Chris McKee, Landisville, PA

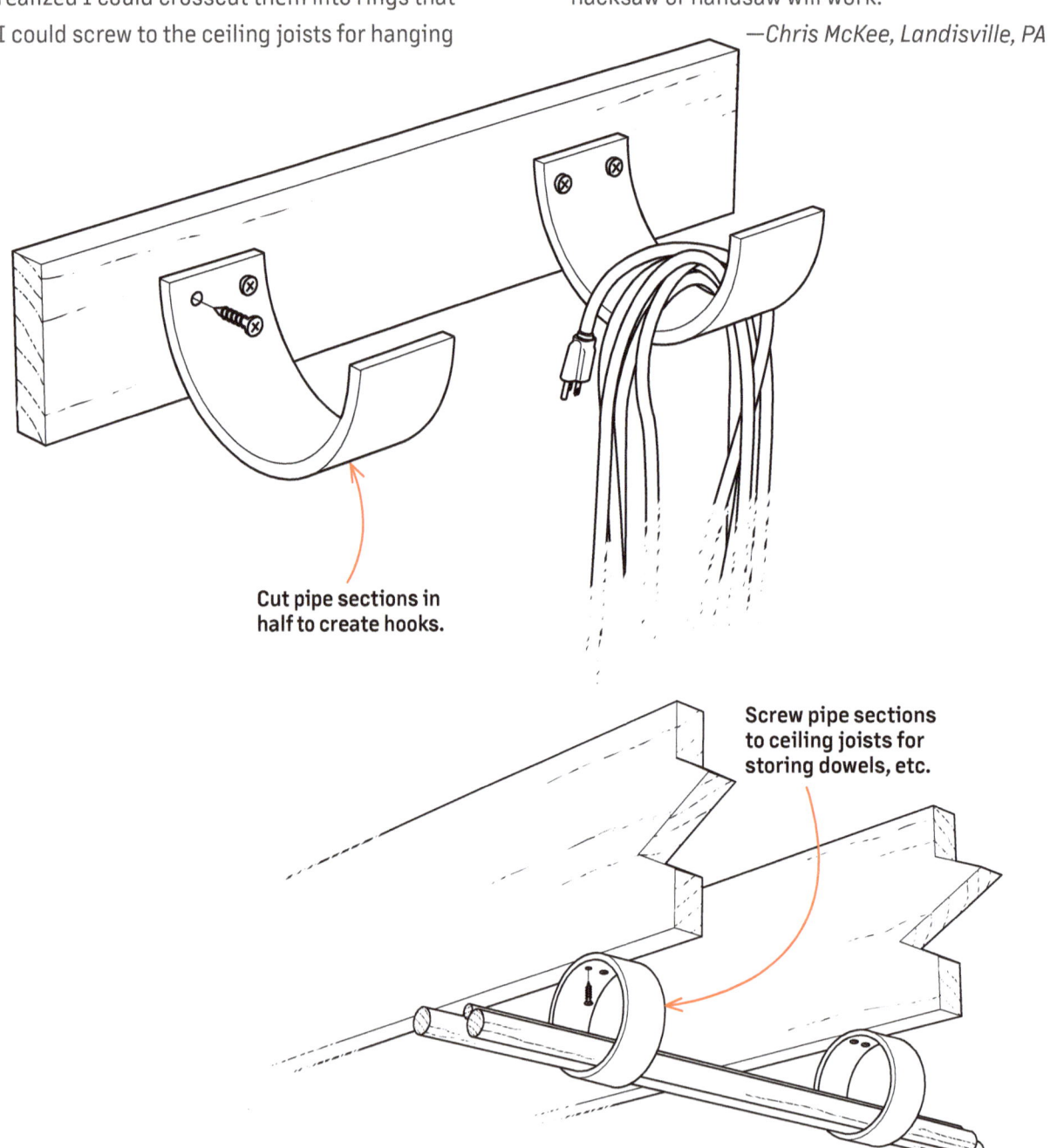

Cut pipe sections in half to create hooks.

Screw pipe sections to ceiling joists for storing dowels, etc.

Pegboard panel pullouts

When outfitting my new shop, I needed a way to store and organize my hand tools. The setup consists of simple 3/4"-thick frames covered on both faces with pegboard and mounted vertically in a cabinet on full-extension drawer slides screwed to cleats. You could fix the cleats directly to a cabinet top and bottom, but I decided to mount them to a case insert, which I then slipped into the cabinet opening after assembling the entire unit. This system works great for storing lots of tools in a compact area.

—Bob Kellenberger, Fairview, TX

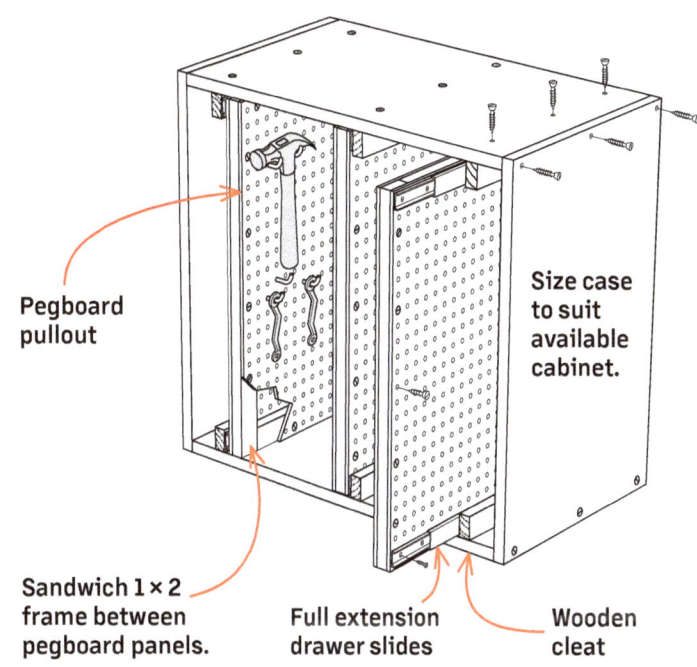

Tape rule hanger

I've managed to accumulate quite a few tape rules in my shop over the years, which tended to pile up on shelves or get lost in the general clutter of the shop. To solve the problem, I screwed a length of 1/8"-thick × 1"-wide flat steel bar to a couple of 2"-thick stand-off blocks fastened to the front of an open cabinet to serve as a hanger for the tapes. Now the tapes are all organized in one place, and I can immediately identify which one I need for the job at hand. As an added benefit, the bar provides a magnet-friendly surface from which to hang shop drawings and notes.

—Jeffry Lohr, Schwenksville, PA

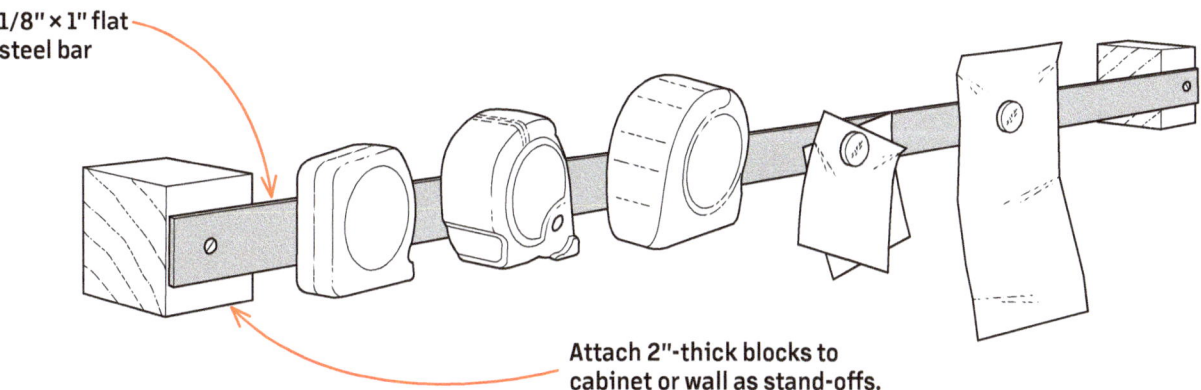

SHOP

Bench caster control bar

I outfitted my workbench with pedal-style casters that attach to the sides of the legs. When disengaged, these wheels allow the bench to sit solidly on the floor. For mobility, stepping on each pedal lifts the bench slightly to transfer the weight onto the casters. They work great for the job, but I find that individual operation of the pedals cocks and tilts the bench, sometimes sending items rolling off the top. Also, raising the pedals to retract the casters can be a bit cumbersome, as there isn't much toe space underneath, so I have to stoop down to lift each pedal.

Turns out the solution was simply to attach a length of 1"-diameter electrical conduit to connect the two pedals on each end of the bench. After cutting the pipe to length, drill 3/16"-diameter holes near each end, and slightly flatten the ends in a vise. Clamp the pipe to the caster pedals; drill the mating holes in the pedals. Finally, make the connections with 3/16" × 1-1/4" machine screws, lock washers, and nuts. Now it's a quick, easy foot-push on each bar to raise that end of the bench. And there's plenty of toe room to lift the bar for retracting the casters.

—*Tom Rosga, Hinckley, MN*

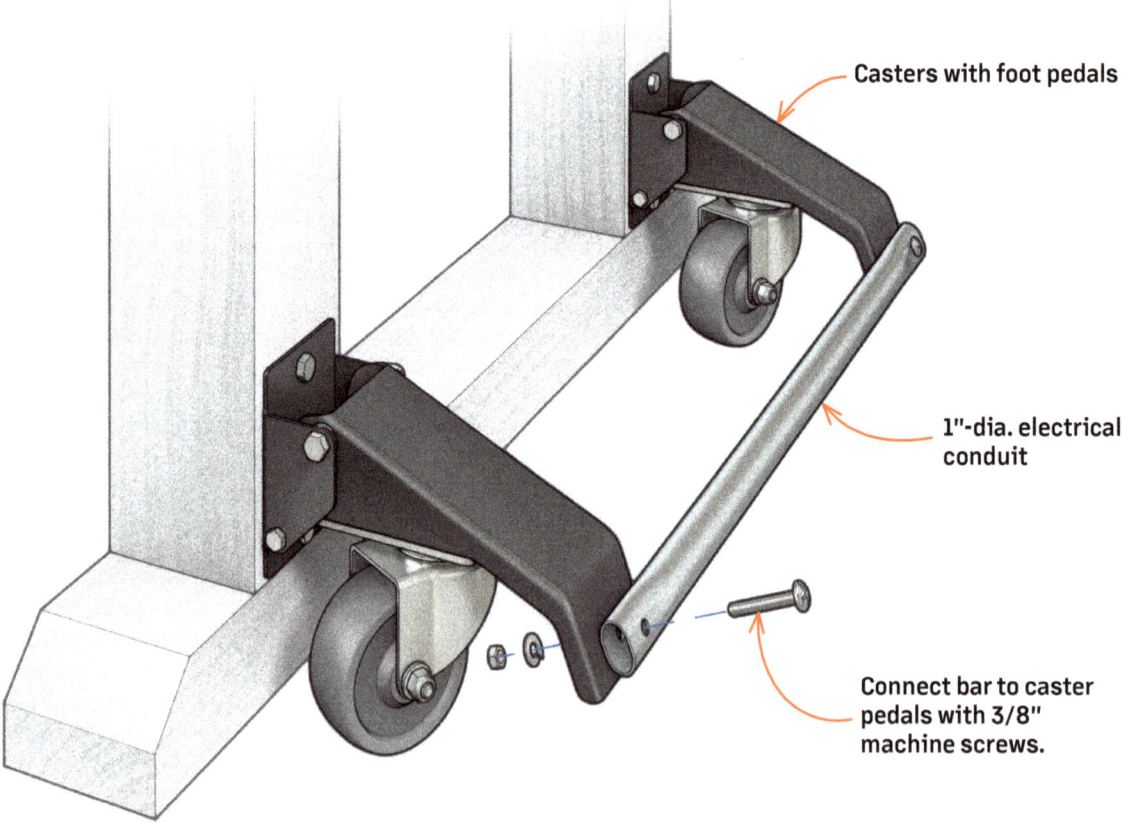

Casters with foot pedals

1"-dia. electrical conduit

Connect bar to caster pedals with 3/8" machine screws.

SHOP < WORKSHOP

Universal magnetic lamp mounting

I have a small lamp with a magnetic base that I use at my drill press, bandsaw, and other metal machines. With its adjustable gooseneck, it's a great task light for all sorts of chores. Unfortunately, I couldn't put it to use on my wooden bench because the base isn't heavy enough to prevent the lamp from toppling. I was getting ready to buy another work light when it occurred to me that all I needed was a portable metal base of some sort. I bought a cheap steel cover for an electric box and screwed it to a scrap of plywood. Now, I can use the light wherever I can clamp or hang that piece of plywood.

—Ken Burton, New Tripoli, PA

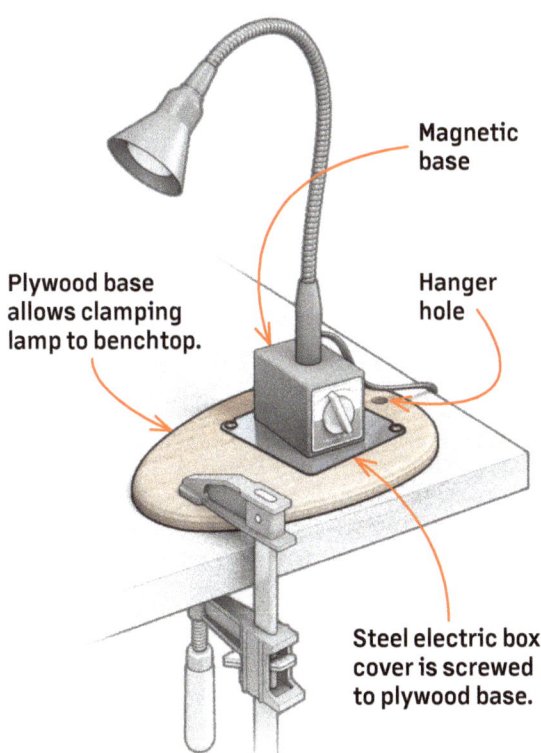

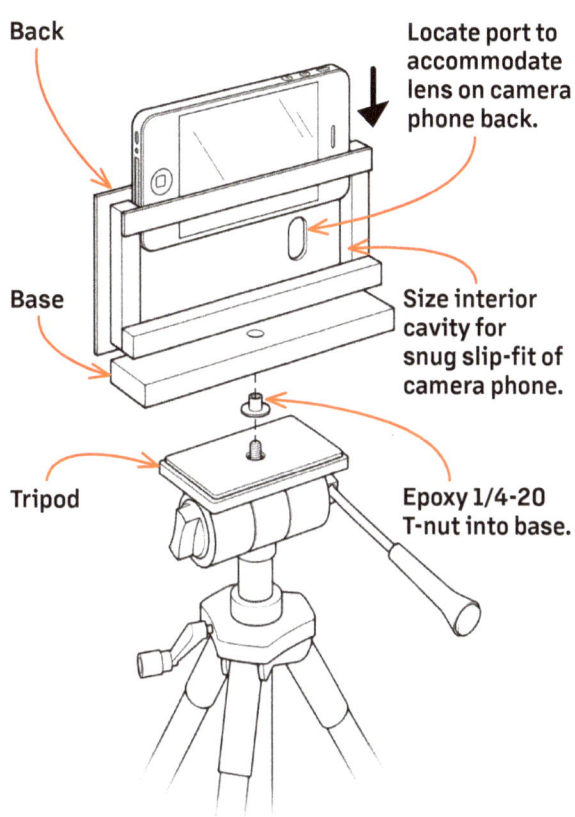

Camera phone tripod mount

A camera phone makes it easy to photograph your completed projects before they slip the shop and your memory. It also allows you to record videos of complicated jig setups and hard-to-remember procedures, making the job easier the next time. I find that using a tripod helps enormously, especially when including hands-at-work to help demonstrate a technique. To mount my phone, I cobbled together the unit shown. To make one yourself, size the pieces and locate the lens port to suit your particular model. Epoxy a 1/4-20 T-nut in the bottom piece to connect to a typical tripod head.

—Lee Wimbs, Greensboro, NC

WOODCRAFT MAGAZINE TIPS & TRICKS FOR WOODWORKING

Packing tape tips

Always have a roll of clear packing tape in the shop. It's inexpensive, but get the premium grade; it only costs a buck or so more and you won't be using that much of it. I've found clear packing tape to be one of the most useful "tools" in the shop, with almost unlimited functions. Here are just three.

It makes a quick drill stop: Use a 1/2" strip to mark the depth you need on a drill bit. If you fold it around the bit so a little flap sticks out on one side, it will also act as a fan and blow chips away from the hole. Conventional stops are a pain; you need so many of them and they take too much time.

Bundle parts for machining: If you have to drill, bandsaw, or even sand several identical parts, tape them together and go at it. Pencil marks show right through, and with experience you will learn where to tape and in what order to do the machining so all parts have some tape holding them until the end of the procedure.

Label tools: It's waterproof and quite durable, so I use it to cover my name tags on the tools I occasionally loan out.

—William McDowell, Syracuse, NY

Comfy jig handles

Jig handles are not unlike any other hand tool; the go-to shop companion must be comfortable and intuitive. Having experimented with dozens of different handle shapes and sizes, I found the perfect solution hanging on my wall: my favorite handsaw. I traced the handle onto a 1-1/4"-thick hardwood blank. (Use whatever scrap you have on hand, but I suggest starting with a blank that's a few inches longer and wider than you might need, so that you can adapt the handle for multiple jigs.)

After cutting the handle to rough shape, invest a little time shaping and sanding it, and you may find that the jig graduates from "one-time" use to "new best friend."

—Andy Rae, Ashville, NC

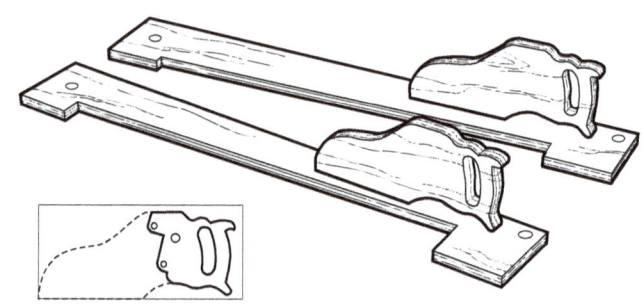

A tab for grabs

Anytime you need to temporarily apply masking tape, cellophane tape, or electrical tape, "tab" one end first by folding the last 1" or so of one end back on itself. This gives you something to quickly grab to remove the tape.

—Paul Anthony, Riegelsville, PA

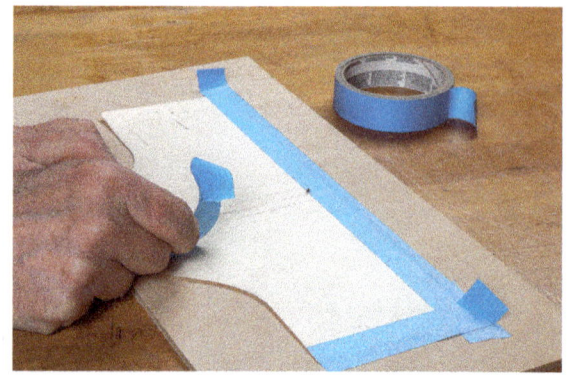

Pre-clean to prevent profanity

Sweep the floor around a bench before working on anything with small parts that might get lost in detritus if they roll off the bench.

—Paul Anthony, Riegelsville, PA

UL-approved lamp cord knot

If you make lamps (or simply repair them on occasion), it's worth knowing how to make an Underwriters Laboratories approved knot. All commercially sold lamps include a UL-approved knot at the end of the electrical cord within the lamp socket. It's designed as strain-relief to prevent a yanked cord from disconnecting from the socket, as the knot cannot be pulled through the socket nipple. As shown in the drawing, it's "knot" hard to tie, so why "knot" use it?

—William Stetson, Roanoke, VA

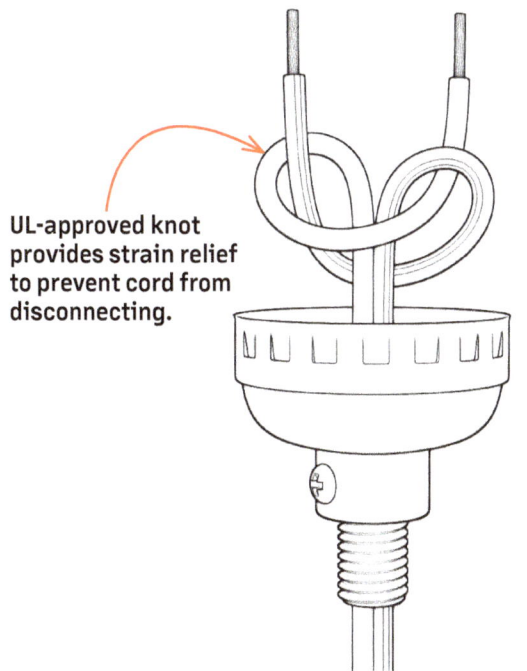

UL-approved knot provides strain relief to prevent cord from disconnecting.

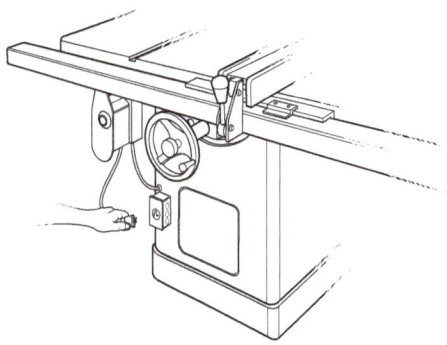

Safer short-tailed tools

I think that one of the biggest enemies of shop safety is inconvenience. For example, everybody knows that machinery should be unplugged before doing any work "under the hood," but when a plug's at the other end of the shop, you may opt to risk it every now and then in order to save time. If this sounds familiar, you need this tip.

To eliminate the temptation—and potential injury—of working while a tool is plugged in, I've wired my workshop so that the electrical receptacles are within an arm's reach of my major power tools and trimmed my machinery's power cords accordingly. With this setup, unplugging my table saw and keeping the exposed plug in sight during any setup operations is as convenient as reaching for a blade-changing wrench.

—Bill Sands, Lubeck, WV

Magnetic tell

Use a magnet to determine whether a screw or other hardware is brass-plated (magnetic), or solid brass, stainless steel, or aluminum (non-magnetic).

—Paul Anthony, Riegelsville, PA

WORKSHOP > SHOP

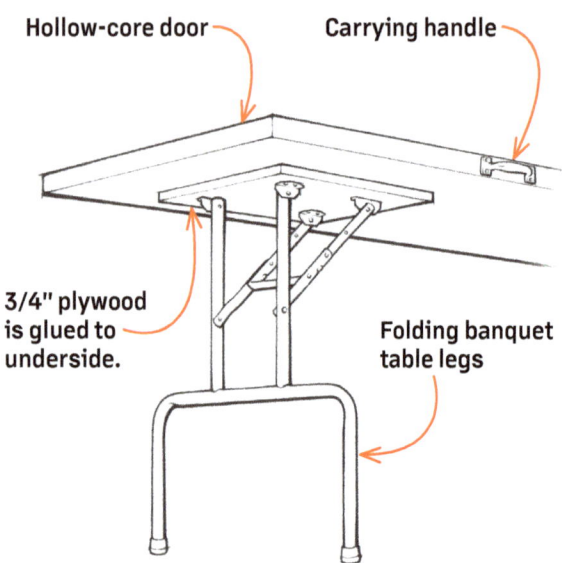

- Hollow-core door
- Carrying handle
- 3/4" plywood is glued to underside.
- Folding banquet table legs

Hollow-core assembly table

When it comes time to assemble or finish a project, I find that there's always a desperate shortage of clear work surface in my shop. To solve that problem, I used to lay a hollow-core door atop a pair of sawhorses, instantly creating a large table surface that's dependably flat.

But I recently upgraded this solution by permanently attaching a set of folding tubular banquet table legs to the door. To provide a solid target for the screws attaching the legs, I glued squares of 3/4" plywood to the underside of the door. Adding a handle at the midpoint of one edge of the door makes it easy to carry the table wherever I need it. When it's not in use, the table stores flat against the wall in my shop, taking up almost no floor space.

If you prefer a shorter table height, it's easy to hacksaw the legs and replace the plastic tips over the cut ends.

—*Frank Sagio, Niagara Falls, NY*

Woodshop card tricks

Tired of discarding those reader-response and subscription cards from your magazines? Save them and use them in your shop:

- Scratch pad—Make notes and calculations.
- Mixing palette—Mix up epoxy or shop-made wood filler from sawdust and glue.
- Card stock—The cards make good templates and patterns for small projects.
- Story stick—Quickly mark the edge for repeated measurements.
- Shims—Fourteen stacked cards measure approximately 1/8".
- Surface protection—Catch dripping glue from glue-ups.
- Glue spreader—Use to insert glue into thin spaces.
- Coaster—Absorb condensation from your cold drinks.

Keep a stack in your shop and you will probably come up with more uses.

—*Ben Pilcher, Georgetown, TX*

Let there be lotsa light

Dim shop lighting will strain your eyes, create shadows, and invite mistakes or injury. Overhead fixtures should cast broad ambient light for general machine work, while adjustable task-lighting fixtures are key to precise work at benches. Small magnetic lights easily attach to lathes, bandsaws, and mortisers.

—*Larissa Huff, Schwenksville, PA*

Rotating carver's easel

When I'm relief-carving panels, I prefer to work at an easel, which reduces the amount this old back has to bend. While working on an intricate design recently, I found myself constantly reorienting the panel to allow carving with the grain. To make the job easier, I screwed a rotating platform to the easel, attaching the carved panel to the platform by wedging it between cleats, as shown. Now, I can simply rotate the platform and workpiece as necessary to gain the best angle of attack.

I find that the single pivot screw creates enough friction between the unfinished easel top and platform to stabilize the platform. However, if I find it shifting under tool pressure, I'll drive an additional locking screw through its corner.

—*Philip Houck, Boston, MA*

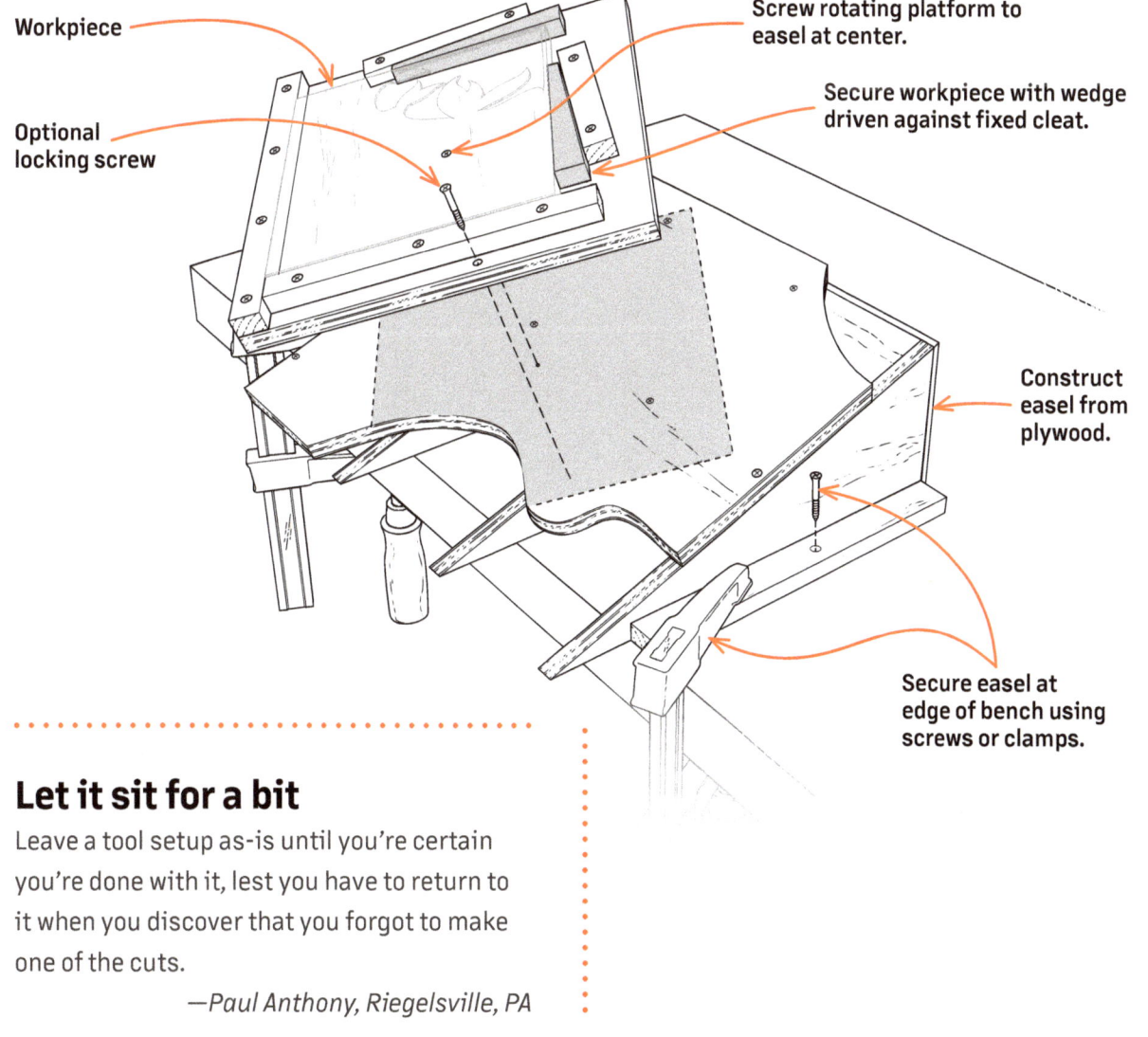

Workpiece

Optional locking screw

Screw rotating platform to easel at center.

Secure workpiece with wedge driven against fixed cleat.

Construct easel from plywood.

Secure easel at edge of bench using screws or clamps.

Let it sit for a bit

Leave a tool setup as-is until you're certain you're done with it, lest you have to return to it when you discover that you forgot to make one of the cuts.

—*Paul Anthony, Riegelsville, PA*

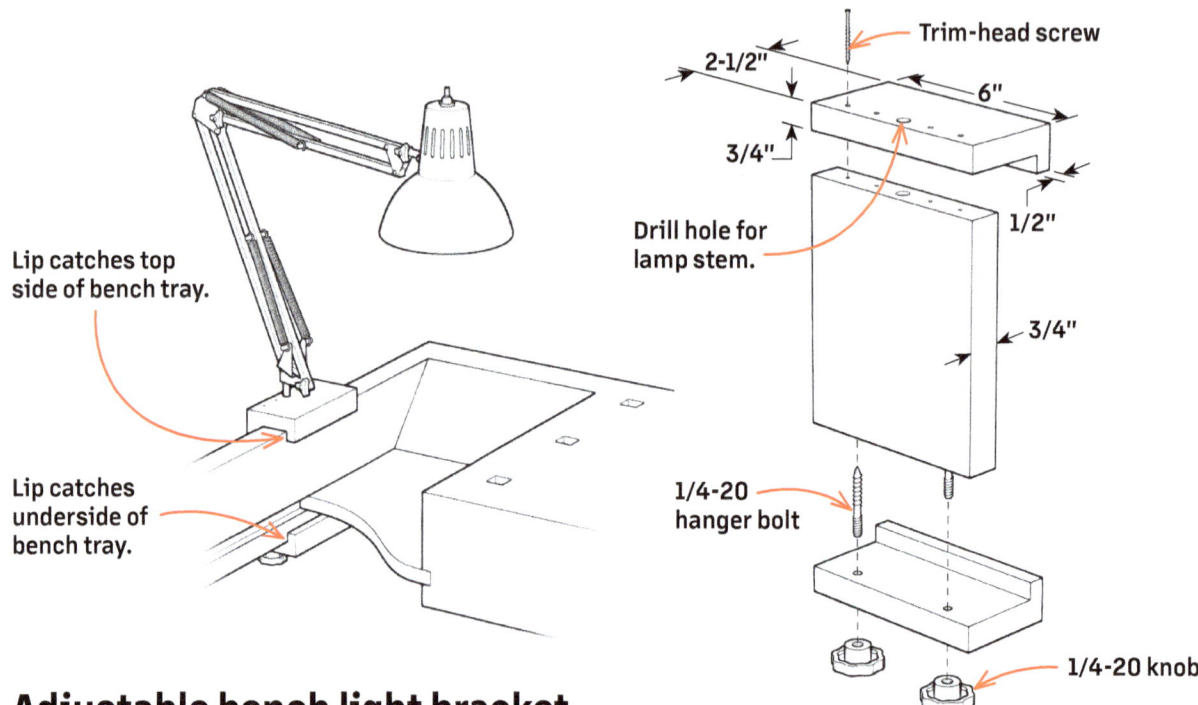

Adjustable bench light bracket

Locating light precisely where it's needed at the bench makes doing detail work much easier, whether it's laying out joints, cutting dovetails, or simply reading wood grain. This sliding bracket lets me position my articulating-arm lamp anywhere along the length of my workbench. The bracket was designed to grip the edge of a recessed tool tray, but it can be easily modified to suit other benches.

To size the bracket to fit your bench, make the vertical block a tad longer than the height of your bench's back rail to ensure an easy, sliding fit. When rabbeting the top and bottom blocks on the table saw, initially work with stock that's oversized in length for safety. Alternatively, create the lipped areas by gluing on separate strips of wood. Don't glue the bottom block, as you'll want to remove the bracket when necessary, such as when laying large panels on your benchtop.

—Andy Rae, Asheville, NC

Anti-fatigue mats

Locate anti-fatigue mats on the floor at your bench and commonly used machines. Your back and legs will thank you for it. As an added benefit, mats pay for themselves the next time you drop your favorite chisel or a freshly sanded workpiece.

—Larissa Huff, Schwenksville, PA

Nuke your tape

Masking tape dries out as it gets old. If you're stuck with a roll that shreds instead of unrolling (like it should), try giving it a 10-second zap in the microwave.

—Jarrod Gentry, Raleigh, NC

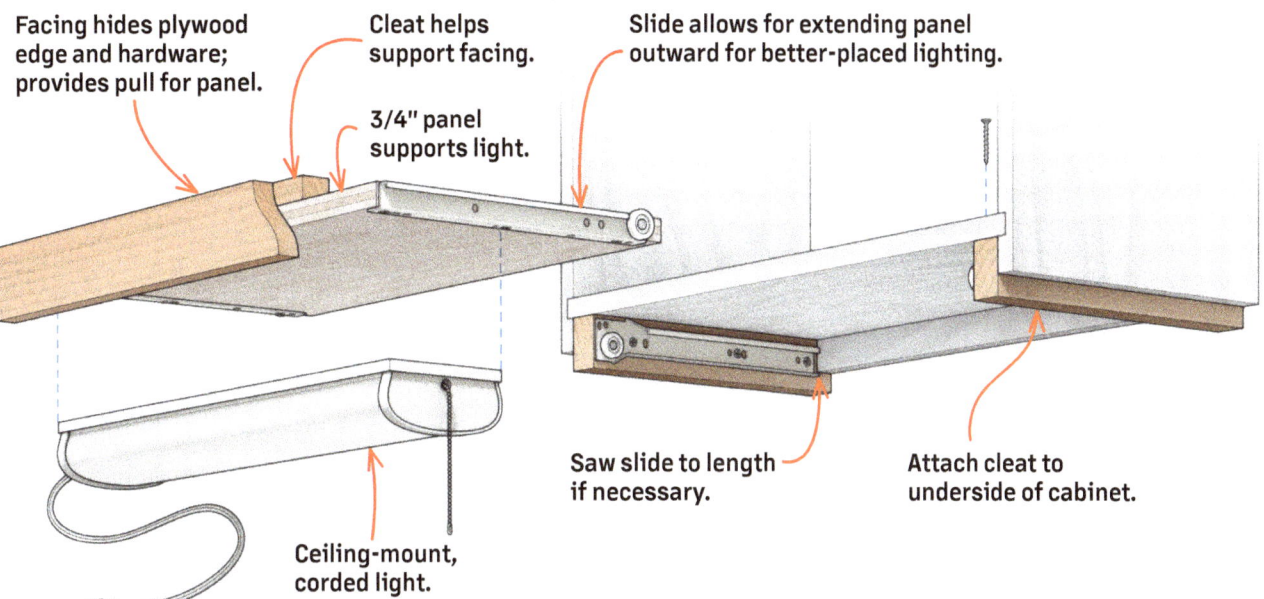

Facing hides plywood edge and hardware; provides pull for panel.

Cleat helps support facing.

Slide allows for extending panel outward for better-placed lighting.

3/4" panel supports light.

Saw slide to length if necessary.

Attach cleat to underside of cabinet.

Ceiling-mount, corded light.

Under-cabinet light extension

Wanting to install some task-lighting at my sharpening station, I tried attaching an LED ceiling-mount, corded light fixture to the underside of the cabinet above the area. Unfortunately, the fixture's close proximity to the wall simply back-lit the area. In order to better illuminate my work, I cobbled up a pull-out mounting surface using a pair of drawer slides and a few wood scraps.

For my purposes, I used 3/4-extension slides that are designed to wrap around under a drawer's sides. I began by cutting them to a length that matched my cabinet depth. Next, I made a pair of thick cleats, to which I attached the case halves of the slides before screwing the cleats to the cabinet bottom. After sawing a piece of 3/4" plywood to suit the drawer slide spacing, I attached the drawer half of each slide. As a finishing touch, I added a facing piece to trim things out and serve as a pull. After attaching the light and finding that everything worked well, I felt pretty bright.

—*Joe Hurst-Wajszczuk, Birmingham, AL*

No loose screws

Need to keep a machine screw or other hardware from loosening due to vibration in use? Brush on a bit of fingernail polish, which will keep it tight while still allowing disassembly if necessary.

—*Paul Anthony, Riegelsville, PA*

Buy extras

Whenever purchasing screws, bolts, and other hardware, buy at least a few more than you need in case of loss or manufacturing defects. Plus, it's always good to have a wide variety of fasteners in store.

—*Paul Anthony, Riegelsville, PA*

Planing edge-to-edge tapers

A recent commission involved making a 12"-wide by 5'-long ramped threshold for a doorway that spanned floors of different heights. One edge needed to be 1-3/8" thick, and the opposite edge 3/4" thick. I realized that the easiest, most accurate way to make the taper would be to plane the board at an angle, raising one edge the appropriate amount with a full-length support strip.

I first milled the stock slightly oversized in width, and just a bit over 1-3/8" thick. I then marked my intended angle on one end of the board and placed it on my bench. I shimmed under the intended thinner edge to bring the marked line parallel to the benchtop and then measured from the underside of the raised edge to the benchtop. After ripping a 5"-long support strip to that measurement, I beveled one edge of it to complement the tilt of the board. All that was left was to attach the support strip with double-faced tape and plane the board down to my line. My client was so delighted with the accuracy of the finished work that he presented me with a fifth of scotch as a bonus.

—Paul Anthony, Riegelsville, PA

Clamps put to other uses

I find that quick-grip clamps have lots of other uses besides holding workpieces together. The strong, deep jaws and long bar on such a clamp makes it a great levered wrench of a sort for loosening everything from jar lids to blanks stuck on the lathe. These clamps are just as useful in the same fashion around the home and garage for wrenching plumbing fittings, oil filters, and many other stubborn parts of different sizes and shapes. To top it all off, I recently discovered that clamping one to an exposed wall stud makes a great paper towel holder!

—Richard Entwhistle, Highland Lakes, NJ

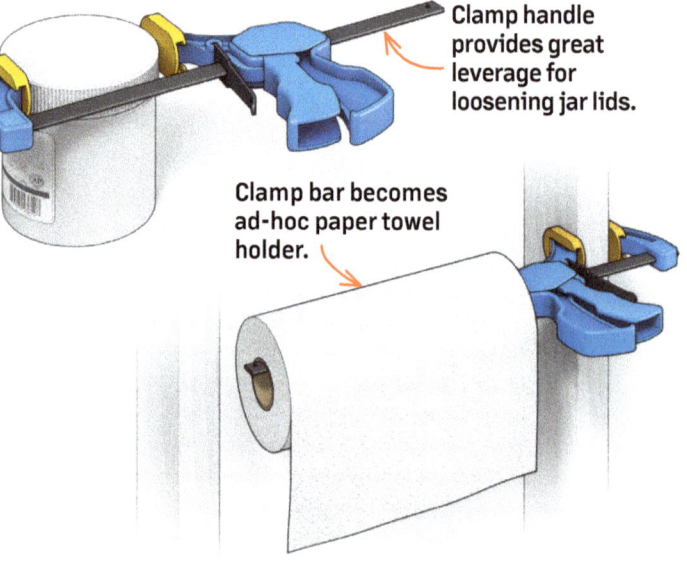

Long live the push broom

Years ago, when sweeping up the shop, it seemed I was always catching my push broom on machine and cabinet bases until the handle eventually broke off in the head. After buying my third replacement handle, I decided to reinforce it with a simple plywood gusset as shown. Twenty years later, I'm still using the same broom and handle, proving the trick a winner.

—Rick Worthington, Spokane, WA

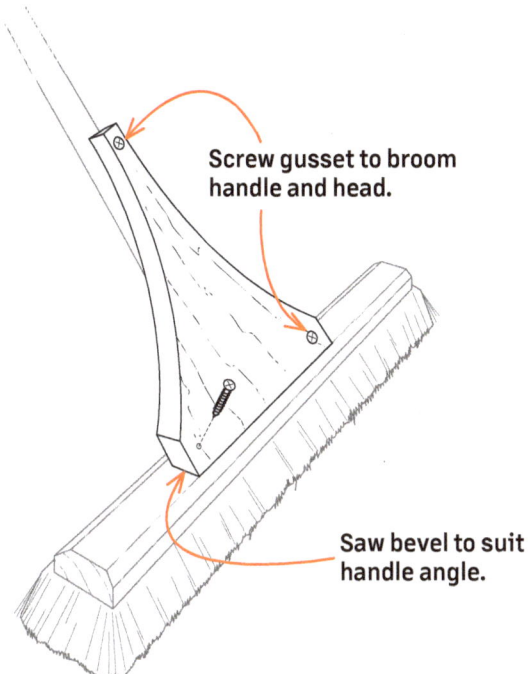

Shop jar opener

Like many woodworkers, I store finishes in appropriately sized jars to prevent them from skinning over in a partially empty can. The problem is that no matter how well I wipe the rim of the jar before closing it, the lid often sticks stubbornly shut afterward. To solve the problem, I designed this jar opener that mounts to the underside of a cabinet, allowing me to twist the jar with both hands while the jig holds the lid firmly in place. It works so well that I made a second one for the kitchen too.

To make the jig, use 2×6 lumber sized to fit under a standard-depth wall cabinet. Shorten a hacksaw blade to fit by scoring it with an abrasive wheel and snapping off the excess. Drill holes in the blade to mount it to the wood strip with #10 pan-head screws, cantilevering the blade 1/8" off the edge.

—Bill Wells, Olympia, WA

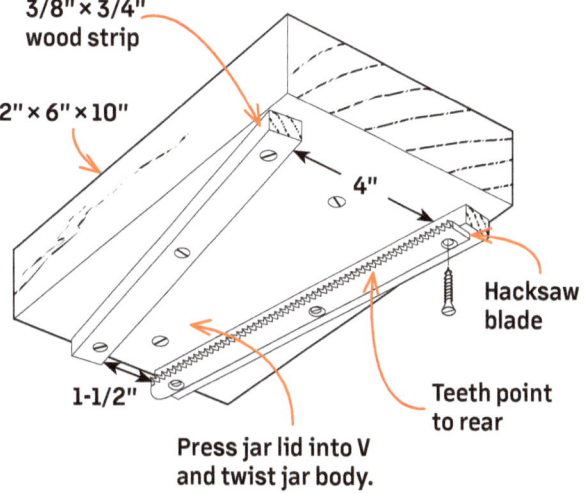

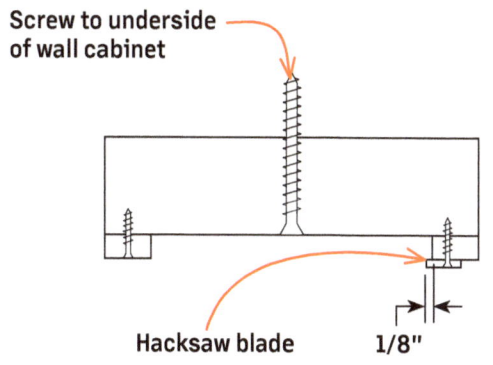

Walker workstation

I had been pondering making a portable, lightweight workstation when my neighbor asked if I had any use for an unneeded walker. I laughed and told him no—not yet, anyway. But then I realized that it would make a great base for my purposes. I easily knifed off the molded plastic handles, and used inexpensive conduit fasteners to attach wood panels to the upper and lower bars. In less than an hour, I had created a small, stable, lightweight workstation that—with the push of a button on each leg—easily adjusts in height from 32" to 40" in 1" increments. It's a great help in the shop or when working on home projects, providing a work surface with staging below for tools and supplies. Walkers are often available at thrift stores.

—Jim Kelly, Trappe, PA

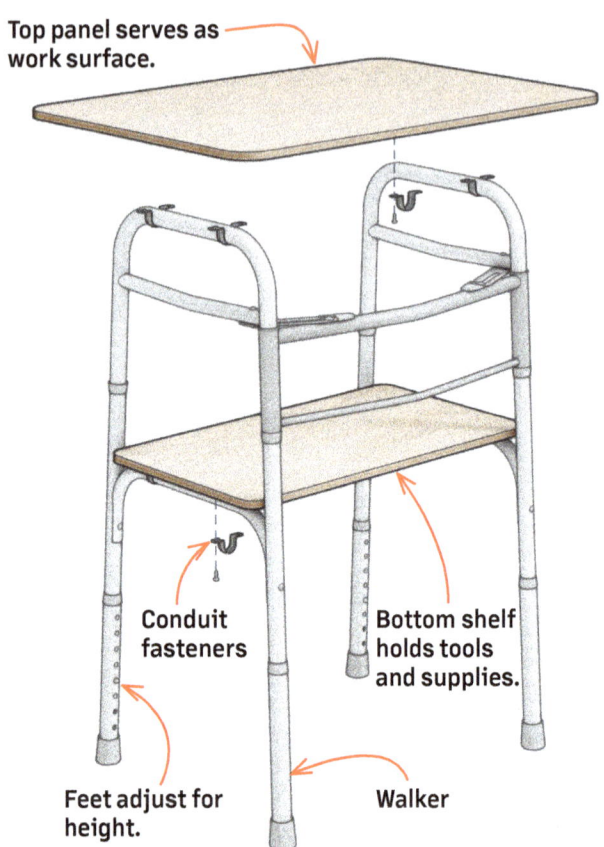

Woodworker's welcome mat

After cleaning up countless shavings and sawdust trails leading from my workshop into my home, I made a heavy-duty boot brush from a few scraps of 3/4" plywood and three 2" × 7" deck scrub brushes. Assemble the base using screws and glue. To fasten the brushes to the base, drive 1-1/4" screws through the bristle-ends of the brushes. To give workshop debris the boot, stand on an end and kick your free foot over the bristles. To make a garden-grade version, use leftover deck boards, waterproof glue, and plastic brushes.

—Kevin Woelfel, Moscow, ID

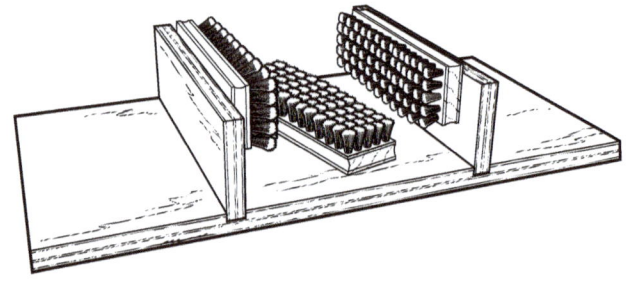

Hear ye, see ye!

Invest in hearing and eye protection that's comfortable, so you're more inclined to wear it. In addition to a good fit, make sure the gear is rated for a woodshop environment. Don't stint on protecting the only eyes and ears you have.

—Larissa Huff, Schwenksville, PA

Wall-mounted lamp arm

At my shop workstations, I like to use swing-arm lamps for adjustable task lighting. For convenience, I mount the lamp on a wooden arm that swings out from a nearby wall. Sometimes, a single arm does the trick, but when I need more reach and flexibility, I create an articulated arm by adding extensions as shown.

Make the primary arm from 1-1/4"-thick hardwood about 5" wide, tapering out to 1-1/2" at the end. Mine is 26" long, but suit yourself. Drill a 3/8"-diameter hole through the wide end on the drill press, using a long bit. Bore as deep as your drill press allows, and then raise the table to complete the hole. Rout or sand a bullnose onto the wide end. You can drill a hole on the narrow end to carry a lamp, or add an extension or two. Make an extension 1-1/4" thick × 1-1/2" wide and attach it to its mating arm with a 3/8" carriage bolt, a washer, a lock washer, and a nylon nut or a pair of nuts jammed against each other. Tighten the hardware enough to provide both friction and adjustability. Mount two metal L-brackets to the primary arm, using a length of 3/8" threaded rod secured at each end with a pair of jam nuts, and then screw the brackets to a wall stud.

—Mike Kehs, Quakertown, PA

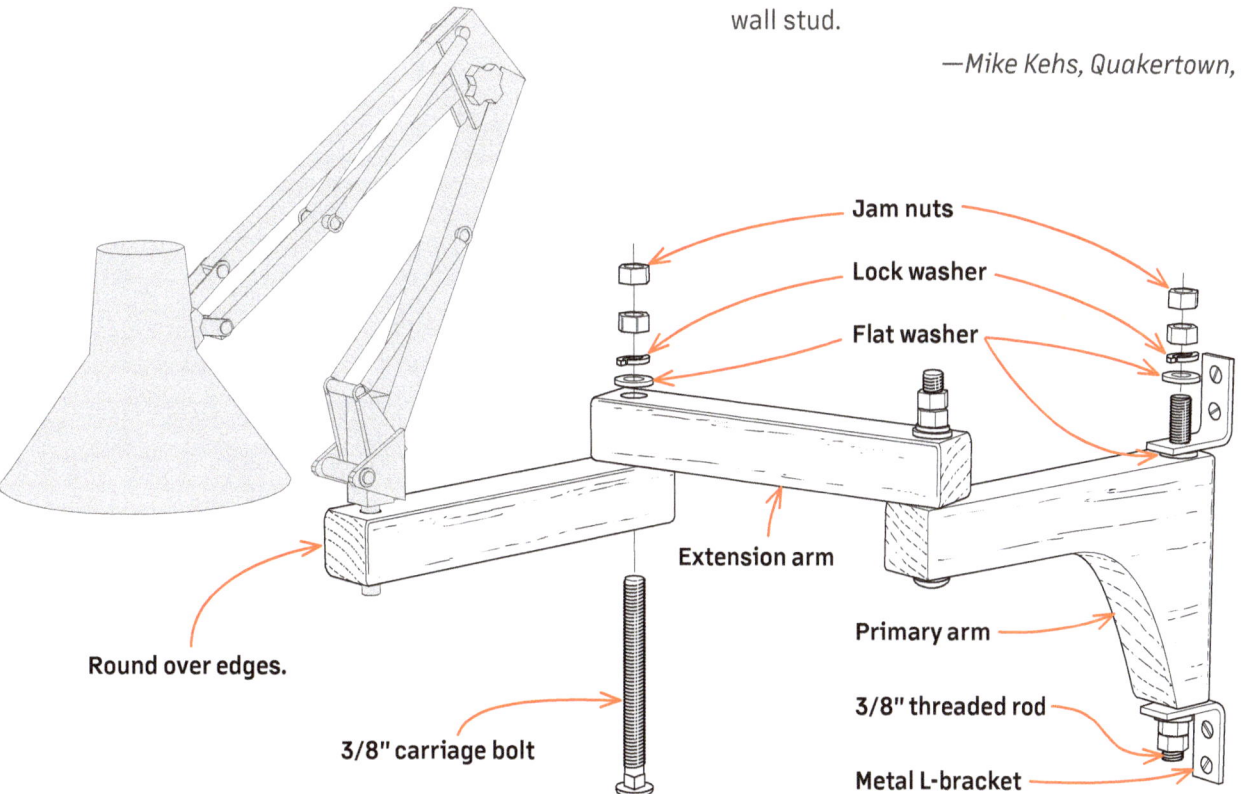

A helper post

When working wood, task lighting is indispensable for really seeing what you're doing, especially with older eyes. Strong, well-positioned light is critical for peering into a router base opening, seeing cutlines, and taking accurate measurements, among other things. I also find that a strong light raking across a work surface in a dimmed shop makes defects really pop out for effective smoothing. To allow perfect positioning of a lamp, I use a simple free-standing post to which I can fix a clamp light at any height. It's just a 2×2 with a base made of scrap plywood panels. I also outfitted it with cup hooks and plywood brackets to support cords and dust collection hoses.

—Paul Anthony, Riegelsville, PA

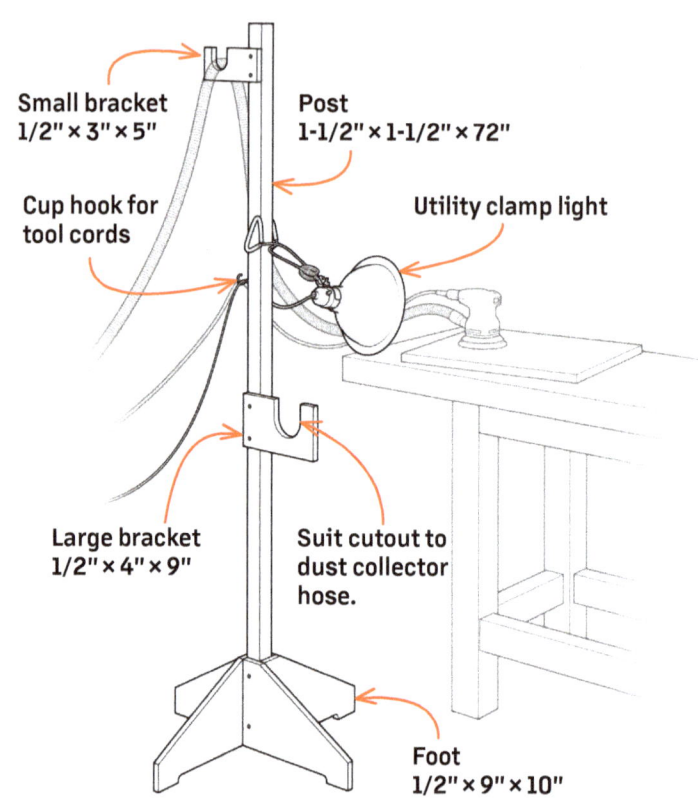

Small bracket 1/2" × 3" × 5"
Post 1-1/2" × 1-1/2" × 72"
Cup hook for tool cords
Utility clamp light
Large bracket 1/2" × 4" × 9"
Suit cutout to dust collector hose.
Foot 1/2" × 9" × 10"

Taking off the gloves without a fight

When hand-applying finishes, I often wear disposable gloves. Unfortunately, removing them usually resulted in tearing or inverting them, making their reuse impractical. One day it dawned on me that compressed air might help me get more life from lightly used pairs. I slipped the air nozzle in at the wrist and pulled the trigger. Sure enough, I was then able to easily slip my hand out of the inflated glove without damaging it or turning it inside out.

—Dennis Beadles, Mount Juliet, TN

Inflate glove with compressed air to remove it without tearing or inverting it.

Mini-carts make moving easy

OK, so they aren't really anti-gravity, but these mini-carts come close. Made from scrap plywood and inexpensive twin-wheeled casters, these handy movers can be used individually for scooting heavy sheets of plywood or MDF, or as a set for moving machinery or cabinets. Larger objects can be placed on top, or set into the mitered notches in the top rail to ensure that the cart doesn't unexpectedly kick out in use. They're also good for schlepping furniture around the house.

Making a set of four is an easy afternoon production run. Start by cutting the 11-1/4" × 11-1/4" × 15-1/2" triangular bases from any scrap-pile piece of 3/4"-thick plywood. Next, attach the 1"-wide top rails with glue and 1-1/4" finish nails. To make the notches, attach one rail, insert a 1"-thick spacer, then tack on the second rail. (Trim the matching rail to match the base after assembly.) Ease the pointed corners with a sander, then attach the wheels with 3/4"-long screws.

—Don Hamrick, Parkersburg, WV

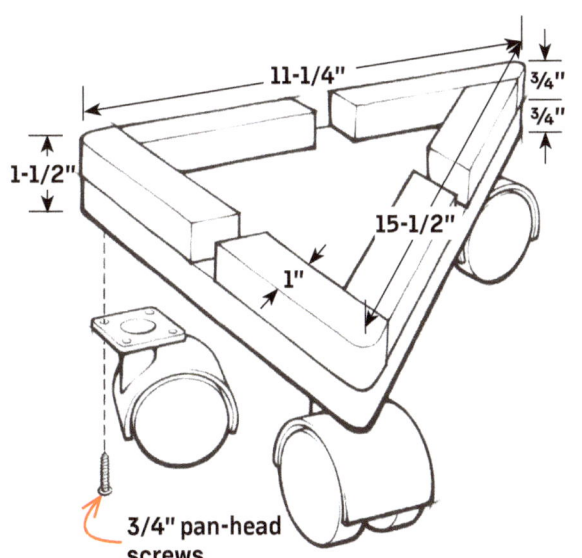

Flattening a plane sole

Flattening a plane sole typically involves rubbing it on an abrasive that's sitting atop a dead-flat surface, like a cast-iron table saw wing or slab of reference granite. For abrasive, I've used wet/dry sandpaper, but it seems to lose its aggressiveness pretty quickly. Alternatively, I've used silicon carbide powder, but that can undesirably abrade my reference surface. I finally realized that combining the two is a better approach. I start off with sandpaper attached with spray adhesive. Then, as the paper dulls, I sprinkle it with silicone carbide powder, adding more as necessary to get the job done. That way, I make the most of the paper and powder while protecting my reference surface.

—Paul Walco, Toledo, OH

Tape rule shims

Like any dusty packrat, I hang on to all manner of scraps, including sections of self-adhesive measuring tape left over from jig-building. I find that this stuff makes great shim material because it's thin, durable, and self-sticking. It's easily cut into appropriately sized lengths for shimming fences and jig parts. It can also be cut into very small pieces if necessary. For example, I have affixed tiny pieces of it along the underside edges of recessed machine table inserts to bring them flush to the table top. Whenever I need to shim something just a bit, it's one of the first things that comes to mind.

—Barton Grimsley, Houston, TX

Elevate books and magazines for easy viewing

If you use books or magazines for reference when building a project in the shop, you know how quickly they can become victim to coffee spills, glue, sawdust, and more. That's because they are typically lying down on the workbench. You can protect them and have them stand tall while taking up less counterspace with this custom holder. The angled back and support rely on a sliding dovetail system for easy adjustment front to back on the base in order to accommodate reference materials of various thicknesses up to 3". When you move the back forward, the publication becomes sandwiched between it and an 11" × 14" shielding piece of 1/8"-thick clear acrylic, keeping it in mint condition.

—Rod Eberly, Livermore, CO

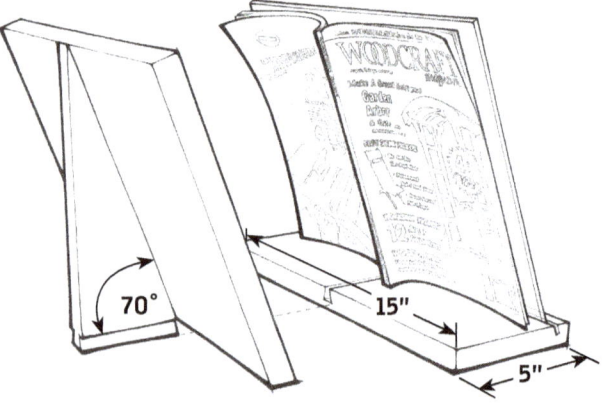

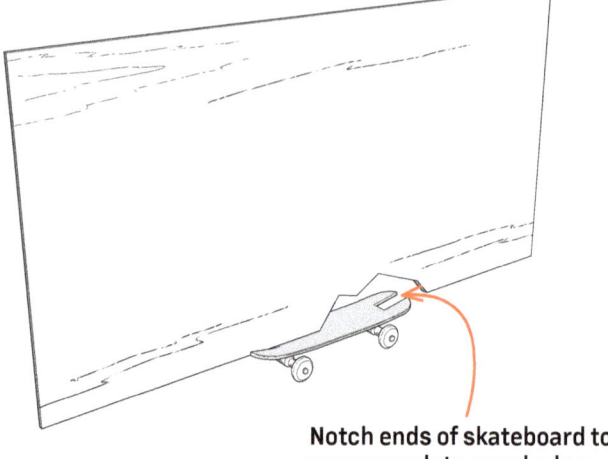

Notch ends of skateboard to accommodate panel edge.

Sheet goods dolly

The older I get, the harder it is to manage full sheets of plywood and MDF. To take some of the pain out of handling sheet materials, I turned a cheap yard-sale skateboard into a valuable shop assistant. As shown in the drawing, I notched both ends of the deck so that the edge of the panel could lay flat on the board.

I can now easily maneuver a 4×8' panel around my shop. When the panel is centered on the board, I find that I can even rock the skateboard enough to skip over electrical cords. If you need to traverse gravel, grass, or other rough terrain, look for an all-terrain board with oversized wheels.

—Leslie Bradshaw, Hartsville, SC

Tennis ball bumpers

For years, I've used heavy-duty shop shelving systems. These systems, with their wall-mounted standards and heavy metal arm supports, serve as great lumber racks. However, I've found that the arms can be pretty sharp. To prevent accidental injury, I outfitted each with a brightly colored tennis ball by slitting and slipping it onto the projecting end of the arm.

—James Kajpust, Freeland, MI

Dog hole cleaner

I was having trouble sliding my 3/4"-diameter metal bench dogs in some of my workbench dog holes. Upon closer examination, I found that a couple of the problematic holes were a hair undersized, and a few were contaminated with glue or paint drips. I tried cleaning up the holes with an undersized dowel wrapped in sandpaper, but with little effect. It seemed to me that I needed a reamer of some sort. An online investigation uncovered a 3/4"-diameter spiral flute "chucking reamer." With its 7"-long shaft and 3"-long HSS cutter, it did a great job of reaching into deep dog holes and quickly shaving their sides to precise diameter.

The only problem was the bit's 5/8"-diameter shank, which wouldn't fit in a standard drill chuck. My solution was to make a 3/4" × 1-3/4" × 4" wooden handle with a 5/8"-diameter hole for the shank. To lock the handle in place, I tapped it to accept a 1/4-20 × 1" machine screw. To use the tool, insert it from the underside of a dog hole, attach the handle, then pull upward while slowly twisting clockwise to slice through the choke points.

—Joe Hurst-Wajszczuk, Birmingham, AL

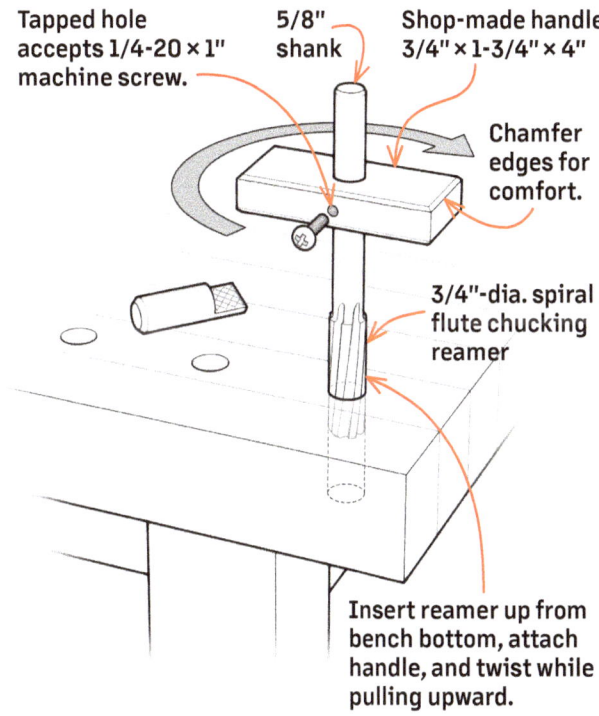

Roller shade dust screens

For years, every time I machined wood in my shop—sawing, planing, sanding—my open-base cabinets and wall-hung shelving units became dust depositories. Emptying the contents of these to clean them out was a chore I never looked forward to, and yet, if I didn't do it, smaller items would get buried in layers of dust, making them impossible to find. I didn't want to make doors of varying sizes to enclose the units; I needed something quick and simple.

While pulling down a common window roller shade in one of our home's bathrooms, it occurred to me: Why not use roller shades to cover the cabinet openings in my shop? They're affordable; better still, you can have the shades cut to whatever length you need. Since the shades are designed to cover sizable windows, length should not be an issue. Simply secure the shade using the accompanying hardware to your cabinet's face frame above the opening.

—Jim Harrold, Norwalk, IA

WORKSHOP > SHOP

Tools at hand

Use rare-earth magnets on machines to keep wrenches, small squares, and other machine-adjustment tools close at hand.

—Paul Anthony, Riegelsville, PA

Shop-made dowel sizer

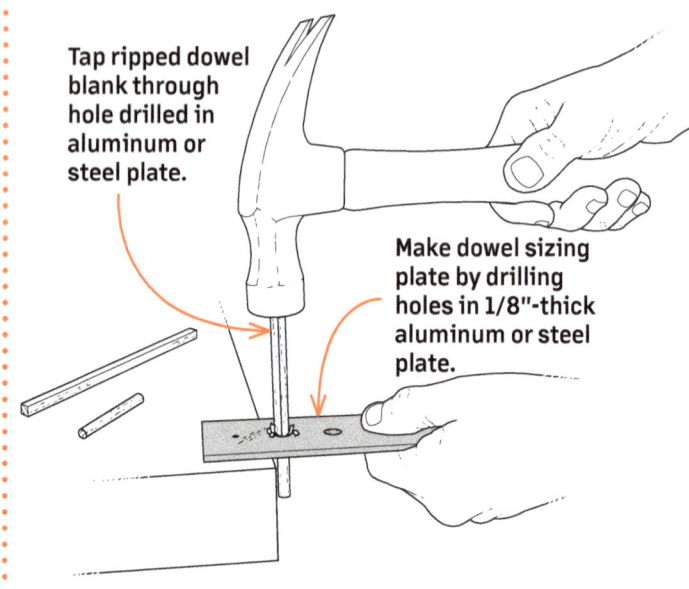

Tap ripped dowel blank through hole drilled in aluminum or steel plate.

Make dowel sizing plate by drilling holes in 1/8"-thick aluminum or steel plate.

Occasionally, I use dowels as pins to join parts or as plugs for inlaid accents. Although dowels are available commercially, they have often swelled too much to fit properly into a hole of the correct size. The other problem is that they're not available in a wide variety of woods.

To solve both issues, I made a dowel sizer by drilling common dowel size holes in a scrap piece of aluminum plate. (Steel works, as well.) To use it, I place the appropriate-size hole over a bench dog hole (or adjacent to the edge of the bench), chamfer one end of the dowel, and then drive it through the appropriate hole. To make a dowel from scratch, I rip a piece of straight-grained wood roughly oversized, chamfer the end, and drive it through the hole.

—Geoff Noden, Trenton, NJ

Buy short boards for big savings

You already know that woodworking is an exercise in turning long boards into short ones, but you may not realize that you can save money by letting someone else do that work for you. The next time you're at your mill or lumberyard, ask about the availability of "shorts." While lengths may vary, the term refers to boards shorter than 8'. (In my last purchase, the short boards were mostly 6-footers and a handful of 5-footers.) While the quality of the wood was the same as 8'-long FAS (first and seconds), the shorts cost 30% less per board foot.

—Robert J. Settich, Gladstone, MO

Bike gloves stop the vibes

My mountain bike hasn't seen many single tracks lately, but my bike gloves still get a workout. I don't recommend wearing any gloves when using jointers, drill presses, table saws, or other large machinery, but they are perfect when doing benchwork, such as sanding and planing. The exposed fingertips help me keep in touch with surfaces, but the gelled palms insulate my hands from vibrations that can cause blisters, or, over time, pain and numbness.

—Chris McKim, Greeley, CO

Easy-split double-faced tape

Double-faced tape can be a woodworker's best friend when it comes to temporarily attaching templates and holding parts together. Unfortunately, it can be maddening trying to remove the backing. Turns out there's a simple solution: Instead of cutting the tape to length, tear it, which roughly separates the tape and backer, providing easy-to-grab layers.

—Serge Duclos, Delson, Québec

Slippery surfaces

Wipe cast-iron machine surfaces with paste wax to make your workpieces glide with ease. Waxing plane soles and router bases will also reduce drag and ease wear and tear on your body.

—Rob Spiece, Berea, KY

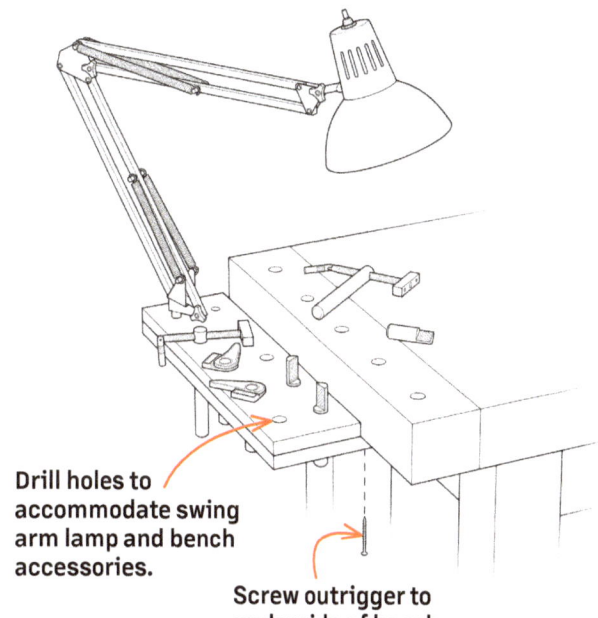

Drill holes to accommodate swing arm lamp and bench accessories.

Screw outrigger to underside of bench.

Workbench outrigger

In order to mount a swing arm lamp at my bench without drilling holes in my benchtop, I decided to attach an outrigger made up of two pieces of 3/4" scrap plywood glued together. Extending the lower piece by a couple of inches allows for screwing the unit to the underside of my bench, while the 5" × 18" cantilevered section offers various light-mounting locations. As a bonus, I quickly realized that the outrigger can also house my various bench dogs, bench clamps, and hold-downs in suitably sized holes. Because the outrigger sits below the bench surface, the accessories are within easy reach without interfering with work underway on the benchtop. They also don't end up buried in shavings and sawdust, as do items in the bench's tool till. Of course, the design is ripe for modifications such as adding a rare-earth magnet, or slots for chisels and squares.

—Joe Hurst-Wajszczuk, Birmingham, AL

Text and art © 2022

All rights reserved. Excepting patterns, no part of this book may be reproduced or transmitted in any form or by any means, electric or mechanical, including photocopying, recording, or by any information storage and retrieval system, without written permission from the Publisher. Readers may make copies of patterns for personal use. The patterns themselves, however, are not to be duplicated for resale or distribution under any circumstances. Any such copying is a violation of copyright law. Text and art previously published in *Woodcraft Magazine*.

Publisher: Paul McGahren
Editor: Kerri Grzybicki
Design & Layout: Robert Schehl

Cedar Lane Press
PO Box 5424
Lancaster, PA 17606-5424

Paperback ISBN: 978-1-950934-61-4
ePub ISBN: 978-1-950934-62-1

Library of Congress Control Number: 2022945139

Printed in the United States of America
10 9 8 7 6 5 4 3 2 1

Note: The following list contains names used in *Tips & Tricks for Woodworking* that may be registered with the United States Copyright Office:
Biesemeyer; Bondo; Jumbo Jaws; Magswitch (MagJig); Masonite; McMaster-Carr (Tap-Flex); Space Balls; Styrofoam; Super Glue; Teflon; Underwriters Laboratories; WD-40, Woodcraft.

The information in this book is given in good faith; however, no warranty is given, nor are results guaranteed. Woodworking is inherently dangerous. Your safety is your responsibility. Neither Cedar Lane Press, Woodcraft, nor the contributors assume any responsibility for any injuries or accidents.

To learn more about Cedar Lane Press books, or to find a retailer near you,
email info@cedarlanepress.com or visit us at www.cedarlanepress.com.

INDEX

A
adhesive-backed sandpaper 67
alcohol swab uses 16
angle calculator 48
anti-fatigue mats 234
assembly 6–13
assembly braces, self-positioning 193
assembly table, hollow-core door 232

B
bandsaw 82–89
    blade buyer's guide 87
    dressing blocks 84
    dust collection 87
    fence, tail-cutting 44
    homemade blocks 83
    lignum vitae blocks 86
    outfeed support 82
    quick-set fence 89
    repurposing a narrow blade 134
    resawing, magnet-assisted 89
    sawing small pieces 85
    secure clamping 87
    segmented rings 83
    setting thrust guides 86
    small strip ripping 85
    tighter turns 84
    wedge cutting jig 88
bar clamp compass 47
bar clamp hold-down 183
belt sander
    chamfering 70
    gap filler 65
bench dogs
    blade-friendly 186
    bumpers 188
    hole cleaner 243
    modification 191
    vise-assist 188
    wedge 203
bench hook
    miter-biscuiting 43
    versatile 195
bench slave 192
bench stops
    dual-purpose 204
benchtop stop 202
bike gloves 245
biscuits
    bench hook for miter 43
    fresh 41
    glue spreader 46
    guide 39
    offset 37
    stale 44

blackboard eraser sanding block 68
block plane, turning with 120
book display 242
book-matched legs 26
boot brush 238
bottle cap keeper 31
brads, holding 8, 10, 11
brass ball catch, locating 13
brass ball catch upgrade 10
brass screws, installing 9
breadboard joint epiphany 41
broom, push 237
brush, adjusting bristle stiffness 22

C
calipers
    gauge block 117
    non-catch 117
card scraper, keeping cool 65
carver's easel, rotating 233
carving vise 200
caster control bar 228
casters 241
cast-iron tool jig magnets 104
cast-iron webbing filler 199
cauls
    corner clamping 182
    miter clamping 184
    taping 184
center finder
    as saddle square 54
    dowel as a 56
    improvised 59
    large scale 120
chalk for layout 48, 60
cheap chisel 209
chipbreaker grinding guide 79
chip collection for drill press 106
chisel guard, nonslip 225
chop saw
    zero-clearance overlay 129
circular saw
    clamp-free guide 133
    clamp-on saw guide 190
    track setup for multiples 130
clamping 182–205
    aluminum square 198
    cantilevered 200
    cocking for square assemblies 187
    corner aid 186
    foam 194
    inner tube 194
    mitered frames 6
    pads, see-through 185
    string-and-sticks 203

clamps, other uses for 236
cleanup 206–209
    brush, small 208
    denatured alcohol 209
    glue detailing 207
combustion prevention 23
compass, bar clamp as a 47
compass, yardstick as a 58
continuous hinge piloting 109
cord management, hook-and-loop for 215
countertops, perfect alcove-fit 50
cup holder, no-tip 30
cyanoacrylate 33
cyclone dust collector, muffler for 213

D
deburring tool 67
dehumidifier distilled water 24
depth gauge block 59
distilled water 24
dogwood 118
door assembly 12
double-faced tape, easy-split 245
dovetails
    perfect formula for 38
    platform 40
dowel
    boring 91
    extracting blind 42
    grooving 45
    grooving collar 45
    sizer 244
    slimming down 93
    tenoning jig 140
drawer-planing perch 28
drawer stop
    adjustable 27
    hinge 26
    outward 28
    screw 27
drill
    90° hole jig 101
    bits, color-coded 96
    flat-bottom bit guide 100
    Forstner bit for perfect circles 94
    keeping level 100, 104
    magnetic tip holder 94
    spare bits 91
    stem caster holes 103
    tightening keyless chucks 102
    V-jig centers dowel hole 98
    wooden plug removal 91
drill and drill press 90–112
drill bits
    precision with large-diameter 109

INDEX

drilling out broken screws 106
drilling the ends of long boards 38
drilling tiny parts 108
drill press
    accessory board 92
    angle platform 112
    ball-drilling jig 110
    base platform 108
    boring dowels 91
    chip collection 106
    dowel depth stop 96
    end-boring 99
    handscrew to hold small pieces 98
    handscrew vise 99
    hands-free with lock 94
    height gauge 93
    hold-down 111
    key upgrade 97
    leveling table 105
    magnetic key 91
    step switch 93
    table setter 101
    table-tilt gauge 95
    tiny parts 108
    toothbrush for bit cleaning 95
    twin-flip hinge gauge 97
    vertical drilling jig 107
    V-fence 90
    workpiece support 108
drive belt memory 159
drum sander, makeshift 64
dry-erase cabinet doors 215
drying rack 16
dust collection 210–213
    bag, holding in place 210
    bandsaw 87
    connector, coffee can as a 211
    exhaust port connector, bicycle tube as 212
    filter detector 211
    gate, holding in place 211
    hose storage, hooks for 213
    scrollsaw 132
dust filter 212
dust in finishes, avoiding 22
dyes, custom 17

E

edge clamps 197
    quick-fix 204
emery boards 64
end-boring at the drill press 99
epoxy leveling 138
epoxy shortcut, hot glue as 29
eraser, white polymer 207
European hinges, hanging 10
European hinges, twin-flip drill press gauge 97
extras 235

F

fastener organization 8
finish dipper 18
finish for woodturning 24
finishing 14–24
    gaps, polyurethane glue to avoid 35
    turntable 19
Forstner bits
    make arced cuts with 94
    stop collar 105
frame assembly jig 9
framing square, add an edge 52
furniture construction 25–28
    drawer planing platform 191

G

glove removal 240
glue. *See also* gluing
    application, pipette for 34
    cleanup water 35
    pot brush lid 31
    quick spreading tips 33
    removal, marking knife for 209
    setup extension 35
    spreader for biscuit slots 46
    station 33
    stick to adhere patterns 86
glue bottle
    self-cleaning plugged nozzle 32
    slanted snout 32
glue line depressions 30
glue-ready, getting 36
glue-scoop 206
glue shield, sandwich bag as a 36
glue-sizing end grain 30
glue-ups, winter solutions for 34, 35
gluing 29–36
grain-wrapping 7
grinding station 72

H

hammerless nailing 7
handle layout sketch pad 53
handscrew 96, 98, 99, 108, 148, 185, 189, 196, 200
handscrew, drilling small pieces with a 98
hardware, holding with spray adhesive 12
helper post 240
hinge 10, 12, 26, 28, 97, 106, 109, 112, 128, 216
    honing 8
hold-down, telescoping 205
hollow chisel mortiser
    dead-setting 131
    squaring up 134
honer, double-headed 74
hot-melt glue release 36
HVLP sprayer, spraying less with a 14

I

inside measurements, accurate 52

J

jar opener 237
jig
    90° hole drilling 101
    angle clamping 201
    anti-rack vise 196
    ball-drilling 110
    bandsaw wedge cutting 88
    bottomless crosscut table saw 169
    cast-iron tool magnets 104
    chamfer-sanding 66
    circle-sanding 61, 62
    door assembly 12
    dowel tenoning 140
    drill press dowel hole centering 98
    frame assembly 9
    frames 193
    handles 230
    honing guide 73
    keyhole slot routing 150
    long board drilling 102
    photos for setup 224
    scraper sharpening 78
    stand-up router rule 143
    vertical drilling 107
    wooden spreader 199
jigsaw
    zero-clearance base 130
joinery 37–46
jointer 113–115
    curved tapers 114
    knife life extender 115
    perfect angle 114

K

keyhole slots, marking 13
knife line accuracy 54

L

laminate trimmer 147, 150
lamp cord knot 231
lamp mounting 229, 234, 239, 245
lathe 116–124
    banjo holder 118
    bowl blank template 122
    bowl blank templates 123
    chisel rack 219
    faceplate centering 119
    faceplate mounting 124
    gauge, shop-made 121
    Jumbo Jaw standoffs 119
    live tail center for finials 116
    mobile cabinet 217
    Morse taper as jam chuck 121
    no-marks faceplate 122

INDEX

pen turning blanks 120
piloting a Forstner bit 122
rubber fingertips 121
spindle splint 123
tighter threads 124
lathe-mounted sanding nub 63
layout, curves by clamp-and-rule 56
level case 214
light fixtures 232
lighting 232, 235, 239, 240
linseed oil 24
lock mortise location, marking 7
loose screw prevention 235

M

magnet 8, 11, 65, 69, 87, 91, 94, 103, 131, 134, 158, 162, 164, 187, 207, 210, 216, 227, 231, 245
magnetic pickup 216
mallet, instant soft-faced 11
marking system, triangle 220
masking tape 234
    tab to grab 230
measuring and marking 47–60
measuring center 50
mini drum sander, dowel as 67
mini square, rule depth gauge as a 57
mitered box, grain-wrapping a 7
mitered frames, clamping 6
mitersaw 125–128
    crosscutting short multiples 127
    crosscutting short pieces 126
    flip-stop 128
    long-arm stop 127
    no-fuzz cuts 125
    no-spin dowel sawing 126
mixing cup, disposable 17
mixing surface
    blister package tray 36
    flying disc 32
    sticky notepad 30
mortise
    squaring with a hollow chisel 39
mortising setup 44

N

nail gun
    pins pointing in the right direction 132
nail holes, shoe polish to hide 23
nailing
    unsupported pieces 11
    without a hammer 7

O

offset and depth gauge block 59
organization 214–227
    PVC pipe 226
    stretch wrap 218

P

packing tape 230
panel construction 25
paper bag for finishing 22
parallel jaw clamps, leather clad 205
parts bin I.D. 216
pattern removal 208
patterns, temporarily adhere 86
pegboard 227
phone tripod mount 229
pipe clamp
    avoid stains 192
    spin-free pads 187
    stands 197
pipe clamps
    daisy-chaining 189
pitch removal, using sunscreen for 208
planer 135–137
    chamfering 135
    microfiber grain detector to reduce tear out 137
    mill some extra 137
    riser for thin stock 137
    short boards 136
    snipe avoidance 136
plane, shop-made flush-cut 69
plane sole, flattening 241
planing support 201
planing tapers 236
power tools, other 129–134
power tools, shortening cords 231
practice new methods 23

R

random orbit sander for rubout 15
razor blade as mini-scraper 208
razor scraper, safety 69
roller shade dust screens 243
roller stand wall rack 222
router 138–150
    table saw side-extension table 153
router, handheld
    dadoes 148
    edge stabilizer 139
    flush-routing plugs 147
    flush-routing riser 138
    flush-routing riser for plugs 150
    I-beam risers 147
    keyhole slot routing jig 150
    parking pad 141
    plywood dado shim 142
    through-mortises in thick stock 143
router, plunge
    precision plunging 141
router table
    angled fence for routing discs 145
    block router table sag 150
    corner rout 149
    dowel tenoning jig 140
    flush trim support 146
    handscrew to hold small parts 148
    panel-raising guard 142
    power lift 146
    pushpad upgrade 144
    slide-on top for circles 144
    small parts 149
    Space Ball to prevent bottoming out of bit 139
    stand-up rule jig 143
rub out finishes, random orbit sander for 15
ruler widths for quick reference 54
runaway plugs, preventing 107
rust, avoiding 78
rust blocker, shellac as a 16
rust inhibitor, bike chain wax 161

S

saddle square, center finder as 54
safety equipment 238
sander-grinder 77
sanding 23, 61–71
    backer, cove-matching 68
    cleaner 63
    disc, combo 62
    nub, lathe-mounted 63
    pads, yoga mats as 65
    table, zero-clearance 65
    tight spots 68
sandpaper
    gunk removal 71
    organization 70
    sizer 71
    tearing 71
sawdust filler 17, 18
saw guide 196
scraper, improvised
    block plane blade 208
    glass 207
screwdriver
    magnetizing 103
screws
    shortening 190
    wax for lubrication 98
screw strips for finishing 20
scribing, using a washer for 51, 54
scrollsaw
    repurposing a narrow bandsaw blade 134
    sanding 134
    vacuum attachment 132
seal cans 24
self-adhesive measuring tape 241
shaper
    height adjustment 132
shaping. *See* sanding

INDEX

sharpening 72–79
    facet marker 78
    heat sink 79
    marking gauge wheel 77
    scraper 76
    scraper jig 78
    short blades 74
sharpening station, portable 75
sheet goods dolly 242
shelf-support pins, shaping 64
shellac 24
    measuring 20
shop 228–245
short boards 244
small parts, working with 231
spill absorber 209
spindle splint 123
spindle-spraying rack 21
sprayer, HVLP 14
spreader bar clamp 198
square check 55
square corners, checking for 49
squaring a square 58
squaring sticks 51
stabilizing knots 33
standoffs, finishing
    blind slats 20
    dome-headed upholstery tacks 21
    screw strips 20
steel wool dispenser 221
stickers, lumber 217
sticky notepad mixing surface 30
storage 214–227
    dust brushes 223
    lumber 224
    manuals 222
    milk crates 225
    paper rags 222
    tape rules 227
    veneer and dowel rack 223
subscription card uses 232

T

table saw 151–179
    baby powder for surface slick 155
    bottomless crosscut jig 169
    butcher block fence 174
    crosscut sled skinning 152
    dado blade tray 168
    double-slot zero-clearance hold-down 177
    ergonomic pushstick 158
    extension table as router fence 153
    featherboard riser 176
    fence auxiliary facing 170
    fence-free tapering 163
    fine-tuning sled runners 161
    flush-trimming 161
    kerfing the gauge 165
    laminate-sawing auxiliary fence 178
    magnet featherboard holder 158
    magnetic crosscut standoff 162
    miter gauge quick-slip 168
    miter measure 167
    multipurpose crosscut sled 177
    outdoor safety strips prevent slips 152
    precision alignment for crosscuts 159
    quick rip fence reset 162
    repeatability 165
    reversible dual fence 160
    rip-fence repeater 175
    ripping knife-edge bevels 154
    ripping scrappy-edged stock 160
    ripping thin strips 173
    self-gripping springboard 164
    sharpening indicator 170
    shoe-style pushsticks 167
    small parts hold-down 154
    splining polygons 166
    tapering 156
    tapering boards 151
    thin-plate zero-clearance insert 179
    tongue-and-groove 171
    tooth- and knuckle-saving blade changer 156
    wedge-cutting 172
    wobble-widening a dado 155
    zero-clearance insert refresh 168
    zero-clearance laminate panel 174
    zero-clearance throat plate 157
tabletop spray booth 24
tape residue removal 207
tape rule
    accuracy 49
    gauge 57
    hanger 227
    trammel 49
tenon
    trimming trick 42
    wedges 46
tool holders
    canvas roll with mini sawhorse 218
    conduit clips 218
    strapping 215
tool roll protector, glove fingers as 224
tool tray, detachable 221
toothbrushes 209
tracing mouse 60
trammel, tape rule as a 49
two-faced finishing 15

V

vacuum 84, 106, 212, 213
veneer
    jointing 113
veneer uses for electric iron 36
vise
    Anti-rack jig 196
    handscrew 189, 200
    pinch prevention 197
    power-tool mounting 202
    tall, with handscrew 185
    versatile jaws 195
vise-assistance from sanding sponges 183
vise conversion 185

W

walker workstation 238
wall cabinets, pre-shimming for 55
warp, checking for 115
waterstone holder 73
wax 245
waxed paper, clothes hanger for 220
white boards 221
winding sticks, aluminum angle 53
woodturning. *See* lathe
woodturning finish 24
work-holding 182–205

WOODCRAFT magazine

SUBSCRIBE

2 YEARS FOR JUST $29.99

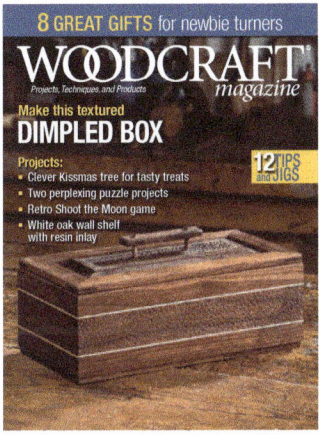
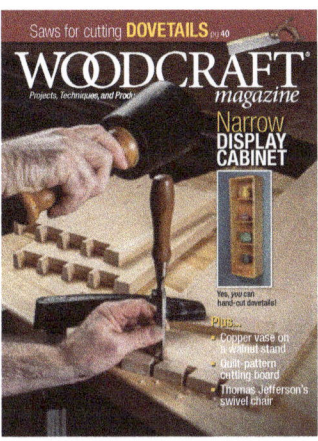
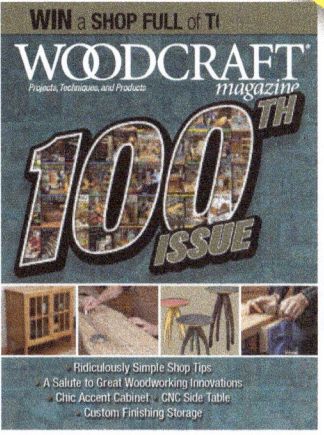
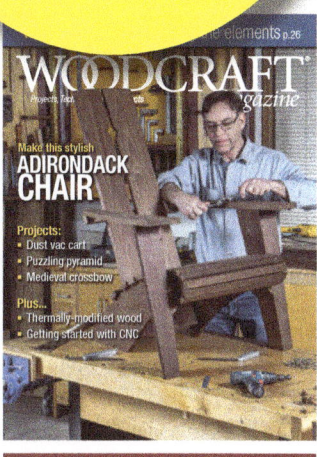

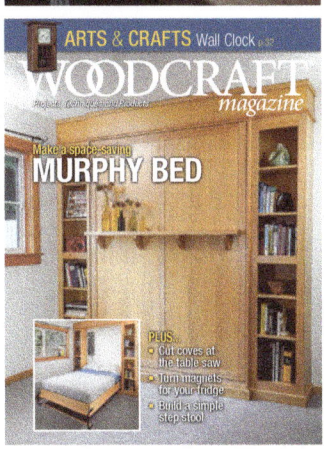
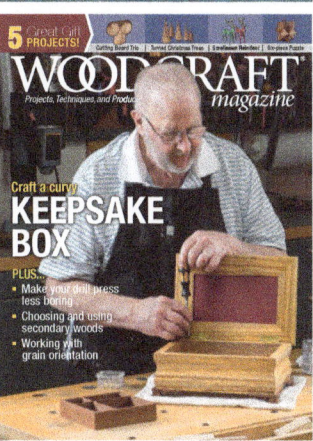
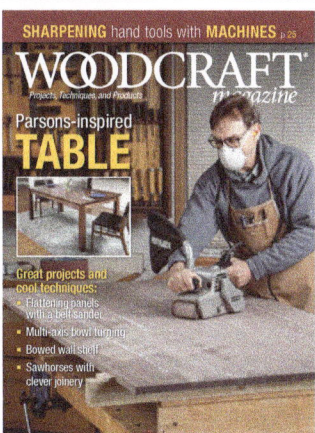
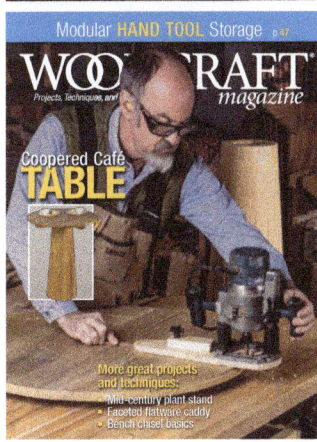
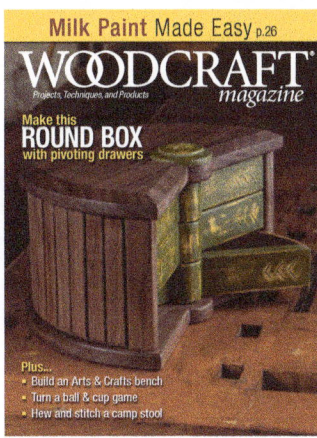
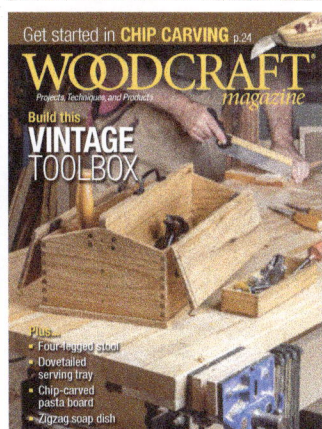
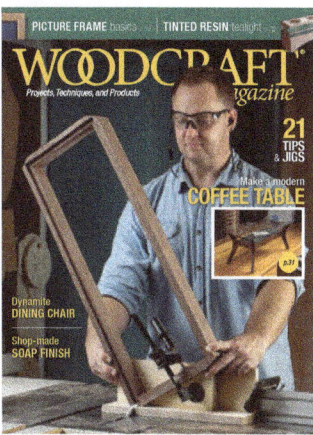

Order online and save at **woodcraftmagazine.com**

www.ingramcontent.com/pod-product-compliance
Lightning Source LLC
Chambersburg PA
CBHW051548220426
43671CB00021B/2976